LOVE, WAR, AND THE GRAIL

LOVE, WAR, AND THE GRAIL

*Templars, Hospitallers, and Teutonic Knights
in Medieval Epic and Romance 1150–1500*

BY

HELEN J. NICHOLSON

BRILL ACADEMIC PUBLISHERS, INC.
BOSTON • LEIDEN
2004

Library of Congress Cataloging-in-Publication Data

Nicholson, Helen J., 1960–
    Love, war, and the grail / by Helen Nicholson
    p. cm.
    Includes bibliographical references and index.
    ISBN 0-391-04218-1
    1. Military religious orders in literature. 2. Literature, Medieval—History and criticism. 3. Grail—Romances—History and criticism. I. Title.

PN682.M57N53 2004
809'.9338255791—dc22

2003069712

Helen J. Nicholson, Love, War, and the Grail,
appeared originally in the series History of Warfare,
edited by Theresa Vann and Paul Chevedden
© Copyright 2001 by Koninklijke Brill NV, Leiden, The Netherlands

ISBN 0-391-04218-1

© Copyright 2001 by Koninklijke Brill NV, Leiden, The Netherlands

All rights reserved. No part of this publication may be reproduced, translated, stored in
a retrieval system, or transmitted in any form or by any means, electronic,
mechanical, photocopying, recording or otherwise, without prior written
permission from the publisher.

Authorization to photocopy items for internal or personal
use is granted by Brill provided that
the appropriate fees are paid directly to The Copyright
Clearance Center, 222 Rosewood Drive, Suite 910
Danvers MA 01923, USA.
Fees are subject to change.

PRINTED IN THE UNITED STATES OF AMERICA

CONTENTS

Preface VII
Abbreviations XIII
Chapter One: Introduction... 1

PART ONE: SURVEY

Chapter Two: Monastic Roles... 35
Chapter Three: Military Activity 76
Chapter Four: The Grail 102

PART TWO: ANALYSIS

Chapter Five: The Appearances Of The Military Orders In Medieval Fictional Literature 187
Chapter Six: Servants Of Christian Knights...................... 222
Chapter Seven: The Predominance Of The Templars 227
Chapter Eight: Some Conclusions...................................... 234

Bibliography 239
Index 263

PREFACE

This is a study of the appearances of the Military Orders in the epic and romance literature of the Middle Ages, 1150–1500. The subject is important for historians of the Military Orders and the crusades because the Orders' appearances in literature give an insight into how they were viewed by the noble knightly class who supported them with money, land and recruits – the same class for which epic and romance literature was composed. The Orders' continued appearance in this literature throughout the Middle Ages is valuable evidence for continued belief in the Orders' vocation – military service in a religious order dedicated to defending Christians and Christendom against their external enemies – and continued support for the crusade, with which the Military Orders were often but not invariably associated in literature.

The subject is also of interest to literary specialists. The Military Orders' appearances in fictional literature, and the changes in their roles in fictional literature throughout the Middle Ages, indicate that while convention was important in the composition of fictional literature, from the late twelfth century onwards it was essential that fiction should reflect actual events: that it should be 'realistic'. While this was not total realism, fictional literature must at least have a context in actuality, and the inclusion of the Military Orders could assist in providing this context.

No study of the Military Orders' roles in medieval fictional literature can be complete without a consideration of the Templars' appearance in Wolfram von Eschenbach's version of the Grail legend, *Parzival*, and the later works based on it. This study reassesses the historical context of *Parzival* and sets out a new historical interpretation of the work. It also reconsiders the connection of the Grail with the Holy Land and with the concept of the 'perfect knight' and considers how these themes were developed during the course of the Middle Ages. While the emphasis here is on the historical rather than the mystical aspects of the Grail legend, it is also shown that Wolfram von Eschenbach's *Templeise*, who bear a symbol of faithful love – the turtle dove – were probably responsible for the development of the image of the Templars in French literature as supporters of lovers.

Certain problems arise in a work of this sort in reconciling the expectations of historians and of literary specialists, who differ in their approaches to their material and in their definitions of key concepts such as 'history', 'reality', 'literature' and 'fiction'. In attempting to define such terms there is a danger of becoming bogged down in an epistemological morass, but at the same time to avoid any attempt at definition will certainly lead to misunderstanding among readers. The stance taken in this study reflects my own background and training as a historian with wide reading in texts which historians would generally label 'literary'. Strictly speaking a 'literary' text is anything that is written (as distinct from, for instance, an artefact) and can include both texts intended primarily as a record of actuality and those intended primarily to entertain. However, historians have tended to use the term 'literature' to mean texts produced primarily to entertain, with no intention to accurately record actuality. This sweeping distinction overlooks the fact that many medieval texts which claim an intention to act as a record of actuality (such as chronicles) include a great deal of material which in present-day scholarship would not be regarded as recording actuality: the most obvious example being miracle stories. At the same time, many medieval texts which are now regarded by historians as having been written primarily to entertain (such as epics or *chansons de geste*) were believed by their contemporaries to record actuality, while others which are now generally regarded as fantasy (such as Arthurian romances) were presented by their writers as recording actuality, and had a clear didactic intention in addition to their function as entertainment. In short, it would be misleading to claim that there is a clear distinction between 'reality' and 'fiction' in medieval writing.

However, as is discussed in part two of this study, my own reading of these texts has led me to conclude that the concern for 'realism', in the sense of reproducing actuality, and the prejudice against 'fiction', in the sense of inventing a literary reality distinct from objective actuality, were important factors in dictating the form of all kinds of literature during the medieval period. It is therefore legitimate to enquire how far writers of works not regarded as 'historical' by modern historians did attempt to reproduce actuality to a greater or lesser extent, and how they went about doing this. This raises the problem of which definition of 'realism' and 'fiction' are to be used in this study. However, while acknowledging that it is impossible to define an objective reality of the past, as our knowledge of the past must be mediated through texts and archaeological evidence, it is an underlying assumption of this study that it is possible through a study of a combination of different forms of evidence (such as government records, letters, archaeological evidence and chronicles) to arrive at an approximation of a past actuality which, while not objective or complete, provides us with a yardstick against which to measure the extent to which texts produced during a particular period in the past reproduce that actuality. The extent to which they correspond or deviate from this modern scholarly approximation of past actuality will be expressed in this study in terms of their degree of 'realism' or 'fiction'. It is acknowledged that this can only be approximate, and that many scholars will consider that any attempt to define 'reality' or 'fiction' is theoretically flawed. However, these are concepts which are regarded as useful measures by many scholars of history and those outside academia, and I can only crave the patience of colleagues who regard such an exercise as essentially pointless.

This study is purely concerned with the appearances of the Military Orders in epic and romantic literature, and not with their appearances in chronicles or other forms of writing which were intended to record actuality. It is clear that chronicle accounts of the Military Orders were governed by convention as well as by actuality, and could present an image of the Military Orders no closer to actuality than that presented in epic and romantic literature. However, I have written elsewhere on this problem as it relates to certain chronicle sources, and will not consider it here.

Moreover, this study does not set out to examine the interrelationship between works which were primarily intended to entertain (such as epic and romance) and those primarily intended to record actual events, i.e. history, but also intended to entertain (such as chronicles). While writers of epic and romance may have drawn on chronicles for their materials, chronicle writers certainly knew epic and romantic literature: as evidenced, for instance, by their references to the epic hero Roland, and to King Arthur. Yet the extent to which the writing of history was affected by the writing of fiction during the Middle Ages is an area of on-going scholarly debate in which it is not yet possible to draw firm conclusions. In order to establish what chroniclers of the Military Orders may have owed to epic and romance it is first necessary to establish the content of epic and romantic tradition regarding the Military Orders. This study sets out to establish this epic and romantic tradition. I will note one instance in where the author of the chronicle attributed to Ernoul may have been influenced by a romantic tradition linking the Templars to romantic love, but it is equally probable that both romance writers and 'Ernoul' took this theme from elsewhere; possibly from papal encyclicals in favour of the Templars. It is, however, hoped that the present study will contribute material for future consideration of the question of the relationship between the writing of 'history' and the writing of 'fiction' in the Middle Ages.

The dates which form the limits of this study may require some explanation. The earliest work considered here dates from the period 1150–1200; hence the starting date for this study. The final date of 1500 was chosen to indicate the end of the medieval period. It is not intended as a sharp cut-off point, but was chosen as a date of convenience to keep this study within reasonable bounds. The Templars, Hospitallers and Teutonic Knights continued to appear in new works of literature after 1500, and so far as I know no thorough scholarly research has yet been done on this subject. The present study does consider reprintings, translations and adaptations of works originally produced before 1500 which continued to appear through the sixteenth, seventeenth and eighteenth century; but study of new works must await further research in this area.

In a study of this type, using literature originally written in several different languages, it can be difficult to decide how best to render names, especially as successive writers may use different spellings for the same name. Some characters' names have English forms while others do not; some have a standard form recognised by scholars while others do not. However, these English versions of names and standard forms are not necessarily familiar to those who are not familiar with this literature. With their needs in mind, I have attempted to use the form of each name as given by each writer, even where there is a common English alternative or a standard form, except in the cases of very familiar characters such as King Arthur where no confusion is likely to arise. I hope that this will be clear and will not lead to audience frustration. In contrast, when rendering the names of historical figures I have followed current British scholarly practice, for instance Roger of Howden, Wolfram von Eschenbach.

Some of my research into the literature of the period 1150–1300 was completed while I held an Open Research Scholarship at Leicester University, 1986–89. Most of the rest of my research was carried out during a year of research leave, 1998–99, from the School of History and Archaeology, Cardiff University. A proportion of my expenses were generously met by the School. I should also acknowledge the tireless assistance of the staff of the Arts and Social Studies Library, Cardiff University. I am indebted to the British Library, London, for providing a photocopy of part of their Additional Manuscript 25434 (*Les Prophecies de Merlin*), and to the Bibliothèque nationale, Paris, for providing a photocopy of part of their MS nouveau acquisition français 10060 (*Theséus de Cologne*) and MS français 1473 (*Le roman de Theséus de Cologne et de Gadifer*). I am also indebted to the staff of the Bodleian and Taylorian Libraries, Oxford. Without the resources of their institutions, this study could not have been completed.

All translations, unless otherwise attributed in the notes, are my own. Except where the precise meaning of individual words is crucial, I have preferred to translate passages into modern English rather than quoting in the original language. This is intended to make this work accessible to non-specialists. Specialists will be well aware that the precise meaning of individual words in medieval languages is a matter for individual interpretation, and no two translators will translate the same passage precisely alike. My translations may therefore differ in some details from other translations. Scholars should not rely on my translations but should go back to the original languages.

I am extremely grateful to Professor Norman Housley of Leicester University, Professor Peter Edbury of Cardiff University, and Nigel Nicholson, who read this work during the various stages of its composition and made valuable suggestions for improvements. Dr Padma Anagol, Dr Alan Forey, Dr Anthony Luttrell, Dr Kari Maund, Dr Karen Pratt, Kate Hamlin and Bill Zajac gave helpful advice on various aspects of the project. To quote the conventional modern academic disclaimer, the errors which remain are my own.

ABBREVIATIONS

BEFAR	Bibliothèque des écoles françaises d'Athènes et de Rome
BLVS	Bibliothek des literarischen Vereins in Stuttgart
CCCM	Corpus Christianorum Continuatio Medievalis
CFMA	Classiques français du moyen âge
EETS	Early English Text Society
GRL	Gesellschaft für romanische Literatur
MGH	*Monumenta Germaniae Historica*, ed. G.H. Pertz *et al.*, Hanover, Weimar, Stuttgart and Cologne, 1826ff.
MGHS	*Monumenta Germaniae Historica Scriptores*, ed. G.H. Pertz *et al.*, 32 vols in folio (Hanover, 1826–1934)
Pat. Lat.	*Patrologus Cursus Completus, Series Latina*, ed. J.P. Migne, 217 vols and 4 vols of indexes (Paris, 1834–64)
OFCC	*The Old French Crusade Cycle*, ed. Emanuel J. Mickel, Jan A. Nelson, *et al.*, 9 vols (Tuscaloosa and London, 1977–)
RHC Occ	*Recueil des historiens des croisades: historiens occidentaux*, pub. L'Académie des Inscriptions et de Belles-Lettres, 5 vols (Paris, 1841–95)
RHGF	*Recueil des historiens des Gaules et de la France*, ed. Bouquet *et al.*, revised edn ed. Léopald Delisle, 24 vols (Paris, 1878)
RS	Rolls Series: *Rerum Britannicarum medii aevi scriptores*, 99 vols (London, 1858–1911)
SATF	Société des anciens textes français
SHF	Société de l'histoire de France
TLF	Textes littéraires françaises

CHAPTER ONE

INTRODUCTION

1 *The Current State of Scholarship*

The Templars, Hospitallers and Teutonic Knights, as well as other religious military orders, make frequent appearances in medieval epic and romance literature. Scholars have puzzled over the Templars' appearance as Grail guardians in Wolfram von Eschenbach's Grail romance *Parzival*, and noted their appearances in crusading epics as well as, for example, the appearance of a Templar in the alliterative *Morte Arthure* and the role of Margon the Templar in *Sone de Nausay* or *Nansay*.[1] However, analysis of these appearances has been limited to individual works, and until recent years there was little attempt to assess them as a whole.

In 1971 Ansgar Konrad Wildermann produced a study of assessments of the trial of the Templars up to the seventeenth century, which included a consideration of some literary evidence. He did not, however, consider epic and romance literature, but concentrated on chronicles and political and

---

[1] For example, on *Parzival*: Willem Snelleman, *Das Haus Anjou und der Orient in Wolframs 'Parzival'* (Nijkerk, 1941), pp. 121–44; Helen Adolf, *Visio Pacis: Holy City and Grail: an attempt at an Inner History of the Grail Legend* (Philadelphia, 1960), pp. 90–123 on the Grail Temple and pp. 203–4 n. 30 on the Templars in particular; Joachim Bumke, *Wolfram von Eschenbach: Forschung seit 1945: Bericht und Bibliographie* (Munich, 1970), pp. 123, 162, 205, 222; Marion Melville, *La Vie des Templiers* (Paris, 1951), pp. 180–84; Alain Demurger, *Vie et mort de l'ordre du Temple, 1120–1314*, 3rd edn (Paris, 1993), p. 282; Stephen Knight, 'From Jerusalem to Camelot: King Arthur and the Crusades', in *Medieval Codicology, Iconography, Literature and Translation: Studies for Keith Val Sinclair*, ed. Peter Roufe Monks and D.D.R. Owen (Leiden, 1994), pp. 223–32, here p. 228; on Templars in the Grail romances in general: Jessie Weston, 'Notes on the Grail Romances – *Sone de Nansai, Parzival* and *Perlesvaus*', *Romania*, 43 (1914), 403–26, here 409, 412–13, 426; James Douglas Bruce, *The Evolution of Arthurian Romance From the Beginnings Down to the Year 1300*, 2 vols (Baltimore, 1923; 2nd edn 1928; repr. 1959), 1, pp. 335, 353 n. 17 where he erroneously states that the Templars do not appear in *Sone de Nansay*. For the alliterative *Morte Arthure*, see: *The Alliterative Morte Arthure: A Critical Edition*, ed. Valerie Krishna (New York, 1976), pp. 176–7, notes on lines 890ff. and 903 (where she notes but fails to identify the crusading references in the text, and overlooks the Templar); William Matthews, *The Tragedy of Arthur: A study of the Alliterative 'Morte Arthure'* (Berkeley and Los Angeles, 1960), p. 24 notes the presence of a Templar and on pp. 63, 184 notes crusading references in the text but does not specifically make the crusading connection for the Templar; see also Claude Lachet, *Sone de Nansay et le roman d'aventures en vers au XIII siècle*, Nouvelle Bibliothèque du Moyen Age, 19 (Paris, 1992), pp. 703–6 on Margon the Templar; David Trotter, *Medieval French Literature and the Crusades (1100–1300)* (Geneva, 1987), pp. 146, 157, 191, 207–8 on Military Orders in medieval literature.

religious works.² In 1987 David Trotter published a study of the crusades in medieval French literature from 1100–1300, which included some reference to the Military Orders. However, most of the Military Orders' appearances in literature before 1300 are not directly involved with crusading, and Trotter did not always mention them even where they did appear. Trotter also made a general contribution towards the study of the subject, pointing out a number of problems in the use of fictional literature as an historical source and underlining the importance of literary convention, rather than 'history' or 'reality' (left undefined), in the creation of characters and plots in crusading literature.³

In 1991, I included a brief description of literary references to Templar protection and sympathy towards romantic lovers as part of a short preliminary study on Templar attitudes towards women. This was followed by a more extensive review of the Military Orders' relations with romantic love and lovers in the romance literature of the thirteenth century (1994). I also included a survey of the Military Orders' roles in epic and romance literature in my study of attitudes towards the Military Orders in the twelfth and thirteenth centuries (1993).⁴ The assumption underlying these studies was not that literature reflected the Orders' actual activities but that the image of the Orders in literature reflected the overall attitude held by the writers, patrons and audiences of epic and romance literature. While it is clear from other evidence that the Orders aroused considerable criticism, they were not as savagely criticised as the Cistercians and the Friars, and after 1250 less criticism was expressed.⁵ As writers of chronicles and satire seldom set out to express positive views on any subject – just as good news is seldom reported, because it is not 'news' – their work contains few positive views of the Military Orders. Hence, although lack of criticism may indicate favour, this cannot be deduced with any certainty from chronicles, satire and documentary sources alone. However, the Military Orders' consistently good image in epic and romance literature is an indication that, no matter how much they might be criticised by individuals for particular reasons, overall the concept of the Military Orders and their chief activities were viewed positively by those who formed the main audience for epic and romance literature, the landed warrior

---

² Ansgar Konrad Wildermann, *Die Beurteilung des Templerprozesses bis zum 17. Jahrhundert* (Freiburg, 1971).

³ Trotter, *Medieval French Literature*, pp. 146, 157, 191, 207–8 on the Military Orders' appearances, and pp. 29, 249 on the importance of literary convention.

⁴ Helen Nicholson, 'Templar Attitudes towards Women', *Medieval History*, 1, 3 (1991), 74–80; idem, 'Knights and Lovers: the Military Orders in the Romantic Literature of the Thirteenth Century', in *The Military Orders: Fighting for the Faith and Caring for the Sick*, ed. Malcolm Barber (Aldershot, 1994), pp. 340–45; idem, *Templars, Hospitallers and Teutonic Knights: Images of the Military Orders, 1128–1291* (London, 1993), pp. 86–98.

⁵ Nicholson, *Templars, Hospitallers*, pp. 48–50.

classes, both men and women, who were also those on whom the Military Orders relied for donations of land and recruits.[6]

It is also clear from epic and romance literature, as is suggested by other evidence, that the Templars were the best-known of the Military Orders – the Military Order *par excellence*, which represented the whole concept of the Military Order. Hence, when the international Military Orders as a whole failed in their vocation by failing to defend the Holy Land to the Muslims, finally losing Acre in 1291, it was the Templars which were most damaged by this failure. As a result it was the Templars, rather than any other religious order, which in 1307 was attacked by a French government in desperate need of financial resources.[7]

Other scholars have considered the appearance of Military Orders in later medieval literature as an indication of continuing western European interest in

---

[6] While scholars have shown that women formed a substantial part of the audience for epic and romance literature, such literature was also enjoyed by men; while women were also important in patronage of the Military Orders and in encouraging crusade recruitment. There has been extensive recent debate over how far women formed the intended audience for literature. See, for example, the papers in *Women, the Book and the Worldly: Selected Proceedings of the St Hilda's Conference, 1993, vol. 2*, ed. Lesley Smith and Jane H.M. Taylor (Cambridge, 1995), pp. 13–23; the papers in *Women and the Book: Assessing the Visual Evidence*, ed. Lesley Smith and Jane H.M. Taylor (London, 1996), pp. 75–93; Peter Coss, *The Lady in Medieval England, 1000–1500* (Stroud, 1998), pp. 165–74; Joan M. Ferrante, *To the Glory of Her Sex: Women's Roles in the Composition of Medieval Texts* (Bloomington, 1997); D.H. Green, *Medieval Listening and Reading: the Primary Reception of German Literature, 800–1300* (Cambridge, 1994), pp. 192, 211–15, 290–315 (particularly on the literacy of noble laywomen); Elspeth Kennedy, 'The Knight as Reader of Arthurian Romance', in *Culture and the King. The Social Implications of the Arthurian Legend; Essays in Honor of Valerie M. Lagorio*, ed. Martin B. Shichtman and James P. Carley (New York, 1994), pp. 70–90; Roberta L. Krueger, *Women Readers and the Ideology of Gender in Old French Verse Romance* (Cambridge, 1993). For women's involvement in recruitment for crusading, see Jonathan Riley-Smith, 'Family tradition and participation in the Second Crusade', in *The Second Crusade and the Cistercians*, ed. Michael Gervers (New York, 1991), pp. 101–8. For women's involvement in crusading, see also: James M. Powell, 'The role of women in the Fifth Crusade', in *The Horns of Hattin*, ed. Benjamin Z. Kedar (Jerusalem and London, 1992), pp. 294–301; Helen Nicholson, 'Women on the Third Crusade', *Journal of Medieval History*, 23 (1997), 335–49. For women in the Military Orders, see Alan Forey, 'Women and the Military Orders in the Twelfth and Thirteenth Centuries', *Studia Monastica*, 29 (1987), 63–92; Roberta Gilchrist, *Contemplation and Action: the Other Monasticism* (London, 1995), pp. 64–5; Helen Nicholson, 'Templar attitudes towards women'; idem, 'The Military Orders and their Relations with Women', in *Expanding the Frontiers of Medieval Latin Christianity: The Crusades and the Military Orders*, ed. József Laszolovsky and Zsolt Hunyadi, Department of Medieval Studies, Central European University, Budapest (forthcoming); Francesco Tommasi, 'Uomini e donne negli ordini militari di Terrasanta: Per il problema delle case doppie e miste negli ordini giovannita, templare e teutonico (secc. XII–XIV)', in *Doppelkloster und andere Formen der symbiose mannlicher und weiblicher Religiosen in Mittelalter*, ed. Kaspar Elm and Michel Parisse, Berliner historische Studien, 18 (1992), pp. 177–202.

[7] Norman Cohn, *Europe's Inner Demons: the Demonization of Christians in Medieval Christendom* (London, 1975, 1993), pp. 86–7; Malcolm Barber, *The New Knighthood: a History of the Order of the Temple* (Cambridge, 1994), pp. 295–301; Nicholson, *Templars, Hospitallers*, pp. 125–8, 133–5.

the crusades in the fourteenth and fifteenth centuries.[8] Yet basic questions remain to be settled. Why did the Military Orders appear in epic and romance literature? Is there a pattern to their appearances, or are they haphazard and *ad hoc*? What exactly are the Templars doing in Wolfram von Eschenbach's *Parzival*? Why did the Templars acquire a literary reputation as protectors of romantic lovers, and was it particularly significant? Was the Military Orders' image in epic and romance literature dictated primarily by convention or by actual contemporary and past events? If the former, then it is of limited use as a guide to contemporary attitudes towards them; but if the latter, then it must reflect the attitudes of writers, patrons and audiences of this literature. As study of the military religious orders has expanded rapidly in recent years, it is clear that a comprehensive survey of the Military Orders' appearances in medieval fictional literature would be worthwhile, as an indication of underlying attitudes towards the Military Orders by the landed warrior classes throughout the Middle Ages.

The answers to these basic questions are considered in the final section of this book; but a few specific questions should be noted in more detail here, as they relate to the importance of this study for historians. A study of the Military Orders' roles in epic and romance literature after 1300 is particularly useful at the present time, as study of the Orders after the dissolution of the Order of the Temple has been expanding rapidly in recent years.[9] Historians are not in complete agreement over exactly why King Philip IV of France brought about the dissolution of the Order of the Temple in 1312, and whether or not the king and his ministers believed the charges against the Order. It is tempting to deduce that the Order's unpopularity was an important factor behind the charges. If this was the case, the literary image of the Order should give some indication of how unpopular the Order was. However, this study will show that the literary image of the Order remained positive even after the loss of Acre in 1291 and up to the time of the trial and after. This reinforces the theory held by most modern historians of the Military Orders, that the Order of the Temple was not dissolved because it was unpopular but to suit the political and financial interests of King Philip.[10] Moreover, an examination

---

[8] Anthony Luttrell, 'The Hospitallers in Cyprus after 1386', in *Cyprus and the Crusades*, ed. N. Coureas and J. Riley-Smith (Nicosia, 1995), pp. 125–41, esp. pp. 135–6; see also Norman Housley, *The Later Crusades: From Lyons to Alcazar, 1274–1580* (Oxford, 1992), p. 362; see also his reference to *Cleriadus et Meliadice* in 'Cyprus and the Crusades, 1291–1571', in *Cyprus and the Crusades*, pp. 187–206, here pp. 190–91.

[9] For an indication of the recent expansion of scholarly study in this field see the published proceedings of the two international Clerkenwell conferences on the Military Orders in 1992 and 1996, *The Military Orders: Fighting for the Faith and Caring for the Sick*, ed. Malcolm Barber (Aldershot, 1994) and *The Military Orders*, volume 2: *Welfare and Warfare*, ed. Helen Nicholson (Aldershot, 1998), esp. Jonathan Riley-Smith's introduction to volume 2, pp. xxv–xxviii.

[10] See, for instance, Barber, *New Knighthood*, pp. 294–301; Forey, *The Military Orders: From the Twelfth to the Early Fourteenth Centuries* (Basingstoke, 1992), pp. 231–9.

of the Military Orders' appearances in fictional literature after 1300 casts light on how attitudes towards the Military Orders changed after the dissolution of the Order of the Temple. This study demonstrates that the dissolution of the Templars had an adverse affect on the image of Military Orders as a whole, because when the principal Military Order ceased to exist writers and audiences of literature became uncertain as to what the Military Orders were.

Yet this is not a subject of relevance only to the historian of the Military Orders. Attitudes towards the Military Orders are also of interest to historians of the crusades, for, as the history of the Military Orders was linked to that of the crusades, views of the Military Orders should also reflect views of crusading. Recent work on the crusade has shown that wide and active interest in crusading continued throughout the Middle Ages from 1095 into at least the sixteenth century; it is therefore reasonable to ask whether and how literary images of the Military Orders changed during this period in response to the changing fortunes of the crusades. This study will show that as the crusading arena expanded, so did the geographical arena in which the Military Orders were depicted in operation: whereas in the twelfth century they were only depicted in the Holy Land, by the late fifteenth century they were also depicted in Prussia and Spain.[11]

The role of the Military Orders in fictional literature is also of significance because of their special position within the history of the development of the concept of knighthood, otherwise known as 'chivalry'. When the first Military Order, the Order of the Temple, was given official Church approval, it was depicted as the apex of knighthood: 'this religious order represents the resuscitation and flowering of knighthood'.[12] Several religious authorities agreed with this depiction, most significantly Bernard, abbot of Clairvaux, who wrote in support of the new Order between 1129 and 1135 his letter *De laude novae militiae*, 'In Praise of the New Knighthood', in which he depicted secular knighthood as an evil, and the knights of the Temple as the true knighthood, both spiritual and physical, fighting the enemies of Christ.[13] As a 'living ideal of Christian chivalry', the Templars should have been central to the development of the ideals of knighthood, and the roles in which they are depicted in fictional literature, we would expect, should indicate to us exactly how knights were supposed to behave. Furthermore, Bernard of Clairvaux'

---

[11] For recent work on the crusades throughout the Middle Ages and into the early modern period see Housley, *Later Crusades*; Christopher Tyerman, *England and the Crusades, 1095–1588* (Chicago, 1988); for changing views of the crusade, see also Elizabeth Siberry, *Criticism of Crusading, 1095–1274* (Oxford, 1985); Silvia Schein, *Fideles Crucis: The Papacy, the West, and the Recovery of the Holy Land, 1274–1314* (Oxford, 1991).

[12] *La Règle du Temple*, ed. Henri de Curzon, SHF (Paris, 1886), p. 11, clause 2.

[13] 'Liber ad milites Templi de laude novae militiae', in *S. Bernardi opera*, ed. Jean Leclercq, C.H. Talbot and H.M. Rochais, 8 vols (Rome, 1957–77), 3, pp. 213–39. For other religious authorities who wrote in praise of the new Order, see Nicholson, *Templars, Hospitallers*, pp. 35–7.

depiction of the Templars as the true form of knighthood has encouraged modern commentators to see allusions to the Templars in medieval literature wherever the ideal of knighthood is under discussion.[14]

If Bernard of Clairvaux' vision of the Templars' vocation was widely shared in twelfth-century society, it would be reasonable to expect the Military Orders to be depicted in fictional literature as an example of the best fighting force which Christendom could produce. It is certainly clear that the Military Orders' military discipline was widely admired.[15] Yet, it is not at all certain that all knights shared Bernard's opinion of the Templars as the best form of Christian knighthood even when the Templars were first founded, and when the Military Orders began to appear in fictional literature, in the last quarter of the twelfth century, they were not generally presented as an ideal for knights to emulate. In other words, even if the Military Orders were indeed initially seen by knights as a 'living ideal of chivalry', they did not long remain so.

Rather than the Military Orders having been regarded by knights as a 'living ideal of chivalry', it appears that the original concept of the Military Orders was a creation of the Church and the clergy, whereas knights' own views of knighthood were rather different.[16] Certainly the warrior classes approved of the Military Orders, endowed them with patronage and even entered the Orders themselves, but they do not appear to have viewed them as the apex of chivalry. The earliest theoretical work on knighthood by a knight, Raoul de Hodenc's *Roman des Eles*, written in around 1215, perceives

---

[14] For the Templars as a 'living ideal of Christian chivalry', see Malcolm Barber, 'The Social Context of the Templars', *Transactions of the Royal Historical Society*, 34 (1984), 27–46: here 46. Albert Pauphilet, *Études sur la Queste del Saint Graal attribuée a Gautier Map* (Paris, 1921), pp. 70–71, suggested that Galaad was the perfection of the Templar ideal, as did James Douglas Bruce: *The Evolution of Arthurian Romance*, 1, p. 421. See also Pauline Matarasso, *The Redemption of Chivalry: a Study of the Queste del Saint Graal* (Geneva, 1979), p. 68. Horst Richter, '*Militia Dei*: a central concept for the religious ideas of the early crusades and the German *Rolandslied*', in *Journeys Towards God: Pilgrimage and Crusade*, ed. Barbara N. Sargent-Baur (Kalamazoo, Michigan, 1992), pp. 107–26, draws a parallel between the Templars and Roland and the twelve peers in Konrad's *Rolandslied*, p. 123. Gregory J. Wilkin, 'The Dissolution of the Templar Ideal in "Sir Gawain and the Green Knight"', *English Studies*, 63 (1982), 109–21 sees the reference to Solomon's Star on Gawain's shield as an oblique reference to the Templars, knights of the Temple of Solomon, whose ideal of knighthood Gawain sets out to emulate but fails.

[15] See, for instance, Odo of Deuil, *De profectione Ludovici VII in orientem*, ed. Virginia G. Berry (New York, 1948), Bk 7, p. 124; Benjamin Z. Kedar, 'The *Tractatus de locis et statu sancte terre ierosolimitanae*', in *The Crusades and Their Sources: Essays Presented to Bernard Hamilton*, ed. John France and Bill Zajac (Aldershot, 1998), pp. 111–33, here pp. 125–6; translated as Anonymous Pilgrim V,2 in *Anonymous Pilgrims I–VIII (11th and 12th Centuries)*, trans. Aubrey Stewart, Palestine Pilgrims' Text Society 6 (London, 1894), pp. 29–30; Ralph of Diss, *Opera historica*, ed. William Stubbs, 2 vols, RS 68 (London, 1876), 1, p. 423; *Itinerarium peregrinorum et gesta regis Ricardi*, in *Chronicles and Memorials of the Reign of Richard I*, ed. William Stubbs, 2 vols, RS 38 (London, 1864–65), 1, pp. 266–7, 371–2: Bk 4, chs 18, 19, Bk 5, ch. 51.

[16] See Maurice Keen, *Chivalry* (New Haven and London, 1984), pp. 44–63, especially pp. 49–51.

knighthood as serving the Church without any need to join a religious order.[17] By the 1230s the knightly ideal portrayed by such contrasting characters as Galaad, Tristan, Palamedes and Meliadus was very different from the ideal of the Templars. Galaad performed deeds of arms in pursuit of his lone quest for God; Palamedes performed his deeds of arms in honour of a lady, Queen Iseut of Cornwall; Meliadus sought honour and glory for their own sake, through deeds of arms without service for a lady.[18] In contrast, the Templars' ideal was a life of chastity, poverty and obedience in a community of brothers dedicated to laying down their lives for Christ in battle in order to win an eternal reward in Heaven.

It is necessary to stress that study of the roles of the Military Orders in medieval fictional literature does not give us any first hand evidence about the Brothers' own attitudes and ideals. The Military Orders produced or commissioned works of spiritual edification and some works of history, and in addition two *sirventes* survive composed by Templar Brothers, which lament the defeats suffered by Latin Christians in the Holy Land and call on the West to send military aid; but no member of a Military Order is known to have written epic or romance literature during this period. In fact, they were discouraged from even reading romance literature.[19] Nor does this literature

---

[17] Raoul de Hodenc, *Le Roman des Eles*, in *Le Roman des Eles by Raoul de Hodenc and L'Ordene de Chevalerie*, ed. Keith Busby, Utrecht Publications in General and Comparative Literature, 17 (Amsterdam and Philadelphia, 1983), pp. 31–49; lines 274–90 on relations between knighthood and the Church; pp. 14–15 on the identity of the author and the date.

[18] On Galaad, see below, pp. 159–60, 169–80; on Palamedes, see below, pp. 207–11; on Meliadus, see below, p. 205.

[19] On works read by brothers of the Military Orders see Alan Forey, 'Literacy and Learning in the Military Orders during the Twelfth and Thirteenth Centuries', in *The Military Orders*, vol. 2, ed. Nicholson, pp. 185–206: here pp. 195–7; Nicholson, *Templars, Hospitallers*, pp. 110–12. For works composed by or for brothers of the Military Orders see K. Helm and W. Ziesemer, *Die Literatur des Deutschen Ritterordens* (Giessen, 1951); *Livländische Reimchronik*, ed. F. Pfeiffer, BLVS 7B (Stuttgart, 1844); Eric Christiansen, *The Northern Crusades: the Baltic and the Catholic Frontier, 1100–1525* (Basingstoke, 1980), pp. 215–17; Peter von Dusberg, *Chronik des Preussenlandes*, ed. K. Scholz and D. Wojtecki (Darmstadt, 1984); *The Hospitallers' Riwle (Miracula et regula Hospitalis Sancti Johannis Jerusolimitani)*, ed. K.V. Sinclair, Anglo-Norman Texts 42 (Oxford, 1984); R.C.D. Perman, ed., 'Henri d'Arci: the Shorter Works', in *Studies in Medieval French Presented to Alfred Ewert in Honour of his Seventieth Birthday* (Oxford, 1961), pp. 279–321; *Le Livre des Juges. Les cinq textes de la version française faite au XIIe siècle pour les chevaliers du Temple*, ed. Marquis d'Albon (Lyon, 1913). For the work of the Templar Brother Ricaut Bonomel see Antoine de Bastard, 'La colère et la douleur d'un templier en Terre Sainte: <I're dolors s'es dins mon cor asseza>', *Revue des Langues Romanes*, 81 (1974), 333–73; for Brother Oliver the Templar, 'Estat aurai lonc temps en pessamen', see *Choix des poésies originales des troubadours*, ed. M. Raynouard, 6 vols (Paris, 1816–21), 5, p. 272; see also Forey, 'Literacy', pp. 198–204; Anthony Luttrell, 'The Hospitallers' Historical Activities, 1291–1400', reprinted in his *The Hospitallers in Cyprus, Rhodes, Greece and the West (1291–1440)* (London, 1978); Jean Delaville le Roulx, *Les Hospitaliers à Rhodes (1310–1421)* (Paris, 1913, reprinted London, 1974), pp. 243–6 (on Grand Master Juan Fernández de Heredia); for discouragement from reading vernacular works, see *Cartulaire général de l'ordre des Hospitaliers de S. Jean de Jérusalem*, ed. Jean Delaville le Roulx, 4 vols (Paris, 1894–1905), no. 3039, clauses 39 and 42 (19 September 1262); Forey, 'Literacy', pp. 205–6. The fact that the Brothers had to be discouraged

necessarily tell us anything about the Brothers' actual activities or about the structure of the actual Orders. The use of literary sources not originally written as a record of contemporary events as historical evidence is deeply problematic. However, the fact that the Military Orders appear in fictional literature is in itself valuable evidence of how these Orders were viewed by the writers and audiences of this literature. It may also tell us something about the composition of literature.

2 Literary sources as historical evidence: the problems

Historians of the middle ages have long made use of literary sources which were not primarily written as a record of contemporary events as a means of obtaining evidence about the actualities of the society in which they were written.[20] The justification for using these sources in this way is that the numbers of manuscripts which survive and frequent references to epic or romantic incidents or characters within sources which were ostensibly written as a record of contemporary events – such as chronicles and royal records – suggest that so-called 'fictional' literature should give insights into the attitudes and prejudices of those who read it or listened to it being read. To judge by what we know of patronage of old French texts, such works were commissioned by members of the upper ruling classes, men and women,[21] but the introduction to Rusticien de Pise's compilation of Arthurian romances indicates that by the late thirteenth century they were being read and listened to not only by monarchs and high and low nobility, but also by the merchant classes. The author of the *Prophecies de Merlin*, probably written in the period 1276–79, refers to 'knights and other lay people' as the intended audience, which may include well-to-do non-noble landholders as well as the merchant classes.[22] Hence, fictional literature should give insights into the attitudes of a wide section of medieval society.

---

from reading vernacular works indicates that they were in fact reading them, but it is impossible to say what proportion of Brothers were doing so or which works they were reading.

[20] For instance, the excellent work of Maurice Keen and Jean Flori on knighthood is underpinned by their use of epic and romance literature: see, for instance, Maurice Keen, 'Chivalry and Courtly Love', *History*, 47 (1964), 1–17, reprinted in his *Nobles, Knights and Men-at-Arms in the Middle Ages* (London, 1996), pp. 21–42; Keen, *Chivalry*, etc.; Jean Flori, 'La notion de chevalerie dans les chansons de geste du XII siècle. Étude historique de vocabulaire', *Le Moyen Age*, 81 (1975), 211–44, 407–45; 'Pour une histoire de la chevalerie: l'adoubement dans les romans de Chrétien de Troyes', *Romania*, 100 (1979), 21–53, etc.

[21] Diana B. Tyson, 'Patronage of French Vernacular History Writers in the Twelfth and Thirteenth Centuries', *Romania*, 100 (1979), 180–222; Green, *Medieval Listening and Reading*, pp. 211–15; Kennedy, 'Knight as Reader', and see note 30 below.

[22] The preface written by Rusticien de Pise (the same Rustichello of Pisa who recorded Marco Polo's travels) is reproduced in the facsimile edition of Anthoine Vérard's 1501 edition of *Gyron le Courtoys*, with an introductory note by C.E. Pickford (London, 1979), f.1c; Eilert Löseth, *Le Roman en prose de Tristan, le roman de Palamède et la compilation de Rusticien de Pise: Analyse*

There are, however, problems in using this sort of literature as evidence for specific events or for 'public opinion', as we generally do not know who composed a work, nor for whom it was composed, nor how far works would have reflected the views of either author, patron or audience, nor how far they followed literary convention.[23] Indeed, the terms 'author' and 'audience' are themselves deeply problematic. The term 'author' implies the originator of the concept of a story. In the Middle Ages writers were often supplied with the concept and basic plot by their patron, as Chrétien de Troyes was given the plot for *Le Chevalier à la charette* by Countess Marie of Champagne, while Girart d'Amiens was given the plot of *Escanor* by Eleanor of Castile, queen of England. Other writers might simply be reworking earlier works of literature, and are more properly called 'redactors'. In fact, writers were unwilling to claim original authorship of a text, preferring to appeal to an 'authority' (such as a Latin author) whose work they claimed to have translated or adapted. In this study, however, I shall use the word 'author' loosely, to mean the person who actually put the story together in the form in which we have it, whether or not they were the originator of the concept. The term 'audience' implies those who listen to a story being read aloud. As the reception of literature changed during the period under consideration from oral to a combination of oral and private reading, here I shall refer to those who read or listened to texts being read as 'the audience', including private readers.

It is easiest to assume that literature was composed by male members of the clergy, simply because they are known to have been literate. However, this assumption rests on dubious foundations. As some writers were undeniably either female (Marie de France) or knights (Wolfram von Eschenbach) or secular administrators (Antoine de la Sale) we cannot assume that others were none of these simply because the authors do not tell us. In particular, the great prose romances of the thirteenth century, with the exception of Rusticien de Pise's compilation, are all anonymous or written under pseudonyms, and some may have been written by knights. In the early thirteenth century, lay men such as Ambroise (a trouvère), Geoffrey de Villehardouin (a noble knight), Robert de Clari (a poor knight) and Ernoul (a squire) were composing histories in the vernacular: Ambroise composed the *Estoire de la guerre sainte*, an account of the Third Crusade; Villehardouin and Robert de Clari composed accounts of the conquest of Constantinople, and Ernoul wrote a history of the events of

---

critique d'après des manuscrits de Paris (Paris, 1890; Geneva, 1974), pp. 423–4, para. 620; *Les Prophecies de Merlin*, ed. Lucy Allen Paton, 2 vols, Modern Language Association of America nos 1026, 1077 (London and New York, 1926–27), 1, p. 57, 2, p. 346; for the audience of literature, see also Philippe Ménard, *Les Fabliaux: contes à rire du moyen âge* (Paris, 1983), pp. 101–2.

[23] On the problems of authorship and audience see Trotter, *Medieval French Literature*, p. 249. For a plea for the validity of crusading literature as a historical source, see Robert Francis Cook, 'Crusade Propaganda in the Epic Cycles of the Crusade', in *Journeys Towards God: Pilgrimage and Crusade*, here p. 167.

1187 in the Holy Land.[24] By the mid-thirteenth century lay nobles in the Latin East such as John of Ibelin and Philip of Novara were writing legal texts[25] and Philip also wrote satirical and other poetry, including a tale of Renard the fox.[26] It is clear that such knights were also readers of romance.[27] As the Prose *Tristan* and *Meliadus-Gyron* are very secular in tone, these works were probably written by a member of the laity. The first author of the *Tristan* claims to be a knight, Luce de Gat,[28] and even if this was untrue it suggests that knights did write romances. The author of *Meliadus-Gyron* (giving this work the titles ascribed to it in the printed editions) claimed to be the author of the *Brait* or *Brut*, which was identified by some later copyists with the prose *Tristan*. This writer names himself as Helie, a companion in arms of Robert de Boron.[29] Again, the religious writings of (for example) both Mechtild of Magdeburg and Marguerite Porete were written in the tradition of romance, telling the story of the romantic love between the soul and Christ. Clearly these women identified their own experience with the romantic tradition; hence it is at least possible that behind some of the anonymous literature of the thirteenth century lie female authors. Heldris de Cornualle, author of *Silence*, has a name which could be either male or female.[30] Some of the scenes in *Gyron le*

---

[24] Ambroise, *L'Estoire de la guerre sainte: Histoire en vers de la troisième croisade*, ed. Gaston Paris (Paris, 1987); Geoffrey de Villehardouin, *La Conquête de Constantinople*, ed. Edmond Faral, 2 vols, (Paris, 1973); Robert de Clari, *La Conquête de Constantinople*, ed. Philippe Lauer, CLMA 40 (Paris, 1924); *Chronique d'Ernoul et de Bernard le trésorier*, ed. L. de Mas Latrie, SHF (Paris, 1871).

[25] Peter Edbury, *John of Ibelin and the Kingdom of Jerusalem* (Woodbridge, 1997), pp. 105–26; Jonathan Riley-Smith, *The Feudal Nobility and the Kingdom of Jerusalem, 1174–1277* (London and Basingstoke, 1973), pp. 121–44.

[26] Filippo da Novara, *Guerra di Federico II in Oriente (1223–1242)*, ed. Silvio Melani (Naples, 1994), pp. 112–16, 120–22, 126, 128–30, 134–44.

[27] Kennedy, 'Knight as Reader', pp. 70–90.

[28] *Le Roman de Tristan en Prose*, ed. Renee Curtis, 3 vols (Cambridge, 1985), 1, p. 39, line 10.

[29] *Meliadus de Leonnoys, 1532*, introduction by C.E. Pickford (London, 1980), fol. 1b; Roger Lathuillère, *Guiron le Courtois. Étude de la tradition manuscrite et analyse critique* (Geneva, 1966), pp. 176–7; and see *La Suite du roman de Merlin*, ed. Gilles Roussineau, 2 vols, TLF 472 (Geneva, 1996), 1, p. 194, lines 30–36.

[30] See Mechtild of Magdeburg, *The Flowing Light of the Godhead*, trans. Frank Tobin (New York, 1998); German text in *Das fliessende Licht der Gottheit. Nach der Einsiedler Handschrift in kritischem Vergleich mit der gesamten Überlieferung*, ed. Hans Neumann, 2 vols (Munich, 1990); Marguerite Porete, *The Mirror of Simple Souls*, trans. Ellen Babinsky (New York, 1993); original Old French text, *Le Miroir des simples âmes anéanties*, ed. Romana Guarnieri and Paul Verdeyen, in *CCCM*, 69 (Turnholt, 1986). On Heldris see *Silence: A Thirteenth-Century French Romance*, ed. and trans. Sarah Roche-Mahdi (East Lansing, Michigan, 1992), p. xi n. 2. If Heldris is from France, Scandinavia or a Germanic country, the 'is' suffix on Heldris' name would suggest a woman's name, as in Helvis, Alis, Adalheidis, Freydis; if Heldris is from Wales, the 'is' suffix could belong to either a man or a woman. Given that *Silence* is about crossdressing and the unreliability of appearances, the ambiguity of the author's name is probably deliberate. On lay literacy and writing in the Middle Ages see also *The Book of Chivalrey of Geoffroi de Charny: Text, Context and Translation*, ed. Richard W. Kaeuper and Elspeth Kennedy (Philadelphia, 1996), pp. 18–19 and note 60, and especially Michael Clanchy, *From Memory to Written Record: England, 1066–1307*, (London, 1979), pp. 182–201; Coss, *Lady in Medieval England*; Green,

Courtoys in particular could well have come from a woman's pen, or at least were intended to appeal particularly to women: for instance, Danayn li Rous' story of the old woman who defeated Henor de la Salve with his own sword,[31] the 'evil damsel' who is a match for Brehus sans Pitié when no knight has ever been able to defeat him,[32] and Guiron, wearing only his underwear, tied to a tree in a snow (his damsel, likewise tied to a tree, is fully dressed).[33] Moreover, the London-Turin continuation of the *Chanson de Jérusalem*,[34] written in the 1290s or early fourteenth century, has a number of scenes which could have been written by a woman or with a mainly female audience in mind, in particular the scenes in which Tancred and Dodequin wrestle in the sand.[35] The young, dashing and romantic yet somewhat hapless character of Tancred in this work would obviously be more attractive to a female than a male audience – for example, he is described at lines 11700–702 as being 'fair and handsome and had a slender body and a fair, clear face with a joyous, happy expression; he was praised and esteemed for his great prowess as a knight'.[36] There are a number of strong female characters: Queen Calabre, her daughter Florie, Margalie (baptised Marguerite) and Margalie's governess, whose good education is stressed[37] – although all these women are well-educated and intelligent.[38] In short, we do not know whose interests these works reflect, but by the 1230s they were not simply the works of clergy trying to persuade the laity to live better lives; they also reflect the interests of laywomen and laymen.

These texts were not intended to be used as a record of their time, but were largely written to entertain, comment on contemporary society and instruct. This is an obvious obstacle to using them as sources for the reconstruction of contemporary events.[39] Yet it must be said that chronicle sources, which were

---

Medieval Listening and Reading, pp. 192, 211–15, 290–315 (particularly on the literacy of noble laywomen). On the female patron of medieval literature see, for instance, Coss, *Lady in Medieval England*, pp. 165–7 and notes; J. Ferrante, 'The Influence of Women Patrons', in *Literary Aspects of Courtly Culture*, ed. D. Maddox and S. Sturm Maddox (Cambridge, 1994); Ferrante, *To the Glory of Her Sex*; Henrietta Leyser, *Medieval Women: A Social History of Women in England, 450–1500* (London, 1995), pp. 240–56; S.W. Ward, 'Fables for the Court: Illustrations of Marie de France's *fables* in Paris, BN MS Arsenal 3142', in *Women and the Book: Assessing the Visual Evidence*, ed. L. Smith and J.H.M. Taylor, pp. 190–203. On women as authors, see also Jeanette Beer, 'Women, Authority and the Book in the Middle Ages', in *Women, the Book and the Worldly*, ed. L. Smith and J.H.M. Taylor, pp. 61–9.

[31] *Gyron*, fols 62a–d; Lathuillère, *Guiron*, p. 258, section 69.
[32] *Gyron*, fols. 227c–233d; Lathuillère, *Guiron*, pp. 305–6, sections 108–9.
[33] *Gyron*, fols. 322b–324d; Lathuillère, *Guiron*, p. 329, section 126.
[34] *OFCC*, VIII: *The Jérusalem Continuations: the London-Turin Version*, ed. Peter R. Grillo (Tuscaloosa, 1994).
[35] Ibid., lines 2011–22, and again at 2811–19.
[36] Ibid., lines 7890–8135, 8049–73, 8466–75.
[37] Ibid., lines 13642, 13873, 14043, 14449–50, 14454, 14481.
[38] Ibid., eg. lines 5275–7 on Calabre, 5813–31 on Florie, 13569–72 on Margalie.
[39] For this argument and a counter-argument, see Philippe Ménard, *Les Fabliaux: Contes à rire au moyen âge* (Paris, 1983), p. 46.

ostensibly written as a record of their time, also present serious problems of interpretation which must be taken into account before they can be used as evidence of actual events. Such problems have been explored in recent scholarly assessments of the twelfth-century historian William of Tyre and the thirteenth-century chronicler Matthew Paris.[40] Whether or not they were intended as an historical record, all forms of written evidence from the past require careful analysis and cannot be taken at face value. The fact that 'fictional' literary sources were not intended to be an historical record does not invalidate them as evidence of the actualities of past societies, but means that scholars must interpret and use them within the limitations the sources present.

Another problem for modern historians in using so-called 'fictional' literary sources for evidence of past actualities is that as popular works were rewritten to a greater or lesser extent each time that they were copied, later copyists may have completely changed the intention of the original writer. Furthermore, the dating of a text or of a specific version of a text can be extremely uncertain. Moreover, although we may assume that the popularity of a particular story might be deduced from the number of manuscripts which have survived, we do not know how many manuscripts have not survived, or how many are still unidentified in private collections. We might conclude that because we know that a manuscript of a particular text was owned by a particular person, that person read and enjoyed the contents; but it does not follow that because someone owns a text they read it or enjoy it, although other members of their household may do so. It might be that the husband would own a book, but his wife and children would read it. In this context it is interesting to note that Eleanor of Provence, queen of Henry III of England, owned a copy of the epic crusading poem *La Chanson d'Antioche*, and apparently read it; but such priceless evidence is seldom available for any one text. Nor do we know how much of a text was read: whether it was read from one end to the other, or only certain favourite incidents were selected for

---

[40] For the problems of using the work of William of Tyre, see, for instance, D.W.T.C. Vessey, 'William of Tyre and the Art of Historiography', *Medieval Studies*, 35 (1973), 433–55; R.H.C. Davis, 'William of Tyre', in *Relations between East and West in the Middle Ages*, ed. Derek Baker (Edinburgh, 1987), pp. 64–76; Peter W. Edbury and John Rowe, *William of Tyre: Historian of the Latin East* (Cambridge, 1988); Peter W. Edbury, 'Propaganda and Faction in the kingdom of Jerusalem: the background to Hattin', in *Crusaders and Muslims in Twelfth-Century Syria*, ed. M. Shatzmiller (Leiden, 1993), pp. 172–89. On Matthew Paris, see Richard Vaughan, *Matthew Paris* (Cambridge, 1958), Marie Luise Bulst-Thiele, 'Zur Geschichte der Ritterorden und des Konigreichs Jerusalem in 13. Jahrhundert bis zur Schlacht bei La Forbie am 17. Okt 1244', *Deutsches Archiv für Erforschung des Mittelalters*, 22 (1966), 197–226; W.R. Thomson, 'The Image of the Mendicants in the Chronicles of Matthew Paris', *Archivum Franciscanum Historicum*, 70 (1977), 3–34; Antonia Gransden, *Historical Writing in England, c. 550 to c. 1307* (London, 1974), ch. 16; R.N. Berard, 'Grapes of the Cask: a Triptych of Medieval English Monastic Historiography', *Studia Monastica*, 24 (1982), 75–103.

reading. If the latter, then any 'message' contained within the text would probably not be noticed or assimilated by the audience.[41]

The influence of literary convention is a particular obstacle to the use of medieval 'fictional' literature as evidence for the nature of the society in which it was produced. Different forms of medieval literature had their own conventions – as, indeed, do different forms of modern literature – to such a degree that it can be argued that 'fictional' literature depicts only the development of a convention, and does not reflect actuality.[42] This theory assumes that most audiences would have been aware of these conventions and, despite the author's conventionalised protestations that the story was true, often complete with reference to a Latin source which the author claimed to have translated, the audience would have made a sharp distinction between their own actuality and the fictional 'reality' of the story. In short, the conventionalised claim that a story was true was no more than a 'literary game'.[43] We must remember, however, that many modern viewers or listeners of television and radio soap operas lose the ability to distinguish between their own actuality and fictional 'reality', coming to identify the actors with the

---

[41] Eleanor of Provence's 'certain large book, in the French language, in which are contained the deeds of Antioch and of other kings, etc.', was kept with the queen's valuables in the house of the Templars in London. On 17 May 1250, King Henry III sent Henry of the Wardrobe to the Temple to fetch it 'for the queen's use': *Close Rolls of the Reign of Henry III preserved in the Public Record Office, 1247–51* (London, 1922), p. 283. On Eleanor's treasure at the New Temple, see also the Annals of Dunstable, *Annales monastici*, ed. H.R. Luard, 5 vols, RS 36 (London, 1864–69), 3, p. 222; although the book is recorded here as belonging to Eleanor, would it simply have been recorded by the Templars as part of the king's treasure? This is the problem with using wills for evidence of readership of literature: ownership does not prove readership, and property could legally belong to the husband while actually belonging to the wife or a child. On evidence from wills, see Philippe Ménard, 'La réception des romans de chevalerie à la fin du Moyen Age et au XVIe siècle', *The Bibliographical Bulletin of the International Arthurian Society*, 49 (1997), 234–73, here 256–7. On similar problems in ascertaining audience reception of a chronicle, William of Tyre's 'History', see Davis, 'William of Tyre', especially p. 75.

[42] See, for instance, Trotter, *Medieval French Literature*, pp. 29, 249.

[43] Jeanette M.A. Beer, *Narrative Conventions of Truth in the Middle Ages* (Geneva, 1981) who argues that the truth assertion was a convention which was deliberately parodied and that a sophisticated audience would recognize it as such: pp. 9, 11, 85. See also Evert van den Berg, 'La littérature chevaleresque dans la Flandre du 14e siècle: épopée ou roman?' in *Aspects de l'épopée romane: mentalité, idéologies, intertexualités*, ed. Hans van Dijk and Willem Noomen (Groningen, 1995), pp. 331–8, here p. 337. On the *exempla* used by preachers, often drawn from epic and romance, which were not intended to be interpreted as truth, see Penny J. Cole, *The Preaching of the Crusades to the Holy Land, 1095–1270* (Cambridge, Mass., 1991), p. 115 and note 54, pp. 123, 125, 131–3, 195–201. On truth assertions in German vernacular writing, see Green, *Medieval Listening and Reading*, pp. 246–65. He argues that 'an autonomous realm of fiction was created' in the twelfth century (p. 265), but in the thirteenth century even 'fiction' had to be shown to have an historical foundation in order to be accepted by audiences: pp. 265–9. See also Trotter, *Medieval French Literature*, pp. 33–4. I return to this problem in Part Two of this study.

roles they are playing, and sending wreaths when a fictional character dies.[44] While there certainly were conventions in all forms of literature, and well-educated audiences would have been aware of this, not all those who heard or listened to 'fictional' literature would necessarily have been aware that aspects of this literature did not reflect present or past actuality but was only part of the convention; and even if they knew that (for instance) there had never been a king named Arthur, perhaps they rather wished that there had been.

In short, the use of 'fictional' literature as an historical source is deeply problematic. Yet, given the evident popularity of the legends of Charlemagne and Arthur, and of other adventure romances, historians cannot simply ignore them. The legends depict largely invented tradition, an invented tradition in the mould of that defined by the British historian Eric Hobsbaum: they established and symbolised social cohesion or the membership of a group (knighthood); they legitimised an institution and its status (knighthood); and they inculcated beliefs, value systems and conventions of behaviour (chivalry).[45] The extent of their popularity is evidenced by the many references to romance and epic literature in chronicles,[46] the political use made of the Charlemagne and Arthurian tradition by kings,[47] their impact on social

---

[44] The famous BBC Radio 4 soap opera 'The Archers' is a particularly notable example of a serial whose fictional characters have become 'real' to their audience, even inspiring a legal campaign to procure the release of a fictional character, Susan Carter, who had been unjustly imprisoned within the fictional story. See, for instance, Roger Ede, 'Why the Archers is no soft soap', *The Times*, 2, Tuesday 16 November 1999, pp. 10–11.

[45] Eric Hobsbaum, 'Introduction: Inventing Traditions', in *The Invention of Tradition*, ed. Eric Hobsbaum and Terence Ranger (Cambridge, 1983), pp. 1–14, here p. 9.

[46] See, for example, Robert Huntingdon Fletcher, *Arthurian Material in the Chronicles, especially those of Great Britain and France*, Studies and Notes in Philology and Literature (Boston, 1906); see also *Itinerarium peregrinorum*, ed. Stubbs, Bk 1, ch. 29, p. 67, Bk 2, chs 5, 11, pp. 143, 154, Bk 3, ch. 5, p. 216, Bk 5, ch. 21, p. 332, Bk 6, ch. 23, 422; *Das Itinerarium peregrinorum. Eine zeitgenössische englische Chronik zum dritten Kreuzzug in ursprünglicher Gestalt*, ed. Hans E. Mayer, MGH Schriften, 18 (Stuttgart, 1962), pp. 331, lines 15–16; Jean Froissart, *Chroniques, Livre 1: Le manuscrit d'Amiens, Bibliothèque municipal no. 486*, ed. George T. Diller, 5 vols (Geneva, 1991–98), 1, pp. 54, 68, 127, 167, 2, pp. 53, 122, 210, 304 (references to Arthur), 2, pp. 56, 430 (references to Roland and Oliver); *Life of the Black Prince by the herald of Sir John Chandos. Edited from the manuscript in Worcester College with linguistic and historical notes*, by Mildred K. Pope and Eleanor C. Lodge (Oxford, 1910), lines 51–2, 4097–100 (Charlemagne and Arthur), 162–4 (Roland, Oliver and Ogier the Dane), 3382–3 (Oliver and Roland). On the various representations of Roland and other epic heroes in art, see Rita Lejeune and Jacques Stiennon, trans. Christine Trollope, *The Legend of Roland in the Middle Ages*, 2 vols (London, 1971).

[47] For the emperor Frederick I and the Charlemagne legend, see Lejeune and Stiennon, *Legend of Roland*, 1, pp. 169–77. For the Capetian kings and the Charlemagne legend, see Hans-Erich Keller, 'The *Song of Roland*: a mid-twelfth century song of propaganda for the Capetian kingdom', *Oliphant*, 3 (1976), 242–58; for the Capetian kings and the Arthurian prose romances, see Rosemary Morris, 'King Arthur and the Growth of French Nationalism', in *France and the British Isles in the Middle Ages and Renaissance: Essays by members of Girton College, Cambridge, in memory of Ruth Morgan*, ed. Gillian Jondorf and D.N. Dumville (Woodbridge, 1991), pp. 115–30. For the English monarchy and Arthurian romance, see Beate Schmolke-

events,[48] the use of anecdotes from these traditions in sermons,[49] the various 'spin-off' works based on them,[50] even the number of children named after the

Hasselmann, *Der arthurische Versroman von Chrestien bis Froissart: zur Geschichte einer Gattung* (Tübingen, 1980), pp. 190–208, 222–32: translated by Margaret and Roger Middleton as *The Evolution of Arthurian Romance: Verse Tradition from Chrétien to Froissart* (Cambridge, 1998), pp. 235–51, 267–77. See also Girart d'Amiens, *Escanor. Roman arthurien en vers de la fin du XIIIe siècle*, ed. Richard Trachsler, TLF (Geneva, 1994), pp. 61–5; Emma Mason, 'The Hero's Invincible Weapon: an Aspect of Angevin Propaganda', *Ideas and Practice of Medieval Knighthood III*, papers from the fourth Strawberry Hill Conference, 1988, ed. Christopher Harper-Bill and Ruth Harvey (Woodbridge, 1990), pp. 121–37. For a contemporary comparing King John of England to King Arthur, see *Histoire des ducs de Normandie et des rois d'Angleterre*, ed. Francisque Michel, SHF 18 (Paris, 1840, reprinted New York, 1965), p. 109: 'puis le tans le rois Artu n'avoit eu roi en Engletierre qui tant fust doutés en Engletierre, en Gales, en Eschoce ne en Yrlande, comme il estoit'. For King Edward I of England and the Arthurian legend, see Roger Sherman Loomis, 'Edward I, Arthurian Enthusiast', *Speculum*, 28 (1953), 114–27. The herald of Sir John Chandos stated that that Edward III of England was the most powerful king since Arthur: *Life of the Black Prince*, lines 1836–81. Recording the death of King Edward III of England, June 1377, Jean Froissart – who used the Chandos herald as one of his sources – lamented that there had never been such a king as his equal since the time of King Arthur (*Chroniques: manuscrit d'Amiens*, 4 (1993), p. 360, ch. 934, lines 41–3). While this was clearly a standard eulogy of a king of England by this time, it does indicate that King Arthur was regarded as the archetypal king of England and Britain, against whom all others were compared. Froissart also declared Queen Philippa of England as the best queen to enter England since Queen Guinevere: Jean Froissart, *Chroniques. Dernière rédaction du premier livre. Édition du manuscrit de Rome, Reg. lat. 869*, ed. George T. Diller, T.L.F. 194 (Geneva, 1972), ch. 35, p. 159. For the interest of kings Henry VII and Henry VIII of England in King Arthur, see David Starkey, 'King Henry and King Arthur', in *Arthurian Literature XVI*, ed. James P. Carley and Felicity Riddy (Cambridge, 1998), pp. 171–96. For the use of Meliadus and Arthurian imagery in the masque 'Prince Henry's Barriers', produced at the court of King James I of England, see Lesley Mickel, *Ben Jonson's Antimasques: a History of Growth and Decline* (Aldershot, 1999), pp. 63–88, esp. p. 81 for the identification of Prince Henry, then heir to the throne of England, with Meliadus.

[48] For example, for the development of tournaments in imitation of those described in Arthurian literature, see Roger Sherman Loomis, 'Arthurian Influence on Sport and Spectacle', in *Arthurian Literature in the Middle Ages: A Collaborative History*, ed. Roger Sherman Loomis (Oxford, 1959), pp. 553–63. See also David Jacoby, 'Knightly Values and Class Consciousness in the Crusader States of the Eastern Mediterranean', *Mediterranean Historical Review*, 1 (1986), 158–86, here 166–8; reprinted in his *Studies on the Crusader States and on Venetian Expansion* (Northampton, 1989), I; David Jacoby, 'La littérature française dans les états latins de la Méditerranée orientale à l'époque des croisades: diffusion et création', in *Essor et fortune de la chanson de geste dans l'Europe et l'Orient latin. Acts du IXe Congrès international de la Société Rencesvals pour l'étude des épopées Romanes* (Padua and Venice, 1982), pp. 617–46, here pp. 629–32; reprinted in his *Studies on the Crusader States*, II. For another link between tournaments and Arthurian literature see Lisa Jefferson, 'Tournaments, Heraldry, and the Knights of the Round Table: a fifteenth-century Armorial with two accompanying texts', in *Arthurian Literature XIV*, ed. James P. Carley and Felicity Riddy (Cambridge, 1996), pp. 69–157, especially pp. 84–7 for a discussion of how these texts illustrate the popularity of the Arthurian legend during the fifteenth century. See also Richard Barber and Juliet Barker, *Tournaments: Jousts, Chivalry and Pageants in the Middle Ages* (Woodbridge, 1989), pp. 110–25.

[49] Trotter, *Medieval French Literature*, pp. 24–5; David Trotter, 'La mythologie arthurienne et la prédication de la croisade', in *Pour une mythologie du Moyen Age*, ed. Laurence Harf-Lancer and Dominique Boutet (Paris, 1988), pp. 155–77; Simon Lloyd, *English Society and the Crusade, 1216–1307* (Oxford, 1988), pp. 96–7.

[50] For instance, *Les Prophecies de Merlin* is a religious and political work, criticising ecclesiastical corruption, promoting obedience to the Church, promoting the Venetians and the

heroes of these stories.[51] Hence, this invented tradition became deeply rooted in the society in which it was developed, and, like Hobsbaum's modern invented traditions, is an important symptom and indicator of problems and developments which would otherwise be difficult to identify and date.[52] It appears that chivalric literature developed for the newly-forming knightly class in response to external pressures: hostile ecclesiastical attitudes towards warriors and the ascendancy of the new literate class which was a product of the twelfth century renaissance and which was taking over government and administration. Chivalric literature should therefore give insights into how the knightly class actually developed and how those who regarded themselves as members of this class saw themselves and the outside world. To use the term employed by Maurice Keen, chivalric literature constituted the 'mythology' of knighthood which told the knightly class what it really was.[53]

However, given the problems set out above, may the historian assess 'fictional' literary works in any meaningful way? The present study is based

---

city of Venice, set against a backdrop of the Arthurian tradition: *Les Prophecies*, ed. Paton, 2, pp. 346–8.

[51] See Roger Sherman Loomis, 'The Oral Diffusion of the Arthurian Legend', in *Arthurian Literature in the Middle Ages*, p. 60 for a list of Arthurian names used in Italy in the twelfth century; Rita Lejeune, 'The Troubadours', in *Arthurian Literature in the Middle Ages*, pp. 392–9, here p. 397 note 3. See also, for example, Beatrice A. Lees, *Records of the Templars in England in the Twelfth Century: the Inquest of 1185 with illustrative charters and documents* (London, 1935), p. 90 (Iwein), p. 102 (brothers named Roland and Oliver); William of Tyre mentions an 'Yvenus', translated by his old French translator as 'Yveins', the name of Chrêtien de Troyes' 'Chevalier au Lion': *Willelmi Tyrensis archiepiscopi chronicon; Guillaume de Tyre, Chronique*, ed. R.B.C. Huygens, CCCM LXIII–LXIIIa (Turnholt, 1986), Bk 22, ch. 29 (30), 2, p. 1056; 'L'Estoire de Eracles Empereur et la Conqueste de la Terre Doutremer', in *RHC Occ.*, 1, p. 1125, Bk 22, ch. 28; one of the leading Frankish Cypriot nobles during the 1220s was one Gauvain de Chenechê: 'Estoire de Eracles Empereur', in *RHC Occ*, 2, pp. 375–7; and see Peter W. Edbury, *The Kingdom of Cyprus and the Crusades, 1191–1374* (Cambridge, 1991), 51–3, 55, 57, 61, 66; his father was named Galganus (ibid., p. 55), a Latin spelling of the same name. In the 1330s, Perceval de Semeries was an active warrior in Hainaut: Froissart, *Chroniques. Dernière rédaction*, pp. 71, 114, 118. In the latter part of the fourteenth century, one Palamedes Giovanni was admiral of the Hospital of St John on Rhodes and the Order's prior of Venice: Malta, National Library, Archives of Malta 321, fol. 160 (new 169); Delaville le Roulx, *Hospitaliers à Rhodes*, pp. 212–13, 225, 229, 272, 278. The French chronicler Perceval de Cagny was writing in 1436: *Chroniques de Perceval de Cagny, publiés pour la première fois*, ed. H. Moranville, SATF (Paris, 1902). There are many other examples, but these will suffice here.

[52] Hobsbaum, 'Inventing traditions', p. 12.

[53] On knightly mythology, see Keen, *Chivalry*, pp. 102–24, especially p. 103. See also Green, *Medieval Listening and Reading*, p. 265; George Duby, 'The transformation of the aristocracy: France at the beginning of the thirteenth century', in his *The Chivalrous Society*, trans. Cynthia Postan (London, 1977) pp. 178–85, especially pp. 181–2. On the growth of the knightly elite and the pressures on knights see also Peter Coss, *The Knight in Medieval England, 1000–1400* (Stroud, 1993), pp. 46–99. See also *The Chivalric Vision of Alfonso de Cartagena: Study and Edition of the Doctrinal de los cavalleros*, by Noel Fallows (Newark, Delaware, 1995), p. 6: 'Fictional romances were often taken literally as codes of chivalric conduct'. For fictional literature as a basis for knightly behaviour see also Jacoby, 'Knightly Values and Class Consciousness' and 'La littérature française dans les états latins'.

on the premise that, despite all the problems, it is possible to use medieval fictional literature to gain insights into medieval views of the Military Orders and other aspects of medieval culture. The reasoning underlying this premise is as follows.

Recent scholarship has argued that such literary works were largely conventionalised, reflecting their own invented reality rather than contemporary or past actuality, although this might be influenced by contemporary or past actuality.[54] Scholars generally agree that the 'truth assertion' in 'fictional' literary works was no more than a convention and was not taken seriously by listeners.[55] Such literary works seldom refer to actually existing institutions or living persons. It is true that living persons occasionally appear, such as Brian des Isles in *Perlesvaus*, but in general even when an institution is mentioned which bears a ressemblance to an institution existing in contemporary society its identity is left undefined. For instance, the 'white brothers' of the *Queste del Saint Graal* and its post-vulgate successors may be intended to be Cistercians, but this is never stated. In fact, were it not for the fact that the *Queste* was composed before the Carmelite friars are known to have became widespread in the West, it would seem more logical for these 'white brothers' to be Carmelite friars, dubbed 'white brothers' because of their white habits. The Carmelites originated in the Holy Land, to which the Grail departs in the last part of the *Queste*.[56]

Lewis Thorpe summed up the conventional nature of medieval fictional literature as follows:

> So much of mediaeval literature is in absolute essence a repeated statement and re-statement of certain folk-lore themes, which can be traced, usually fruitlessly, across the map of Europe and Asia – the Amazon knight, Potiphar's wife, the substituted letter, birth marks, the man disguised as a woman, la princess lointaine, the incubus, the incuba, the incubum.[57]

---

[54] See, for example, Trotter, *Medieval French Literature*, pp. 29, 33, 89, 98, 101, 104–5, 227, 249.

[55] See, for instance, Beer, *Narrative Conventions of Truth*; Berg, 'La littérature chevaleresque dans la Flandre,' pp. 331–8, here p. 337.

[56] Pauphilet, *Études sur la Queste del Saint Graal*, pp. 54–6; *La Queste del Saint Graal, roman du XIIIe siècle*, ed. A. Pauphilet, CFMA 33 (Paris, 1980), pp. ix–x, and, for instance, p. 26, lines 26–9; Matarasso, *Redemption of Chivalry*, pp. 14, 216, 224–41; Karen Pratt, 'The Cistercians and the *Queste del Saint Graal*', *Reading Medieval Studies*, 21 (1995), 69–96, here 72–88; Jill Mann, 'Malory and the Grail Legend', in *A Companion to Malory*, ed. Elizabeth Archibald and A.S.G. Edwards (Cambridge, 1996), pp. 203–20, here pp. 207–8. The Carmelites are generally believed to have begun expansion in the West in 1238. Only one historian, John Bale, writing in the sixteenth century, dated their expansion from 1187: see Andrew Jotischky, *The Perfection of Solitude: Hermits and Monks in the Crusader States* (Philadelphia, 1995), p. 132.

[57] *Le Roman de Silence: A thirteenth-century Arthurian verse-romance by Heldris de Cornuälle*, ed. Lewis Thorpe (Cambridge, 1972), p. 35 note 93.

Hence, when certain works of medieval literature repeatedly break from convention to name and cite a specific, existing institution in particular well-defined roles, then this should lead us to ask why contemporary actuality has impinged upon literary convention. Moreover, when an actually existing institution repeatedly appears in different 'fictional' literary works which differ widely in type, content and date, it is necessary to ask what this appearance may tell us about the composition of this literature: for this appearance indicates that contemporary actuality, rather than convention, was becoming important in 'fictional' literature by the late twelfth century and increased in importance throughout the rest of the Middle Ages. It should be useful to examine the roles given to this actually-existent institution in the invented literary world, and to ask what these roles might tell us about how this institution was viewed by at least the patrons of this literature, or perhaps by a wider band of society, and whether we can deduce from this anything about the patrons or society at large. As the appearances of this institution are very widespread over a long period of time, the problems of precisely defining patron, author and audience of any one work do not have a material impact on the conclusions: the sample is large enough to compensate for this.

The particular medieval institutions in question are the Military Orders. This study, therefore, sets out to examine the roles of the Military Orders in certain categories of fictional medieval literature with a view to not only gaining insights into medieval views of the Military Orders and of crusading but also of gaining insights into the beliefs and value systems of the knightly classes and evidence of changes in the composition of fictional literature from the late twelfth century, when the Military Orders first began to appear in such literature.

3 *A brief introduction to medieval fictional literature*

The period considered in this study is 1150–1500. In the first half of the twelfth century vernacular 'fictional' literature in France, Germany and England was almost invariably written in verse. This vernacular literature may be divided into several broad categories; this study will consider epic and romance literature and omit satire, love poetry and the scurrilous *fabliaux* except where they provide valuable supporting evidence or help to illustrate a point.

In the twelfth century French was the language of Western European secular culture and the bulk of epic and romance literature which survives was composed in French. All the English nobility spoke it and read French; hence, for instance, in the first half of the thirteenth century the author of the first part of the prose *Tristan* claimed to be an English knight, while the Vulgate *Lancelot*, *Queste del Saint Graal* and *La Mort le Roi Artu* claimed to have been written by the Anglo-Welsh cleric Walter Map.[58] German literature was often translated or adapted from French works of epic or romance, such as the version of the 'Roland' story written by the Priest Konrad for Duke Henry the Lion of Saxony (the *Rolandslied*), or the *Erec* and the *Iwein* composed by Hartmann von Aue. French fictional literature remained influential throughout the Middle Ages, but national differences in literature became much more marked. In England by the end of the fourteenth century English was becoming reestablished as a literary language for the noble classes, and French literature was being read in English translation rather than the original. In Germany by this period some German literature was still translated from French romance, but D.H. Green has argued that German literature after 1200, even more than French literature, centred on demonstratively historical works, which included epic, and on religious legend.[59] As a result, few French romances were translated into German after 1200, and German literature became much more independent of French literature than was English literature. In short, whereas at the beginning of the period under consideration in this study most of the 'fictional' literary works to be considered were composed in French, in the later period original works of German literature and fictionalised history and also some works of English literature – original compositions or translated from French – must additionally be considered.

The subject-matter for literature could be taken from classical sources, such as the stories of Alexander or the history of Troy (the so-called 'Matter of Rome' or 'Matter of the Orient'); from history, such as the reigns of Charlemagne or Louis the Pious (the 'Matter of France'); from legend with its roots in history, such as the stories of Arthur (the 'Matter of Britain'); from oriental legends, as in the case of the cycle of the Seven Sages of Rome (also regarded as part of the 'Matter of Rome' or 'Matter of the Orient'); from folklore, or from contemporary events and settings. Works could combine various elements from different sorts of sources. Some works were written to fit into an already-existing tradition, such as Arthurian legend or the epics of Charlemagne, but others were independent, combining traditional elements with a present-day setting to produce an original story. Although many writers wrote anonymously, and many did not name their patron, they were usually anxious to identify a written source for their work, often a Latin chronicle which they claimed to have translated.

In the twelfth century epic literature was written in epic metre, consisting of groups (*laisses*) of long lines each with a caesura. The exact form of epic

---

[58] *Tristan*, ed. Curtis, 1, p. 39, lines 10–14; *Lancelot, roman en prose du XIII siècle*, ed. Alexandre Micha, 9 vols, TLF 247 etc. (Geneva, 1978–83), 6, p. 244, line 16; *Queste*, p. 280, lines 1–3; *La Mort le Roi Artu, roman du XIII siècle*, ed. J. Frappier, TLF 58 (Geneva, 1964), p. 2, lines 1–16.

[59] Green, *Medieval Listening and Reading*, pp. 265–9.

metre varied. In Old French epic verse, the last word of each line of a laisse assonates, while Middle English epic verse is made up of alliterating words rather than assonating or rhyming lines.

The epic or *chanson de geste* is generally described as being concerned with the history of a family rather than of an individual, although stories generally concentrated on a certain individual who played a central role, such as Roland in *La Chanson de Roland*, Guillaume d'Orange in *Aliscans*, Sebille in the *Chanson des Saisnes*, and la Belle Hélène de Constantinople in the epic poem named after her. The central theme is conflict, either between parent and children, lord and vassal or Christian and non-Christian. The epic is characterised by long descriptions of scenes of general battle, although single combats also occur. Epics in general also have a lesser degree of fantasy and love-interest than romances. However, magic and love do appear in some epic works, and scholars often prefer to use the term 'romance-epic' to refer to these.

French epic poets usually composed within the confines of an existing tradition, with some basis in the actual past. Hence, epic works can be grouped into 'cycles'; the cycle of Charlemagne, the cycle of Guillaume, of Dagobert, of the Crusade, and so on. For the convenience of scholars, André Moisan has listed the works in each of these epic cycles and drawn up family trees of the characters who appear in them.[60]

Epic poetry remained popular throughout the Middle Ages. In the fourteenth century new works were still being composed, while some of the older epics, such as *Renaut de Montalban*, were rewritten to produce stories in the style now demanded by audiences: longer, with more involved plots and more development of character and motivation. There was also a movement towards including middle class and working class heroes, such as Hugh Capet the butcher in *Hugues Capet*, and Regnier the charcoalburner in *Theséus de Cologne*. This may reflect the widening of the audience for epic to include the bourgeoisie and the better-off artisan class, or, more likely, a greater awareness on the part of the nobility of the importance of non-nobles in society, perhaps prompted by non-noble movements such as the 'Jacquerie' in France and the 'Peasants' Revolt' in England.[61] In the fifteenth century in France verse epics were rewritten into prose with still more complexity of plot and development of character and motivation. Overall, works became increasingly reflective of

---

[60] André Moisan, *Répertoire des nons propres de personnes et de lieux cités dans les chansons de geste françaises et les oeuvres étrangères dérivées*, 2 tomes in 5 vols (Geneva, 1986), 1.1, pp. 72–97; 2.5, pp. 959–1025.

[61] *Hugues Capet: chanson de geste du XIV siècle*, ed. Noëlle Laborderie, CFMA 122 (Paris, 1997); Robert Bossuat, 'La Chanson de Hugues Capet', *Romania*, 71 (1950), 450–81; on Regnier the charcoalburner see Elizabeth E. Rosenthal, 'Theséus de Cologne: A General Study and Partial Edition', PhD thesis, Birkbeck College, University of London, 1975; pp. 337, 378, and on attitudes towards the middle and working classes in fourteenth century epic poetry see pp. 300–301, 352, 364, 378D, 378H, 378K, 378L and note 2.

contemporary actuality, although remaining within the literary conventions of the epic.

Vernacular romances first appeared in the twelfth century. 'Romances' centre upon the career of one individual or – in longer works – a series of individuals. The central character is usually a man but occasionally a woman (such as Silence in *Le Roman de Silence*) and the story focusses on their search for assimilation, recognition and fulfilment, either in this world through renown and/or marriage or in the next through a search for God, as in the Grail romances. As the focus is on a single named individual, single combats occur more frequently than general battle, and the love between two individuals often forms an important part of the plot. Magic is more likely to appear than in epics. However, as stated above, the epic and romance genres could be very similar, and the term 'romance-epic' is more appropriate for some works, such as the Romance of Alexander, or the later parts of the epic First Crusade Cycle.

French verse romances were written in octosyllabic rhyming couplets. The most famous French verse romances were the Arthurian romances written by Chrétien de Troyes in the period 1160–92. He records that he wrote his poem *Le Chevalier de la Charrette* for Marie, countess of Champagne, while his *Conte du Graal* was written for Philip of Alsace, count of Flanders. Chrétien's sources remain a subject of scholarly debate. Verse romances continued to be written throughout the thirteenth century, becoming progressively longer and more complex, with greater development of character in the better adventure romances such as *Sone de Nausay* or *Nansay*. They might be part of a 'cycle', for instance, being based around King Arthur or Tristan, but many stories were not. Verse romances remained popular in England and in Germany, where Ulrich Füetrer was writing in verse in the 1480s. In France, however, although verse epics continued to be composed until at least the late fourteenth century (such as *Theséus de Cologne*), prose became the preferred medium for the romance. Fewer romances were composed in verse in the fourteenth century: the *Roman du Comte d'Anjou* appeared in 1316, and *Le Chevalier au papegau*, an Arthurian romance, in the late fourteenth century. The last Arthurian verse romance in French was *Meliador*, composed by the chronicler-historian Jean Froissart at the end of the fourteenth century.[62]

Even in the early thirteenth century, French verse romances were being put into prose, and new romances were written in prose. The great bulk of prose romances were centred on King Arthur, or connected with the legend of Arthur in some way. For reasons that scholars are still debating, the plot of the French Arthurian prose romance became fixed by 1250. The best known form of the Arthurian legend, referred to by scholars as the 'Vulgate Cycle', was composed between 1210 and 1250. In its final form it consists of a prose

---

[62] Ménard, 'La réception', 239–40. Works mentioned here are either referenced by Ménard or are listed in the bibliography, below.

version of Robert de Boron's verse *Estoire dou Graal* or *Joseph* and a prose version of his *Merlin*, followed by a sequel to the *Merlin* describing Merlin's death and the early years of King Arthur's reign (the 'Suite du Merlin'), a romance of Lancelot, the story of the Quest for the Holy Grail, and the story of the death of Arthur. The 'Vulgate Cycle' seems to have been the work of a number of authors, and scholars debate whether it was originally conceived as a whole or composed piecemeal with each part being written by different authors as separate works and put together by later redactors. A later or 'Post-Vulgate' version of the Arthurian story was composed in the 1230s by one author who called himself 'Robert de Boron' and called his work *Le Roman du Graal*. Modern scholars assume that this author used the name 'Robert de Boron' as a pseudonym.[63] The *Roman du Graal* was followed by a long prose romance about King Meliadus of Leonnois and Guiron le Courtois, set in the early days of King Arthur's reign with 'flash-backs' to the reign of his father Uther, and a long prose romance of Tristan, in which Tristan is closely connected with King Arthur's court. Although there were at least three different sequels to the *Merlin* – the Vulgate, the Post-Vulgate and another version now known as the *Livre d'Artus* – and later redactors such as Rusticien de Pise reworked and combined these romances, no new French Arthurian prose romances were written after 1250.[64] Some early thirteenth-century French

---

[63] On the *Roman du Graal* see Fanni Bogdanow, *The Romance of the Grail – a Study of the Structure and Genesis of a Thirteenth-Century Arthurian Prose Romance* (Manchester, 1966).

[64] The following editions of the Arthurian prose romances have been used for this study. The prose *Lestoire del Saint Graal* and the vulgate *Merlin* from *The Vulgate Version of the Arthurian Romances, edited from Manuscripts in the British Museum*, ed. H. Oskar Sommer, 8 vols (Washington, 1908–16), 1 and 2; *Lancelot, roman en prose du XIII siècle*, ed. Alexandre Micha, 9 vols, TLF 247 etc. (Geneva, 1978–83); *La Queste del Saint Graal, roman du XIIIe siècle*, ed. A. Pauphilet, CFMA 33 (Paris, 1980); *La Mort le Roi Artu, roman du XIII siècle*, ed. J. Frappier, TLF 58 (Geneva, 1964). A critical edition of the prose *Estoire del Saint Graal* is now available: *L'Estoire del Saint Graal*, ed. Jean-Paul Ponceau, 2 vols (Paris, 1997). The editor suggests that the work was composed before the *Queste del Saint Graal*, which will certainly provoke debate among scholars. For post-vulgate version of the Arthurian romances, I have used the following editions: *La Suite du Roman de Merlin*, ed. Gilles Roussineau, 2 vols, TLF 472 (Geneva, 1996); *La Version Post-Vulgate de la* Queste del Saint Graal *et de la* Mort Artu*: troisième partie du* Roman du Graal, ed. Fanni Bogdanow, 3 vols to date, numbered 1, 2 and 4 part 1, SATF (Paris, 1991); *A Demanda do Santo Graal*, ed. Augusto Magne, 3 vols and 1 vol. (Rio de Janeiro, 1944–49, 1955); *Le Livre d'Artus*, in *Vulgate Version*, 7; the prose *Tristan*, in two parts: *Le roman de Tristan en prose*, ed. Renée L. Curtis, 3 vols (Cambridge, 1985), and *Le roman de Tristan en prose*, ed. Philippe Ménard *et al.*, 9 vols, TLF 353 etc. (Geneva, 1987–97); there is no critical edition of 'Meliadus' and 'Guiron li Cortois', collectively also known as 'Palamedes', although V. Bubenicek is preparing an edition of part of the work (Ménard, 'La réception', 224 note 2). The printed editions referred to in this study are facsimiles of the sixteenth-century editions: *Meliadus de Leonnoys, 1532*, introduction by C.E. Pickford (London, 1980); *Gyron le Courtoys, c. 1501*, with an introductory note by C.E. Pickford (London, 1979). Although Lathuillère, *Guiron*, p. 17, insists on the title *Guiron le Courtois* for the whole work, I have used the title *Meliadus-Gyron* because these are the titles of the only published edition currently available. The printed editions are based on a manuscript very like B.N. f. fr. 355, a mixed manuscript which corresponds to Lathuillère's analysis sections 1 to 48, 158, 53, 58–78, 159–60, 104–32. I have tried to ensure the validity of my analysis of the printed editions by checking them to Lathuillère's analysis. The

Arthurian prose romances, the so-called 'Didot' *Perceval* and *Perlesvaus* or *Le Haut Livre du Graal*, stood outside this standardised tradition, but no more were written after 1250. However, works connected to but separate from this tradition were composed, such as *Les Prophecies de Merlin* and the *Roman de Perceforest*; the former in the 1270s, the latter between *c.* 1335 and 1344.

Not all French prose romances dealt with Arthur; the cycle of the Seven Sages of Rome, composed in the second half of the thirteenth century, contains an Arthurian episode in *Le Roman de Laurin*, but much of the material elsewhere in the cycle is from oriental folklore. In the fifteenth century French prose adventure romances appeared, full of detailed description and far more rooted in contemporary actuality than were the old Arthurian prose romances. These works included *Jehan de Saintré*, *Jehan d'Avesnes*, and *Cleriadus et Meliadice*; these might refer to the Arthurian legend, but were independent of it.[65]

In England and Germany, verse remained a favoured medium for fictional literature. Verse metres varied. Some works were translated or adapted from French. Wolfram von Eschenbach's *Parzival*, written in the first decade of the thirteenth century, is based on a translation of Chrétien de Troyes' *Conte du Graal*, written *c.* 1185–92.[66] The French prose *Lancelot* was translated into German prose in the thirteenth century; the French fifteenth-century prose *Pontus et Sidoine* was translated into German prose in the same century.[67] Thomas Malory's *Morte Darthur*, published in 1485, is a compilation, redaction and translation into English of some of the thirteenth-century French Arthurian prose romances, with additional material such as the alliterative *Morte Arthure*.[68] The French prose *Merlin* and its vulgate sequel were translated into English prose in 1450–60.[69] In contrast, in Germany in the second half of the fifteenth century Ulrich Füetrer was compiling and rewriting thirteenth-century German romance works in verse and prose, rather than using French sources, such as his *Prosaroman von Lanzelet* from the German prose *Lanzelet*, and his verse *Buch der Abenteuer* from Wolfram von Eschenbach's *Parzival*, Albrecht's *Jüngerer Titurel*, and the anonymous *Lohengrin*.

'vulgate' text of *Guiron le Courtois* has not yet been published; it may be that when it does appear some of the arguments on pages 205–7 below will be shown to be based on false dating, but this will not affect my overall conclusions.

[65] See Ménard, 'La réception', 240–41.

[66] On these works, see Chapter 4, below.

[67] *Pontus und Sidonia*, ed. K. Schneider (Berlin, 1961), a translation of *Le Roman de Pontus et Sidoine*, ed. M.-C. de Crécy, TLF 475 (Geneva, 1998).

[68] Thomas Malory, 'The Tale of King Arthur' in *The Works of Sir Thomas Malory*, ed. Eugène Vinaver, 3 vols, 2nd edn (Oxford, 1967).

[69] *Merlin: the Early History of King Arthur: a prose romance about 1450–1460 AD, edited from the unique manuscript in the University Library Cambridge*, ed. Henry B. Wheatley, 2 vols, EETS (London, 1899).

4 *The Military Orders: a brief history*

The Military Orders were religious orders set up in the Holy Land in the twelfth century, in the wake of the conquest of Jerusalem by the First Crusade in July 1099. The First Crusade itself was a combination of holy war (war in the name of God for the defence of the faith), and pilgrimage (a penitential journey to a sacred site, for which participants were promised partial or complete remission of sins). At that time and throughout the Middle Ages commentators did not always distinguish between 'crusade' and 'pilgrimage', and scholars are not agreed on the precise definition of crusade. Some scholars hold that the only true crusades were those to defend the Holy Land, and that these ended in 1291 when the last Latin Christian strongholds in the Holy Land fell to the Mamluk sultans of Egypt. Others argue that a crusade was any military expedition proclaimed or supported by the papacy for which participants were promised the crusade indulgence of remission of their sins and privileges of Church protection, and in which combatants wore the sign of the cross and took vows.[70] It is important to distinguish between the broad definition of 'holy war', which does not necessarily require formal Church participation and in which there is no formal promise of remission of sin – although participants expect remission of their sins if they are killed – and the more specific definition of 'the crusade', a holy war which required active Church involvement and approval and the taking of formal vows, and for which the spiritual rewards were set out by the papal bull which called the crusade and by the preachers who were appointed by the Church authorities to publicize the crusade. Crusades were holy wars, but they were a specific type of holy war.[71]

The Military Orders' major function was to carry on the work of the crusaders in defending Christians and Christian territory against aggressive non-Christians. They attracted volunteers from all ranks of society. The most prominent members were knights, but also included *servientes*, non-knightly fighting men, craftsmen and servants, as well as clergy and women, who might be nuns or might be nursing sisters, depending on the order. Members were not crusaders, because they were committed to God's service for life, unlike crusaders who were only bound to fight for the duration of the expedition. Full members of the Military Orders were fully professed religious, taking the three

---

[70] This is the definition given by Norman Housley in *Later Crusades*, p. 2.

[71] For the definition of crusading, see, for instance, Jonathan Riley-Smith, *What were the Crusades?*, 2nd edn (Basingstoke, 1992); Christopher Tyerman, *The Invention of the Crusades* (Basingstoke, 1998). On crusades as holy wars, see John Gilchrist, 'The Papacy and the War against the "Saracens"', *International History Review*, 10 (1988), 174–97.

monastic vows of poverty, chastity and obedience. The Military Orders continued to attract volunteer recruits throughout the Middle Ages.[72]

The concept of the Military Orders, warriors serving God on the battlefield, was a natural development of the Catholic European society of the twelfth century. Catholic tradition allowed the papacy to declare wars in defence of Christendom to be holy wars, in which those who died fighting for Christendom would receive forgiveness of their sins. During the religious reforms of the eleventh and twelfth century new forms of religious orders appeared which were no longer limited to noble men and women enclosed in a single house and following a well-defined rule, but included hermits, houses of priests, hospitals and which – in the case of the Cistercian Order – allowed non-nobles to enter a religious house as laybrothers and work out their salvation through manual work rather than contemplation. To win salvation through fighting was not particularly revolutionary next to such radical new developments. The First Crusade (1095–99) had allowed Christian warriors to win forgiveness of their sins in return for fighting against the enemies of Christendom; the Military Order made this a permanent means to salvation for the warrior classes. While there were some objections to the concept of the Military Orders on the grounds that religious men should not shed blood, the only strong objections came from the heretical Waldensians and Cathars, who were pacifists. Hence James of Vitry declared in the thirteenth century that to question the concept of the Military Order was a sign of heresy. The Military Orders were orthodox Catholics, and their vocation was regarded as essential to the defence of Christendom.[73]

The direct predecessor of the first Military Order may have been a knightly confraternity. During the eleventh century these associations of knights became quite common: members would band together for some good purpose, such as maintaining the peace in their area, the protection of a monastery, or mutual support on an expedition. These were informal, secular groupings which might involve the Church in that the knights took oaths of fidelity to the group and promised to use their swords only to fight for good, but otherwise had no formal connection with Church institutions. It is possible that such an

---

[72] The best introduction to the Military Orders in English is Alan Forey, *The Military Orders: From the Twelfth to the Early Fourteenth Centuries* (Basingstoke, 1992).

[73] Alan Forey, 'The Emergence of the Military Order in the twelfth century', *Journal of Ecclesiastical History*, 36 (1985), 175–95, and reprinted in his *Military Orders and Crusades* (Aldershot, 1994), I; for the new monasticism, see C.H. Lawrence, *Medieval Monasticism: Forms of Religious Life in Western Europe in the Middle Ages*, 2nd edn (London, 1989), pp. 149–237; Henrietta Leyser, *Hermits and the New Monasticism: a Study of Religious Communities in Western Europe, 1000–1150* (London, 1984); for the long tradition of the concept of holy war in Catholic Christianity see Gilchrist, 'The Papacy and the War against the 'Saracens'; for criticism of the concept of the Military Order, see Nicholson, *Templars, Hospitallers*, pp. 37–40; for James of Vitry's defence of the concept, see his thirty-eighth sermon, in *Analecta novissima spicilegii Solesmensis: altera continuatio 2, Tusculana*, ed. J.B. Pitra (Paris, 1888), p. 419.

association of knights in the Holy Land, seeking the blessing of the patriarch of Jerusalem for their military activity in defence of the pilgrim routes, became – with Church approval and support – the Order of the Temple.[74]

The three leading international Military Orders, in order of militarisation, were the Order of the Temple of Solomon of Jerusalem (or Templars), the Order of the Hospital of St John of Jerusalem (or Hospitallers) and the Hospital of St Mary of the Teutons (or Teutonic Knights). The Order of the Temple of Solomon was so called because its headquarters in Jerusalem was the al-Aqsa mosque, which the Latin Christians identified, erroneously, as Solomon's Temple. Before being given to the Order, it had served as a royal palace for the Latin kings of Jerusalem. The Order was military from its first official foundation, probably at the Council of Nablūs in January 1120. The Hospital was named after the hospice for poor sick pilgrims which the Order ran in Jerusalem. The Order's role of guarding pilgrims on the pilgrim routes within the Holy Land was a natural development of this role. When the Hospital became militarised is a matter of scholarly debate, but it was certainly becoming involved in military activity by the 1130s and was fully militarised by the 1160s, while maintaining its role as a Hospital. The Teutonic Order, which originated during the siege of Acre (1189–91) during the Third Crusade, also began as a hospice for sick pilgrims and did not become a Military Order until 1198.

These three international Orders also became involved in defending Christian territory in Europe: the Templars and Hospitallers in Spain, and the Teutonic Order in Prussia and Livonia, where 'defence' became an offensive war against the pagan Prussians and Lithuanians and the Christian Orthodox Russians. Their military operations on the frontiers were supported by a vast network of estates in Europe, from which money, warriors and other supplies were sent to the frontier. As a result of their need to collect resources in the West for supplying their centres of operations on the frontiers, the Military Orders also became involved in trade and other economic activities and banking. They also became servants and advisors of popes, kings and nobles throughout Europe. They were therefore very much 'in the public eye' and attracted a good deal of comment from contemporaries, favourable and unfavourable.

After the final loss of the Latin Christian territories in the East to the Muslims in May 1291, the Orders of the Temple and Hospital removed their

---

[74] See Forey, 'Emergence', 189; for one such confraternity, see Marcus Bull, 'The Confraternity of La Sauve-Majeure: a Foreshadowing of the Military Order?' in *The Military Orders: Fighting for the Faith*, ed. Barber, pp. 313–19; Bull points out that this was rather different from the later Military Orders, but that nevertheless the existence of such confraternities forms the background to the emergence of the Military Orders. On the beginnings of the Templars see Barber, *New Knighthood*, pp. 6–8.

headquarters to Cyprus, while the Teutonic Order moved its headquarters to Venice. The Hospitallers went on to conquer Rhodes from 1306 onwards; the Teutonic Order moved its headquarters to Marienburg in Prussia in 1309. The Order of the Temple, on the instigation of King Philip IV of France, was dissolved by the pope in 1312 and its properties transferred to the Order of the Hospital. There were also national Military Orders in Spain. The most famous of these were the Order of Santiago, also known as the Order of St James of Compostella, and the Order of Calatrava.

From 1300 to 1522 the Hospital of St John was involved in naval and land action against the Mamluks and, later the Ottoman Turks, in the Eastern Mediterranean, Asia Minor, Greece and the Balkans. It finally lost Rhodes to the forces of Suleiman the Magnificent at the beginning of 1523. In 1530 the Order accepted an offer from the Emperor Charles V to use the island of Malta as its base, and continued hostilities against the Ottoman Turks from Malta until the surrender of the island to Napoleon in 1798. The Teutonic Order continued to wage war against the pagan Lithuanians from its bases in Prussia and Livonia. Both Orders were assisted by forces from the West; the Hospital took part in various naval leagues with Venice, Genoa and other naval powers, while western European knights came out to Rhodes to give military and naval assistance. The Teutonic Order's Prussian base became a popular destination for knights who wanted military experience against the pagans. The Orders' regular expeditions against the Lithuanians, *Reisen*, were deliberately promoted by the Order as a means of winning honour and glory as well as serving God against the pagans. The *Reisen* continued even after the official conversion of Lithuania to Christianity in 1386. However, after the Order was defeated by the allied forces of Poland-Lithuania at Tannenberg (Grunwald) in 1410 and the ideology underlying its wars came under attack at the Council of Constance, 1414–18, the number of western Europeans prepared to come to the Prussian front was greatly reduced. Economic and political crises within Prussia as well as continued conflict with Poland-Lithuania resulted in the destruction of the Teutonic Order's hegemony in Prussia. In 1466, with the Second Treaty of Thorn, the Teutonic Order in Prussia became a vassal of the king of Poland, although its Livonian branch retained considerable independence.[75]

---

[75] See Anthony Luttrell, 'The Military Orders, 1312–1798', in *The Oxford Illustrated History of the Crusades*, ed. Jonathan Riley-Smith (Oxford, 1995), pp. 326–64; Housley, *Later Crusades*, pp. 214–33, 322–75, 399–402.

5 *Plan of this Study*

The military religious orders did not play a leading or dominant role in knightly epic and romance literature, but from around 1175 until the latter part of the fifteenth century and later they repeatedly appeared by name in certain conventionalised roles. They did not appear in every form of epic and romance literature: they did not appear in the great prose Arthurian romances of the thirteenth century, the Vulgate Cycle and its post-vulgate reworkings, or in the prose *Tristan*, *Meliadus* or *Gyron le Courtoys*. The spiritual aspect of the Military Orders' vocation received little attention: although they were knights of Christ, men of great courage and piety, this was not stressed but simply taken for granted. Their image was almost invariably good, and remained almost undamaged throughout the Middle Ages. This was ironic in light of the severe criticism that the Teutonic Order, for instance, received in eastern Europe and the Baltic States from the late thirteenth century onwards;[76] but the western and central European audiences for whom the works examined here were written did not share these criticisms.

From their first appearance, the Military Orders' roles in epic and romance literature developed and multiplied with time. Firstly, they appeared as monks, fulfilling one of the traditional roles of monks: providing a place of penance for wrongdoers. This was later expanded to being a place of retirement from the world, either at the end of one's life, as a thankoffering to God, or for a person grieving at a personal loss. The Templars in particular appeared helping lovers. The Orders also performed various charitable duties, guiding pilgrims, giving lodging and giving burial to the dead. Secondly, they appeared as knights of Christ, fighting at the hero's side against the enemies of the faith. As a corollary to their role as knights they appeared as counsellors of kings and of the hero. However, while their spiritual virtues were always taken for granted as prerequisite for these roles, they were seldom stressed to the extent of making the Military Orders the spiritual guides of the Christian knight. The assistance which they gave the hero was secular and physical rather than spiritual.[77] Thirdly, the Templars appeared as guardians of the Grail castle in Wolfram von Eschenbach's masterpiece *Parzival* and in some of the later adaptations of this work. This study suggests that this role should be interpreted in a specific historical context.

Part One of this study surveys the development of each of these roles in turn, and considers how these relate to the actual Orders in contemporary

---

[76] See, for example, Michael Burleigh, *Prussian Society and the German Order. An Aristocratic Corporation in Crisis, c. 1410–1466* (Cambridge, 1984), esp. pp. 111–13; Eric Christiansen, *Northern Crusades*, pp. 145–7, 223–32; Norman Housley, *The Avignon Papacy and the Crusades, 1305–1378* (Oxford, 1986), pp. 267–70; Housley, *Later Crusades*, pp. 331–2, 344–7, 358–62.

[77] There are a few exceptions, for which see pp. 70–72 below.

society or in the past. In particular, the historical context for Wolfram von Eschenbach's *Parzival* is reconsidered and a new historical interpretation of this work suggested. Overall, I trace how each of the Military Orders' literary roles developed with time and whether roles changed in later adaptations of each work. Part Two analyses why the Military Orders appear in some works but not in others, and the function that their appearance seems to have performed. I then consider what the Military Orders' appearances indicate of patrons' or audiences' views of the actual Orders in contemporary society, and what the results of this were for the actual Military Orders.[78]

Before beginning this survey, it is necessary to establish what constitutes a reference to a Military Order in literature. For the purpose of this study, the Military Order must be mentioned by name, as a description without the name would not necessarily have been interpreted by patron or audience as referring to a Military Order. For example, as will become clear in relation to the Grail legend, a reference to a knight with a red cross on his shield is not a specific reference to a Military Order but to any warrior of Christ. Certainly some readers or listeners may have interpreted such a reference as referring to a Military Order, but we cannot be sure that they did. In addition, if the appearance or organisation of the named Military Order is described, the description should correspond to what is known of the actual Orders, and should follow the ideal set out above. The brothers should have sworn chastity, poverty and obedience and follow a religious rule; they should live in a community of brothers; they should be devoted to laying down their lives for Christ in battle for an eternal reward in Heaven. Some of the general allusions to knights of Christ which might or might not refer to a Military Order have considerable interest in themselves and are given consideration.

The literature under examination is epic and romance; this study refers to satire and to chronicles when necessary to illustrate a point, but in order to keep within manageable limits it is necessary to limit the literature under discussion. As stated in the preface to this study, to divide 'fictional literature' sharply from 'historical writing' is to make a false distinction for this period, as much writing now regarded as 'history' was written in the style of 'fictional' literature, much 'fiction' in the style of history, and both were written to edify as well as to entertain. As this is a subject which has been studied by others

---

[78] Some of the references which follow were originally traced from E. Langlois, *Table des noms propres de toute nature compris dans les chansons de geste* (Paris, 1904); L.-F. Flutre, *Table des noms propres avec toutes leurs variantes figurant dans des romans du moyen âge* (Poitiers, 1962); Moisan, *Répertoire*; Helmut Birkhan, 'Les croisades contre des païens de Lituanie et de Prusse. Idéologie et réalité', in *La Croisade: réalités et fictions*, ed. Danielle Buschinger (Göppingen, 1989), pp. 31–50; Danielle Buschinger, 'La signification de la croisade dans la littérature allemande du moyen âge tardif', in *La Croisade*, pp. 51–60; Bernd Schirok, *Parzivalrezeption im Mittelalter* (Darmstadt, 1984); Friedrich-Wilhelm Wentzlaff-Eggebert, *Kreuzzugsdichtung des Mittelalters: Studien zu ihrer geschichtlichen und dichterischen Wirklichkeit* (Berlin, 1960).

elsewhere I do not propose to discuss it in detail here.[79] Some of the works I consider could also be classified as history; but I have included them where the work includes a substantial fictional content and the role of the Military Order corresponds to that found in works normally classified as 'fiction'. Most of the evidence comes from Old French literature, with some from Middle High German and a little from Valencian Catalan and Middle English literature.

No survey of this kind may claim to have found every relevant reference from the period under consideration, as many works remain unpublished or do not have a modern critical edition. However, without claiming to be the final word on the subject, sufficient evidence has been discovered to establish a pattern in the literary images of the Military Orders in the Middle Ages, and to draw certain conclusions.

In this study frequent reference is made to the so-called 'knightly class' or 'knightly classes'. This is a deliberately vague expression, for what constituted a knight in law and the status of knights changed considerably during the period under consideration. By the mid-thirteenth century there also existed alongside knights those who were entitled by birth to take up knighthood but who preferred not to do so, for example for reasons of cost. These squires were from a similar social background to some knights and shared their outlook and aspirations but not their rank. While by the late Middle Ages to be a knight was necessarily to hold high social rank, in the twelfth century many knights were of relatively low social status. In this study, the term 'knights' or 'knightly class' is used to refer to those individuals or families who expected to fight as professional or semi-professional warriors on horseback in armour and with their preferred weapons the sword and the lance – although in practice they might fight on foot, semi-armed or armed with a bow or axe, or might pass through their adult careers hardly ever fighting at all. Their professional or semi-professional fighting skills gave them a certain social status, although within this group or class a minority, the high nobility, were of very high social status, while the majority were of relatively low social status in comparison. It is clear that the aspirations and values of these individuals and families might be shared by merchants and by the better-off free farmers, but contemporaries would be well aware which individuals and families had the social status of skilled warriors and which did not, although for modern historians studying these people it may be difficult to distinguish between them. It was these individuals and families who held these ideals of skilled professional mounted warriors which constituted the social group for which the epics and romances

---

[79] On this problem for one of the works which will be mentioned below see *A Critical Edition of the Estoires d'Outremer et de la Naissance Saladin*, ed. Margaret A. Jubb (London, 1990), pp. 293–307; see also, for instance, Maurice Keen, 'Chivalry, Heralds and History', in *The Writing of History in the Middle Ages: Essays Presented to R.W. Southern*, ed. R.H.C. Davis and J.M. Wallace-Hadrill (Oxford, 1981), pp. 393–41 and reprinted in his *Nobles, Knights and Men-at-Arms*, pp. 63–81; Trotter, *Medieval French Literature*, pp. 20–28.

were written, and who adopted the 'invented tradition' or 'mythology' developed within this literature.[80] This was also the social group which supplied the 'knightly' element of the Military Orders, although in general only the knights of lower status actually joined the Orders in person, while the higher nobility supported them with donations of lands and privileges.[81]

---

[80] The literature on the development of knighthood is vast and can only be touched on here. See, for instance, Keen, *Chivalry*; Coss, *Knight in Medieval England*; Jean Flori, *Idéologie du glaive: préhistoire de la chevalerie* (Geneva, 1983); Jean Flori, *L'Essor de la chevalerie, XIe–XIIe siècles* (Geneva, 1986); Georges Duby, *The Chivalrous Society*, trans. Cynthia Postan (London 1977); and the other works by these authors listed in the bibliography to this book.

[81] Dieter Wojtecki, *Studien zur Personengeschichte des Deutschen Ordens im 13 Jahrhundert*, Quellen und Studien zur Geschichte des östlichen Europa, ed. Manfred Hellmann, vol. 3 (Wiesbaden, 1971), pp. 78–80, 88–91; Alan Forey, 'Recruitment to the Military Orders (twelfth to mid-fourteenth centuries), *Viator*, 17 (1986), 139–71: here 143–7; reprinted in his *Military Orders and Crusades*, II; John Walker, 'Crusaders and Patrons: the Influence of the Crusades on the Patronage of the Order of St Lazarus in England', in *The Military Orders: Fighting for the Faith*, ed. Barber, pp. 327–32.

PART ONE

SURVEY

CHAPTER TWO

MONASTIC ROLES

The first roles in which the Military Orders appeared in literature were essentially monastic. They first appeared as a place of penance, then as a place of retirement, and went on to appear giving hospitality, ransoming prisoners, and burying the dead, all roles that the Orders performed in actuality. The Templars also appear supporting lovers, and occasionally giving spiritual leadership; as will be seen, these were roles which developed from contemporary actuality, although they did not correspond to actuality.

1 *A place of penance*

The earliest reference to the Military Orders in an epic or romance appears in *Raoul de Cambrai*, written between 1175 and 1200. This was a popular tale, to judge from the number of references to it in other twelfth- and thirteenth-century texts. The story is set in the tenth century AD, and describes the career of Bernier, squire and illegitimate brother of Raoul de Cambrai. In the course of attempting to regain his patrimony, Raoul sets fire to the convent where Bernier's mother is abbess, and in a scene of horrific starkness the audience and Bernier watch Bernier's mother dying in the flames. In his terrible grief, Bernier pursues and kills Raoul; and with a deft twist of the pen the author reminds us that Raoul, despite his evil deed, was a handsome young man and a good knight and that his death, too, is a tragedy. Raoul's uncle Guerri then threatens to kill Bernier for killing his lord. In response, Bernier offers to sail to Acre and serve with the Templars there in penance.[1]

Service with the Templars as penance for a crime was a theme taken from contemporary events. Criminals were indeed sent overseas to serve at the Temple of Solomon in penance for their crimes, or were required to send knights to serve there. Criminals of previous generations had faced penance in a religious house or a requirement to go on pilgrimage; a pilgrimage to Jerusalem followed by penance in a religious house that consisted of fighting the enemies of Christians and possibly being killed in service was a reasonable

---

[1] *Raoul de Cambrai, chanson de geste*, ed. P. Meyer and A. Longnon, SATF (Paris, 1882), pp. xxxiii–lv; lines 3427–8; Moisan, *Répertoire*, 1.1, p. 58, for date.

development from this.² Bernard of Clairvaux wrote of 'villains and impious men, robbers and sacrilegious, homicides, perjurers and adulterers' going to fight with the Templars by the early 1130s; he does not state that they were sent in penance, but as he explains that Europe was glad to see them go it seems probable that some were sent in penance.³ Following the murder of Thomas Becket, archbishop of Canterbury, in December 1170, King Henry II of England was absolved by the Church on condition that he provide two hundred knights to serve for a year with the Templars in the Holy Land. In fact, Henry provided the money to pay two hundred knights, rather than sending the knights himself.⁴ The four knights responsible for the murder of the archbishop were condemned to go overseas and fight for the defence of Jerusalem. According to the later Lansdowne Codex MS 398 in the British Library, the knights were given penance by the pope, to go to the holy places of Jerusalem and fight fourteen years with military arms in the Temple against the pagans. The contemporary chronicler Roger of Howden tells us that they were sent by the pope to Jerusalem in penance and after their deaths they were buried in Jerusalem before the door of the Temple. He does not specify whether this is the Lord's Temple or the Temple of Solomon, but the latter seems more likely in the context. In fact, however, it is not clear whether the murderers did actually ever go to Jerusalem.⁵ In a similar vein, Peter the Venerable, abbot of Cluny, told in his *Miracula* how a local lord, Humbert of Beaujeu, who had inflicted much damage on local churches, especially the abbey of Cluny, received a vision in which he was warned to mend his ways or he would end up in the tortures of Hell. Terrified, Humbert went on pilgrimage to Jerusalem, where he joined the Order of the Temple – although he later left the Order and returned home again.⁶ In 1224 Pope Honorius III told the master of the Temple to receive a knight, Bertran, who had killed a bishop, into the house of the Templars for seven years to do penance for his crime.⁷ Clearly doing penance in the Order of the Temple was a suitable punishment for a

---

² Jonathan Sumption, *Pilgrimage: an Image of Medieval Religion* (London, 1975), pp. 98–113; pp. 99, 101 for pilgrimages before the foundation of the Military Orders. After the loss of Jerusalem in 1187, criminals were sometimes sent instead to Cyprus to fight the Muslims: pp. 105–6.

³ *De laude novae militiae*, p. 223.

⁴ Jonathan Phillips, *Defenders of the Holy Land: Relations Between the Latin East and the West, 1119–1187* (Oxford, 1996), p. 214; *Itinerarium peregrinorum*, ed. Stubbs, Bk 1, ch. 12, p. 26; *Das Itinerarium peregrinorum*, ed. Mayer, p. 269; lines 10–16.

⁵ 'Excerpta e codice ms⁽ᵗᵒ⁾ Lansdowniano', in *Materials for the History of Thomas Becket*, ed. J.C. Robertson, 7 vols, RS 67 (London, 1875–85), 4, p. 163; Roger of Howden, *Chronica*, ed. William Stubbs, 4 vols, RS 51 (London, 1868–71), 2, p. 17; see also Frank Barlow, *Thomas Becket* (London, 1986), 258–69; C. Tyerman, *England and the Crusades*, p. 43 and note 27.

⁶ On Humbert's early career, see Peter the Venerable, *Miracula*, Bk 1, ch. 27, in *Pat. Lat.*, 189, cols. 901–3; for his joining and leaving the Order of the Temple, see *The Letters of Peter the Venerable*, ed. Giles Constable, 2 vols (Cambridge, Mass., 1967), 1, pp. 407–13, nos. 172–3.

⁷ *Regesta Honorii papae III*, ed. Petrus Pressutti, 2 vols (Rome, 1888, reprinted Hildesheim, 1978), 2, p. 289, no. 5219.

knight accused of murder; presumably an honourable one, given that there was strong justification for Bernier's crime.

The literary role of the Order of the Temple as a place of penance appears again in *Orson de Beauvais*, written between 1180 and 1185, or early in the thirteenth century. This work was not well known, although it probably remained popular at Beauvais beyond the thirteenth century, as it was used by the author of *Valentin et Orson*, a prose romance composed between 1475 and 1489 and printed at Lyons by Jacques Maillet in 1489. *Orson de Beauvais* was also known in Lorraine, where the only surviving manuscript was copied at the end of the thirteenth century. It is set in the eighth century, in the reign of Charles Martel. Here the Templars appear in a false account given by Hugh, count of Berri, of the fate of his companion, Orson, whom Hugh has in fact sold to the Muslims. Hugh claims that Orson, on pilgrimage to Jerusalem, confessed to him that he had planned to assassinate King Charles, and then entered an abbey of the Holy Sepulchre; he later alters this account, saying that Orson entered the Order of the Temple. The bishop of Beauvais in the 1180s was an enthusiastic crusader, which may have encouraged the poet's interest in the actual city of Jerusalem and the Order of the Temple.[8] The fifteenth-century prose romance contains an episode with a similar theme: here the villainous Hugh persuades Orson and his brother-in-law the Green Knight to accompany him on pilgrimage to Jerusalem, where he has them arrested at Jerusalem by the Muslims and imprisoned. He then forges letters which state that they have decided to remain in Jerusalem to fight the Muslims.[9] The theme of penance had been slightly changed to reflect contemporary actuality: as the Latin Christians no longer held territory in the Holy Land by the late fifteenth century, the audience would not appreciate the reference to joining a religious order in Jerusalem, whereas taking part in wars against non-Christians in penance for sin and to win spiritual merit was still a popular concept among the nobility.

The Order of the Temple appears again as a place of penance in the immensely popular works *La Chevalerie d'Ogier de Danemarche* and *Renaut de Montauban*. Both works are set in the ninth century, in the reign of Charlemagne. *Ogier* was written around the end of the twelfth century; the original version of *Renaut* has been dated less precisely, to the twelfth century. In *Ogier*, Charlemagne's son Callot offers to visit the Holy Sepulchre with two

---

[8] *Orson de Beauvais, chanson de geste du XIIe siècle*, ed. G. Paris, SATF (Paris, 1899), lines 3319–21, pp. lxii–lxviii, lxxviii–lxxx; Moisan, *Répertoire*, 1.1, p. 56, for date. For the bishop of Beauvais as a crusader, see: *Itinerarium peregrinorum*, ed. Stubbs, Bk 1, ch. 29, p. 67; *Das Itinerarium peregrinorum*, ed. Mayer, p. 311, lines 13–16.

[9] *Valentin et Orson* (Jacques Maillet, Lyons, 1489), Chapter 71, fol. 103a–104b; Arthur Dickson, *Valentine and Orson: a Study in Late Medieval Romance* (New York, 1929), pp. 162, 165, 171, 175, 251, 265. *Valentin et Orson* was translated into English: *Valentine and Orson, translated from the French by Henry Watson*, ed. Arthur Dickson, EETS 204 (London, 1937).

hundred well-armed men and serve *al l'ospital au temple*, 'at the Hospital at the Temple' for seven years for the soul of Ogier's son Baldwin, whom he has killed in a rage during a game of chess. This obviously refers to the Hospital of St John as well as the Order of the Temple, and implies that the Hospital was part of the Order of the Temple, or was on the site of the Temple of Jerusalem – neither of which was correct. It is possible that *au temple* should read *ou temple*, and that Callot is saying that he will go to serve at the Hospital or the Temple. Nevertheless, *au temple* may be correct, for the Hospital of St John and the Order of the Temple worked in co-operation in military affairs, and the Hospital may have had some involvement in the foundation of the Order of the Temple. Later writers confused the two Orders, and this may simply be an example of such confusion. In any case, this reference in *Ogier* is the first mention of the Order of the Hospital in epic literature.[10]

In *Renaut*, Renaut offers to go to overseas as a penitent with his cousin Maugis and serve at the Temple in penance for killing Charlemagne's son. However, in this instance it is unclear when the Order of the Temple was introduced into this role; in the oldest surviving manuscript, copied in the mid-thirteenth century, it is the Holy Sepulchre, not the Temple, which is cited as a place of penance. Possibly the Order of the Temple was introduced at this point in place of the Holy Sepulchre by a later redactor who considered that a literary hero accused of murder should offer to go overseas and serve at the Temple, as occurred in *Raoul* and *Ogier*. Alternatively, it indicates that the writer identified the Temple of Solomon with the Holy Sepulchre, or believed that they were very closely related; this is also the case in *Orson de Beauvais*, where Count Hugh first claims that Orson joined the Holy Sepulchre and then that he joined the Templars. In fact, the confusion was perfectly understandable. There is some evidence that the Order of the Temple and the Order of the Hospital were at first dependent on the canons of the Holy Sepulchre. The two Orders' own iconography underlined their connection with the Holy Sepulchre: the seal of the master of the Order of the Temple clearly shows the dome of the church of the Holy Sepulchre, while a number of the churches which both the Templars and Hospitallers built in the West were constructed with round naves, on the model of the church of the Holy Sepulchre. These images formed a visual reminder to onlookers that these Orders were involved

---

[10] *La Chevalerie Ogier de Danemarche*, ed. M. Eusebi (Milan and Varese, 1953), line 10427, and pp. 34–5: five manuscripts survive. For early relations between the Hospital and the Order of the Temple, see *Chronique d'Ernoul et de Bernard le trésorier*, ed. L. de Mas Latrie, SHF (Paris, 1871), pp. 7–8; Anthony Luttrell, 'The Earliest Templars', in *Autour de la première Croisade*, ed. Michel Balard (Paris, 1996), pp. 193–202. For the Hospital of St John as a place of punishment, see *Cartulaire général de l'ordre des Hospitaliers*, no. 1598 (Brother J., a clerk); *Close Rolls of the reign of Henry III, 1234–1237* (London, 1908), pp. 151, 291, 324, 325, 361–2, 364, 366 (Geoffrey Bauzan was accused of robbery and breaking the king's peace; in October 1236 he was released from gaol and handed over to the Hospitallers at Clerkenwell).

in the defence of the Holy Sepulchre. The importance of the Holy Sepulchre as a Christian symbol can hardly be overstated: it is the empty tomb, the material evidence of Christ's triumph over death, and its defence against unbelievers was the fundamental reason for the Latin Christian presence in the Holy Land. Hence, a Templar messenger in the late-fourteenth-century long version of *Theséus de Cologne*, bringing news of Jerusalem to France, begins by stating that he and his companion have come from the Sepulchre where Christ was laid: not from Jerusalem or from the Temple of Solomon, but from the Sepulchre, the central relic of the Christian faith, as if this represented Jerusalem and the Temple of Solomon as well.[11]

Renaut was a popular story throughout the Middle Ages, and was translated into Flemish, German, Spanish, Italian, English and Icelandic. In the German verse translation, *Reinolt von Montelban*, Reinolt's offer to Charlemagne is slightly different to his offer in the French verse versions: he will go overseas with his three brothers and remain there for seven years, serving in a temple or a hospital: '*in eym tempel oder in eym hospital*'. This offer is more reminiscent of Callot's offer to Ogier in *La chevalerie Ogier* than Renaut's offer in the French verse versions of *Renaut*, but the translator does not seem to have realised that specific religious houses in Jerusalem were intended. What was

---

[11] *Renaus de Montauban, oder die Haimonskinder, Altfranzösisches Gedicht*, ed. H. Michelant, BLVS 67 (Stuttgart, 1862), p. 337, line 10; *La Chanson des quatre fils Aymon, d'après le manuscrit la Vallière*, ed. Ferdinand Castet (Montpellier, 1909, reprinted Geneva, 1974), line 12818, and see pp. 253–65 on the distribution of the story; for the oldest manuscript, see *Renaut de Montauban, édition critique du manuscrit Douce*, ed. J. Thomas, TLF 371 (Geneva, 1989), line 11000, etc., and p. 9; for date, see Moisan, *Répertoire*, 1.1, p. 58. *Renaut* survives in 13 manuscripts. On early connections between the Templars, the Hospitallers, and the canons of the Holy Sepulchre see Luttrell, 'The Earliest Templars'; Anthony Luttrell, 'The Earliest Hospitallers', in *Montjoie: Studies in Crusade History in Honour of Hans Eberhard Mayer*, ed. Benjamin Z. Kedar, Jonathan Riley-Smith and Rudolf Hiestand (Aldershot, 1997), pp. 37–54. For the Templars' master's seal, see Marie Luise Bulst-Thiele, *Sacrae domus militiae templi Hierosolymitani magistri: Untersuchungen zur Geschichte des Templerordens 1118/9–1314* (Göttingen, 1974), plates, facing page 416, no. 1b (seal of Master Bertrand de Blanchefort, 1168); and Barber, *New Knighthood*, p. 180. Comparison of these images to a modern photograph of the dome of the Church of the Holy Sepulchre (available in any good guidebook to Jerusalem) show a striking similarity. In contrast, the image on Bertrand de Blancfort's seal bears little ressemblance to the dome on the al Aqsa mosque, the Templars' base in Jerusalem, or even to the Dome of the Rock, the crusaders' 'Templum Domini'. The most striking difference is that on the al Aqsa mosque the supporting drum, the wall supporting the dome of the mosque above the roof of the mosque, is relatively low, with shallow arches set into the stonework in relief; whereas the drum supporting the dome of the church of the Holy Sepulchre is taller, with distinctive arches containing windows – as on the Templars' seal. In addition, whereas the seal shows a round building, neither the al Aqsa mosque nor the Dome of the Rock have a round floor plan; only the central part of the church of the Holy Sepulchre fits this description. On Templar and Hospitaller round-naved churches see Michael Gervers, 'Donations to the Hospitallers in England in the Wake of the Second Crusade', in *The Second Crusade and the Cistercians*, ed. Michael Gervers (New York, 1991), p. 159; Gilchrist, *Contemplation and Action*, pp. 71–2, 77, 94–5. Many British round-naved churches have no connection with the Military Orders but were built by crusaders as a visual reminder that they had visited the Holy Sepulchre, for instance, those at Ludlow, Northampton and Cambridge. For *Theséus de Cologne* see Bib. nat. nouv. acq. fr. 10060, fol. 260v.

originally an undertaking to serve in specific religious houses has become a general, stereotyped promise to perform penance in Jerusalem.[12]

A revised French version of *Renaut* was written in the second half of the fourteenth century. In this, Regnaut (as he is here) proposes in his peace terms to Charlemagne that he will go overseas to Acre to fight against 'la gent maufé' (meaning the Muslims), and to visit the Holy Sepulchre and conquer it. However, in recounting his offer to his wife, he says that he has vowed to go overseas to the Temple of Solomon, to conquer the city and the whole region. Obviously this writer did not intend 'going to the Temple' to mean 'serving with the Templars'. Instead, this writer, like the earlier writers, identified the Temple of Solomon and the Holy Sepulchre as being the same place, and identified both with Jerusalem itself. He understood 'going to the Temple of Solomon' or 'going to the Holy Sepulchre' to mean 'to go on crusade'. In the same way in the contemporary verse epic *Florent et Octavian* Florent decides to go overseas to the 'Temple of Solomon' as the equivalent of going to Jerusalem. Regnaut in fact goes on to capture the city of Jerusalem and becomes king. He later crowns his son Yvon as king of Jerusalem.[13]

The role of the Temple was amended again in the prose version of *Renaut*, composed during the fifteenth century, and printed several times. In around 1489 William Caxton produced his English translation of the prose version of *Renaut*, entitled *The Right Plesaunt and Goodly Historie of the Foure Sonnes of Aymon*: in this Renaut declares 'And soo shall I goo in to the holy londe, I and Mawgys, where we shall serve to the temple of our lorde'. Later, his cousin the enchanter Maugis says: 'And so wylle I goo to the holy londe, for to serve to the temple of Iherusalem, and for to vysite the holy sepulcre of our lorde …' The Lord's Temple was not identical with the Temple of Solomon, which was what was meant in the original work.[14] In fact, however, although here as in all versions of the story the two cousins visit Jerusalem and fight the Saracens to recapture Jerusalem for the Christians, they do not specifically serve at the Temple. It seems most probable that the writer understood 'to serve at the Temple' to mean simply 'to fight the Muslims', which was what the Templars did, and what Renaut and Maugis had done in earlier versions of

---

[12] *Reinolt von Montelban oder die Heimonskinder*, ed. Fridrich Pfaff, BLVS 174 (Tübingen, 1885; reprinted Amsterdam, 1969), lines 12594–7, esp. 12597. Two fifteenth-century manuscripts survive, dating from 1474–80: pp. 468–9. For the Dutch version of *Renaut*, see pp. 488–548.

[13] *<Renaut de Montauban>: edition critique du ms de Paris, B.N., fr. 764 (R)*, ed. Philippe Verelst (Ghent, 1988), lines 8361–2, 8365–9, 8421–4; for date, see p. 6. For the identification of the Temple of Solomon with the city of Jerusalem, see, for instance, lines 2064–6, 16495–6, 23548. See also *Florent et Octavien. Chanson de geste du XVI siècle*, ed. Noëlle Laborderie (Paris, 1991), line 11994.

[14] *The English Charlemagne Romances: parts X, XI: The Right Plesaunt and Goodly Historie of the Foure Sonnes of Aymon, Englisht from the French by William Caxton, and printed by him about 1489*, ed. Octavia Richardson, EETS Extra Series 44/45 (London, 1885), 2, pp. 409, 466, and 1, pp. xii–xiv.

the story. In the German prose version published in 1618 the author changed and clarified the hero's original offer, so that Reinolt now simply offers to take the cross and serve in the Holy Land for seven years.[15]

A very similar case occurs in the fifteenth-century manuscript of *Le Roman de Baudouin de Sebourc*. The poem was composed between 1350 and 1360 in the Valenciennes region; one of the surviving manuscripts used by the nineteenth-century editor dates from the fourteenth century, the other from the fifteenth. Towards the end of the poem, Baudouin is locked in single combat with the villain Gaufroit, who has not only poisoned the king of France but also inflicted numerous wrongs on Baudouin and his family. In the fifteenth-century manuscript, Gaufroit interrupts the battle to propose peace terms, which include a proposition that he and Baudouin should go to the Temple of Solomon and avenge Jesus Christ on the Muslims. Baudouin refuses, and eventually succeeds in defeating Gaufroit, who is put to death. In this poem the Temple of Solomon is the place where kings of Jerusalem are crowned, and, as is appropriate for the period in which it is set (the first and second decade of the twelfth century) the Templars do not yet exist. Obviously, the fifteenth- and fourteenth-century manuscripts represent different recensions: Edmond-René Labonde, in his study of the poem, concluded that the fifteenth-century manuscript was based on a later, revised version of the story. If this was the case, then the later redactor must have deliberately introduced this theme of penance at the Temple of Solomon into an episode where it did not exist in the original – although here, once again, going to the Temple is clearly only a synonym for going on crusade. This redactor must have been familiar with the earlier literary tradition in which penance at the Temple was appropriate for a wrongdoer, such as Callot in *Ogier* and the seneschal in *Guillaume de Dole*, of whom more below.[16]

The same theme of penance at the Temple of Solomon is described in a little more detail in *La Fille du Comte de Ponthieu*, a popular legend which linked the descent of Saladin with the counts of Ponthieu. The count of Ponthieu is depicted making a pilgrimage to the Holy Land and serving for

---

[15] Paul von der Aelst, *Die vier Heymons Kindern*, Bibliotheca Anastatica Germanica (Berne, Frankfurt am Main, New York, 1986; reprint of 1618 edition), p. 205 for Reinolt's offer: pp. 227–36 for Reinolt and Malegys in the Holy Land.

[16] *Li Romans de Bauduin de Sebourc, IIIe roy de Jhérusalem; poëme du XIVe siècle, publié pour la première fois d'après les manuscrits de la Bibliothèque Royale* [ed. anon: in fact ed. Louis Napoléon Boca], 2 vols (Valenciennes, 1841), 2, p. 365, no line numbering: lines 14–15 on page. For this manuscript, see 1, pp. iii, v and note. A new edition being prepared by Robert Cook and Larry Crist, to be published by SATF. Edmond-René Labande, *Étude sur Baudouin de Sebourc, chanson de geste. Légende poétique de Baudouin II du Bourg, roi de Jérusalem* (Paris, 1940), pp. 53–62, 69. For date, see Larry S. Crist, 'On Structuring *Baudouin de Sebourc*', in *Romance Epic. Essays on a Medieval Literary Genre*, ed. Hans-Erich Keller (Kalamazoo, Michigan, 1987), pp. 49–55: here 49. It is possible that the Templars are omitted from this work because it was composed after the dissolution of the Order; however, they do appear in other works composed after the dissolution of the Order, as will become clear below.

a year with the Templars in penance for a murder, in this case the murder of his own daughter. As the daughter eventually turns out to be the great-grandmother of Saladin, these events are presumably supposed to have taken place in the late eleventh century. The date that this tale was composed is unclear except that it belongs to the first half of the thirteenth century. It may date from before 1230, as it was used by the author of the *Estoires d'Outremer et de la Naissance Saladin*: the editor of this latter text dated it to the 1230s, although it may in fact have been written post-1250. In the version of the story in the *Estoires* the Templars appear in the same role as in *La Fille*.

The story of *La Fille* was rewritten between 1465 and 1468 to form part of the story of *Jehan d'Avesnes*, probably written for Charles, count of Charolais, later duke of Burgundy, or for his father Philip the Good. The fifteenth-century writer does not seem to have known what was meant by serving at the Temple. The count and his companions stay at the Temple of Jerusalem for a year in the service of God, in devoted prayers and giving alms, and when the count departs, he bids farewell to the priests (*prestrez*). In the *Estoires*, in contrast, he bids farewell to the people of the Temple, that is, the Templars. Clearly the fifteenth-century writer did not know exactly what the Templars were and assumed that they were priests attached to the Lord's Temple (the Muslim Dome of the Rock).[17] The conventional theme survived, but was no longer understood.

In other forms of literature, however, the theme was adapted in line with contemporary events. In one of the stories in Giovanni Boccaccio's *Decameron*, written in the mid-fourteenth century, the highwayman Ghino di Tacco is made a brother of the Hospital of St John by Pope Boniface VIII as a reward for his good treatment of the abbot of Cluny.[18] On the one hand this can be regarded as a form of penance for Ghino, who spends the rest of his days in the Order. On the other hand, however, there is a note of humour in sending a highwayman to join the Order whose activities upon the high seas, attempting to prevent trade between Muslims and Christians, was earning it a reputation among the Italian naval cities for piracy.

---

[17] *La Fille du Comte de Ponthieu: nouvelle du XIIIe siècle*, ed. C. Brunel, CFMA 52 (Paris, 1926), p. 22, lines 305–10 and 402–9. One manuscript survives. A lost manuscript belonged to the library of Philip the Good of Burgundy: *La Fille du Comte du Ponthieu, conte en prose, versions du XIIIe et du XVe siècle*, ed. Clovis Brunel, SATF (Paris, 1923, reprinted New York and London, 1968), p. ix, note 1; Barber, 'Social Context', 41; Trotter, *Medieval French Literature*, pp. 145–53, esp. p. 146. *Critical Edition of the Estoires d'Outremer*, p. 74; for date, see p. 8. However, its many errors in its historical 'facts' indicate that this work is actually much later, although it must have been written before 1300 because this is the date of the earliest surviving manuscripts: p. 1. For the fifteenth-century version, see *La Fille du Comte du Ponthieu, conte en prose, versions du XIIIe et du XVe siècle*, ed. Clovis Brunel, SATF (Paris, 1923, reprinted New York and London, 1968), p. 100. Two manuscripts survive. For its date and patron, see Brunel (1923), pp. xlviii–liv, and Geert H.M. Claasens, 'Some notes on the Proto-Saladin', in *Aspects de l'épopée romane*, p. 132; Trotter, *Medieval French Literature*, pp. 151–2.

[18] Giovanni Boccaccio, *Decameron*, day 10, story 2.

In Jean Renart's *Roman de la Rose* or *Guillaume de Dole* (written between 1208 and 1218) the theme of penance is slightly altered. Here it is not a hero who is to go overseas to the Temple, but the villain, the emperor's seneschal who sought to block the path of true love.[19] Only one manuscript survives; it was dedicated to Milon de Nanteuil, who was elected bishop of Beauvais in 1217. Jean's depiction of the Temple as a place particularly suited for penance relating to romantic love was probably influenced by the development of another strand of literary convention around the Order of the Temple; that the Templars assisted lovers. This is discussed below.

2 A place of retirement

Another of Jean Renart's works also mentions the Templars: *L'Escoufle*, which was dedicated to a count of Hainaut. Rita Lejeune has demonstrated that this must have been Baldwin VI of Flanders and Hainaut, who took the cross in 1200 and departed on the Fourth Crusade in 1202. She dated the text to 1200–1202.[20] Like Jean Renart's later *Guillaume de Dole*, this poem survives in only one manuscript, and was not, apparently, known outside the court of the poet's patron. In the *Guillaume de Dole*, Jean reworked one familiar image of the Order of the Temple; in *L'Escoufle*, he also depicted the Order as a place of retirement from the world, and the Brothers as knights of Christ, both images which again reflected the Order's actual role in the world.

In *L'Escoufle*, the knight who is to retire into the Order of the Temple is the hero's father, lying on his deathbed. The doctors in fact suggest that the dying knight should take this step: 'for it would be a great shame if such a doughty man should die in his bed like a beast.'[21] In the third French version of the epic poem *Bueve de Hantone* (written after 1220), the hero's father-in-law enters the Order of the Temple specifically to do penance for his sins: he states that during his life he has destroyed many cities, burned many towns and destroyed many towers, making many orphans and widows. *Bueve of Hantone* was a popular hero, but this particular version of his adventures survives in only three manuscripts and two fragments.[22]

---

[19] Jean Renart, *Le Roman de la Rose ou Guillaume de Dole*, ed. Félix Lecoy, CFMA 91 (Paris, 1962), line 5589; Rita Lejeune, *L'Oeuvre de Jean Renart*, Bibliothèque de la Faculté de Philosophie et Lettres de l'Université de Liège, fascicule 61 (Liège, 1935), pp. 34–170, esp. pp. 79–82 for date and dedication, on p. 217 she dates it to 1212–13; for a later dating see *L'Escoufle, Roman d'aventure*, ed. F. Sweetser, TLF 211 (Geneva, 1974), pp. vii–viii, xiii.

[20] Lejeune, *L'Oeuvre de Jean Renart*, pp. 171–238, esp. pp. 217–20.

[21] *L'Escoufle*, lines 2390–95, pp. vii, xii.

[22] *Der festländische Bueve de Hantone, Fassung III*, ed. A. Stimming, 2 vols, GRL 34, 42 (Dresden, 1914–20), 1, lines 16279–82, 16297–9, 2, pp. 1–11; Moison, *Répertoire*, 1.1, p. 36 for date (BH 11).

Contemporary practice was similar: in the biography of William Marshal, earl of Pembroke, written in the 1220s, the hero dedicates himself to the Order of the Temple on his deathbed, but in this case he had given his body to the Order many years before. The biography is based on the testimonies of those who knew the Marshal, but adapted according to the conventions of romance. It was sufficiently popular among the English nobility for Guy de Beauchamp, earl of Warwick, to own a copy in the early fourteenth century.[23] Likewise, in 1236, John of Ibelin, the Old Lord of Beirut, joined the Order of the Temple in his old age for the salvation of his soul.[24]

In 'La Chanson des rois baudouin' (a continuation of *La Chanson de Jérusalem* written in the mid-thirteenth century and regarded as the 'Second State' of the First Crusade Cycle), noble women retire into a Military Order, but in this case the Order of the Hospital. In reality and in literature noble women often did retire into a religious order, and obviously to enter a Military Order would be particularly appropriate for a leading character in the Crusade Cycle. However, the rule of the Order of the Temple did not allow women to enter that Order, whereas the Order of the Hospital had houses of women; and perhaps the writer regarded the Order of the Hospital as more appropriate for a noblewoman in that social convention demanded that respectable women should not have to become involved in fighting except in case of emergency. Alternatively, perhaps the patron of this continuation was a patron of the Hospital. In this story, Beatrice daughter of King Baldwin is left as a hostage for her father after his capture by the Muslims. While she is held prisoner she is violated by one of the Muslims. She declares that as she now cannot marry a noble man she will enter the Hospital at Acre, an Order to which her father has already donated a castle. King Baldwin gives the Order another castle, Sidon, as her dowry. Later her sister Ida, now twice widowed, enters the Hospital to join her sister. Her two husbands, Amaury and Baldwin de Sebourc, are both buried there. By the time this work was written Acre was the actual location of the Order's headquarters, as Jerusalem had been lost to the Muslims, although in the 'Chanson' Jerusalem is still held by the Christians. In this respect, this work reflects the actual contemporary situation despite literary convention.[25]

---

[23] *L'Histoire de Guillaume le Maréchal, comte de Striguil et de Pembroke*, ed. Paul Meyer, 3 vols, SHF (Paris, 1891–1901), lines 18351–78, 18233–42; M. Blaess, 'L'abbaye de Bordesley et les livres de Guy de Beauchamp,' *Romania*, 78 (1957), 514. Another Anglo-Norman noble who retired into the Order of the Temple, before 1160, was the powerful Marcher lord Gilbert de Lacy. He apparently joined the Order in middle age to seek honour and glory, although he had had a successful career in the West, and had succeeded in recovering his patrimony in the Marches. Wightman suggests he was bored with life as a provincial landlord: see W.E. Wightman, *The Lacy Family in England and Normandy, 1066–1194* (Oxford, 1966), pp. 188–9, 213.

[24] Filippo da Novara, *Guerra di Federico II in Oriente*, section 116 (212), p. 210.

[25] *OFCC, VII: The Jérusalem Continuations*, part 2: *La Prise d'Acre, La Mort Godefroi, and La Chanson des Rois Baudouin*, ed. Peter R. Grillo (Tuscaloosa and London, 1987), pp. xxxi–xxxv on the date, and lines 4683–5, 5103–42, 5198, 5865–9, 5872–5. Only one manuscript

The First Crusade Cycle also depicted knights retiring into a Military Order, but in this case they entered the Order of the Temple. At the end of some manuscripts of the *Chanson de Jérusalem*, it is announced that Harpin de Bourges is to retire into the newly-formed Order of the Temple 'pour servir': no other motive is given.[26] In the third part of *Les Chétifs*, the Christian Baldwin and Muslim Corbaran undertake to serve at the Temple for a year as a thankoffering if they are preserved from their present peril: the implication is that these are two of the first knights of the Temple.[27] However, in the London-Turin continuation of the *Chanson de Jérusalem*, composed at the very end of the thirteenth century or the beginning of the fourteenth (known as the 'Third State' of the First Crusade Cycle), Harpin de Bourges enters the Order of the Temple not simply in retirement but following the death of his wife.

> Count Harpin was very upset and troubled and was so distressed at the death of his wife, and he hated the world so much, that he said to himself that he would never have another wife all the days of his life. Harpin the redoubtable gave himself to the Temple; but this was not the end of his boldness. As long as he lived he brought grief on the Saracens and Slavs.[28]

Taking this example alongside the entry of Queen Ida into the Hospital of Acre in the earlier 'Chanson des Rois Baudouin', it is clear that by the end of the thirteenth century entrance into a Military Order as a result of personal loss had become a common literary theme. Again, it was a theme which reflected contemporary practice. In the 1130s a knight named Guy Cornelly joined the

---

survives recording this episode. On women in Military Orders see A. Forey, 'Women and the Military Orders'; Tommasi, 'Uomini e donne negli ordini militari di Terrasanta'.

[26] *OFCC, VII: The Jérusalem Continuations*, part 1: *La Chrétienté Corbaran*, ed. Peter R. Grillo (Alabama, 1984), pp. xvi–xvii, and note 14. Harpin's entry to the Order of the Temple is mentioned in MSS Bib. nat. 786, Bib. nat. 795, Bib. nat. 1621, Bib. nat. 12569, Arsenal 3139 [MSS B, C, D, E, G in this series] and Bib. nat. 781 [MS P]. It is not mentioned in Bib. nat. 12558, which was used as the base manuscript for the edition of the *Chanson de Jérusalem* which forms vol. VI of *The Old French Crusade Cycle*. Nor is Harpin's forthcoming retirement, nor the forthcoming foundation of the Hospital and Temple, mentioned in manuscripts of London and Turin [here MSS I and T] in which Harpin does actually enter the Order of the Temple: see below.

[27] *OFCC, V: Les Chétifs*, ed. Geoffrey M. Myers (Alabama, 1981), lines 2147–8, 3058; this is thought to have been written around 1180: S. Duparc Quioc, *La Chanson d'Antioche: Étude critique* (Paris, 1978) pp. 132–9; cf. G.M. Myers, '*Les Chétifs* – Étude sur le développement de la chanson', *Romania*, 105 (1984), 65–75, where it is shown that the third part was a later interpolation written to extol the knights of Beauvais. Ten manuscripts survive.

[28] *OFCC, VIII: TheLondon-Turin Version*, lines 13375–7 for Harpin's marriage to the queen of Nubia; lines 13438–41 for her death from illness; lines 13442–8 for Harpin's entry into the Order of the Temple. For the Military Orders assisting lovers, see also Nicholson, 'Knights and Lovers'. Although the later version of this story, written soon after 1350 and forming part of the so-called 'Second Crusade Cycle', *Le Chevalier au Cygne et Godefroid de Bouillon*, ed. Frederic A.F.T. Baron de Reiffenberg and A. Borgnet, 3 vols (Paris, 1846–54) is based on a version of the first Crusade Cycle very like the London-Turin continuation, in this later poem Harpin does not enter the Order of the Temple, although here the Templars were already in existence before the First Crusade: 2, lines 5423–5.

Order of the Temple 'to exercise knighthood in the service of Christ' after his wife had contracted leprosy and had been segregated from normal society.[29] Previously, in 1125, Count Hugh of Champagne had joined the Order of the Temple, apparently to escape an unhappy marriage: he believed that his wife Elizabeth had been unfaithful to him.[30]

This theme first appeared in fiction in the work of the poet Gontier de Soignies, writing in the early thirteenth century. His work is mentioned by Jean Renart in his *Guillaume de Dole*, which would date it to before the period 1208–18. Lamenting his failure in love, Gontier declares:

> So, to finish, if he cannot do any better, Gontier wishes to leave all these evils and leave this world. Oh, love! I will cross the sea for love of God and join the Temple, for I want to go where I will never hear of love every day, increasing and doubling my pain.[31]

A similar story also appeared in historical literature at around the same time, in the chronicle attributed to Ernoul, squire of Balian of Ibelin. Balian, who died *c.* 1193, was one of the leading nobles in the Latin kingdom of Jerusalem. In the form in which it survives, the 'Chronicle of Ernoul' probably dates from the 1220s. The story also appears in the Genoese *Regni Iherosolymitani brevis historia*, the date of which is uncertain but which may date from the early thirteenth century, and in the *Estoires d'Outremer*, which drew much of its material from the chronicle attributed to Ernoul. According to these sources, Gerard de Ridefort, the tragic Master of the Temple who was partly responsible for the disastrous Christian defeats of 1187, had originally joined the Order as a direct result of his failure to win the hand of the heiress of Botron. However, in another version of the story appearing in a work of the 1240s, it is stated that Gerard joined as a result of illness: presumably retirement when in fear of death, as in the examples quoted above. The fact that one version of the chronicle attributed to Ernoul has a different version of the incident, and the fact that no existing version of these chronicles can be shown to date from before 1208, arouses suspicion that the whole story of Gerard de Ridefort's entry into the Order of the Temple as a result of disappointment in love arose, not because this was what actually happened, but because of the literary convention that the Order of the Temple was a suitable place for disappointed lovers.[32]

---

[29] *Cartulaire général de l'ordre du Temple, 1119?–1150*, ed. le marquis d'Albon (Paris, 1913), no. 27; Guy entrusted his wife and daughters to the care of the Church.

[30] *Chronica Albrici monachi Trium Fontium*, ed. Paul Scheffer-Boichorst, in *MGHS* 23, p. 826; see also Malcolm Barber, 'The Origins of the Order of the Temple', *Studia Monastica*, 12 (1970), 219–40: here 223.

[31] *Gontier de Soignies: il canzoniere*, ed. L. Formisano (Milan and Naples, 1980), no. XVIII 'Lan quant voi esclarcir,' p. 130, lines 63–4, and p. lx; on date, see also Lejeune, *L'Oeuvre de Jean Renart*, p. 159.

[32] *Chronique d'Ernoul*, p. 114; 'Regni Iherosolymitani Brevis Historia', in *Annali Genovesi di Caffaro e de'suoi continuatori dal MXCIX al MCCXCIII*, ed. L.T. Belgrano and C.I di

The theme reappeared in the immensely popular *La Chastelaine de Vergi*, probably written around 1240. This tale of secret love, jealousy and betrayal ends with all the major characters except the duke dead of grief or violence. In all but one manuscript of the story, the heartbroken duke enters a Military Order. In most versions he enters the Order of the Temple, but in two manuscripts he enters the Order of the Hospital. The two 'Hospital' manuscripts are Paris Bib. nat. nouv.acq. fr. 4531 (start of the fourteenth century) and Paris, Bib. nat. fons fr. 25545 (fourteenth century), but as all the manuscripts used for the modern printed editions date from the late thirteenth century or fourteenth century, it is clearly not the case that later copyists replaced the reference to the Templars with a reference to the Hospitallers.[33] Presumably the patrons who paid for these two manuscripts to be copied preferred the Hospital in this romantic role.

The Hospital appears again in such a role in a short poem by Jean de Condé (*c.* 1275–*c.* 1345), *Le Dis dou chevalier à la mance*. A knight rejected by his lady-love goes overseas to the Holy Land to visit the Holy Sepulchre and help defend the land against the Muslims; his lady, regretting his departure, dresses as a young man and seeks him out. Reunited, they return home and live happily until her death, when the knight is so sad that he decides to serve God for the rest of his life, and joins the Order of the Hospital. Jean de Condé concludes,

---

Sant'Angelo, new edn, 5 vols, Fonti per la Storia Italia nos. 11–14bis (Rome, 1890–1929), 1, pp. 137–8; 'Regni Iherosolymitani brevis historia', ed. G.H. Pertz, *MGHS*, 18, p. 3; *Estoires d'Outremer*, p. 175. For the non-romantic version of the story, see *La Continuation de Guillaume de Tyr (1184–97)*, ed. M.R. Morgan (Paris, 1982), p. 46 para. 33; 'L'Estoire de Eracles Empereur', *RHC Occ.*, 2, p. 52. The composition and dating of the chronicle of Ernoul is a complex problem. M.R. Morgan's study, *The Chronicle of Ernoul and the Continuations of William of Tyre* (Oxford, 1973), elucidated the problem to some degree, but her conclusions have been subjected to severe criticism by Peter Edbury: 'The Lyon *Eracles* and the Old French Continuations of William of Tyre', in *Montjoie*, ed. Kedar *et al.*, pp. 139–53. John Gillingham has suggested that 'Ernoul' is only contemporary for the events of 1187, and the rest of the chronicle was compiled in the 1220s: 'Roger of Howden on Crusade', in *Medieval Historical Writing in the Christian and Islamic Worlds*, ed. D.O. Morgan (London, 1982), pp. 60–75, here pp. 72–3, note 33; reprinted in his *Richard Coeur de Lion, Kingship, Chivalry and War in the Twelfth Century* (Londin and Rio Grande, 1994), pp. 141–54. Certainly, other chronicles of the Third Crusade seem to date from the early 1220s: Helen Nicholson, *Chronicle of the Third Crusade: a Translation of the Itinerarium peregrinorum et gesta regis Ricardi* (Aldershot, 1997), pp. 10–11; and the fact that the romantic story about Gerard de Ridefort fits so neatly into literary convention of the 1220s supports this dating for 'Ernoul'. For the dating of *La Continuation de Guillaume de Tyr*, see Edbury, 'The Lyon *Eracles*', pp. 140–41.

[33] *La Chastelaine de Vergi, poème du XIII siècle*, ed. G. Raynaud, 2nd edn revue par L. Foulet, CFMA 1 (Paris, 1912), p. iii and lines 941–3; *La Chastelaine de Vergi. Edition critique du ms. B.N. f. fr. 375 avec introduction, notes, glossaire et index, suivie de l'edition diplomatique de tous les manuscrits connus du XIIIe et du XIVe siècle*, ed. René Ernst Victor Stuip (The Hague and Paris, 1970), p. 99, lines 931–3 (Templar), p. 241, lines 940–42 (Templar), p. 261, lines 933–5, (Templar), p. 280, lines 931–4 (Hospitaller), p. 299, lines 917–9 (Templar), p. 318, lines 944–6 (Templar), p. 338, lines 939–41 (Hospitaller), p. 358, lines 912–14 (Templar), p. 394, lines 933–5 (Templar); the Rennes MS does not mention either Order (p. 375). For date, see Stuip, pp. 63–5. There were also two middle Dutch versions of the poem (Stuip, pp. 24–30). On the various manuscripts, see Stuip, pp. 35–47.

'*Prions pour ces ii vrais amans / qui d'amours tinrent les commans*': let us pray for these two lovers, who obeyed the commands of love.[34] Two manuscripts of this work were known when it was printed in 1886, and the date is unclear. The appearance of the Hospitallers rather than the Templars in this role may indicate that it was written after the dissolution of the Order of the Temple in 1312, although it is firmly set in the period immediately before Saladin's conquest of the Holy Land in 1187.

The familiarity of the theme is underlined by its appearance in the romance *Sone de Nausay* or *Nansay* (written during the second half of the thirteenth century, probably between 1267 and 1280). Here the noble young lady Ydain is informed by her nurse Sabine that because she has refused Sone's love, he will go overseas and give himself to the Temple, as if this were an act expected from disappointed young lovers, tantamount to killing himself.[35] In a later age, he would have joined the French foreign legion.

Turning this theme on its head, in the second and third French versions of *Bueve de Hantone* (written after 1220) the countess of Hantone tells her lover, Doon of Mayence, murderer of her husband, that she will send her son Bueve overseas to the Persians or the Templars in order to prevent his taking vengeance on Doon.[36]

These references, and that in Jean Renart's *Guillaume de Dole* to the Temple as a place of punishment for a man who opposed the way of true love, indicate that the writers and audiences of epic and romance literature saw a close connection between the Military Orders, especially the Order of the Temple, and love, courtly or otherwise. It is hardly surprising that the Military Orders appear in stories with a romantic element, for – like modern literature –

---

[34] 'Le Dis dou chevalier à la mance', in *Dits et contes de Baudouin de Condé et de son fils Jean de Condé, publiés d'après les manuscrits de Bruxelles, Turin, Rome, Paris et Vienne et accompagnés de variantes et de notes explicatives*, ed. Auguste Scheler, 3 vols: vol. 2, *Jean de Condé, première partie* (Brussels, 1866), pp. 167ff. and 419ff. for notes: lines 2330–37, 2343–4, and p. 436 note on line 2336; lines 1625–707 for setting. This work is cited, but without mentioning the Military Orders, by Suzanne Duparc-Quioc, *Le Cycle de la Croisade* (Paris, 1955), pp. 208–9.

[35] *Sone von Nausay*, ed. M. Goldschmidt, BLVS 216 (Tübingen, 1899), lines 8705–6. The poem most probably dates from after 1264, as it assumes that a lady rules Beirut: pp. 552–4. Trotter does not date the text, and does not mention the Templars: *Medieval French Literature*, pp. 159–63. The dates 1267–80 are deduced by Lachet, *Sone de Nansay*, pp. 53–61. Lachot considers most of the Templars' roles in this poem, although not Sabine's suggestion to Ydain. However, although Lachot can account for the Templars' and Hospitallers' military roles, he does not consider why the Templars should appear as helpers of lovers, apart from the humorous aspect of this role: pp. 57–8, 96–8, 122, 130, 239, 305, 395, 474, 477, 485, 576 note 133, 659, 703–6, 718, 750.

[36] *Der festländische Bueve de Hantone, Fassung II*, ed. A. Stimming, 2 vols, GRL 30, 41 (Dresden, 1912–18), line 536 (dated to 1225 by Moisan, *Répertoire*, 1.1, p. 36); *Fassung III*, 1, line 470, note; this only appears in one manuscript of the three manuscripts and two fragments surviving. In the other two manuscripts the countess intends to send Bueve to the Persians or the turcopoles.

much of medieval literature had a romantic element. However, what is surprising is that the Brothers are depicted as sympathetic towards lovers, and as giving them active help. Given that the Brothers were members of religious orders, bound by the three monastic vows of poverty, chastity and obedience, and that the Templars in particular were forbidden by their Rule to admit women to the Order or even to have any contact with women,[37] this literary role requires explanation.

3 *The Templars and lovers*

It was the Templars who first appeared in literature assisting lovers, and who appeared most often in this role. The literary connection between the Templars and romantic lovers may have originated in the Templars' reputation as an ideal example of Christian love in action. Christian love, *caritas* or charity, is not the same as romantic love, *amor*, but in the work of Wolfram von Eschenbach and his contemporaries and later adaptors Christian love for God is paralleled with faithful romantic love between innocent lovers, such as Sigûne and Schîanatulander, or Parzivâl and Condwîrâmûrs. The *Templeise*, Wolfram's version of the Templars, who serve God and represent faithful Christian love, were hence connected also with faithful romantic love. It appears that the Templars' literary image developed from this parallel between Christian love and faithful romantic love, to make them the protectors of romantic lovers.

The Templars were first depicted dedicated to self-sacrifice for love of God in their own Rule, which received official ecclesiastical approval in 1129 at the Council of Troyes, and in the *De laude novae militiae* of Bernard, abbot of Clairvaux. However, although both these documents circulated outside the Order, they were not widely known outside educated clerical and monastic circles. The Brothers were first depicted as an ideal of Christian love by Pope Innocent II in his great bull of exemption for the Order (1139), 'Omne datum optimum'. The Templars, he wrote, were aflame with Christian love, charity: '*verae charitatis flamma succensi*'.

> As true Israelites and warriors equipped for divine battles, aflame with the true flame of charity, your deeds fulfill the saying of the Gospel, where it is said: 'Greater love has no man than this, than a man lay down his life for his friend'. Following the voice of the supreme shepherd, you are not afraid to lay down your lives for your Brothers and to defend them from the incursions of the pagans, and, in order that you might be given the name 'Knights of the Temple', you have

---

[37] On women in the Order of the Temple see Forey, 'Women and the Military Orders', 63–6; Tommasi, 'Uomini e donne negli ordini militari di Terrasanta'; Nicholson, 'Templar Attitudes Towards Women'; Nicholson, 'The Military Orders and their Relations with Women'.

been established by the Lord to be defenders of the Catholic Church and attackers of the enemies of Christ.[38]

Indeed, by a similar analogy, crusading itself could be seen as an act of love. This bull was reissued regularly by later popes, and later popes frequently described the Templars in other bulls and letters for the Order as laying down their lives for their Brothers.[39]

It is difficult to establish how well known this papal image of the Templars as 'aflame with Christian love' would have been in the early thirteenth century, when the connection of Templars with romantic love first appears in literature. It is possible that the Brothers themselves publicised the papal description of their Order. The Templars and Hospitallers had the privilege of having a confraternity of lay people who paid an annual sum to their Order in return for a remission of one seventh of their penance. Those collecting confraternity payments could even open churches which were under interdict once a year in order to preach and collect alms. The bull of Celestine II which gave the Templars this privilege compared the Templars to the Maccabees – who, before the time of Christ, fought to defend the Temple of Jerusalem against defilement from pagans – and emphasized that the Templars laid down their lives for their Brothers.

> The Knights of the Temple of Jerusalem, new Maccabees in the time of grace, denying secular desires and leaving their own possessions, have taken up their cross and followed Christ. They are those through whom God liberates the Church in the East from the filth of the pagans and attacks the enemies of the Christian faith. They do not fear to lay down their lives for their Brothers and to defend the pilgrims who proceed to the holy places from the incursions of the pagans as they go and return.[40]

The Templars' almscollectors would have had to quote from this bull to justify their alms-collecting, and it would have been reasonable for them to have taken this opportunity to press home to their listeners that the Templars were a perfect expression of Christian love. However, as most of those from whom they were collecting would not have been able to understand Latin, translations into the vernacular would have been required. In fact, one such translation has been found.

A twelfth-century French translation of this bull survives on the last blank sheet of a manuscript containing Old French lives of the saints. It follows the

---

[38] *Papsturkunden für Templer und Johanniter, Archivberichte und Texte*, ed. Rudolf Hiestand, Abhandlungen der Akademie der Wissenschaften in Göttingen, phil-hist Klasse, dritte Folge, no. 77 (Göttingen, 1972), no. 3. The Gospel reference is to John ch. 15 v. 13.

[39] *Papsturkunden* (1972), nos 17 (Eugenius III), 27 (Hadrian IV), 93, 121, 133 (Alexander III), 208, 217, 222, 224 (Clement III), 233 (Celestine III); Jonathan Riley-Smith, 'Crusading as an Act of Love', *History*, 65 (1980), 177–92. See also Bernard of Clairvaux, 'Liber ad milites Templi', pp. 220–21 on the piety and comradeship of the Templars.

[40] 'Milites Templi': *Papsturkunden*(1972), no. 8 (1144) for the Temple. See also 'Christianae Fidae Religio' *Cartulaire général de l'ordre des Hospitaliers*, no. 122 (1137) for the Hospital.

original bull word-for-word until it comes to Celestine's comparison between the Templars and the Maccabees; it then explains, as if for the benefit of those not familiar with the Old Testament, who Judas Maccabaeus and his brothers were.

> This was the best knight that lived at that time. All the days of his life he waged war on the enemies of the Lord God and at the end he was killed in the service of the Lord God. For this reason, those lords renounced all earthly desires for the love of God and abandoned their own to fight against God's enemies and willingly let themselves be killed for love of Him. [In the same way,] these lords [of the Temple] have renounced all earthly desires for the love of God and abandoned their own possessions and taken up the cross and followed our lord Jesus Christ ...[41]

This translation then continues in the same words as the original bull, to emphasise that the Templars lay down their lives for their fellow-Christians.

The translation, therefore, places particular emphasis on the Templars' love of God, with the repetition of the phrase 'for love of God', *pur amor Deu*, and underlines their self-sacrificing vocation, which is precisely what we would expect if this papal bull was to be used to stress to potential donors that the Templars were the perfect expression of Christian love. It is not possible to say to what use this translation was put, but it must have been used to justify the Templars' privilege to some audience which did not understand Latin – otherwise, there would have been no point in having the translation made – and it was probably aimed at a non-clerical audience who were not fully familiar with the Bible and did not know who the Maccabees were. This is compatible with its having been used to encourage lay people to give alms to the Order of the Temple. Those who heard this bull read out would have been given a vivid impression of the Templars as examples of faithful, self-sacrificing Christian love.

There were also a number of anecdotes in circulation by the first two decades of the thirteenth century depicting the Templars as prominent examples of love for God; these obviously circulated outside the Order as they were recorded by non-Templars. The author of the original *Itinerarium peregrinorum*, an account of the Third Crusade, recorded in the early 1190s accounts of the martyrdom of the Templar Jakelin de Mailly at the battle at the Spring of Cresson, 1 May 1187, of the Templar Nicholas after the Battle of Hattin, 4 July 1187, and of the Master Gerard de Ridefort, in battle outside Acre, 4 October 1189. This work was circulating in the West before 1200, as it or a work derived from it was used by the chronicler William of Newburgh. A

---

[41] *Papsturkunden für Templer und Johanniter, neue Folge*, ed. Rudolf Hiestand, Abhandlungen der Akademie der Wissenschaften in Göttingen, phil-hist Klasse, dritte Folge, no. 135 (Göttingen, 1984), pp. 252–3, no. 35.

slightly different, but equally heroic, version of the martyrdom of Gerard de Ridefort was known to the Anglo-Norman historian and poet Ambroise, writing at the end of the twelfth or start of the thirteenth century. Another version appeared in a contemporary Latin poem about the siege of Acre, possibly composed by a crusading priest. James of Vitry, bishop of Acre, writing between 1216 and 1228, recorded an anecdote of a Templar who rode eagerly to death against the Muslims, bidding his horse carry him to Paradise. Caesarius of Heisterbach, writing his *Dialogus miraculorum* between 1219 and 1223, recorded a tale of Templar steadfastness at prayer, demonstrating their piety and courage in the face of Muslim attack.[42]

The Templars' connection with Christian love first appears in fictional literature in Wolfram von Eschenbach's Grail romance *Parzival*, written in the first decade of the thirteenth century. Wolfram's *Templeise*, who guard the Grail castle, bear on their shields a turtle dove, a symbol of pure and faithful love. Wolfram himself laid great stress on fidelity in love, favourably contrasting the faithful Sigûne, who died of love after her faithful lover Schîanatulander was killed, with the unfaithful Lunete of Chrétien de Troyes' *Yvain*, who urged her mistress Laudine to marry Lord Yvain after he killed her husband.[43] The love associated with the Grâl, which comes from God, must necessarily be faithful love, since God is faithful and God is love. While Wolfram's *Templeise* are not 'real' Templars, as is shown below, it is clear that Wolfram meant his audience to understand that his imaginary Order was intended to parallel the actual Order: like the actual Templars, the *Templeise* guard holiness from those who are not worthy to approach.

Albrecht, identified by his modern editor as Albrecht von Scharfenberg, writing in around 1260–76, based his *Jüngerer Titurel* on Wolfram's *Titurel*. Albrecht certainly saw Wolfram's *Templeise* as associated with love; not only love for God, but also faithful, pure, romantic love. Tschionotulander, proposing to lead his intended bride Sigune to the Grâl, states that he fears no argument with the *Templeise*, for his journey is inspired by his love for Sigune and for God: '*den strit ich furhte niht der tempeleise, wan durch die liebe dine und ouch durch got laz ich gen in die reise*'.[44]

---

[42] *Itinerarium peregrinorum* 1: *Itinerarium peregrinorum* ed. Stubbs, Bk 1, chs 2, 5, 29, pp. 7–9, 16–17, 70; *Das Itinerarium peregrinorum*, ed. Mayer, pp. 180–81, p. 248, line 6– p. 249 line 20, p. 260, lines 3–7, p. 313, line 31–p. 314, line 3; Ambroise, *Estoire*, lines 3021–34; 'Ein zeitgenössisches Gedicht auf die Belagerung Accons', ed. Hans Prutz, *Forschungen zur deutschen Geschichte*, 21 (1889), 449–94, here 478–9, lines 767–86; James of Vitry, Sermon 37, pp. 412–13 and Sermon 38, p. 420; *Caesarii Heisterbachensis monachi ordinis Cisterciensis dialogus miraculorum*, ed. J. Strange, 2 vols (Cologne, Bonn and Brussels, 1851), 2, p. 119.

[43] Wolfram von Eschenbach, *Parzival*, ed. K. Lachmann and W. Spiewok, 2 vols (Stuttgart, 1981), 253.9–18, 435.13–436.25.

[44] Albrecht von Scharfenberg, *Jüngerer Titurel*, ed. Werner Wolf, Deutsche Texte des Mittelalters, 45 (1955), 55 (1964), 61 (1968), 73 (1984), 77 (1992): here 3/1, p. 163, strophe 5045.

Within a hundred strophes, however, Tschionotulander is dead and Sigune is weeping over his body. She goes to King Arthur's court, where she informs King Arthur that she intends to take her lover's corpse and go to the land of the Grâl, *Salvaterre* – the land of salvation. At this point a *Templeise* arrives, to help her on her journey to the Grâl. When they arrive in *Salvaterre*, Sigune sends the *Templeise* to find her friend Kundrie.[45] The *Templeise* here are more than simply guardians; they are active helpers and protectors of faithful lovers.

At the end of the thirteenth century, the author of *Reinfrid von Braunschweig* remarked *àpropos* of a turtle dove offered as a prize at a tournament that he thought that this had come from the Grâl, where, on many occasions, in battles and expeditions, the *Templeise* were seen bearing the chaste turtle dove, and went on to add that only the chaste could serve at the Grâl.[46]

In German literature, therefore, the Templars were connected with love for God and with pure, faithful romantic love. This image was very well known, for Wolfram's *Parzival* circulated widely. Bernd Schirok calculated that eighty-six manuscripts survive from the medieval period, forty-four from the thirteenth century, thirty-two from the fourteenth, and ten from the fifteenth – demonstrating that the work was still being read in the fifteenth century. Wolfram's work was adapted and reworked by many other writers, including Ulrich Füetrer in the late fifteenth century. Albrecht's *Jüngerer Titurel* survives in fifty-seven manuscripts and fragments from the thirteenth to the fifteenth centuries, so that his depiction of the Templars as friends of faithful, chaste lovers was scarcely less well-known in German-speaking lands than Wolfram's image of them bearing the symbol of faithful love. Again, his work was used by Ulrich Füetrer.[47] In French literature the connection with love was with romantic love rather than love for God. This was usually faithful love, but in the Templars' most developed role of this type, in *Sone de Nausay* or *Nansay*, it includes encouraging a one-night stand.

The Templars' connection with romantic love first appeared in French literature in the work of Gontier de Soignies and his contemporaries, as discussed above, before 1208–18. The thread continued throughout the thirteenth century. Not only was the Temple of Solomon as a place of refuge for lovers, as described above, in *La Chastelaine de Vergi*, *Sone de Nansay*, and elsewhere, but it was also a suitable place of lodging for lovers. In *Sone* the Templars of Ireland take in the fugitive Sone, his Norwegian sweetheart Odee, and his horse Morel, then assure their guests' safe escape from the country without the knowledge of the amorous queen.[48] Sone eventually marries Odee. In *Le Roman de Laurin*, the third part of the cycle of the Seven Sages of Rome,

---

[45] Albrecht, *Jüngerer Titurel*, 3/1, pp. 192–3, strophes 5160–64.
[46] *Reinfrid von Braunschweig*, ed. K. Bartsch, BLVS 109 (Tübingen, 1871), lines 780–91.
[47] Schirok, *Parzivalreception*, p. 57; Albrecht, *Jüngerer Titurel*, 1, pp. xliv– cviii.
[48] *Sone von Nausay*, lines 5995–6916.

a house of the Temple lodges the count of Provence on his way to ask for the hand in marriage of Dyogenne, daughter of the king of Aragon. In this case, however, the count fails in his suit.[49]

As in Albrecht's *Jüngerer Titurel*, the Templars also appear as undertakers for lovers. In the fictional *vida* of the troubadour Jaufré Rudel, written just before the middle of the thirteenth century, the hero takes the cross and crosses the sea in order to set eyes on the countess of Tripoli, whom he loves but has never seen. Becoming ill on the voyage, he has one glimpse of her beauty before expiring in her arms. Heartbroken, she has him buried in the Temple of Tripoli and becomes a nun.[50] The Templars also appeared in this role in the Arthurian verse romance *Claris et Laris*, which may be dated from the evidence of its introduction to the period 1261–68.[51] This text survives in only one manuscript. The author's anxiety over the situation in the Holy Land and his concern to give his story a context in actual events may have been factors which led him to place the Templars in the role of hosts and undertakers for wandering knights, a role usually assigned in Arthurian romance to hermits.

The Templars appear in *Claris et Laris* during the course of the adventures of the *Lai Hardi*, the brave, ugly knight, who undertakes to avenge a young lady whose lover has been murdered. The Templars bury the dead man and lodge the *Lai Hardi* and the lady. After her lover has been avenged, the lady returns to the grave and falls dead upon it. 'The Templars laid her in the grave alongside her lover and then wrote letters which explained her death; they were of fine enamelled gold'.[52] Perhaps this writer put the Templars into this role because of the tragic romantic setting, which fitted their role elsewhere in French literature. Hermits, the usual undertakers in romance, were only concerned with love for God, and in fact often appear in romance condemning physical love, as do the hermit Ogrin in Beroul's *Tristan* and the hermits who advise Lancelot in *La Queste del Saint Graal*.[53]

The connection between Templars and lovers in French romance is most marked in *Sone*, where the Templar master of Ireland, Margon, appears as a lovers' go-between, arranging a meeting between his queen and the fugitive Sone. The following extract illustrates this episode:

---

[49] *Le Roman de Laurin, fils de Marques le sénéchal*, ed. Lewis Thorpe (Cambridge, 1958), p. 111, lines 4613–14. This work was written in prose by an anonymous writer in the 1250s or 1260s and survives in eight manuscripts.

[50] *Les Chansons de Jaufré Rudel*, ed. A. Jeanroy, CFMA 15 (Paris, 1924) pp. vii, 21.

[51] *Li Romans de Claris et Laris*, ed. J. Alton, BLVS 169 (Tübingen, 1884; reprinted Amsterdam, 1966), lines 40–49.

[52] *Claris et Laris*, lines 9863–71, 9907–22.

[53] *The Romance of Tristan by Beroul, a poem of the twelfth century*, ed. A. Ewert (Oxford, 1977), lines 1362–422, 2265–448, 2481–509, 2656–744; *Queste*, pp. 63–71, 122–9, 132–9; for a more positive view of hermits in medieval literature, see J. Leclercq, 'Monks and Hermits in Medieval Love Stories', *Journal of Medieval History*, 18 (1992), 341–56.

Sick with the pain which grieved her, the queen led the Templar to counsel, not concealing her desire from him. She said to him: 'Master, I have loved you in good faith and have shown it. Now it seems to me that I have fallen into misfortune. I shall not conceal this from you, for I have great faith in you. I have fallen in love with this knight, and my heart is greatly troubled as a result. If I see him leave me, I could well go mad. Show me how much you love me; help me with your advice'.

The Templar said: 'I will give you the best advice that I know. You have a fine hall here which was built a long time ago by the kings. Go and eat there now and stay there tonight. When it gets dark, have your bed made up in such a place that no one knows where it is except the one commanded to make it. I will bring this knight in by a wicket gate, but first I will inform him'.

'If you do this,' she said, 'you will have my love forever.'[54]

The result of this liaison is a son, whom Margon later brings to Sone in Norway, where he acts as its godfather. Unusually, the Templar Margon plays a leading role in the story and becomes a well-defined character, although a rather dubious one, for he unquestioningly fulfils the demands and needs of his secular ruler despite his religious vows. Claude Lachet must be correct as seeing Margon's role as essentially humorous, but his role is far from the role of the Templars supporting pure, faithful love in the German romances.[55]

The Templars, in fact, appear in more French romances as supporters of lovers than in German romances, but these French romances survive in only one or two manuscripts each, indicating that individual works were not well known; in contrast to the enormous success of two of the German works in which the Templars appear supporting lovers. Overall, however, it is clear that the Templars' connection with love, Christian or otherwise, was well known by writers in the thirteenth century.

Did the French writers know of the Templars' role defending Love in *Parzival*? Alternatively, did the writer of *Sone*, writing between 1267 and 1280, know the work of Albrecht, writing in 1260–76 – or *vice versa*? The fact that Margon the Templar in *Sone* acts as chief minister for Sone and is left in a position of authority when Sone goes overseas, which would involve responsibility for the protection of the Grail castle, suggests that this author – a man of Brabant, living within the Empire and thus understanding German as well as French – at least knew Wolfram's *Parzival*. Unfortunately, because of a missing folio it is not possible to be sure what Margon's full responsibilities involved.[56] Did Albrecht know *Claris et Laris*, where the Templars also appear acting as undertakers for a knight slain wrongfully and assisting his

---

[54] *Sone von Nausay*, lines 6541–70.
[55] *Sone von Nausay*, lines 6372–916, 17525–676. See also Nicholson, 'Knights and Lovers', pp. 340–41; Lachet, *Sone de Nansay*, pp. 703–6.
[56] *Sone von Nausay*, lines 17607–18, 17659–60. The abbot of the Grail Castle is entrusted with the care of Sone's heir, but Margon, Sone's chief adviser, is left behind in Norway and is last seen recording the sorrow of the people at Sone's departure: lines 18005–6.

heartbroken lady? As various French romances were translated or reworked into German from the late twelfth century onwards it is at least possible that this German poet may have known *Claris et Laris*.[57]

Alternatively, it is possible that both French and German writers produced the literary image of Templars as defenders of Love and lovers independently of each other, basing this image on the papal description of the Order as 'aflame with the flame of charity', and the Templars' defence of the Holy Sepulchre and Christ's city of Jerusalem and, hence, of Christ and His love, for Jerusalem was viewed as being Christ's patrimony.[58] Yet such near-simultaneous invention – between 1200 and 1220 – of this particular image of the Templars by both French and German writers independently would have required some sort of stimulus.

The obvious stimulus would have been papal letters in favour of the Order as an example of Christian charity, bolstered by the Order's own newsletters and funding-raising efforts in the West. Eye-witness reports of the Order's self-sacrificing courage during the Third Crusade, as recorded in the original *Itinerarium peregrinorum*, for example, would have supported such an image of the Order. It is clear from other evidence that in the early thirteenth century, in the wake of the losses of territory in 1187, the Templars and Hospitallers were very active raising donations in the West.[59] Therefore if the Templars were promoting an image of the Brothers as aflame with Christian love, it would be reasonable to find this image first starting to appear in literature in the first decade of the thirteenth century.

Alternatively, it may be that the literary image of the Templars as being connected with romantic love was first conceived by Wolfram von Eschenbach, the earliest dateable user of this literary image. Wolfram himself may have derived it from accounts of Templars martyrdoms in the East, or papal bulls in the Order's favour, or simply the fact that the Templars, as

---

[57] On German translations or reworkings of French romances, see Green, *Medieval Listening and Reading*, pp. 255–67.

[58] Jonathan Riley-Smith, *The First Crusade and the Idea of Crusading* (London, 1986), pp. 21, 48–9.

[59] For the Hospital, see *Die Register Innocenz' III*, ed. Othmar Hageneder and Anton Haidacher, vol. 1 (Graz and Cologne, 1964), no. 450; *Cartulaire général de l'ordre des Hospitaliers*, no. 1050; for the Temple, see Innocent III, 'Liber registorum sive epistolarum', 3 vols, *Pat. Lat.* 214–16, Year 10, no. 121, vol. 215, cols. 1217–18. The fact that the pope complains that the Orders are misusing their privilege of collecting alms indicates that the Orders were collecting alms more vigorously than in the past. See also Karl Borchardt, 'Two Forged Alms-Raising Letters used by the Hospitallers in Franconia', in *The Military Orders: Fighting for the Faith*, ed. Barber, pp. 52–6. For the 'news machine' of the Latin East, including newsletters from the Military Orders to the West, see R.C. Smail, 'Latin Syria and the West, 1149–1187', *Transactions of the Royal Historical Society*, 5th series, 19 (1969), 1–21; Phillips, *Defenders of the Holy Land*; Jonathan Phillips, 'Archbishop Henry of Reims and the Militarization of the Hospitallers', in *The Military Orders*, vol. 2, ed. Nicholson, pp. 83–8; Lloyd, *English Society*, pp. 24–31, 36–41, 248–52; Nicholson, *Templars, Hospitallers*, pp. 102–24.

defenders of God's city of Jerusalem, were effectively defenders of Love. Wolfram's image of the Templars was then taken up by French writers. However, this does suppose a greater degree of cross-cultural exchange from German writers to French writers in the early thirteenth century than scholars have generally conceived, and it must be said that the German writers only connect the Templars with pure and faithful love, while the French works – especially *Sone* – put no particular emphasis on chastity, and do not always emphasize fidelity.

A comparison with the literary image of the Hospitallers, however, helps to illuminate the problem. The Hospitallers also 'laid down their lives for their Brothers', and in addition cared for the poor and sick. A description of the Hospital, possibly written in the 1180s but certainly before 1187, begins with a long encomium to charity; for the Hospital was an outstanding example of Christian charity. The Hospitallers certainly made much of their charitable work when seeking patronage in the West.[60] Yet, nevertheless, the Hospitallers have far less to do with lovers than the Templars in medieval literature. This discrepancy between image and actuality strongly suggests that the literary image of the Templars as defenders of lovers was not simply derived from the Order's own propaganda and papal support but was the invention of one particular writer, Wolfram von Eschenbach. Wolfram chose the Templars as a model for his knights who defend Love, and ever afterward it was the Templars, rather than the Hospitallers, who were given literary roles which were closely connected with love and lovers.

A few instances occurred in literature of Hospitallers being connected with romantic love. They appear in two manuscripts of *La Chastelaine de Vergi* and in *Le Dis dou chevalier à la mance*, as noted above. In Jean d'Arras' version of the legend of Mélusine, the legendary good demon ancestress of the Lusignan family, written between 1382 and 1394, the Master of the Hospital of Rhodes and the captain of Rhodes explain to Urien of Lusignan, son of Mélusine, that the sultan of Damascus has attacked Cyprus because he wishes to marry Hermine, daughter of the king of Cyprus, but has been refused unless he accepts baptism. 'Since the sultan has undertaken this enterprise under pressure from love', Urien says, 'he is all the more to be feared.' Here, however, the Hospital is opposing a lover rather than helping him. After triumphing over the Saracens with the Hospitallers' assistance, Urien marries Hermine himself and becomes king of Cyprus.[61]

The Hospitallers gave Jean's version of the Lusignans' conquest of Cyprus

---

[60] Benjamin Kedar, 'A Twelfth-Century Description of the Jerusalem Hospital', in *The Military Orders*, vol. 2, ed. Nicholson, pp. 3–26, esp. pp. 15–18; Nicholson, *Templars, Hospitallers*, pp. 120–21; Phillips, 'Archbishop Henry of Reims'.

[61] Jean d'Arras, *Mélusine: Roman du XIVe siècle*, ed. Louis Stouff (Dijon, 1932, reprinted Geneva, 1974), pp. 93–4, 121–2. Five manuscripts survive, as well as a printed edition of 1478. The Hospitallers do not appear in other versions of the legend.

apparent authenticity and historicity and transferred his version of the tale of Mélusine from the realm of fairytale into contemporary actuality. In fact it was the Templars rather than the Hospitallers who had been involved in the Lusignan acquisition of Cyprus, as Richard I of England – who conquered the island in 1191 – had initially sold it to the Templars. The Templars failed to hold it and sold it back to him, on which Richard sold it to Guy of Lusignan. Jean d'Arras' tale, however, has the Lusignans acquiring Cyprus through the heroism of Mélusine's sons. His version of events reflected contemporary needs, in particular the political needs of his patrons. He was writing for Jean de Berri and his sister Marie, duchess of Bar; Jean de Berri had been given Lusignan by his brother, King Charles V of France, in 1357 and was anxious to establish his connection with the original Lusignan family, to which he was distantly related. This version of the Lusignans' rise to power in Cyprus would have been more palatable to the French king and nobility of the late fourteenth century than the true historical link with the kings of England. Jean d'Arras' work was translated into English in around 1500 and into Spanish twice, complete with the deeds of the Hospitallers.[62]

The Hospitallers appear assisting a marriage in one manuscript of *Theséus de Cologne*, the last work in the 'Dagobert' cycle; although here they are confused with the Templars. *Theséus* was a well known work, surviving in two versions dating from after 1364. In her long study of *Theséus*, Elizabeth Rosenthal traced various references to the poem surviving from the late fourteenth and early fifteenth centuries, including references to paintings in the queen's apartments at the Hôtel Saint Pol in Paris which illustrated scenes from the story and records of a tapestry by Nicolas Bataille, ordered in 1379. In addition, she dated to 1374 a miracle story retelling part of *Theséus*.[63] The Military Orders appear in the long version of the poem, which was probably written after 1376.

The Hospitallers appear in connection with the adventures of Osane, queen

---

[62] See also Luttrell, 'The Hospitallers in Cyprus after 1386', pp. 135–6, for the context and Jean's sources for the Hospital of Rhodes. For a general study of the work, see Laurence Harf-Lancner, *Les Fées au Moyen Age. Morgane et Mélusine. La naissance des fées* (Geneva, 1984), pp. 83–5, 155–78, esp. p. 170 on the patron of the work; there is no discussion of the Hospitallers. On the conquest of Cyprus, the Templars and the Lusignans in Cyprus see Edbury, *Kingdom of Cyprus and the Crusades*, esp. pp. 7–9. For the English translation see *Melusine, compiled (1382–1394 AD) by Jean d'Arras, englisht about 1500, edited from a unique manscript in the library of the British Museum*, by A.K. Donald, EETS 68 (London, 1895), pp. 114–81, 265–92, for the Brothers' deeds in the eastern Mediterranean. For the Spanish translation see *Historia de la linda Melosina*, ed. I.A. Corfis (Madison, 1986), pp. 54–89, 129–47 (1489 translation on verso pages, 1526 translation on recto pages). Hans Sachs wrote a short version of the story based on Jean d'Arras' version, but he left out the Hospitallers: 'Tragedie mit 25 personen zu agiern, die Melusina, und trat 7 actus', in *Hans Sachs*, ed. Adelbert von Keller, vol. 12, BLVS 140 (Tübingen, 1879), pp. 526–64; for the episode in Cyprus see Act 3, pp. 537–42.

[63] 'Theséus de Cologne, a general study and partial edition', by Elizabeth E. Rosenthal, PhD thesis, Birkbeck College, University of London (1975), pp. i–ii, 6, 8, 515–22, 1127–247, 1722–8.

of Constantinople. Gadifer, son of Theséus, captures Constantinople, killing the king, Griffon. Subsequently Gadifer's wife Osane is betrayed by Clodas, Griffon's widow. Osane goes to Jerusalem, where she takes on the running of a pilgrim hospice near the Temple of Solomon. In the long version of the poem this hospice becomes the Hospital of St John, as Hospitallers are associated with it. The author of this also calls them Templars, but the fact that they wear black indicates that they are actually Hospitallers. Hospitallers knights, sisters and 'serving Brothers' wore black mantles over a long black tunic, whereas the Templar knights wore white mantles, although their 'serving Brothers' wore black. This author's confusion between the two orders is understandable, as this version of *Theséus* was written over sixty years after the dissolution of the Order of the Temple. As the Hospitallers had been given the Templars' property, by the late fourteenth century some writers thought that the two Orders had always been the same.[64]

Osane's long-lost son Renechon comes to Jerusalem and fights a single combat with a Muslim emir in order to prove Lady Florinde's claim to the throne of Jerusalem. Florinde is a secret convert to Christianity, and she and Renechon are in love. After Renechon has won his battle, he and Florinde meet at Osane's hospice. The Hospitallers and the Patriarch Clement are also present; the Patriarch marries Renechon and Florinde, while the Templars (*sic*) in the hospice celebrate Renechon's victory over the Muslim emir. This writer managed to combine contemporary actuality – the Hospitallers were still in existence while the Templars had been abolished – with literary tradition, with the Templars again assisting lovers.[65]

The long version of *Theséus* was so popular that an abridged prose version had been produced by the early sixteenth century. This survives in a single manuscript. A printed edition was produced by Jehan Trepperel at Paris in 1504, a fragment of which was discovered and transcribed by F.W. Bourdillon *c*. 1918. This version of the story was highly abbreviated, written in an historical style, and downplayed the more fantastic elements of the story. Interestingly, the Brothers here are Hospitallers throughout, and most of the references to them are omitted. They do not appear in the marriage scene. The redactor of this version of *Theséus* accounted for the appearance of the Hospitallers by the fact that Osane is *hospitaliere* of Jerusalem, lodging

---

[64] On this, see Chapter 7, pages 230–33, below.
[65] Bib. nat. nouv. acq. fr. 10060, fol. 210r–v; for the black habits, see fol. 341r; Rosenthal, 'Theséus de Cologne', for Osane at the pilgrim hospital near the Temple of Solomon in Jerusalem, see p. 100, laisse 347, p. 107, laisse 384, p. 115, laisse 427; for confusion between Hospitallers and Templars, see pp. 7–8 and entries on p. 1033, lines 15702–3, p. 1055a, line 15725; for date, see p. 9; this work is cited by Moisan, *Répertoire*, 1.1, pp. 63, 588, 1.2, p. 913. At the time of writing, there is no critical edition of this work. I am indebted to Rosenthal's study for an introduction to the plot and the various editions of Theséus, See also R. Bossuat, 'Théseus de Cologne', *Le Moyen Age*, 65 (1959), 97–133, 293–320, 539–77, esp. 295, 297, 299, 301–2, 319–20 for the Military Orders.

Christian pilgrims in her hospice, and therefore her assistants must be Hospitallers; but their role was reduced to a handful of minor appearances.[66] Various historical works were also based on *Theséus*, which concentrated on the parts of the story which took place in Europe and did not involve the Hospitallers and Templars.[67]

The long version of *Theséus* was also 'put into prose' in its entirety, possibly in the second half of the fifteenth century.[68] This long prose version was printed for Jehan Longis and Vincent Sertenas in 1534. In this version, the Hospitallers have vanished from the marriage scene, and are replaced by Templars. The 1534 version was reprinted for Jehan Bonfons in 1550; this edition omits the last part of the story and thus some of the events including the Templars and Hospitallers, but includes the wedding, where only Templars appear.[69] In 1781 André Guillaume Contant d'Orville included a summarised version of *Theséus* in the eighth part of his seventy-volume *Mélanges tirés d'un grande Bibliothèque*. In this version of the story, the Templars do not live in Osanne's hospital but are her neighbours. A priest attached to the Templars baptises Florinde and (presumably) performs her marriage with Regnesson.[70] It is unsurprising that the Hospitallers were gradually eased out of their involvement in this romantic scene and replaced by the Templars, as literary convention expected the Templars rather than the Hospitallers to be assistants in love affairs.

Later in *Theséus*, Osane calls two Templars and sends them to Constantinople, Rome and France to discover the truth about the betrayal of her marriage and to inform her husband Gadifer that his son Renechon is in a

---

[66] Bib. nat. fr. 1473, pp. 125, 140; for Osane as *hospitaliere* of Jerusalem, see pp. 70, 83, 99, 137, 166. A transcription of the Trepperel edition survives in a typescript in the National Library of Wales and the British Library: *Theseus de Cologne: Fragment of a lost edition, and unknown version of the Romance. Printed apparently by or for Jehan Trepperel, Paris, 1504*, ed. F.W. Bourdillon. For a very brief appearance of the Hospitallers see p. 4, ch. 23; their role in the verse romance and later long prose version is much more extensive. On the short prose version of *Theséus* and the Trepperel fragment see Rosenthal, 'Theséus de Cologne', pp. ii, 1340–403, 1475–83, citing F.W. Bourdillon, 'Notes on a fragment of a lost edition and an unknown version of the romance', *The Library*, 3rd series, no. 33, vol. 9, Jan. 1918, 73–83.

[67] Rosenthal, 'Theséus de Cologne', pp. i–ii, 1248–339, 1404–74.

[68] Rosenthal, 'Theséus de Cologne', p. 1509.

[69] *Hystoire Tresrecreative: traictant des faictz et gestes du Noble et Vaillant chevalier Theseus de Coulongne par sa prouesse Empereur de Romme. Et aussi de son filz Gadifer Empereur de Grece. Pareillement des trois enfans dudit Gadifer cest ascavoir Regnault, Regnier et Regnesson: lesquels firent plusieurs beaulx faictz darmes comme pourrez veoir cy apres. On les vend au Palais en la Gallerie par ou on va a la Chancellerie A la bouticque de Jehan Longis et de Vincent Sertenas* (1534), Bk 2, fols 38b–c; *Hystoire Trescreative ... Jehan Bonfons à Paris* (1550), fols 236a–b; discussed by Rosenthal, 'Theséus de Cologne', pp. 1484–526. On the long lacuna in the 1550 edition see Rosenthal, pp. 1476, 1526.

[70] André Guillaume Contant d'Orville, *Mélanges tirés d'une grande Bibliothèque. De lecture des livres français, huitième partie: livres de Philosophie, Sciences et Arts du Seizième Siècle*, vol. 14 (1781), pp. 176, 184; cited by Rosenthal, 'Theséus de Cologne', pp. 1607, 1610–11, 1701 n. 443.

Muslim prison. They are not to mention that his wife, Osane, is in Jerusalem; although in the event they tell Gadifer everything. It is two Hospitallers rather than two Templars who set off for Constantinople; a few lines later they are called 'pilgrims', which could simply mean 'travellers'. Two Hospitallers arrive in Greece, but when they reach France and deliver the message they are Templars, described as '*senes*', wise. The Templar delivering the message first tells Gadifer that Renechon has married Florinde of Edessa and has been made king of Jerusalem, but has been captured by the sultan of Damascus. Then, after quoting a proverb about the consequences of marrying a good woman as against marrying a bad one, he goes on to tell Gadifer that Osane is in Jerusalem:

> 'We have come here to tell you the whole situation, so you will go to aid your son and Florinde his wife who is in danger, and come to beg mercy from your wife, because you have wrongfully made her undergo such great danger.' When Gadifer heard him, he began to weep ...

Although these messengers should be Hospitallers because they are the religious men who live in Osane's Hospital (except on fol. 263v, where they live in the Temple of Solomon), obviously Templars were more suitable in this role, which was concerned with faithful marital love and which would eventually bring about the reconciliation of wife and husband.[71]

The short prose version of *Theséus* called these messengers simply 'messagiers', although as Osane is *hospitaliere* of Jerusalem the reader could deduce that they were meant as Hospitallers. They obey instructions and do not give Gadifer news of Osane.[72] In the prose versions of 1534 and 1550, the transformation of the Templars into pilgrims, Hospitallers and then Templars follows the same pattern as in the long verse version. Again Templars actually deliver to Gadifer the message which will tell him the whereabouts of his long-lost wife.[73] In the eighteenth-century edition, they are Templars throughout; but this time they actually obey instructions and do not tell Gadifer where his wife is, only giving him news of his son and the charcoalburner, Regnier.[74] In this affair of love, again, the Templars replaced the Hospitallers.

In Joanot Martorell's 'true-to-life' adventure story *Tirant lo Blanc*, written between 1460 and 1468, a Hospitaller appears as a lover. A beautiful and gallant lady of Rhodes is loved by many Brothers of the Order, but especially by *Frare Simó de Far*, Brother Simon de Far, a native of Navarre, who has long begged her for her love, without success. She is also courted by a

---

[71] Bib. nat. nouv. acq. fr. 10060, fols 240v–241r, 260r–262r: quotation from fol. 262r; summarised by Rosenthal, 'Theséus de Cologne', pp. 124, 126.
[72] Bib. nat. fr. 1473, pp. 99, 118.
[73] *Hystoire Tresrecreative* (1534), Bk 2, fols 53c–d, 65a–66a, 67d; *Hystoire Tresrecreative* (1550), fols 258d–259b, 275c–277b (foliated in error as 265c–267b), 279d.
[74] Contant d'Orville, *Mélanges*, 14 pp. 176, 184, 198–9; Rosenthal, 'Theséus de Cologne', pp. 1616, 1619.

Genoese, who tells her that the Genoese, with the consent of the Genoese Brothers of the Order and in alliance with the Muslims, are about to conquer Rhodes and destroy the Order and the people. She sends a messenger to Brother Simon, who is in church with the Master and Brothers. Leading Brother Simon out of church, the messenger asks him to come to the lady's house at once. Inspired by his love for her, he complies eagerly. Here she accepts his love on condition he pass on to the Master the news of the plot against Rhodes. He pours out his eternal gratitude to her, kissing her hands, and vows himself and his property and honour to her service.

There follows a vivid description of Brother Simon's journey to find the Master that night. This account develops Brother Simon's character and that of the Master as pious men, devoted to their Order and the service of God despite their personal shortcomings. They and their Order thus appear more sympathetic to the audience, rendering Tirant's later service for the Order all the more glorious. Equally important for the modern reader is the fact that Brother Simon's journey appears to be an accurate description of the Order's customs and procedures, and it is therefore worthwhile setting it out in some detail here.

As it is now after dark, the Order's fortress is shut up, and Brother Simon has to hammer on the gates and give an account of himself to the Brothers on guard. They are not inclined to let him in, but eventually one goes to fetch the Master, who is at his prayers. The Master is very angry to hear that Brother Simon has been out of the House after dark and threatens to punish him severely. 'Never since I was master has it been seen or heard of for anyone to be outside the fortress at this hour!' He is not to be permitted to enter.

Brother Simon pleads humbly with the guards to ask the Master to allow him to enter, for this is a matter of great necessity; and when he has been heard they may give him the penance he deserves. The Master again refuses to allow him in, but a aged knight reasons with him and points out an earlier occasion where, if the gate of the fortress had not been opened at midnight the castle of St Peter would have been lost to the Turks, who had come at that unexpected hour. The Master then agrees to the gate being opened, and Brother Simon is allowed to come before the Master, who upbraids him in no uncertain terms for going out of the fortress at these *'hores indispostes e no honestes'*. He gives orders for him to be thrown into prison and given only bread and water. However, Brother Simon points out that the Master is not accustomed to condemn anyone before they have been heard, and declares his devotion to the Order: 'I would willingly die a martyr to maintain our Order'. The Master finally agrees to let him tell him what he has heard in private. Brother Simon goes down on one knee and kisses the Master's hand, then tells him that the Genoese Brothers of the Order have conspired with the Genoese to capture Rhodes the very next day; among other things, ammunition has been removed and replaced by soap and cheese, so that the Brothers will not be able to defend themselves. On investigation, this is found to be true. The Master then puts defensive measures in train, so that Rhodes is saved, but remains under siege from the Sultan. The Master appeals to the West for help, and Tirant comes in response to the appeal.[75] In this work the Hospitallers are not connected with romantic love because of any literary tradition; rather, the romantic episode gives additional interest to the plot, and makes the Hospitallers themselves appear more interesting and sympathetic.

Joanot Martorell was born between 1413 and 1415 in Valencia, and travelled to England, Portugal and Naples, dying in 1468. His work was revised by his friend Martí Joan de Galba and published at Valencia by Nicolau Spindeler in 1489. Joanot's description of the Order, its organisation and procedures is very close to the actual contemporary situation, and is clearly based on eyewitness information. He may have used Francesc Ferrer's poem *Romanç de l'armada del Soldà contra Rodes* as a source; Ferrer was a Catalan or Valencian who was present on Rhodes during the siege of the island by the Mamluks in 1444. In addition, also present on Rhodes at that time was Jaume de Vilaragut, who is known to have been a friend of Joanot Martorell, and may have provided him with information on the Order. The work is dedicated to the *infant* Prince Ferran of Portugal. It is a work in the fifteenth-century renaissance pattern, rationalistic and emphasizing actuality, commencing with reference to the heroes of the Bible, classical history and the early Church – all 'historical' figures whose historical accuracy was well-attested in written sources – with only a brief reference to 'Lancelot and other knights'. The appearance of the Hospitallers reinforces and underlines this emphasis on truthful history and actuality, as well as reflecting the long involvement of Aragon in the crusade.[76]

Overall, the involvement of the Templars in romantic love in literature can be explained by the image which papal bulls portrayed of them as the epitome of self-sacrificing Christian love, adapted by Wolfram von Eschenbach and then by later writers. The Hospitallers, although they too were examples of self-sacrificing Christian love, were not depicted in so many such roles in literature, and when they did appear in *Theséus de Cologne* they were gradually 'squeezed out' in later redactions by the Templars. Unlike their other literary roles, which were directly based on their actual deeds, the depiction of Templars as supporters of romantic love was a genuine literary convention with no direct roots in reality. However, when the emphasis was on strict

---

[75] Joanot Martorell, *Tirant lo Blanc*, ed. Marti de Riquer and Maria Josepa Gallofré, 2 vols, 2nd edn (Barcelona, 1985), 1, pp. 159–67, chapters 98–9. For recent studies and a full bibliography see *Tirant lo Blanc: New Approaches*, ed. Arthur Terry (Woodbridge, 1999).

[76] Joanot Martorell, *Tirant lo Blanc*, pp. 7–9, 12 for date and sources, pp. 19–22, 23 for dedication and references to past heroes.

realism, as in *Tirant lo Blanc*, then the Hospitallers could be lovers as well as any other religious.

4 *Hospitality*

The Military Orders also appeared in other monastic or religious roles, fulfilling their real-life charitable and hospitable functions. The charitable function first appeared in literature after the Fifth Crusade, around 1225, in the French versions of the romance of *Bueve de Hantone*. In the second French version, a Templar guides a pilgrim to the land of 'Hermine' to find King Bueve; in the third French version, Templars greet the fugitive Bueve and direct him to Jerusalem, where in the Temple of Solomon he offers his warhorse and armour, in return for a pilgrim's garb. The patriarch gives him a meal, a mule and a hundred shillings, while the Templars give him twenty pounds.[77] Again, in *La Fille du Comte de Ponthieu*, and in the version of this story included in the fictional-historical *Estoires d'Outremer*, the Templars of Brindisi lend money to the destitute count and his entourage. This does not occur in the fifteenth-century version of the story.[78]

A different sort of fugitive receives Templar hospitality in the version of *Saladin* included by Brother Jean la Gougue, prior of St Gildas, in his book *L'Histoire des princes de Déols et seigneurs de Chasteauroux*, composed in the late fifteenth century. Here two of the leading nobles of the Third Crusade, Andrew of Chavigny and William des Barres, leave the forces of King Philip of France at Acre and set out to attack Jerusalem with 500 mercenaries; Andrew carries the banner of the king of France, and William the banner of Richard, king of England. When the two kings discover that their subordinates have been using their banners they are very angry and William has to flee to Jerusalem (currently in Muslim hands), where he takes refuge with 'an uncle of his, who was Master of the Templars'. Clearly Everard des Barres is meant, who was actually Master of the Temple during the Second Crusade, rather than the Third. What the Master of the Temple was doing inside Jerusalem while it was in Muslim hands is not explained; like the earlier author of *Le Chevalier au Cygne et Godefroid de Bouillon* and the writer of the 1460s version of *La Fille du Comte de Ponthieu*, this writer seems to have assumed that the Templars were clergy attached to the Temple, who would have remained there whoever held the city. The original version of *Saladin* was probably composed in verse in the second half of the fourteenth century, but the original version has not survived.[79]

---

[77] *Bueve de Hantone, Fassung II*, 1, line 17578; *Fassung III*, 1, lines 3180–97, 3240–45, 3249.
[78] *Fille du Comte de Ponthieu*, p. 39, lines 570–73, 715–16; *Estoires d'Outremer*, p. 85.
[79] *Saladin, suite et fin du deuxième cycle de la Croisade*, ed. Larry S. Crist, TLF (Geneva, 1972), pp. 258–60, esp. p. 260. Andrew de Chavigny was an ancestor of the lords of Châteauroux,

In real life, the Templars and Hospitallers were sometimes criticized for offering hospitality to fugitives from justice.[80] The Templars also appear giving lodging to lovers, as described above. In contrast, although the Hospitallers lodge knights they do not lodge lovers. It is not always possible to tell whether a 'hospital' in literature is the Hospital of St John or simply a local independent hospital. When the kings Arthur, Ydier, Urien and Neutre in *Le Livre d'Artus* lodge at a hospital, this is probably meant to be simply a local hospice.[81] In the fourteenth-century Middle English verse romance *Richard Coeur de Lion* King Richard I of England, *en route* to the Holy Land on the Third Crusade, lodges at the house of the Hospital outside Messina in Sicily; here the Hospital of St John is probably meant, given the crusading context.[82] In the collection of half-historical, half-legendary tales attributed to the 'Minstrel of Reims' of the mid-thirteenth century, the great Muslim sultan Saladin appears lodging at the Hospital of St John in Acre in the guise of a sick pilgrim. He has come to discover whether the Hospitallers are really as hospitable as they are said to be, and tells the Hospitallers that the only thing he can bear to eat is the right front foot of Morel, the good horse of the Grand Master, and that this should be cut off before his own eyes. After some thought, the Grand Master agrees, the horse is brought and preparations are made to cut off the hoof, but at the last moment Saladin changes his mind and asks for mutton instead, so the horse is saved. A similar story, but shorter, appears in a manuscript containing a collection of *exempla* by the Dominican Stephen of Bourbon; but in this case Saladin visits the Temple at Acre. The story celebrates the Orders' hospitality and selfless care for pilgrims, and goes on to repeat the legend that Saladin later became a Christian; but it also

---

hence his prominence in the story. On the 'Second Crusade Cycle' of which this work forms part see Robert F. Cook and Larry S. Crist, *Le Deuxième Cycle de la croisade* (Geneva, 1972); Duparc-Quioc, *Le Cycle de la croisade* (Paris, 1955), and *Le Bâtard de Bouillon: chanson de geste*, ed. Robert Francis Cook, TLF (Geneva, 1972), pp. xxxiv–lx. Scholars now agree that the so-called 'Second' Cycle was not a cycle at all, but a series of unconnected stories which fit only roughly into a chronological sequence. Nevertheless the title is still used as a term of convenience. See, for instance, Claasens, 'Some notes on the Proto-Saladin', p. 131.

[80] See Hugh, lord of Berzé, *La 'Bible' au seigneur de Berzé*, ed. Félix Lecoy (Paris, 1938), lines 261–93 (possibly writing in the early 1220s: pp. 24–5; five manuscripts are known, p. 7); Gregory IX to the Hospital of St John, *Cartulaire général de l'ordre des Hospitaliers*, 2186, 13 March 1238.

[81] *Le Livre d'Artus*, p. 229, lines 21–3, p. 230, lines 23–5, p. 233, lines 37–8, p. 273, lines 5–6, p. 303, lines 5–6. The date of this text is uncertain, but possibly 1240–50. The description of the Saxon horde, pp. 3–21, is very similar to the description of the Mongol horde of 1236 recorded by a contemporary observer, printed in: 'Ex historia regum Franciae continuatione Parisiensi', ed. O. Holder-Egger, *MGHS*, 26, pp. 604–5. It survives in one incomplete version and fragments, and is part of a 'suite du Merlin'.

[82] *Der mittelenglische Versroman über Richard Löwenherz: kritische Ausgabe nach allen Handschriften mit Einleitung, Anmerkungen und deutscher Übersetzung*, ed. Karl Brunner (Vienna and Leipzig, 1913), line 1768.

reminds us that the Military Orders and the Hospitallers in particular were famed for the quality of their horses.[83]

In the fourteenth-century version of *Renaut de Montauban*, Regnault arrives penniless at Acre, and is taken to the 'Ostel Dieu', a lodging-place for poor pilgrims run by a master and sisters. The 'Ostel Dieu', or God's lodging-house, was a common institution in the cities of this period, and could be attached to any religious Order, or be independent, although all were religious in nature. This one, however, with its master and sisters, bears a faint resemblance to the Hospital of the 'Second State' of the First Crusade Cycle into which Beatrice and Ida retired, and in fact later it is referred to as 'l'ospital'. As the Hospital of St John was certainly the most famous hospice for the poor in Acre, it is most probable that the 'Ostel Dieu' is intended to be the Hospital of St John. This hospital, however, does not come out well in the story – far from curing Regnault or taking good care of him, by the time that Maugis finds him he is in a pitiable state and close to death, although Regnault later returns to the hospital to hear mass, in gratitude for the house's care for him when he was destitute.[84]

The Hospitallers and/or Templars also appear in connexion with Osane's pilgrim hospice in Jerusalem in *Theséus de Cologne*, as described above. Here they are obviously good and well-respected hosts.

5 *Ransoming prisoners*

The charitable role of the Military Orders developed further in later literature, to include another actual charitable role of the Military Orders, ransoming prisoners. In Jean d'Arras' *Mélusine*, written between 1382 and 1394, Mélusine's son Guy of Lusignan gives the Master of the Hospital of Rhodes a hundred Saracen prisoners to enable him to ransom Christians and Hospitallers captured by the Muslims.[85] In the version of *Saladin* which formed part of the story *Jehan d'Avesnes* the Templars and Hospitallers appear briefly, helping

---

[83] *Récits d'un ménestrel de Reims au treizième siècle*, ed. Natalis de Wailly, SHF (Paris, 1876), pp. 104–9, 112, sections 198–208, 213. Written in 1260 and never completed, six manuscripts survive, but only one of these is definitely thirteenth century (pp. xxxiff, lxiii: and see the edition in *MGHS*, 26 p. 525) The editors call the author 'a minstrel', but in fact his identity is unknown. For the story of Saladin visiting the Temple, see Cook and Crist, *Deuxième Cycle*, pp. 166, 184; the story appears in Tours MS 468 (old 205), fol. 161r. It does not appear in the published edition of Stephen of Bourbon's anecdotes, and perhaps was a later addition to the collection, not composed by Stephen; Stephen of Bourbon was writing around 1230. On the Orders' horses, see Nigel Wireker, *Speculum stultorum*, ed. Thomas Wright, 2 vols, RS 59 (London, 1872), 1 p. 82, 95; 'Sur les états du monde', verse 25, in *Anglo-Norman Political Songs*, ed. Isabel S.T. Aspin, Anglo-Norman Texts 11 (Oxford, 1953), p. 123; 'Ordre de Bel Ayre', lines 71–8, in ibid, pp. 130–31.

[84] <*Renaut de Montalban*>, lines 9437–69, 9800, 22643–4.

[85] Jean d'Arras, *Mélusine*, p. 129.

to ransom Christian prisoners after the surrender of Jerusalem to Saladin in October 1187. This is based on the chronicle of Ernoul, discussed above. Interestingly, although Ernoul cast doubt on the Orders' enthusiasm to ransom the poor, in *Saladin* there is no such criticism.[86]

In the late-fourteenth-century *Theséus de Cologne*, Renechon asks for the Templars' prayers while he is a prisoner of the sultan of Damascus. His plea is carried to the Templars by his foster-father Regnier the charcoalburner.[87] However, the Templars do not bring about his release; it is Regnier who eventually liberates Renechon, by a trick and force of arms.

6 *Burying the dead*

This was a role closely connected to the role of hospitality, which in actuality was performed by all the Military Orders.[88] In fiction, this role was first assigned to the Templars after the Fifth Crusade, around 1225, in the third French version of *Bueve de Hantone*.[89] Here the Brothers bury the hero's uncle, killed in battle by the Muslims. In 'La Chanson des rois Baudouin' two kings of Jersualem, Amaury and Baldwin of Sebourc, are buried in the Hospital at Acre.[90] In a different twist to the theme of bereavement, in the Provençal poem of the death of Roland, *Ronsavals*, Charlemagne founds the Hospital and Temple in commemoration of those killed in the battle of Roncesvalles (AD 778).[91] In the fourteenth-century Middle English verse romance *Richard Coeur de Lion* the master of the Hospital, here 'Gawter of Naples' (historically Garnier de Nablūs), is sent with his knights to retrieve the body of the noble knight 'Jake de Neys' (Jacques d'Avesnes) after the battle of 'Arsour' (Arsūf), and to see to its worthy burial. This incident is drawn from the contemporary and near-contemporary accounts of the Third Crusade on which this romance was ultimately based.[92] Other appearances of the Military

---

[86] *Saladin*, p. 66, ch. x, sections 50, 55; *Continuation de Guillaume de Tyr*, p. 70, sections 57–8. On the Orders' actual role in this area see Alan Forey, 'The Military Orders and the ransoming of captives from Islam (twelfth to early fourteenth centuries)', *Studia Monastica*, 33 (1991), 259–79, reprinted in his *Military Orders and Crusades*, VI. For date of this version of *Saladin*, see Claasens, 'Some notes on the Proto-Saladin', p. 132.

[87] Bib. nat. nouv. acq. fr. 10060, fols 223v, 230v; see also *Hystoire Tresrecreative* (1534), Bk 2, fols 45c, 49a; *Hystoire Tresrecreative* (1550), fols 246c–d, 252a.

[88] See, for example, R.B. Pugh, 'The Knights Hospitallers as Undertakers', *Speculum*, 53 (1978), 566–74.

[89] *Bueve de Hantone, Fassung III*, line 15828.

[90] *OFCC, VII: Jérusalem Continuations*, part 2, lines 5198, 5865–9.

[91] Mario Roques, 'Ronsavals: poème épique provençal', *Romania*, 58 (1932), 1–28, 161–89, lines 1444–5. Roques dated this to the fourteenth century, but a date of before 1250 has recently been proposed: Elisabeth Schulze-Busaker, 'La datation de *Ronsavals*', *Romania*, 110 (1989), 127–66, 396–425.

[92] *Der mittelenglische Versroman über Richard Löwenherz*, lines 5175–84; for the historical sources for this incident see Ambroise, *Estoire*, lines 6697–734; *Itinerarium peregrinorum*, ed. Stubbs, Bk 4, ch. 20, pp. 276–7.

Orders in connection with bereavement and burial were linked to erotic love and are described above.

7 *Supporting the conversion of Muslims to Christianity*

This role only appears in the 1534 printed prose edition of *Theséus de Cologne*, although presumably it also appeared in the late fifteenth-century long prose version of *Theséus* on which the printed edition was based. Following his recapture of Jerusalem, Regnesson announces that all the pagans (that is, Muslims) who wish to be baptised will not lose their possessions and may remain safely in Jerusalem, although all others must leave the city. More than twelve thousand pagans have themselves baptised: '*parquoy les templiers en demenerent une moult grande ioye parmi la ville*' – 'so that the Templars celebrated very joyfully throughout the town'. However, while the Templars support the conversion of Muslims, they are not actually involved in the conversion process.[93]

This was also the situation in actuality. The Military Orders were established to protect Christians and Christian territory, not to convert the heathen; the actual process of preaching and baptising converts was the responsibility of the preachers appointed by the relevant bishop. The Military Orders did sometimes work alongside preachers, as did the Swordbrothers in Livonia, and they did assist in producing an environment in which Christian preaching could safely take place, as the Templars did in the locality of their castle of Saphet after they had began rebuilding it during the 1240s. On the rare occasions when rulers and popes referred to the Military Orders as converting the heathen, it was probably this military assistance given to preachers which they had in mind.[94]

It is not clear why the long prose version of *Theséus de Cologne* inserted this reference to the Templars' interest in converting Muslims when there was

---

[93] *Hystoire Tresrecreative* (1534), Bk 2, fol. 121b; this reference to the Templars does not occur in the equivalent part of the verse version, Bib. nat. nouv. acq. fr. 10060, fol. 383.

[94] For the Swordbrothers in Livonia, see *The Chronicle of Henry of Livonia*, translated with an introduction and notes by James A. Brundage (Madison, 1961), pp. 7–8, 11–16, and see also pp. 69, 104, 178–80; Henry of Livonia, *Chronicon Livoniae*, 2nd edn, ed. Leonid Arbusow and Albert Bauer, MGH Scriptores rerum Germanicarum in usum scholarum separatim editi (Hanover, 1955), XI (3), pp. 48–9, XIV (11), p. 84, XXIII (7), pp. 160–62; Christiansen, *Northern Crusades*, pp. 76–7, 90–93, 122–6. For the Order of the Temple and Saphet, see 'Un nouveau texte du traité "De constructione castri Saphet"', ed. R.B.C. Huygens, *Studi Medievali*, 4 (1965), 355–87: esp. 386, lines 262–6. For rulers and popes making reference to the Military Orders being involved in the conversion of non-Christians see *Cartulaire général de l'ordre des Hospitaliers*, nos. 181, 1603, 1742; *Les Registres d'Innocent IV*, ed. Élie Berger, 4 vols, BEFAR (Paris, 1884–1921) no. 7641; Alexander IV in *Tabulae ordinis theutonici ex tabularii regii Berolinensis codice potissimum*, ed. Ernest Strehlke (Berlin, 1869; reprinted Toronto and Jerusalem, 1975), no. 610, p. 407; Alan Forey, *The Templars in the Corona de Aragón*, (London, 1973), p. 377 (1208). On the Military Orders and conversion see also Forey, *Military Orders*, pp. 33, 46–9.

no such reference in the verse version of the story. Possibly this reference reflects the Hospitallers' successes against the Muslims in the eastern Mediterranean in the later fifteenth century: the successful defence of Rhodes in 1480 and the treaty of 1482 with Jem, the pretender to the Ottoman throne.[95] These successes had raised the Order's profile and prestige in the West, and might have prompted the prose redactor of *Theséus* to give the Order a wider role in this work. Yet the problem remains that the Hospitaller-Templars of *Theséus* bear little ressemblance to the actual Hospitallers of St John in the late Middle Ages; they do not fight, and in the long prose version they are almost invariably referred to as Templars. The prose redactor of *Theséus* may have given the Templars an interest in the conversion of Muslims simply to underline the importance of the conversions, and because such an interest would be appropriate for religious men.

8 *An example of spiritual knighthood*

Military Orders, then, especially Templars, appeared in literature in a variety of roles more-or-less linked to their monastic function. They were not generally used, however, to give spiritual advice to Christian knights. This was not surprising, as the Military Orders did not usually hold positions of spiritual leadership in the real world. Very few Brothers were made bishops: Brother Garin the Hospitaller was made bishop of Senlis in 1213, a handful of other Templars and Hospitallers became bishops, while a number of priests of the Teutonic Order became bishops in sees which the Order controlled: Kurland, Culm and Samland.[96] In general, however, and unlike Brothers of other

---

[95] Housley, *Later Crusades*, pp. 111–15, 227–9.

[96] On Brother Garin, see: Charles Petit-Dutaillis, *Étude sur la vie et le règne de Louis VIII (1187–1226)* (Paris, 1894), pp. 335–6; for Brother Stephen de Fulbourn of the Hospital, bishop of Waterford and later archbishop of Tuam, see *Calendar of Documents Relating to Ireland preserved in Her Majesty's Public Record Office, London*, ed. W.S. Sweetman, 5 vols (London, 1875–86), 2, p. 174, no. 1009, and see the index entries, pp. 726–8; ibid., 3, pp. 317, 326, and index p. 652; for his earlier career in England, see *Calendar of the Patent Rolls preserved in the Public Record Office, Henry III, AD 1266–1272* (London, 1913), pp. 190, 348. For Joan de Laodicea, Hospitaller bishop of Limassol *c.* 1312–22, see Anthony Luttrell, 'The Hospitallers in Cyprus, 1310–1378', in *Kypriakai Spoudai*, 50 (1986), 155–84: reprinted in his *The Hospitallers of Rhodes and their Mediterranean World* (Aldershot, 1992), IX, pp. 157, 176–7. For Richard, Templar bishop of Lavello, see *Regesta Honorii papae III*, 2, p. 429, no. 5969; Umbert, Templar bishop of Paneas: Bulst-Thiele, *Sacrae domus*, p. 254. For Hospitallers as bishops of Valenia (a diocese in territory controlled by the Hospital), see: *Cartulaire général de l'ordre des Hospitaliers*, no. 999; Jonathan Riley-Smith, *The Knights of St John in Jerusalem and Cyprus, c. 1050–1310* (London, 1967), p. 413. Teutonic Knights also appear as bishops in north-eastern Europe, in dioceses controlled by the Teutonic Order: C. Eubel, *Hierarchia catholica medii aevi*, 2nd edn (Münster, 1908), p. 433; *Registres d'Innocent IV*, nos. 4855, 7998, 8041; *Les Registres d'Urbain IV*, ed. Jean Guiraud *et al.*, 5 vols, BEFAR (Paris, 1899–1958), nos. 213, 711; 'Menkonis Chronicon', ed. L. Weiland, *MGHS*, 23, p. 553; 'Cronica S. Petri Erfordiensis Moderna', ed. O. Holder-Egger, *MGHS*, 30, p. 423.

religious orders, the priests of the Military Orders were not promoted to bishoprics. Possibly this was because they were not regarded as being as spiritual and well-educated as the priests of other Orders,[97] but it must be remembered that the Military Orders were always short of manpower and it is likely that they could not spare their priests to govern bishoprics.

One occasion when a member of a Military Order does appear giving spiritual advice occurs in the 'Third State' of the First Crusade Cycle, the so-called London-Turin continuation of the *Chanson de Jérusalem*. Having become a Templar on the death of his wife, Harpin de Bourges is captured by the *amulainne* during a siege of Ascalon, along with Abilan of Damascus, who has recently converted to Christianity from Islam. The pair are imprisoned in the tower of the noble Muslim maiden Margalie, an intelligent and well-educated young lady who has already decided to become a Christian and so treats them kindly; and there is an element of humour in the chaste Templar being held prisoner by the lovely Muslim maiden. Before they realise that Margalie is kindly disposed towards them, Harpin and Abilan expect that they are about to be killed. Harpin makes a speech of encouragement to Abilan:

> Noble man full of prowess, don't be dismayed. If you die for God who remains in Trinity, your soul will be put into holy majesty next to Jesus Christ, at his right side! Don't concern yourself about serving the demon [Mohammed, whom Abilan has abandoned] but have true faith in Christianity.[98]

Later he speaks again in the same terms:

> Abilan, dear friend, I am very troubled for you! I beg you, noble man, don't be worried; if God wills that we die, be grateful for it. You will have taken a good step, for our souls will be saved. If the body is martyred, happy the day that it was born.[99]

Is this Harpin speaking as a Christian encouraging a new convert, or as a Templar? His words certainly echo the sentiments of the Templar Nicholas following the Christian defeat at the battle of Hattin in July 1187:

> A certain Templar named Nicholas had been so successful in persuading the rest to undergo death willingly that the others struggled to go in front of him and he only just succeeded in obtaining the glory of martyrdom first – which was an honour he very much strove for.[100]

---

[97] On the generally low level of learning among the brothers of the Military Orders and evidence that the Orders discouraged learning, see Forey, 'Literacy', pp. 185–206. Only a handful of Templars who testified during the trial of the Order had any professional legal qualifications, which may have been an important factor in the destruction of the Order: see James Brundage, 'The Lawyers of the Military Orders', in *The Military Orders: Fighting for the Faith*, ed. Barber, pp. 346–57, esp. pp. 351–2 and note 21.
[98] *OFCC, VIII: The London-Turin Version*, lines 15267–74.
[99] Ibid., lines 16704–8.
[100] *Itinerarium peregrinorum*, ed. Stubbs, Bk 1, ch. 5, p. 16; *Das Itinerarium peregrinorum*, p. 260, lines 3–7.

The Templars' fame for 'laying down their lives for their Brothers' has been noted above; Christian martyrdom was a central part of the Order's vocation. Harpin de Bourges, therefore, is speaking as a Templar in the tradition of Templar martyrs such as Nicholas, encouraging Christians to die in the name of Christ. It is very interesting that the poem which depicts him speaking these words was written after the final loss of Acre to the Muslims, when the Templars were trying without success to organise another crusade to the East, and less than a decade before the beginning of the trial which would destroy the Order. That a Templar could still be depicted in this way, as a faithful and self-sacrificing knight of Christ, at this late date might cause us to question the date of the poem; but this image is repeated in other works of the same period, as will be shown in the next chapter.

The only other work which clearly depicts the Military Orders as an example to Christian knights, encouraging them in their Christian life, is Ulrich von Etzenbach's *Wilhelm von Wenden*. The hero, a Muslim prince, wishes to become a Christian and sets off for Jerusalem to seek baptism, accompanied by his wife, but loses both her and her newborn children *en route*. In Jerusalem he receives baptism from the patriarch and joins the Christian army riding out to fight the Muslims, with the Teutonic Brothers, the Hospitallers and the Templars; Wilhelm is described alongside these last, wishing to be their comrade in their prize of salvation.

Ulrich, who was for a long while court poet of King Waclaw II of Bohemia, wrote this poem between 1287 and 1297. It survives in only two manuscripts. In view of the fact that the Hospitallers and Teutonic Knights received more patronage in Bohemia than the Templars, it is surprising that Ulrich singled out the Templars as the epitome of Christian knighthood for Wilhelm's emulation. The discrepancy suggests that literary convention – which gave prominence to the Templars over the other Military Orders – could be more important than a patron's personal preference. Alternatively, the Templars appear here because, as the first Military Order and the only international Military Order which had been militarised since its original foundation, the Order of the Templar was viewed as representing all the Military Orders.[101]

In both the case of Harpin in the London-Turin continuation and in *Wilhelm*, the Templars are encouraging a Muslim who has recently converted to Christianity. In this respect, they represent the whole of Christendom, showing the Muslims how they ought to live, rather than being an example to the Christian knight who is seeking to advance in the spiritual life. It is notable

---

[101] Ulrich von Etzenbach, *Wilhelm von Wenden*, ed. H.-F. Rosenfeld, Deutsche Texte des Mittelalters 49 (Berlin, 1957), lines 3784–93, 3841–8; Wentzlaff-Eggebert, *Kreuzzugsdichtung des Mittelalters*, pp. 280–83, 393. For the Hospitaller and Templars in Bohemia, see Libor Jan and Vít Jesensky, 'Hospitaller and Templar commanderies in Bohemia and Moravia: their Structure and Architectural Forms', in *The Military Orders*, vol. 2, ed. Nicholson, pp. 235–49. The Teutonic Order held even more properties in Bohemia than the Hospitallers.

that the Templars were not given this spiritual role in fictional literature until late in the life of the Order – not until nearly two centuries after the foundation of the first Military Order, and less than two decades before the beginning of the trial of the Order. Like other roles, however, this role of spiritual leadership did see some development in later literature, so that the Templars were also allowed to encourage Christians on their spiritual path. The Templars appeared again briefly encouraging Christian knights to seek salvation in *Le Chevalier au Cygne et Godefroid de Bouillon* (written *c.* 1350), as they urge Peter the Hermit to call the First Crusade in order that knights might find salvation; and urging the Christian King Arthur to attack a pagan giant in the alliterative *Morte Arthure*, written between 1350 and 1440.[102] Here, however, they are acting as ambassadors for the defence of Christendom, a role which will be considered in the next chapter. As noted above, the Templars are asked for their prayers on behalf of a prisoner in *Theséus de Cologne*, which indicates that their spirituality was respected.[103]

On the other hand, there is some indication in works of the later Middle Ages that the spirituality of the Military Orders, particularly the Templars, fell short of what should be expected of religious warriors.

In *Theséus de Cologne*, one of the Templars who accompanied Regnier the charcoalburner to Antioch is amazed when he sees him threatening the Christian prisoners; not realizing Regnier's clever plan to fool the Muslims, he fears that Regnier is going to have all the Christians killed. In the prose editions of 1534 and 1550, his fear is more serious: he fears that Regnier has abandoned the Christian faith. Queen Florinde rebukes his lack of faith in Regnier, and in due course Regnier is able to take over Antioch and force all the Muslims to convert to Christianity. This is a humorous scene, but the impression we are given of the Templar is that he is foolish and lacks faith in his fellow-Christians.[104] Later, the two Hospitallers (Templars in the printed prose edition of 1534) who accompany Regnier the charcoalburner on his mission to the West to seek aid for the Christians of Antioch are amazed by his courage and determination. They ask him how he has the courage to undertake such deeds. He retorts that they are wrong to ask such questions, for he does not perform them in his own strength but in the strength of God. In contrast to Regnier's strength, the Templars are absolutely worn out by the time that they reach Constantinople, and they cannot keep up with him – although in the 1534 and 1550 versions this contrast is played down, as both Regnier and the Templars are exhausted on arrival in Constantinople. Again, in Rome, the

---

[102] *Le Chevalier au Cygne et Godefroid de Bouillon*, 2, pp. 84–5, lines 5397–425, especially 5422–5; *The Alliterative Morte Arthure*, lines 840–87.
[103] Bib. nat. nouv. acq. fr. 10060, fols 223v, 230v.
[104] Bib. nat. nouv. acq. fr. 10060, fol. 287r; Rosenthal, 'Theséus de Cologne', p. 129; *Hystoire Trescreative* (1534), Bk 2, fol. 79a; *Hystoire Trescreative* (1550), fol. 297b–c.

Templars (in the original verse and in the 1534 edition) are horrified at Regnier's intention of going to confront the usurping pope and his nephew and accuse him of trying to get them killed. He tells them to go to the hostellry, eat and drink and take things easy, and if he dies they can pretend that they didn't know him – a suggestion with which they readily comply. The Hospitaller/Templars are absolutely horrified and terrified at what Regnier goes on to do in Rome; they hate violence and killing, although they do love good food.[105] One of them remarks at last, as Regnier goes to unmask the treachery of the French nobles to the emperor Théséus and King Ludovic that it is the devil who does Regnier's deeds for him. In the 1534 version this is slightly amended to saying that the devil would not dare to anger Regnier.[106]

While understandable in non-combatants, the Hospitaller/Templars' physical weakness, terror at the sight of violence, and tendency to attribute the power of the Christian warrior to diabolical inspiration is hardly what we would expect from the spiritual and physical warriors envisaged by Bernard of Clairvaux, or of the potential martyrs described by the popes of the twelfth and thirteenth centuries and depicted in the character of Harpin de Bourges. Either the author or authors of this part of *Théséus* believed that although the Templars were not guilty of the heresy of which they were accused in 1307 they were not as enthusiastic in the service of God as they should have been, or that the Templar/Hospitallers were purely religious men and did not fight.

While the former is certainly a possibility, the latter seems more likely. The fact that earlier in the poem Renechon asks the Templars for their prayers while he is in prison indicates that the poet did regard the Templars/Hospitallers as spiritual men in other respects. Moreover, the Templars can certainly recognise Osane's holiness, saying that she should be a saint after her death.[107] Again, their caution is significant within the context of the story, for it throws into relief the charcoalburner's sometimes repulsive violence (for example, on fol. 297 where he slaughters a nursing Muslim mother and her baby). Although Regnier is brave and a good Christian, he is impulsive and often makes serious errors which cause him and other Christians great problems, and he does not fight according to the usual rules of holy war, slaughtering the enemy mercilessly rather than sparing non-combatants and giving the defeated the opportunity to convert to Christianity. The Templar/Hospitallers' reaction to him is an indication that his behaviour, while humorous, is in fact unacceptable.

---

[105] Bib. nat. nouv. acq. fr. 10060, fols 302v (Hospitallers set out), 310r (exhausted Templars reach Constantinople), 312v (Templars), 318r (Hospitallers question Regnier), 319v (Templars at Rome), 323v–324r (Hospitaller/Templars), 327r (Templars), 330r (Templars dislike Regnier fighting), 339r, 342r (Templars exhausted); *Hystoire Tresrecreative* (1534), Bk 2, fols 84d, 89a, 92b–c, 93a; *Hystoire Tresrecreative* (1550), fols 308, 313.

[106] Bib. nat. nouv. acq. fr. 10060, fol. 346r; *Hystoire Tresrecreative* (1534), Bk 2, fol. 104b.

[107] Bib. nat. nouv. acq. fr. 10060, fol. 285r.

In fact, in *Theséus* the Military Orders never take on an active military role. In depicting the Templars/Hospitallers as noncombatants lacking in physical courage the author was depicting them as the equivalent of monks, like the 'fourpenny monks' of *La Chanson de Roland*; men who are sent to the monasteries to pray for humanity's sins because they are too weak to be knights and not able to fight.[108] In this respect they represent the Church rather than warriors. Yet the Templar/Hospitallers' excessive caution is not helpful for Christendom: Regnier's rash courage saves the situation at Constantinople, where Clodas' brothers are about to usurp the empire, and at Rome. The author or authors of the long version of *Theséus* regard Regnier as excessively violent, yet clearly it is also possible to be too cautious. The message to the audience is that Christian warriors can be too violent, yet the Church is too cautious; in order to advance Christendom, a combination of both is needed. Yet it would be odd if this author did not know that the Hospitallers of his own day were involved in holy war against the Muslims.

The German verse romance *Orendal* does not depict the Templars as noncombatants, but very much involved in holy war. Yet it also depicts the Templars as lacking spiritual awareness and in courage, for they ignore the hero on his first arrival at the Holy Sepulchre and refuse to ride out with him into battle on the grounds that he is not wearing armour – while in fact he is wearing Christ's robe, whose wearer cannot be harmed. On the other hand, the Templars are the loyal servants of Bride, queen of Jerusalem and ride out to assist their queen the moment that they see that she has ridden into battle; and they accept Orendal as their king as soon as they realize the truth of the situation, setting him honourably on the throne.[109] Once again, they appear in connection with a love affair, although their role is neutral rather than actively supportive.

Orendal has been variously dated to before 1170, after 1196, and 'the late Middle Ages'. Certainly, its composition appears to have been linked with the veneration of the relic of Christ's robe at Trier, which dated from 1197. However, only one manuscript of the verse romance survives, dated to 1477, as well as two later printed versions, one in prose. The simplistic style, language and storyline suggest that the poem was composed in the twelfth century, but this is incompatible with the appearance of the Templars, as it is hardly likely that the Order would have appeared in romances written in Germany, where the Order was not well known in the twelfth century, before it began to appear in epics written in France, where it was extremely well known. There are also errors in the description of the Order, such as the banner (described as green and red at 884.5 – the Order's banner was in fact black and

---

[108] *La Chanson de Roland*, ed. F. Whitehead (Oxford, 1946), lines 1876–82.

[109] *Orendal*, ed. H. Steinger, Altdeutsches Textbibliothek 36 (Halle, 1935), pp. iii–vi, and lines 836–43, 866–70, 884–91, 1201–4, 1340–41, 1676–85, 1949–2016, 2161–86.

white), which indicate that the Order was no longer in existence when this version of the poem was written.[110] In short, *Orendal* as it survives is a fifteenth-century medieval romance which may or may not ressemble a lost earlier work. In its view of the Templars' lack of spiritual awareness, it is certainly closer to the late fourteenth-century *Theséus de Cologne* than to any work written before the dissolution of the Order in 1312.

The Military Orders appear in many roles in fictional literature which underline or assume the fact that they were religious orders. Although in a few later works they are depicted as falling short as religious warriors (as in *Theséus* and *Orendal*) or in their caring vocation (as in the fourteenth-century *Renaut de Montalban*), elsewhere the quality of their spirituality is not in question. In fact, in general the quality of their spirituality is not of central importance to the story, as they hardly ever appear in roles where they are required to offer spiritual leadership. In the great majority of their appearances in literature, the Military Orders accompany the hero and give merely physical assistance, either charitable or military.

---

[110] See, for instance, *Geschichte der Deutschen Literatur 1: Der Deutsche Literatur von Karl dem Grossen bis zum beginn der Höfischen Dichtung, 770–1170*, ed. H. de Boor (Munich, 1949), pp. 256–7; see also Wentzlaff-Eggebert, *Kreuzzugsdichtung*, pp. 379–80. This gives a bibliography of critical works up to 1960. Wentzlaff-Eggebert argued that the original version of the poem was written before 1196, but the present form of the poem is a late medieval redaction. Green, *Medieval Listening and Reading*, assumes a date of before 1300: see, for instance, pp. 76–7, 85, 107.

CHAPTER THREE

MILITARY ACTIVITY

The Military Orders appear in medieval fictional literature involved directly in holy war against the Muslims, initially in the Holy Land, but in fifteenth-century literature also in Spain and Prussia. They also appear in supporting roles, advising kings and lending them money, acting as messengers and, finally, acting as ambassadors for Christians in need of help against pagans. All of these are roles which the Orders performed in actuality.

1 *Active participants in holy war*

The Templars first appeared in a military role alongside Richard of Montivilliers, fighting the Muslims in the Holy Land in *L'Escoufle* (1200–1202).[1] Shortly after this they appeared in a different guise as the *Templeise* in Wolfram von Eschenbach's *Parzival*, where their role, in defence of the Grail Castle, *Munsalvaesche* or *Munsalvatsche*, was primarily military. It will be demonstrated in Chapter 4 that this castle actually represented Jerusalem: hence the need for 'Templars' to defend it. Two of Wolfram's adaptors, Albrecht in the late thirteenth century and Ulrich Füetrer in the late fifteenth, continued the depiction of 'Templars' in this role.[2]

The Templars reappeared fighting Muslims, this time as genuine Templars with the Hospitallers, supporting the hero in Gautier de Tournai's *Gille de Chyn*, written in the 1230s. This work, surviving in only one manuscript, was apparently commissioned by the monks of St Ghislain to publicize the career of their noble patron, whose body lay buried in the abbey church. It is not known when Gilles de Chyn was in the Holy Land, but he died in 1137, before the Hospital became a major force in the army of the kingdom of Jerusalem, and before the Templars had become prominent. These two Orders may have helped him if and when he was in the Holy Land, but their role in battle was probably less prominent than Gautier later imagined it.[3]

---

[1] *L'Escoufle*, lines 1060–65; Trotter, *Medieval French Literature*, pp. 132–4, discusses this work but does not mention the Templars' role.
[2] See below, pp. 109–110, 120–47.
[3] *L'Histoire de Gille de Chyn by Gautier de Tournay*, ed. Edwin B. Place, Northwestern University Studies in the Humanities no. 7 (Evanston and Chicago, 1941), for date, see pp. 5–11; lines 2355–7, 2365–6, 2372, 2478, 2506–7, 2614–15. Trotter, *Medieval French Literature*, pp. 142–5.

One of the Templars' most striking appearances in the military role was in the Anglo-Norman poem *Du bon William Longespee*. This was written to commemorate William Longespee's death at the battle of Mansurah in 1250, possibly at the request of his family and particularly of his mother Ela, countess of Salisbury, whose vision of his translation to heaven is recorded by the contemporary St Alban's chronicler Matthew Paris; or, as has been argued by Simon Lloyd, by the brothers of William's comrade Alexander Giffard, who survived the battle. Although based on actual historical events, this is a fictionalised account in epic metre and the epic tradition, reminiscent of *La Chanson de Roland* or the epics of Guillaume d'Orange. For instance, the Master of the Temple is depicted as fighting with great skill and courage, wreaking much damage on the Muslims before he himself is slain and his soul carried at once to God; whereas at the actual Battle of Mansurah the Master of the Temple was not killed. The soul of a Templar who is slain assisting the Master is said to have been carried off by St Michael, 'singing, to paradise, where he will be in glory with Almighty Jesus', while another Templar, Brother Richard or Wymound of Ascalon, an English Brother, is one of five companions who fight to the death at William's side. The poet praises him warmly: *'li noble guerrer'*, *'mult vaillant'*, *'hardi fust e vaillant'*, *'li hardi combataunt'*. Brother Richard encourages William in the name of God and His Mother, and swears never to desert him while he is alive; only after William's death does he finally fall, over his companion's body. This poem enjoyed some success among the English nobility, as Guy de Beauchamp, earl of Warwick, possessed a copy in the early fourteenth century.[4] The much briefer version of these events recorded by the contemporary 'Minstrel of Reims' is similar in tone, depicting the Masters of the Temple and Hospital dying valiantly fighting the Muslims.[5]

Harpin de Bourges appears several times fighting as a Templar in the London-Turin continuation of *La Chanson de Jérusalem*, although there is

---

[4] Simon Lloyd, 'William Longespee II: The Making of an English Crusading Hero', *Nottingham Medieval Studies*, 34 (1991), 41–70, 35 (1992), 79–125: a new edition of the text appears in 35 (1992), 110–20; for the old edition see 'Du bon William Longespee', in A. Jubinal, ed., *Nouveau recueil de contes, dits, fabliaux, et autres pièces inédits des XIIIe, XIVe et XV siècles, pour faire suite aux collections Legrand d'Aussy, Barbazan et Méon, mis au jor pour la première fois*, 2 vols (Paris, 1839–42), 2, pp. 339–53. Trotter, *Medieval French Literature*, p. 209, discusses this work, but does not mention the role of the Military Orders. For the possible patronage of this work see Lloyd, 35 (1992), 85–99; for Countess Ela, see Matthew Paris, *Chronica majora*, ed. H.R. Luard, 7 vols, RS 57 (London, 1872–83), 5, pp. 153–4: 'the very noble lady countess and abbess of Laycock'. The fact that Matthew mentions her vision in the context of his account of William's death suggests that she was one of his informants on William's martyrdom, and that she was concerned to perpetuate the memory of his noble death. For Guy de Beauchamp see M. Blaess, 'L'Abbaye de Bordesley', 513; and Lloyd, 'William Longespee II', 36 (1992), 79 note 129, 91 note 184.

[5] *Ménestrel de Reims*, pp. 197–9, sections 382–6.

no mention of any other Templars with him. He is 'the good Templar' who is *gentil* and *ber*, good-looking, a good commander and a brave fighter. Although he is also taken prisoner, he conducts himself bravely, encouraging his companion Abilan, and speaking confidently to the sultan of Persia. He is pious and brave and trusts in Jesus, but perhaps he is rather disaster-prone; at one point he complains that he has always been very unlucky. While this is true for Harpin within the poem, perhaps the poet meant that it was also true for the Templars.[6] Later in the poem the Master of the Temple, John, is actively involved in King Amaury's Egyptian campaign; he is 'the Master of the Temple, who much loved the king' and 'a knight proven in law and in arms'.[7]

The Hospital makes no appearance in this poem, but both Orders appear in *Esclarmonde*, written between 1250 and 1300. They are depicted as fighting valiantly, but, when the Muslims have been put to flight, the Templars pursue the hero, Huon de Bourdeaux, who is chasing the fugitives, and forbid him to follow them any further. No criticism is expressed, although the situation is reminiscent of events in the Gaza campaign of 1239 during the crusade of Theobald of Champagne and Navarre. On that occasion the Orders were criticised by some French crusaders for hindering them from winning prestige in deeds of prowess against the Muslims. The Military Orders had advised them not to fight because it was dangerous, but the French set out nevertheless to attack the Muslims and were defeated. This criticism is also reminiscent of events of 1250 at the battle of Mansurah, during the first crusade of Louis IX of France: the Templars and Hospitallers advised Robert, count of Artois, not to advance against the Muslims, but the count ignored their advice and the Christian army was cut to pieces.[8] *Esclarmonde*, then, shows a departure from literary tradition and reflects actual contemporary events, in that the Military Orders did not only help Christian warriors to fight the Muslims, but occasionally advised against it. Nevertheless, the depiction of the Military Orders in this work is positive.

In 1454 *Esclarmonde* was rewritten in prose. The prose version was printed in 1513, while an English translation of the prose version was published in 1534. In the prose version and its translation the details of Huon de

---

[6] *OFCC, VIII: The London-Turin Version*, lines 13822, 13967, 15014, 15070–95, 15117, 15150, 15267–74, 15588–9, 15778–9 (Harpin the Templar who trusted in Jesus), 16675–84, 16692–708 (on his bad luck), 16718–19, 17499 (Harpins *le meschins* – the unlucky), 17593–7 (addressing the sultan), 18652–5, 19173–4, 19213–15, 19242, 19313, 19320–22, 19377 (*qui tant es avenans* – good-looking), 19505, 19846, 19932.

[7] *OFCC, VIII: The London-Turin Version*, lines 26373, 26483–4.

[8] *Esclarmonde, Clarisse et Florent, Yde et Olive, drei Fortsetzungen der chanson von Hugh de Bordeaux*, ed. M. Schweigel, Ausgaben und Abhandlungen aus dem Gebiete der romanischen Philologie, 83 (Marburg, 1889), pp. 111–12, lines 1942–2035, esp. 1944, 2010, 2013–14, 2020–21 (survives in only one manuscript); for date, see Moisan, *Répertoire*, 1.1, p. 45. See also, 'Rothelin', in *RHC Occ.*, 2, pp. 539–40, 604–6; Matthew Paris, *Chronica majora*, 5 pp. 148–54; *Ménestrel de Reims*, pp. 197–9, sections 382–6.

Bourdeaux's expedition to the East have changed, and the Military Orders do not appear.[9]

It is notable that many works written in France and Germany in the decades immediately before the trial of the Temple, c. 1270–1307, were very favourable towards the Military Orders in general and the Templars in particular. This is not as surprising as it might seem, as the plans for new crusades which were being drawn up during this period regarded the involvement of the Military Orders as essential to the recovery of the Holy Land, although they also suggested that some reforms were needed.[10] The fictional French literary works from this period which contain positive depictions of the Military Orders include the London-Turin continuation of the *Chanson de Jérusalem* and *Sone de Nansay*. The German works are even more favourable to the Military Orders.

For example, in the long version of *Wolfdietrich*, written between 1280 and 1300, the Teutonic Order receives particularly favourable treatment. Arriving at Acre during the course of his adventures, Wolfdietrich is met by the Master of the Teutonic house, who greets him warmly. The Master informs him that the house has been suffering great damage from the Muslims, at which Wolfdietrich declares that he will ride out and destroy the Muslim army with the assistance of forty of the Brothers, which he does. At the end of his life, Wolfdietrich, in retirement in the monastery of St George at Tischâl, leads a military force in order to repel a Muslim army. His force, he says, consists of 'five hundred lords of the Temple', but apparently this is a joking reference to his own monks; like the actual Templars, they are both monks and knights. Although this is not praise for the actual Order, it implies general approval of the actual Order.[11]

Wolfdietrich was a popular tale, surviving in four different versions. The long version of the poem was the last to be composed, and survives in ten manuscripts, all dating from the fifteenth century. This is an impressive number of manuscripts for a romance epic originally written more than a hundred years previously. The long-enduring popularity of this version of

---

[9] *The English Charlemagne Romances: The Boke of Duke Huon of Burdeux, done into English by Sir John Bauchier, Lord Berners, and printed by Wynkyn de Wade about 1534 A.D.*, ed. S.L. Lee, EETS Extra Series, 4 vols bound as two, nos. 40–41, 43, 50 (London, 1882–87), 1, pp. xxxvi–xxxviii.

[10] See, for example, Alan Forey, 'The Military Orders in the crusading proposals of the late-thirteenth and early-fourteenth centuries', *Traditio*, 36 (1980), 317–45; reprinted in his *Military Orders and Crusades*, VIII; Schein, *Fideles Crucis*, esp. pp. 196–233; Silvia Schein, 'The Templars: the Regular Army of the Holy Land and the Spearhead of the Army of its Reconquest', in *I Templari: Mito e Storia, Atti del Convegno Internazionale di Studi alli Magione Templari di Poggibonsi-Siena, 29–31 Maggio 1987*, ed. Giovanni Minnucci and Franca Sardi (Siena, 1989), pp. 15–25.

[11] *Ortnit und die Wolfdietriche nach Müllenhofs vorarbeiten*, ed. A. Amelung and O. Jänicke, 2 vols, Deutsches Heldenbuch 3, 4 (reprinted Dublin and Zurich, 1968), 3, pp. iii–iv, 4, pp. xv, 227, X line 65.2, p. 229, X line 79, pp. 56–62, V lines 106–40.

Wolfdietrich is significant, for it illustrates the fact that after the existence and importance of the Teutonic Order became recognized in German literary tradition, and even long after the destruction of the Templars, the Templars retained a niche in German literature as outstanding knights of Christ. Presumably the work of Wolfram von Eschenbach was largely responsible for this; it is clear that the Templars appear in Ulrich Füetrer's work, for instance, only because they appeared in Wolfram's *Parzival*. It is worth noting, however, that the trial of the Temple had not been popular in Germany, an indication that the Order continued to enjoy a positive image in German-speaking lands.[12]

All three Military Orders appeared in two German historical or semi-historical works written in the early years of the fourteenth century, *Die Kreuzfahrt des Landgrafen Ludwigs des Frommen von Thüringen*[13] and Ottokar's *Österreichische Reimchronik*[14]. These works will be examined at some length, because they give a very positive view of the Military Orders' role in holy war despite having been written after the final loss of Acre in 1291, and, in the case of Ottokar's *Reimchronik*, after the beginning of the trial of the Temple and possibly also after the beginning of the papal investigation of the Livonian branch of the Teutonic Order for heresy.

The *Kreuzfahrt* survives in one manuscript, written early in the fourteenth century. Some scholars argue for a date between 1301–1305, others judge that it is later. Its very positive view of the Templars certainly indicates a date before the beginning of the trial in October 1307. In the sixteenth century, someone wrote on the manuscript: 'Wolfram von Eschenbach wrote this book'.[15] Obviously he did not, but this assertion may have been prompted by the crusading subject, the positive view taken of Saladin (lines 7651–78), and the very favourable image which is given of the Templars. The writer certainly

---

[12] Marie Luise Bulst-Thiele, 'Der Prozess gegen den Templerorden', in *Die geistlichen Ritterorden Europas*, ed. Josef Fleckenstein and Manfred Hellmann, Vorträge und Forschungen 26 (Sigmaringen, 1980), pp. 375–402, here p. 292; idem, *Sacrae domus*, pp. 372–7; and see the German sources quoted in Wildermann, *Die Beiurteilung des Temperprozesses*, pp. 98–105. For late-thirteenth-century donations to the Order of the Temple in Germany, see: Helmut Lüpke, *Untersuchungen zur Geschichte des Templerordens im Gebiet der nordostdeutschen Kolonisation: Inaugural-Dissertation* (Bernburg, 1933); Helmut Lüpke, 'Das Land Tempelburg. Ein historisch-geographische Untersuchung', *Baltische Studien*, 35 (1933), 43–97; and see the table in Michael Schüpferling, *Der Tempel-herren Orden in Deutschland. Dissertation zur Erlangung der Doktorwürde von der philos. Fakultät der Universität Freiburg in der Schweiz* (Bamberg, 1915), pp. 240–41.

[13] *Die Kreuzfahrt des Landgrafen Ludwigs des Frommen von Thüringen*, ed. Hans Naumann, *MGH Deutsche Chroniken (scriptores qui vernacula lingua usi sunt)*, 4, 2 (Berlin, 1923; Munich, 1993).

[14] *Ottokars Österreichische Reimchronik nach den Abschriften Franz Lichtensteins*, ed. Joseph Seemüller, 2 vols, *MGH Deutsche Chroniken (scriptores qui vernacula lingua usi sunt)*, 5, parts 1 and 2 (Dublin and Zurich, 1974).

[15] *Kreuzfahrt*, p. 180.

knew Wolfram von Eschenbach's work, as he refers to him and to his poem *Willehalm*.[16]

The story confuses Ludwig IV of Thuringia, brother of the Conrad of Thuringia who became master of the Teutonic Order in 1239, with Ludwig III of Thuringia, who took part in the Third Crusade, but left the siege of Acre in autumn 1190 and died on his way home.[17] Historically, Ludwig IV set out on crusade with the emperor Frederick II in 1227 but died early in the voyage, leaving a young widow, Elizabeth of Hungary. Both Ludwig IV and Elizabeth were later canonised.

In the story, Landgrave Ludwig sets out on crusade with his brother Hermann and arrives at the siege of Acre. This must be the Third Crusade of 1189–92, as this is the only crusade in which a Landgrave Ludwig of Thuringia took part, and in which he played a leading role. In fact, however, Hermann did not accompany his brother; he took part in the German Crusade of 1197–98.

At Acre, Ludwig is assisted by the Military Orders: the Hospital of St John, the Templars and the Teutonic Order – although the last Order was actually founded in 1190 and did not become a Military Order until 1198. These three Orders, with the Military Order of St Lazarus, are depicted as among the leading Christian powers in the Holy Land (lines 7878–81). Again and again, the author praises the three leading Military Orders' courage and determination in battle.[18] The masters of the Orders also give sound advice.[19]

During the course of the crusade the emperor Frederick I (who in historical fact died during his land journey to the Holy Land) and the duke of Austria (Duke Leopold V) arrive by sea, with Ludwig's brother Conrad, master of the Teutonic Order (lines 3566–8). The first two did take part in the Third Crusade, but the third did not, as he was brother of Ludwig IV, not Ludwig III. In actual fact, Conrad did not become Master of the Teutonic Order until 1239.

With these three leaders comes (line 3571) Jâkop von Aveine, alias Jacques d'Avesnes, who was historically a major leader during the Third Crusade. A reference to an earlier crusade at Damietta (lines 3599–602) presumably refers to the Fifth Crusade – although this crusade did not take place until 1217–21.

The Master of the Temple is named as Walther von Spelten, a count.[20] He is very close to the landgrave and friendly with the emperor, informing the latter of the doughty deeds of the Landgrave Ludwig and how he has saved the lives of the Christians. The emperor orders him to record the landgrave's deeds in

---

[16] Ibid., lines 955, 1797.
[17] On the historical basis of the poem see *Kreuzfahrt*, pp. 199–202.
[18] *Kreuzfahrt*, lines 921–30, 1147–9, 1153–6, 1659–66, 1769–78, 3845–50, 3954–5, 4046–52.
[19] Ibid., lines 1595–600.
[20] Ibid., line 3647–9, and note. Walther von Spelten appears to be a totally fictional character, the invention of the author. Note that the author depicts him as a German – in reality, none of the masters of the Temple were German.

writing.[21] He negotiates with the Muslims, and acts as an interpretor.[22] In addition, the editor of the text, Hans Naumann, believed that it was Brother Walther von Spelten who is depicted as the only man able to see St George when he comes to help the Christians. This holy brother is described as '*ein ritter, als der het ein heilic leben, er was ein sâlic man begeben*' (lines 6884–6), '*der begebene man*' (line 6920), '*der brûder*' (line 6921), '*ein brûder daz / sach, des er lop sprach gote*' (lines 7198–9), '*der brûder*' (line 7208), '*der eine begebene man*' (line 7293), '*der begebene brûder*' (line 7498). In fact this holy Brother is never named, and while he is clearly a Brother of a Military Order, being both '*ritter*' (knight) and '*brûder*' (brother), he is not specifically identified as the Master of the Temple.[23]

The view of the Military Orders in *Die Kreuzfahrt des Landgrafen Ludwigs* is undeniably extremely favourable. The view taken by Ottokar in his *Österrreichische Reimchronik* is more thoughtful and includes criticism, but overall it is reflective of contemporary events and situations and is surprisingly positive, given that it seems to have been written after the beginning of the trial of the Temple: at one point Ottokar remarks that now the pope and the king of France have been made aware of how the Templars deceived the world in refusing to help the Christians defend Acre.[24] However, there is no reference to the crimes of which the Order was accused in 1307. This part of the chronicle was presumably written before 1317, when Pope John XXII finally gave permission for the annulled Order's properties in the Iberian peninsula to be used to found new Orders. Ottokar, in contrast, envisages the Templars continuing to fight in the Iberian peninsula as Templars (lines 51886–910). It is, however, possible that Ottokar was writing after 1317 and believed that the new Spanish Orders were merely extensions of the Order of the Temple, Templars in a new habit.

The portion of Ottokar's chronicle under consideration in this study is his account of the final loss of Acre to the Muslims in 1291, which marked the end of the kingdom of Jerusalem. However, it is not strictly a chronicle, but fictionalised history. Although actual persons and incidents are included, the historical course of events was rather different. A study of Ottokar's treatment of the loss of Acre was published by Mary Fischer in 1986, but I will consider Ottokar's work again here because it fits into the overall pattern of the Military Orders' involvement in holy war in literature. Although it gives a more

[21] Ibid., lines 3667–715, 5975.
[22] Ibid., lines 5242, 5279–88, 6786, 7717.
[23] Ibid., lines 6884–6, 6919–20, 6959–61, 7198–202, 7208–10, 7290–95, 7497–520, and pp. 291 note 3, 295 note 3.
[24] *Ottokar*, lines 48518–23. See also Mary Fischer, 'Criticism of Church and Crusade in Ottokar's Osterreichische Reimchronik,' *Forum for Modern Language Studies*, 22 (1986), 157–71. Ottokar's discussion of the Templars is mentioned by Bulst-Thiele, *Sacrae domus*, p. 293.

detailed and thoughtful account of the Military Orders than is generally found in more fictional literature, Ottokar's analysis may cast light on the more general attitude towards the Military Orders at the time of the trial of the Templars, and help to explain why it is that despite the dissolution of the Order for heresy it continued to appear in literature – albeit less frequently and in a smaller variety of roles.

Ottokar's account shows one man's analysis of the Military Orders' position in the Holy Land, their role and importance and how far they were to blame for the loss of the city of Acre in 1291.[25] In most of his account, Ottokar is extremely sympathetic towards the three leading Military Orders and their problems they faced, and in his account the blame for the loss of the city falls principally on the papal legate. The military role and importance of the Templars, Hospitallers and Teutonic Order is stressed (lines 44634–43, 51622–9, 51660–77) as is their political influence (lines 44810–14, 44833–41). They have to be taken into account when a truce was being made with the Muslims (lines 44782–91), and the Muslim sultan negotiates directly with them (lines 45331–45). The Military Orders negotiate on the sultan's behalf with the other Christian leaders and the papal legate (lines 45488–95, 45530–45). When the legate decides to renew the war with the sultan and refuses to listen to the Military Orders, the Masters of the Temple, Teutonic Order and Hospital attempt to reason with him (lines 45560–80, 45637–96, 45729–33).

Ottokar, however, was well aware of the realities of the Military Orders' predicament in the Holy Land; the need to balance holy war with co-existence and to find a *modus vivendi* with the Muslims. In the past this had led to accusations in the West that the Military Orders were not sufficiently enthusiastic about reconquering the holy places, and some accused them of being in allegiance with the Muslims. In the 1250s, the English chronicler Matthew Paris described an exchange between the Masters of the Temple and Hospital and Count Robert of Artois before the battle of Mansurah in 1250, in which the count accused them of being traitors to Christianity. The Military Orders hotly denied the charge, and to prove their innocence rode to their deaths against the Muslims. A similar story was recounted by the 'Ministrel of Reims'.[26] In Ottokar's account of the events of 1291 the legate likewise rejects the Masters' advice, complaining that the Orders were set up to defend the Holy Land against the Muslims, but now they try to keep in with the sultan. It is their duty to aid the legate, but instead they are opposing him (lines 45773–817). The Masters of the Hospital and the Teutonic Order protest that the Brothers are good Christians, and many of them have been martyred or

---

[25] On the fall of Acre and the Military Orders' role in events, see Riley-Smith, *Knights of St John*, pp. 195–7; Schein, *Fideles Crucis*, especially pp. 112–39; Nicholson, *Templars, Hospitallers*, pp. 125–8.

[26] Matthew Paris, *Chronica majora*, 5, pp. 148–54; *Ménestral de Reims*, pp. 197–9, sections 382–6.

have shed their blood for Christ. They add that the legate, as a cleric, does not get involved in the fighting, and is in no position to criticise, and they refuse to break the truce with the Muslims (lines 45829–922, 46125–95). The legate's response is to excommunicate everyone who opposes him (lines 46196–240).

Ottokar carefully sets out the Military Orders' dilemma in this situation. The Teutonic Order in particular does not wish to incur the wrath of the pope, because his chief personal ministers are Brothers of the Teutonic Order. Hence the Order's loyalties are divided, a situation which is a direct cause of the loss of Acre (lines 46414–35, 48548–53).[27] All the Military Orders share this problem; they finally agree that as religious orders they are bound to obey the pope, even if his commands are foolish or unpleasant (lines 46480–514). They appeal to the pope against the legate (lines 48036–7, 48138–66), but are forced to agree to war with the Muslims. The Military Orders gather their forces from all over Europe. The Teutonic Order calls Brothers from Prussia, while the Masters of the Hospital and Temple ride round Europe urging people to join the Orders and serve God for His reward (lines 48190–244).

So Ottokar sees and describes the Military Orders' actual problems: they wanted to maintain a *modus vivendi* with the Muslims, insofar as this was to the benefit of the Christians in the Holy Land, but they were unable to maintain their wise policies because they were bound to obey the pope, who wanted holy war. This led to the fall of the Holy Land. He saw that they also had faults. Ottokar shows that the Orders have pride, and are well aware that they are essential for the defence of the city. Hence, when the final battle is about to begin, the Hospitallers and Templars at first refuse to fight (lines 48488–504, 48514–23, 48668–89) and only the Teutonic Brothers agree to help defend the city (lines 48590–640, 48659–63). Eventually the three Military Orders send their forces into the field and individual Brothers are depicted as fighting valiantly (lines 50234–379, 50423–5, 51754–72, 51924–64, 51534–45, 51636–9). However, when the Master of the Temple is killed the Christians fall back (50426–32) and major forces of each Order eventually flee, taking their treasure with them to their ships (50574–7, 51434–74).

Ottokar observes that the differences of opinion among the Military Orders were a factor in the final fall of the city (lines 48776–80) and he regrets that they finally agreed to fight the Muslims after they had promised to keep the truce (lines 50775–8, 51622–9). The Military Orders were doughty, and won much honour in the world and God's reward (lines 51434–42), but in the end,

---

[27] For Brothers of the Military Orders as servants of the pope, see Marie Luise Bulst-Thiele, 'Templer in königlichen und päpstlichen Diensten', in *Festscrift Percy Ernst Schramm*, ed. P. Classen and P. Scheibert, 2 vols (Wiesbaden, 1964), 1, pp. 289–308; Klaus Militzer, 'From the Holy Land to Prussia: the Teutonic Knights between Emperors and Popes and their Policies until 1309', in *Mendicants, Military Orders and Regionalism in Medieval Europe*, ed. Jürgen Sarnowsky (Aldershot, 1999), pp. 71–81; Nicholson, *Templars, Hospitallers*, pp. 21–2.

despite their courage, they had to leave their honour and their property to the Muslims (lines 51680–82, 51683–705).

The Hospitallers are depicted as being the first to flee, although Brother Matthew, the commander, remains to fight and to die (lines 51723–77, 51924–64). The Hospitallers are followed by the Teutonic Order (lines 51782–823), and finally the Templars (lines 51824–910). The Master of the Teutonic Order declares before he departs that, although it has been driven out of the Holy Land, the Order will continue to fight the heathen in Prussia and Livonia instead (lines 51795–817). Likewise, the Master of the Temple, Brother Anne, declares that the Templars will go to fight the king of Morocco; they will go to Spain and help the king of Spain to recover that land (lines 51886–910).

Overall, then, although Ottokar did not see the Military Orders as blameless in the loss of Acre, his depiction of them was very positive. The dilemma he described is a reasonable assessment of the Military Orders' actual problems in the Holy Land, and he considered that the final blame for the loss of the city must fall on the papal legate rather than the Orders. Certainly, if the Orders could have withstood the legate's demands that they break the truce, the city would not have been lost; but, given that they had to obey the pope, they had no choice. He made it very clear that their current predicament was ironically due to their loyalty to the pope. As Ottokar seems to have been writing his 'chronicle' during the trial of the Temple, when the Teutonic Order in Livonia was also under papal investigation for heresy,[28] it is impressive that he succeeded in producing such a balanced assessment of events. It is also interesting that he made a point of describing how the Order of the Temple and the Teutonic Order were still fighting the Muslims, in Spain and Prussia respectively; they were still essential for the defence of Christendom. He made no such point for the Hospitallers.

The Military Orders play a far more minor but almost wholly historical role in the fourteenth-century Middle English verse romance *Richard Coeur de Lion*, which survives in seven manuscripts and two sixteenth-century printed editions. The Templars and Hospitallers are mentioned as part of the crusading army of King Richard I of England during the Third Crusade. They are given the command of the vanguard at the battle of Arsour (Arsūf), and they both play a role in the battle which led to the capture of the great caravan in June 1192, although only the Templars are mentioned assisting King Richard at the relief of Jaffa, 1–5 August 1192, and riding to help him as he hacks his way through the Saracen ranks. The romance also refers to the Hospitaller's castle of 'Gybelyn'; historically this was Bait Gibrin, or Beth Gibelin, given to the Hospital by King Fulk of Jerusalem in 1136. In this romance it also belonged to the Templars. Clearly, like other authors writing after the dissolution of the Templars, the composer of this romance had difficulty in differentiating

---

[28] On this see Housley, *Avignon Papacy*, pp. 267–70.

between the two Military Orders. The Military Orders' role in this romance mirrors their actual role in the Third Crusade, as described by contemporary and near-contemporary accounts.

However, they are not depicted as faultless. The writer notes that the Templars and Hospitallers gave no help to Jakes de Neys and his two sons when they were surrounded by Saracens at 'Arsour'. In one late fifteenth-century manuscript of the romance the redactor added a scene in which the master of the Hospital, here Gauter of Naples (in reality Garnier of Nablūs) advises Richard for strategic reasons not to attack Jerusalem. The redactor who added this incident observed: 'Ther was he no good consailer'. Contemporary and near-contemporary historical accounts of the Third Crusade agree that both the Hospitallers and Templars advised Richard against attacking Jerusalem: some writers agreed with this advice, pointing out that the city could not have been held if it were captured, although others were critical. In adding this incident, therefore, the redactor improved the historicity of the poem; although by omitting the Templars he threw the blame for this supposedly bad advice entirely on to the Hospitallers.[29]

After the dissolution of the Order of the Temple in 1312 the Order made few appearances in depictions of holy war in new works of French literature. The Templars and Hospitallers are mentioned by Jean de Condé in his poem *Le dis dou chevalier à la mance*, which may have been composed after 1312: here the hero fights alongside the Templars and Hospitallers against the Muslims while he is in the Holy Land in the service of Kings Baldwin V and Guy in the years 1185–87. The mention of the Templars and Hospitallers helped to give originality and historical authenticity to this poem, an otherwise conventional love story.[30] The verse epic *Baudouin de Sebourc* in the 'Second Crusade Cycle', composed 1350–60, mentions the Templars' involvement in holy war briefly when it explains that Saladin would go on to destroy Christianity: 'Through him the Templars perished and died, and all the Christians that God held dear'.[31] Despite the annulment of the Order its past Brothers could still be depicted in literature as worthy knights of Christ of a past era. However, the

---

[29] *Der mittelenglische Versroman über Richard Löwenherz*, lines 3151–2, 3948, 4981–2, 5019–22, 6479–80, 6855–8, 7057 (in battle); lines 6321–4 (Beth Gibelin); lines 5061–2 (for death of Jake de Neys), pp. 381–2, ms b, lines 7–24 for the master of the Hospital's bad advice. For the Orders' roles in the actual crusade, see, for instance, Ambroise, *Estoire*, lines 6147–8, 6155–6, 6376–438; *Itinerarium peregrinorum*, ed. Stubbs, Bk 4, chs 12, 14, 15, 17–19; pp. 253, 255, 257, 260, 265–9; For contemporary and near-contemporary historical accounts of the Hospitallers' and Templars' advice not to attack Jerusalem, see Ambroise, *Estoire*, lines 7689–716, 7761–80, 10213–24; *Itinerarium peregrinorum*, ed. Stubbs, Bk 4, ch. 35, Bk 5, ch. 1, Bk 6, ch. 2, pp. 305–6, 308–9, 381 (favourable accounts); Roger of Wendover, in *Roger de Wendover liber qui dicitur flores historiarum: The Flowers of History by Roger of Wendover*, ed. Henry G. Hewlett, 3 vols, RS 84 (London, 1886–9), 1, p. 209 (a critical account).

[30] 'Le dis dou chevalier à la mance', lines 1621–4, and 1625–707.

[31] *Li Romans de Bauduin de Sebourc*, 1, pp. 383–4, chant 13, verses 934–7; also quoted by Cook and Crist, *Deuxième Cycle*, p. 105.

Templars' other appearances in original literature first composed after 1312 do not generally involve them actually fighting Muslims. The exception is the German poem *Orendal*, the date of which is uncertain.

When Military Orders appeared fighting in literature first composed after 1312, the Hospitallers and Teutonic knights generally appeared rather than the Templars. This indicates that contemporary events had some influence over the Orders' appearance in literature, whatever the requirements of convention.

One of the Hospital's major appearances in late medieval literature is in Jean d'Arras' *Mélusine*, which has already been discussed in connection with the Hospitallers' opposition to a marriage. In *Mélusine*, Urien and Guy of Lusignan, two of Mélusine's sons, go to the East to fight the Muslims, and are assisted by the Hospitallers of Rhodes, Rhodes having been the Order's headquarters since 1310. The Hospitallers welcome them and lodge them on Rhodes, keep the Brothers informed of Muslim movements, act as messengers, and cooperate with the Brothers and with the kings of Cyprus and Cilician Armenia. Later, when Urien and Guy have been installed as kings of Cyprus and Armenia respectively, the Hospitallers of Rhodes fight under the command of Urien and Guy's brother Geoffrey 'Big Tooth' when he comes to the East.

The Hospitallers are clearly a major military and naval power in the eastern Mediterranean, and their support, on land and at sea, is essential for anyone campaigning against the Muslims. They have valuable contacts among the Muslims: a spy among the Muslim army which is coming to invade Armenia and Rhodes warns the Master of Rhodes of the invasion. It is clear that they are both religious and military: the Brothers are *freres de religion*, and the Master calls them *sergens de Crist*, servants of Christ. However, their role in the story is as assistants of the brothers Lusignan, although they are clearly independent agents. The inclusion of the Hospitallers in this work probably reflects the Hospitallers' involvement in the campaigns of Peter I of Lusignan, king of Cyprus, against the Muslims in the years 1361–66.[32]

The Hospitallers of Rhodes in Joanot Martorell's *Tirant lo Blanc* also play a supporting military role. Tirant arrives at Rhodes with his companions Felip, the younger son of the king of France, and the king of Sicily, who is on pilgrimage to Jerusalem. Tirant has come to save Hospitallers of Rhodes from the Genoese and Muslims. The Master of the Order and all the knights come to the port, and the Master sends two of the leading Brothers on board his ship to greet him. The Master gives instructions that everyone in the land is to obey Tirant as if he were the Master himself, and sends him the keys to the Brothers'

---

[32] Jean d'Arras, *Mélusine*, pp. 89–95, 98, 101, 117, 123–44, 213–38, esp. pp. 122–3 for Urien of Lusignan becoming king of Cyprus, pp. 142–4 for Guy becoming king of Armenia, p. 139 for the Brothers as servants of Christ, pp. 213–4 for contact with Muslim spies. See also Luttrell, 'The Hospitallers in Cyprus after 1386', pp. 135–6; Edbury, *Kingdom of Cyprus and the Crusades*, pp. 161–70.

fortress and the city of Rhodes. Tirant comes ashore and is greeted by the Master; Tirant greets him as if he were a king, by kneeling before him and trying to kiss his hand, but the Master will not allow this, raises him from the ground and kisses his mouth in greeting, as if Tirant were his equal in rank. The Master gives Tirant an account of the Order's problems, the siege by the sultan by land and the Genoese by sea, and the severe famine among the besieged of the city: 'the little children are dying of hunger'. Tirant provides food which he has brought on his ships.

Tirant considers the military situation and takes counsel with the Master. As earlier, an aged Brother of the Order gives advice: he advises that they send food to the sultan, to show him that they are not suffering from famine. The sultan then doubts whether his siege will be successful. Meanwhile, Tirant bribes a sailor of the Genoese fleet to set fire to the Genoese fleet at night for payment of 3,000 gold ducats. As the fleet burns, Tirant leads his troops out of the city and attacks the sultan's forces. Thus Rhodes is saved from the infidels by Tirant's efforts alone. Ascribing the Order's very survival to Tirant, and vowing eternal gratitude on behalf of the whole Order, the Master declares: 'You have liberated our house of Jerusalem at the Temple of Solomon' – like the author or authors of *Theséus de Cologne*, Joanot Martorell was obviously confused about the relationship between the Hospital of St John and the Order of the Temple. Tirant's gracious reply, however, refers more correctly to Saint John the Baptist, the Hospital's patron. Tirant and his companions then continue with their pilgrimage to the Holy Land.[33]

Later in the story, in gratitude for the service he did the Order, the Master of Rhodes sends to Tirant in Constantinople 'the good Prior of St John with many knights with the white cross' (the white cross of the Hospital of St John), as well as 2000 other knights and men on foot. The Prior of St John presents himself and his troops to the emperor of Constantinople, but he and his warriors are under Tirant's command.[34] The Hospitallers, then, support the knight from Europe, but are subordinate to him; they appear in the story to serve his interests and support and highlight his chivalric deeds, not to play a role in their own right.

The Hospitallers were also referred to in 'travelogues' of this period. *Le Saint Voyage de Jherusalem du seigneur d'Anglure*, describing the pilgrimage of Ogier VIII, lord of Anglure, in 1395, remarks that the emperor of Constantinople had ruled the island of Rhodes, but when the populace rebelled he gave the island to the lords Brothers of Rhodes (i.e., the Hospitallers) if they could conquer it. This reads like a justification by the Order for its having conquered the island from the Christian Orthodox Greeks, while it claimed to be waging

---

[33] *Tirant lo Blanc*, 1, pp. 180–95, esp. p. 191, chapters 104–8. On confusion between the Temple and Hospital, see below, pp. 230–33.

[34] *Tirant lo Blanc*, 1, pp. 282–4, chapters 138–40.

war on Muslims. It is followed by a rather fantastic account of the Brothers' capture of the island. After a great deal of effort, they had captured the whole island except for one city in the mountains, which they besieged for seven years. In the end they bribed a herdsman from the city to allow them to kill and flay some of his animals, and dress themselves in the skins. Disguised as animals, they were able to enter the city with the rest of the herd, then leapt up and captured the gates of the city. So the city fell at last, after seven years! One is reminded of the ten-year siege of Troy, or the seven-year siege of Falmar in *Perceforest*.[35] As the writer records that he heard this story on Rhodes, this must be one of the Brothers' own legends about their capture of the island. The writer also describes the pilgrims' visit to Rhodes, the buildings and the relics held by the Order.[36] Following his visit to Mount Sybilla in 1420 and describing the legend of Queen Sybille and her cavern for Agnes of Burgundy, duchess of Bourbon and Auvergne, Antoine de la Sale made a passing reference to the Hospitallers of Rhodes in his *Le Paradis de la Reine Sibylle* as a destination for knights seeking adventure.[37]

Antoine de la Sale was an expert on the theory and practice of knighthood. He wrote a treatise on knightly weapons and acted as a judge at a tournament, and also fought the Muslims in a Christian expedition against the Moroccan port of Ceuta, on the southern side of the Straits of Gibraltar.[38] It is not surprising that the Military Orders appear more than once in his writings. The Teutonic Order makes a brief appearance in his work *Jehan de Saintré*. This was written before 1456 and survives in ten manuscripts, indicating some popularity. During the course of the hero's adventures (set in the mid-fourteenth century) he takes part in a crusade to Prussia, against a large Muslim army. Historically, this should have been an army of Lithuanians, but by convention all non-Christians could be referred to as 'Saracens' and even the Teutonic Order tended to call their pagan enemy 'Saracens'. In the course of a long description of the magnificent crusading army, the 'Master of Prussia and the whole Hospital' and their forces are given a brief mention at the end of the list of prelates of Germany. The banner of the Order of Prussia is mentioned second in the list of banners, after the banner of France: 'all of silver with a black cross'.[39] Considering that the Teutonic Order had controlled

---

[35] *Perceforest: deuxième partie*, ed. Gilles Roussineau, vol. 1, TLF 506 (Geneva, 1999), pp. 83, 142, lines 20–22. Written between 1335 and 1344; see below, pp. 147–50, for further details of this romance.

[36] *Le Saint Voyage de Jherusalem du seigneur d'Anglure*, ed. François Bounardot and Auguste Longnon, SATF (Paris, 1878), pp. 91–5, paras 318–23, esp. p. 92, paras 318–19; pp. 8–10, paras 30–34.

[37] Antoine de la Sale, *Le Paradis de la reine Sibylle*, ed. Fernand Desonay (Geneva, 1930), p. 43, lines 32–41. Two manuscripts and two printed editions survive: pp. xi–xiv.

[38] Barber and Barker, *Tournaments*, pp. 116, 153, 161; Housley, *Later Crusades*, p. 362.

[39] Antoine de la Sale, *Jehan de Saintré*, ed. J. Misrabi and C.A. Knudson TLF (Geneva, 1967), pp. 211 lines 7–9, 215 lines 5–6. As well as ten manuscripts, four printed sixteenth-century editions survive: p. xvi.

and led the crusade in Prussia, this seems a very brief reference, and no mention is made of the Order in the battle which follows, where Saintré emerges as the hero. The reference to the Order in this work seems to have been inserted to give some authenticity to Saintré's chivalric adventures in Prussia, an essential part of his development as a knight (as Madame makes clear to him in urging him to take part), and to emphasize that the hero really is on an actual crusade. Without the mention of the Teutonic Order this part of the story would bear little relationship to the actual world; it is clear that la Sale had very little idea of how the crusade in Prussia had been organised and waged in practice, for it was past history by the time he was writing. From 1454 to 1466 the Teutonic Order in Prussia was at war with its Christian rivals, the Prussian Estates, Poland and Lithuania, and in the Second Treaty of Thorn (1466) it lost control of western Prussia.

The Teutonic Order appeared again in *Les Cent Nouvelles Nouvelles*, probably written between 1464 and 1467, and dedicated to Duke Philip the Good of Burgundy (duke 1419–67), who had taken the cross in 1454 and was planning a crusade to the East against the Ottoman Turks. The 'cent nouvelles' are reworkings of familiar *fables*, or farces. In the sixteenth 'nouvelle', a noble knight in the service of the duke of Burgundy and count of Artois decides to devote his body to God and, taking leave of his wife and his relatives and friends, goes 'towards the good lords of Prussia, true champions and defenders of the most holy Christian faith' – ironic words in light of the Order's true position by the 1460s; but this story is set a little in the past, *nagueres*. In Prussia the knight has several adventures and performs great deeds of prowess which bring him great renown, fighting the *Sarrazins*. Meanwhile, his wife has taken a noble squire as her lover, and the author contrasts the harsh life being led by the husband in the field with the pleasant life being led by the wife at home, not much caring whether her husband returns or not. At last the husband, seeing that the Saracen attacks have reduced, *la Dieu mercy*, decides to return home. This is a similar theme to *Jehan le Saintré*, whose lady also deserts him for another, although in *Jehan* the lady does not desert while the hero is on crusade, as she told him to go; what causes the estrangement is that Jehan plans an expedition to seek honour in Germany without consulting her, which angers and distresses her. Jehan and his lady are not reconciled, but in the '*nouvelle*' the wife welcomes the husband back and he is left ignorant of her infidelity. The crusade background adds a realistic edge to the familiar theme of farce, and gives a reason for the husband's original departure. It is reasonable that a writer working for a patron who was a vowed crusader should have introduced the crusade as a motivation for the husband's absence, necessary for the story. This story is balanced by '*nouvelle*' 69, where the husband is a knight of Flanders captured by the Ottoman Turks at the battle of Nicopolis in 1396. His wife is forced to remarry against her will. When she hears that he is alive and returning home, she is so distressed by her forced infidelity that she dies of grief.[40]

Around the same time these works were being composed, an anonymous author was composing *Le Livre du tres chevalereux conte d'Artois et de sa femme, fille du conte de Boulogne*, which survives in three manuscripts and was written before 1467, again most probably for Philip the Good, duke of Burgundy. This is a lively reworking of the popular tale of the woman who dresses up as a man to seek her errant husband/boyfriend, a tale which was certainly already well known at the duke's court. The immediate source for the version told in *Le Livre du conte d'Artois* was apparently the story of Gillette de Narbonne in Boccacio's *Decameron*, but earlier versions of the theme included Nicolette in the late twelfth-century tale *Aucassin et Nicolette*, where Nicolette disguises herself as a minstrel, Josiane in *Bueve of Hantone* (written in the 1220s), the heroine of *Le Dis dou chevalier à la mance*, who cuts her hair and disguises herself as a *bacelier*, and Neronés-Steelheart and Malaquin-Circe in *Perceforest* (written 1335–44), who disguise themselves as squires – although Malaquin also acts as a knight. A copy of *Perceforest* was held in the library of the dukes of Burgundy, while another copy was made for Philip the Good.

The author of *Le Livre du conte d'Artois* gave the old, almost too-familiar story immediacy and interest by using historical figures (Philip of Burgundy, 1323–46, and his wife Jeanne of Boulogne, 1326–60) and genuine place names, and involving the hero in the campaigns of the king of Castile, Alfonso XI, against the Muslim king of Granada. The Spanish Military Orders appear in the context of the campaign against the Muslims: the Grand Master of the Order of St James of Santiago is mentioned as one of those who advises the king of Castile, who is involved in mustering the Christian forces, and who, with the Master of Castile (presumably Calatrava is meant) leads one of the Christian batallions into battle. He and the Master of Calatrava are also mentioned in passing in the course of one of the battles, bringing their forces in at an appropriate moment to inflict most damage on the enemy. Here the role of the Military Orders is to give historical authenticity and colour to what would otherwise be a conventional tale of the hero's prowess in battle in a very familiar storyline, and the roles that they play are those which they performed in actual life.[41]

---

[40] *Les Cent Nouvelles Nouvelles*, ed. Franklin P. Sweetser, TLF (Geneva, 1966), pp. x–xi, 107–14, especially lines 19–21, and pp. 422–5. See also Housley, *Later Crusades*, p. 362 (for Prussia) pp. 76–9 (for Nicopolis).

[41] *Le Roman du comte d'Artois (XVe siècle)*, ed. Jean-Charles Seigneuret, TLF 142 (Geneva, 1966), pp. 68–9, lines 65–6, p. 71 line 136, p. 90 line 14, p. 94 lines 143–4; for manuscripts, date and historicity see pp. xi–xxiii, xxviii, xxix, xxxi–xxxv, xxxviii–xxxix. It is interesting that the heroine of this tale, Jeanne of Boulogne, is also a major character in *Jehan le Saintré*, there on her second marriage and queen of France. This suggests that the ideal chronological gap for an historical novel of the mid-fifteenth century was a century. *Aucassin et Nicolette*, ed. Jean

All the works which have been described so far give a generally positive view of the Military Orders in their wars against the infidel. Although Ottokar had some criticism in his *Reimchronik*, he saw that other factors were to blame for the Orders' failings – in particular, the policies of the papacy. The Orders in *Richard Coeur de Lion* failed to save Jake de Neys and in one version of the romance the master of the Hospital gives King Richard bad advice, but in general their prowess and dedication to the Christian cause is irreproachable. Tirant's Hospitallers lack initiative and may appear incompetent and too obsessed with their own regulations, but they are devoted to God and the defence of Christendom. There are, however, a few works in which the Templars are blamed for obstructing holy war. The precise dating of all of these works is unclear.

The poem *La Déliverance Ogier le Danois* survives only in a fourteenth-century fragment and a fifteenth-century manuscript. The dating is uncertain; the language is thirteenth century, but this may be because of convention. The poem mentions that the Christian knight Guy, Ogier's brother, is guarding at Jerusalem *les maus Templiers*, the evil Templars who had betrayed Ogier at Acre. The editor of the text believed that this must have been written after the loss of Acre in 1291, which some blamed on the Templars' quarrels with the Hospitallers. This is certainly true, but in addition it is probable that it was written after the arrest of the Templars in France in October 1307. The Templars' failure to hold Acre came under scrutiny during the trial of the Order, when it was said that their supposed sins were to blame for the loss of Acre.[42]

The epic poem *Gaufrey*, dated to 1250–1300 or the early fourteenth century, includes a brief reference to a Saracen king named 'Templier', i.e., Templar. This character never appears, and does not appear in other works. At first glance it appears that an opponent of Christianity is being called a

---

Dufornet (Paris, 1984), pp. 150–62: Nicolette is daughter of the king of Carthage; for Josiane, see *Der Anglonormannische Boeve de Hauntone*, ed. Albert Stimming (Halle, 1899); 'Le dis dou chevalier à la mance', lines 1804–5, 1823–4, etc.; Neronés: *Perceforest: Troisième partie*, ed. Gilles Roussineau, vol. 2, TLF 409 (Geneva, 1992), ch. 41, pp. 299–312, 340–69; Malaquin: ibid., pp. 288–91. For Gillette of Narbonne, see Giovanni Boccaccio, *Decameron*, day 3, story 9; *Le Roman du comte d'Artois*, pp. xxxiii–xxxiv. For some studies of women who dress as men in medieval romance and epic see Peggy McCracken, '"The Boy Who Was a Girl": Reading Gender in the *Roman de Silence*', *The Romanic Review*, 85 (1994), 517–36; Michele Perret, 'Travesties et Transexualles: Yde, Silence, Grisandole, Blanchandine', *Romance Notes*, 25 (1985), 328–40; and also E. Jane Burns, 'Refashioning Courtly Love: Lancelot as Ladies' Man or Lady/Man?', in *Constructing Medieval Sexuality*, ed. Karma Lochrie, Peggy McCracken and James A. Schulz (Minneapolis and London, 1997), pp. 111–34.

[42] 'La Déliverance Ogier le Danois, fragment d'un chanson de geste', ed. Adrien de Longpérier, *Journal des Savants* (April, 1876), 219–33, esp. 230, lines 192–6. For the Templars being blamed by Philip IV's ministers during the trial of the Order for the loss of the Holy Land, see the speech of 29 May 1308 by William de Plaisans published in *Le Dossier de l'affaire des Templiers*, ed. Georges Lizerand (Paris, 1923), pp. 122–3, no. 4.

Templar, as if the Templars did not promote holy war but opposed it. However, it would be rash to draw such a conclusion, as the most probably explanation for this name is that it is not a reference to the Military Order, but a variation on the word *tempier*, meaning tumult, noise and confusion, which would be an appropriate 'joke' name for a Muslim in French epic.[43]

Another work which is rather hostile, although not completely opposed to, the Templars is *Orendal*, which was considered above as it depicts the Templars as lacking in spiritual awareness. As was said above, the surviving form of this work dates from the late fifteenth century, and it is not known how the Templars were depicted in any earlier form of the poem, or whether they appeared at all. In *Orendal*, the Templars are at first unaware of the significance of Orendal's robe, and therefore refuse to help him fight the Muslims. However, they remain faithful to their supreme commander, for they hurry to Queen Bride's assistance as soon as she rides into battle to aid Orendal. In their reluctance to fight under the command of an apparently unarmed stranger they are reminiscent of Ottokar's Templars: aware of their own importance and unwilling to commit themselves to battle when they are likely to suffer heavy losses, but overall excusable, although undeniably they have not served Christ as well as they should have done.

2 Advisers and messengers in holy war

Alongside their role as knights of Christ, the Military Orders perform an advisory role. In actuality, this was a very important role for the Orders, both in the Holy Land and in Europe. In literature they usually appear as advisers in the Holy Land, but in *Sone* the Templar Margon acts as chief minister to Sone and is left in a position of authority when Sone is summoned to Rome to become emperor. Margon had previously been the trusted adviser of the queen of Ireland.[44] In *Sone*, the Hospital and Temple also appear in positions of responsibility in the Holy Land, acting to choose a new king.[45] They perform a similar role in the first and third French versions of *Bueve de Hantone*.[46] Similarly, in *L'Escoufle*, the Templars appear with the patriarch and barons as part of the king's council.[47] In the London-Turin continuation of *La Chanson*

---

[43] *Gaufrey, chanson de geste publié pour la première fois d'après le manuscrit unique de Montpellier*, ed. F. Guessard and P. Chabaille (Paris, 1859), lines 9510, 9559; cited by Moison, *Répertoire*, 1.2, p. 913 and 1.1, p. 49 for date. 'Templier' is used as a substitute for 'tempier' in *Florent et Octavien*, lines 2118, 6544.

[44] *Sone von Nausay*, lines 17607–18, 17659–60.

[45] Ibid., lines 20527–30, 20580–82, 20601–4.

[46] *Der festländische Bueve de Hantone, Fassung I*, ed. A. Stimming, GRL 25 (Dresden, 1911), lines 10554–7 (one manuscript survives: p. xi); dated to 1220–25 by Moison, *Répertoire*, 1.1, p. 36; *Fassung III*, lines 15552–3.

[47] *L'Escoufle*, lines 798–801.

de Jérusalem, Harpin the Templar appears at court, and encourages King Baldwin. Later, under King Amaury, Master John, Master of the Temple and 'a good lettered clerk' from Douai in Picardy, is one of those called to the king's council when the *amulainne* of Egypt asks him for help against Saladin; and after the Egyptian campaign he and the archbishop of Tyre advise the king to send for people from France to colonise the land he has conquered.[48] Moreover, the master of the Temple lends King Baldwin II money to pay his ransom from the Muslims.[49] Lending money to kings was another important role played by the Military Orders, particularly the Templars, in the real world.[50] In *Richard Coeur de Lion* the Hospitallers act as depositors for King Henry II of England's money in the kingdom of Jerusalem, a role which they and the Templars performed prior to the actual Third Crusade.[51] The Hospital also give strategic advice to King Richard I in one manuscript of this romance, although the redactor criticised this advice. In the *Kreuzfahrt des Landgrafen Ludwigs* and Ottokar's *Reimchronik* the three leading Military Orders play an important advisory role, although Ottokar's papal legate ignores their advice. In Jean d'Arras' *Mélusine* the Master of Rhodes advises the Lusignan brothers.[52] In the *Livre du conte d'Artois* the Grand Master of St James of Santiago advises the king of Castile.[53]

In contrast, the reference in the fourteenth-century epic *Florent et Octavien* to a squire 'of Solomon's Temple', who had served King Amaury for a long period, probably refers to the Temple's original function under kings Baldwin I and II of Jerusalem as a royal palace, or as the place of where kings were crowned, as in the poems of the Crusade Cycles. There is no mention of Templars as such, although possibly this writer thought that those who 'served at the Temple' were royal servants.[54]

In later works of fictionalised history, the Military Order's realistic advisory role was developed further to include other duties which Military Orders routinely performed for kings. In the real world, both the Templars and

---

[48] *OFCC, VIII: The London-Turin Version*, lines 20690, 23318–19, 25981–3, 26816–25.
[49] Ibid., lines 23834–5.
[50] See for example Forey, *Military Orders*, pp. 115–17.
[51] *Der mittelenglische Versroman über Richard Löwenherz*, lines 3264–8. For the historical background to this see Ambroise, *Estoire*, lines 1369–72; *Itinerarium peregrinorum*, ed. Stubbs, Bk 1, ch. 12, p. 26; *Itinerarium peregrinorum*, ed. Mayer, p. 269, lines 10–16.
[52] *Mélusine*, pp. 91–4, 127, 135–6.
[53] *Le Roman du comte d'Artois*, pp. 68–9, lines 65–6.
[54] *Florent et Octavien*, lines 9909–10. The original function of the 'Temple of Solomon' as a royal palace was stated in the French translations of the work of William, archbishop of Tyre (the 'Estoire de Eracles Empereur'), and in the chronicle attributed to Ernoul. The Old French translation of William of Tyre appears to have been very widely known in western Europe: Davis, 'William of Tyre', p. 71: E.A. Babcock and A.C. Kray, *A History of Deeds Done Beyond the Sea*, 2 vols (Columbia, 1944), 1, p. 43. On this, see Chapter 5 section 3, below. Hence the author of *Florent et Octavien* could well have been aware of this fact.

Hospitallers acted as ambassadors for kings.[55] In the work of the 'Minstrel of Reims', Brother Garin of the Hospital, bishop of Senlis, historically vice-chancellor of France and advisor to Philip II, Louis VIII and Louis IX, appears as a wise and cunning ambassador and advisor of the French king. However, the 'Minstrel' never referred to his membership of the Hospital, and apparently did not know that the historical Brother Garin was a Hospitaller.[56] Garin also appears here negotiating on behalf of King Philip II with the count of Flanders before the Battle of Bouvines, 1214. In the prose work *Le Livre de Baudoyn, conte de Flandre*, printed in 1485, this role is instead given to a Templar, who is sent by King Philip and William des Barres, the great French hero, to defy Ferrant, count of Flanders. While this is historically inaccurate, the author of this work obviously believed that this was an appropriate role for a Templar, for the battle is depicted as a sort of holy war: the holy cause being the defence of God's realm of France against its arrogant enemies. This Templar, although he is *moult ireulx et hardi*, extremely fierce and bold, is a positive character; he speaks calmly and rationally to Ferrant, tries to reason with Ferrant when the latter declares his intention of fighting on a Sunday, tells him that God always defends the kingdom of France and that no pagan or Saracen may capture it, and warns him that his pride will be his downfall. When Philip shrugs off the danger of a surprise Sunday attack, the Templar emphasizes the danger and encourages the king to fight. In serving Philip, the Templar is acting on behalf of God and right; in contrast, Ferrant is depicted as having a dubious claim to the county of Flanders, as his wife murdered her father, the previous count; and his rash pride is made clear to the reader in the scene when the Templar finds him and his nobles playing dice for the towns of France as if they had already conquered it.[57] In this case the Templar combines acting for the king with acting on behalf of God.

The Hospitallers and Templars in the long version of *Theséus de Cologne* also play an important role carrying messages. Their first appearance in this role is connected with the state of Osane's marriage to Gadifer of Constantinople, but here and later they are also sent to request aid against the Muslims. Appealing for military aid against the Muslims was historically an important role for the Military Orders. In particular, they played a crucial part in the

---

[55] Bulst-Thiele, 'Templer in königlichen und päpstlichen Diensten', pp. 289–308; H. Nicholson, 'The Military Orders and the Kings of England in the Twelfth and Thirteenth Centuries', in *From Clermont to Jerusalem: the Crusades and Crusader Societies, 1095–1500*, ed. Alan V. Murray, International Medieval Research, 3 (Turnhout, 1998), pp. 203–28: here pp. 210–11 and note 23; Nicholson, *Templars, Hospitallers*, pp. 21–2.

[56] *Ménestrel de Reims*, pp. 141–2, 146, 168; sections 269–71, 276–8, 323.

[57] *Ménestrel de Reims*, pp. 145–6, sections 276–8; *Le Livre de Baudoyn, conte de Flandre*, ed. C.P. Serrure and A. Voisin (Brussels, 1836), pp. 91–5; cited by Duparc-Quioc, *Le Cycle de la croisade*, p. 251. Although this work contains many references to crusading, scholars do not generally regard it as part of the 'Crusade Cycle'. The Military Orders do not appear in the crusading scenes.

transfer of information from the Holy Land to Europe during the twelfth and thirteenth centuries.[58]

In *Theséus de Cologne*, two Templars, also called Hospitallers, take a message from Osane in Jerusalem to her husband Gadifer in France; later, two Hospitallers (later called Templars) accompany the charcoalburner Regnier, foster-father of Osane's children and king of Antioch, to the West to seek aid for the Holy Land. The 'Templars' supply Regnier's credentials in France when his identity as king of Antioch is challenged: as well as stressing his courage they also emphasize the value of his crown. At one juncture, Regnier disguises himself as a 'Templar' in order to pass unrecognised among enemies. Ten Templars also accompany Osane, Queen Florinde and Regnier when they leave Jerusalem for Antioch; in this case their role is to provide an honourable escort for Queen Florinde. As usual, the Military Orders' role is purely supportive, and they do not even fight; when Regnier and his two Templars/Hospitallers find a dangerous situation in Rome, the two 'Templars' are afraid and stay in a safe place while Regnier goes to aid the empress Flore. The Templar/Hospitallers in Jerusalem in Osane's hospice do not fight in holy war, although they do support and encourage those who do. They congratulate Renechon for his victory over the Muslim emir, and when Renechon recaptures Jerusalem towards the end of the story, the Templars within Jerusalem rejoice and congratulate him. Again, two Templars accompany Regnier when he goes to release the Christian prisoners at Antioch prior to launching his *coup d'état* of the city.[59] This depiction of the Military Orders may be a result of the ignorance of the author or authors of the work. Some post-1312 authors clearly did not know what the actual role of the Templars and Hospitallers had been in Jerusalem; they knew that they looked after

---

[58] For general discussion of newsletters sent between the crusader states and the West and some specific examples of the Military Order's newsletters, see Smail, 'Latin Syria and the West, 1149–1187', 1–21; Barry John Cook, 'The transmission of knowledge about the Holy Land through Europe, 1271–1314', unpublished PhD thesis (University of Manchester, 1985), pp. 402ff., esp. pp. 419–20, 453–5, 477–88, 490–92; Phillips, *Defenders of the Holy Land*, pp. 9, 104–6, 129, 145, 151–3, 246–7; see also for the Military Orders, Lloyd, *English Society*, pp. 24–31, 36–41, 248–52, 256–61; José Manuel Rodríguez García, 'Alfonso X and the Teutonic Order: an Example of the Role of the International Military Orders in Mid-Thirteenth Century Castile', in *The Military Orders*, vol. 2, ed. Nicholson, pp. 319–27; Nicholson, *Templars, Hospitallers*, pp. 105–7.

[59] Bib. nat. nouv. acq. fr. 10060 fols 210rv (in Osane's hospice), 240v–241v (sent by Osane to France), fols 260r–262r (deliver message), fol. 285r, 286r (ten Templars/Hospitallers go to Antioch), fol. 289 r (two Templars accompany Regnier at Antioch), fol. 302v (two Hospitallers set out with Regnier), fol. 310r (two Templars arrive at Constantinople with Regnier), fol. 312v (Regnier, not the Templars, gives a report on events in the Holy Land), fols 319v, 323v–324r (Templar/Hospitallers are terrified by Regnier's actions at Rome), fol. 325r (a Templar lends Regnier his habit as a disguise), fols 331v–332r (Templars provide Regnier's credentials), fols 382v–383r (Templars rejoice at recapture of Jerusalem); Rosenthal, 'Theséus de Cologne', pp. 122, 124–5, 126, 129, 130–35, 141 (esp. p. 132 for frightened Templars, p. 133 for Regnier's disguise as a Templar), and see p. 1033, 'Hospitaller' P.f. 318a, p. 1055a, 'Templars', P.f. 318a, P.f. 319b; Bossuat, 'Théseus de Cologne', 297, 299, 301–2, 319–20.

pilgrims and that they were a religious order, but not that they fought the Muslims. However, it is more likely that as *Theséus* is set in a period long before the First Crusade, these Templar/Hospitallers are supposed to depict these Orders during their early history, before they were militarised.[60]

In the short prose edition of *Theséus*, only Hospitallers appeared, in a much reduced role. Ten Hospitallers accompany Regnier, Florinde and Osane to Antioch. The Hospitallers Regnier takes with him to the West supply his credentials in France.[61] In the long prose versions, the Hospitaller/Templars carry a message for Osanne to France as in the verse version. However, later in the long prose versions the Hospitallers who set out with Regnier the charcoalburner in the verse version are transformed to Templars throughout, the Templars provide Regnier's credentials in Constantinople in addition to providing them in France, and Regnier does not disguise himself as a Templar. The number of Templars who travelled to Antioch increases to eighteen. The Templars still congratulate Renechon for his success against the Muslim emir, and, as in the verse version, the Templars who accompany Regnier the charcoalburner are timid and do not fight. The Templars rejoice at Regnesson's recovery of Jerusalem, but also at the conversions which result.[62] In the version by Contant d'Orville, Templars are sent by Florinde and Osane to Gadifer in France solely to ask for help for the Holy Land, and only fifteen Templars go to Antioch. The Hospitallers do not appear.[63]

In short, although the Hospitallers and Templars appear in *Theséus* as messengers and supporting God's warriors, the Hospitallers were displaced by the Templars in the long prose redactions of the work, and what the Brothers actually did changed slightly with each new redaction.

Regnier's disguise as a Templar or Hospitaller is a detail that appears only in the long verse version of *Theséus*, and vanished from later versions of the story. Elizabeth Rosenthal, in her detailed study of the poem, pointed out that this disguise is only a variant on the more common literary theme of the person disguised as a pilgrim in order to travel incognito.[64] As the Hospitallers are also called 'pilgrims', in effect Regnier is disguised as a pilgrim. The concept that the Hospitallers' habit was a convenient disguise for a man wishing to travel inconspicuously also appears in an odd detail of the final continuation of the Latin chronicle of Guillaume de Nangis. Here John, duke of Normandy

---

[60] For the legendary early history of the Hospitallers and Templars, see *The Hospitallers' Riwle*, lines 1–368; Borchardt, 'Two Forged Thirteenth-Century Alms-Raising Letters'; Nicholson, *Templars, Hospitallers*, pp. 112–15.

[61] Bib. nat. fr. 1473, pp. 125, 140; *Theséus de Cologne: fragment of a lost edition*, p. 5.

[62] *Hystoire Trescreative* (1534), Bk 2, fols 53c–d, 65a–d, 67d, 78a, 85d, 90b, 92a–b, 93a, 95c, 96a, 97c, 98b, 99c, 101b, 102c, 103a, 103c, 104a–b, 121b; *Hystoire Trescreative* (1550), 258d–259b, 275c–277a, 279d, 296a, 308a, 315a.

[63] Contant d'Orville, *Mélanges tirés*, pp. 198–9, 203, 207; Rosenthal, 'Theséus de Cologne', pp. 1616, 1619, 1621.

[64] Rosenthal, 'Theséus de Cologne', p. 439.

(the eldest son of King Philip VI of France) is depicted retreating from the siege of Aiguillon in the Agenais in 1346 dressed in the habit of a Hospitaller. This extraordinary detail, written by the continuator who took the work down to 1368, is certainly reminiscent of the charcoalburner in *Theséus de Cologne*. It does not appear in the far more detailed account in Froissart's chronicles, nor in the contemporary chronicle of Jean le Bel, which leads one to suspect that it is invented.[65] Some chroniclers recorded a story that Richard the Lionheart had disguised himself as a Templar when he was travelling back from the Holy Land in autumn 1192, because he knew that his enemies were lying in wait for him. This story seems to have arisen from the fact that Richard had Templars in his entourage.[66] Historically, both Templars and Hospitallers themselves sometimes travelled in disguise when they were on ambassadorial missions for kings.[67]

A Templar again appears as a messenger seeking aid for Christians in the alliterative *Morte Arthure*, written between 1350 and 1440; most scholars prefer to date this work to the early fifteenth century. Here a Templar meets King Arthur on the king's arrival in Brittany and informs him that a giant has been ravaging the land and eating children, and has now carried off the duchess of Brittany. In view of the Templars' role elsewhere assisting lovers, it is interesting to see a Templar depicted as trying to bring aid to a noblewoman, even though he seems almost as much concerned about the giant's treasure as he is about the lady. The battle which follows between Arthur and the giant is depicted as a battle of Christian against pagan, an appropriate matter for a Templar's involvement. Arthur tells his men that he is going on a pilgrimage, a common term for a crusade during the Middle Ages; we are told that his armour comes from Acre and the Jordan – a clear reference to the holy war in the East – and it is emphasized that the babies which the giant is eating are baptised Christians; baby-eating is a characteristic activity of the religious enemy. Hence the appearance of the Templar was a signal to the audience that what followed was a holy war, depicting Arthur as a champion of Christianity.[68]

---

[65] See Duparc-Quioc, *Le Cycle de la croisade*, p. 116; *Chronique latine de Guillaume de Nangis, 1113 à 1300 avec les continuations de cette chronique de 1300 à 1368, nouvelle édition*, ed. H. Géraud, 2 vols, SATF (Paris, 1843, reprinted New York and London, 1965), 2, p. 204.

[66] *Chronique d'Ernoul*, pp. 296–7; see also Ralph of Coggeshall, *Chronicon anglicanum*, ed. J. Stevenson, RS 66 (London, 1875), p. 54.

[67] Nicholson, 'The Military Orders and the Kings of England', pp. 210–11.

[68] *The Alliterative Morte Arthure*, lines 840–87, especially line 841. For Arthur's pilgrimage, see line 896, for his armour, lines 903, 905, for the Christian babies, lines 1065–6, 1051, and see also 1187. For the crusade as a pilgrimage, see Riley-Smith, *The First Crusade and the Idea of Crusading*, pp. 22–5; Riley-Smith, *What were the Crusades?*, pp. 2, 6, 36; Tyerman, *The Invention of the Crusades*, pp. 9, 20–23, 26–8; J.G. Davis, 'Pilgrimage and Crusade Literature', in *Journeys Towards God*, pp. 1–30, esp. p. 23; for accusations of baby-eating aimed at religious enemies or deviants, see Cohn, *Europe's Inner Demons*, pp. 1–4, 6–9, 11–15, 35–78. For Arthur's battle with the giant as holy war and Arthur as a champion of Christianity, see also John Finlayson,

This is reasonable in an English romance, given previous and contemporary English involvement in the Crusades, whether to the Holy Land, Prussia, Spain or elsewhere. Henry Bolinbroke, earl of Derby, and from 1399 King Henry IV of England, was on crusade in Prussia in 1390–91 and 1392, and also visited Jerusalem. He was the most illustrious, but far from being the only English nobleman actively involved in crusading during this period. Chaucer depicted his Knight in his *Canterbury Tales* as an active crusader, who had campaigned in Prussia against the Russians and Lithuanians, in Granada, in Morocco, Asia Minor, and had been at the capture of Alexandria by Peter I of Cyprus in 1365. English involvement and interest in crusading is also reflected in other literature of this period.[69] If the alliterative *Morte Arthure* was written in the first decade of the fifteenth century, the date preferred by most scholars, then it was written when the king, Henry IV, believed himself to be – and depicted himself as – a champion of Christianity; he had campaigned against the external enemies of Christendom before he became king, and had initiated strong measures against the internal enemies of Christendom, the Lollard heretics, since becoming king of England.[70] So it was to be expected that Arthur, the predecessor of the kings of England, should be depicted as a champion of Christendom.

However, when Thomas Malory inserted this episode into his *Morte Darthur*, he replaced the Templar with a 'husbandman', and all but omitted the references to holy war in the battle between Arthur and the giant: his expedition is still a 'pilgrimage', but his armour no longer comes from the Holy Land and the babies whom the giant is eating are not specifically described as Christian. Clearly, Malory's concept of Arthur did not allow Arthur to be an outstanding champion of Christendom; this privilege was reserved for the family of Lancelot, at the very end of the work.[71] It may be that

---

Morte Arthure (London, 1967), pp. 16–19, pp. 41–2 note on line 851, p. 50, note on line 1073, p. 52 note on line 1136, p. 54 note on lines 1200–221. Finlayson stresses the significance of this episode for the whole work, calling it 'a central part of a fairly well-constructed narrative'. On Arthur and holy war in this work, see also Matthew, *The Tragedy of Arthur*, pp. 63, 184, 128–9, 145–6. Matthew points out the importance and popularity of the Lithuanian crusade for the English nobility at the period that this work was written.

[69] Geoffrey Chaucer, *The Canterbury Tales*, General Prologue, lines 49–67, in *The Riverside Chaucer*, 3rd edn, ed. Larry D. Benson (Oxford, 1987); Maurice Keen, 'Chaucer's Knight, the English Aristocracy and the Crusade', in *English Court Culture in the Later Middle Ages*, ed. V.J. Scattergood and J.W. Sherborne (London, 1983), pp. 45–61; Tyerman, *England and the Crusades*, pp. 259–301; Mary Hamel, 'The Siege of Jerusalem as a crusading poem', in *Journeys Towards God*, pp. 177–94.

[70] For Henry IV's persecution of heresy see Peter McNiven, *Heresy and Politics in the Reign of Henry IV: the Burning of John Badby* (Woodbridge, 1987).

[71] 'The Tale of King Arthur' in *The Works of Sir Thomas Malory*, ed. Eugène Vinaver, 3 vols, 2nd edn (Oxford, 1967), Bk 5, ch. 5:1, pp. 198–205; Thomas Malory, *Le Morte d'Arthur*, 2 vols (Harmondsworth, 1969), 1, pp. 173–6: contrast with the end of Bk 21, ch. 13. On the crusade of Lancelot's relatives see also Beverly Kennedy, *Knighthood in the Morte Darthur*, 2nd edn (Cambridge, 1992), pp. 347, 351.

Malory shortened this episode and omitted the crusading references purely for structural reasons, because he did not wish to make it a central episode in his story. But the fact that he did not wish to make it a central episode is significant. Perhaps the omission of the crusade here reflects the reduction in active involvement in crusading by the English nobility during the fifteenth century. But it is more likely that it reflects Malory's own views of kingship and knighthood, for despite the lack of active involvement, the English kings, nobles and people still aspired to fight the enemies of Christendom and gave donations for the purpose, even if they did not go themselves in person.[72] The fact that Malory's Arthur is not involved in crusading, whereas the family of Lancelot are, reveals the moral and spiritual superiority of Lancelot's lineage – in Malory's view – over the lineage of Arthur.

Another appearance of the Templars urging holy war appears in *Le Chevalier au Cygne et Godefroid de Bouillon*, written soon after 1350. Peter the Hermit comes on pilgrimage to the city of Jerusalem and finds that the Christians have been evicted from the Holy Sepulchre by the king of Jerusalem, Cornumarans, and made to live in the Temple, while the Sepulchre is used as a stable. Peter is very distressed at this situation and declares that he will go back to Europe and urge the pope to call a crusade. 'Then the Templars who heard him speak said, 'Lord Peter the Hermit, hurry! Make the Christians come and win their own salvation.'[73] The author, who probably could not remember the historical Order of the Temple, clearly did not know exactly what the Templars were; an ignorance shared with the author of the fifteenth-century redaction of *La Fille du Comte de Ponthieu* and the author or authors of *Theséus de Cologne*. However, he knew that the Templars were somehow connected with the Holy Sepulchre as well as the Temple, and that they played a role in encouraging the crusades.

The Military Orders frequently appear in epic and romantic literature in roles connected with military activity, either actively involved in fighting or promoting holy war, or giving advice and lending money for holy war. Interestingly, they appear less often and in a smaller variety of roles than in religious or monastic roles. Their military roles relate directly to actual contemporary and past events, so much so that the Templars almost completely disappear from literary depictions of active fighting in works first composed after 1312.

The presence of the Military Orders in a work of literature underscored the fact that a conflict was a holy war, between rival faiths or between 'right' and

---

[72] Tyerman, *England and the Crusades*, pp. 302–23.
[73] *Le Chevalier au Cygne et Godefroid de Bouillon*, 2, pp. 84–5, lines 5397–425, especially 5423–5. For date, see Edmond A. Emplaincourt, 'Le Parfait du Paon', *Romania*, 102 (1981), 396–405, here 396 and note 3.

'wrong'. Sometimes they were criticised for being too cautious, too proud or too interested in money, and there is one reference to treachery. However, in general they were depicted as dedicated to advancing or protecting Christendom.

CHAPTER FOUR

THE GRAIL

In many non-academic works on the Grail, the association between the Grail and the Templars is assumed to be so obvious and so well-established that it requires no detailed justification.[1] It may therefore come as a surprise to those not familiar with the Grail romances themselves that of all the various versions of the Grail legend, the Templars appear by name in only Wolfram von Eschenbach's *Parzival* and some later works based on it. It has been suggested by various writers that other Grail stories in which the Templars do not appear by name include the Templars under another guise, bearing symbols such as a white shield with a red cross. This theory assumes that this symbol was the unique property of the Templars. Yet, as will be shown below, this is by no means the case.

Some scholars have assumed that certain Grail heroes, in particular Galaad, were intended to be representations of Templar knights. This assumption is based both upon the symbolism which they carry and their actions during the course of the narrative.[2] Again, however, careful examination of the heroes in question demonstrates that although the Grail heroes are certainly knights who are seeking God, they are not intended to be Templars.

Others have suggested that 'a Grail knighthood' which guards the Grail was an integral part of the Grail legend, and that this knighthood was the knighthood of the Temple, the Templars.[3] As the Grail romances were written for a knightly audience and some were written by knights it is not surprising

---

[1] For example, Michael Baigent, Richard Leigh and H. Lincoln, *The Holy Blood and the Holy Grail* (London, 1976) and Michael Baigent and Richard Leigh, *The Temple and the Lodge* (London, 1990), pp. 77–83.

[2] Pauphilet, *Études*, pp. 69–71; Bruce, *Evolution*, 1, p. 421; see also the sources listed by Wilkin, 'The Dissolution of the Templar Ideal', 111, note 9. Matarasso, *Redemption of Chivalry*, p. 68.

[3] Jessie L. Weston, *From Ritual to Romance: An account of the Holy Grail from ancient ritual to Christian Symbol* (new edition, New York, 1957), p. 100 (and see pp. 91–3): 'Is it not possible that in these armed youths ... notably in that of the Salii, at once warriors and priests, we have the real origin of the Grail Knights? ... From Salii to Templars is not after all so "far a cry" ...', p. 187: 'the puzzling connection of the Order [of the Templars] with the Knights of the Grail ...'; *The Elucidation: a Prologue to the Conte del Graal*, ed. Albert Wilder Thompson (New York, 1931), p. 76: 'the conception of divinely appointed guardians of the Grail'; Margaret Fitzgerald Richey, *Studies of Wolfram von Eschenbach* (London, 1957), p. 141–2: 'the ideal of an order of Knights dedicated to the service of the Graal and associated with the order of the Knights Templar seems to me, on this evidence, to have been an integral part of the basic tradition'.

that the major characters in the Grail stories are knights. However, where the patrons of these romances are known, they were members of the highest nobility, and while the high nobility were patrons of the Military Orders they did not form a high percentage of the members of the Military Orders. In other words, the Grail romances were not written for the same section of society which made up the Military Orders. It is necessary to stress that modern scholarship does not consider that any of the Grail romances were written by members of the Military Orders.[4]

The present study argues that although some of the the Grail stories are concerned with a fraternity of knights who seek the Grail, the knights of the Round Table, these knights are not Templars but are based on the secular confraternities and orders of knights which were founded frequently during the Middle Ages. Although they may take general vows, such as vowing to persist in the quest until they see the Grail, the Grail knights retain their individual freedom of action; they are not members of a religious order who have given up their own wills to serve the Order, but each seeks God alone. While they are often, although not invariably, celibate, they do not espouse personal poverty. They are not, therefore, following a religious form of life as the Templars did. Thus they represent a development of knightly conceptions of knighthood which surpasses the earlier ecclesiastical concepts of knighthood which led to the formation of the Templars. They are, then, a progression from the Templars, rather than a reflection of the Templars.

In short, detailed examination of the Grail romances merely reemphasizes the original point that the Templars only appear in *Parzival*, and that other Grail romances have no direct connection with the Templars. However, there is another possible line of enquiry which should be investigated before it can be stated categorically that there is no fundamental connection between the Templars and the Grail romances as a whole. This is the question of the connection between the Holy Land and the Grail. Is the Grail itself essentially linked to the Holy Land and Jerusalem?[5] Indeed, given that legal treatises and other literary works were being composed in the Holy Land in the thirteenth century, might it be that some of the Grail romances were actually written in the Latin East? If the concept of the Grail was linked to the Holy Land, it may be that the author intended some sort of connection between the Grail hero and the Templars, who were based in the Holy Land. Indeed, if it could be established that any of the Grail romances which include Templar-like heroes

---

[4] In fact, members of the Military Orders produced relatively little writing in comparison with other religious orders; some histories were produced, but nothing ressembling a work of fictional literature. See Forey, 'Literacy', pp. 200–204; Nicholson, *Templars, Hospitallers*, pp. 110–12.

[5] Knight, 'From Jerusalem to Camelot', surveys the Grail romances and deduces connections with the crusades and the Holy Land, but he is more concerned with the development of the concept of the Grail than with the development of the concept of ideal knighthood in relation to the concept of the Templars, which is my intention in this study.

were originally written in the Holy Land, then it would be possible that the heroes of these works were indeed based upon the actual Templars. In any case, having been written within the milieu in which the Templars operated, such Grail romances would reflect the interests and opinions of the nobility of the Holy Land, who fought alongside the Templars in their defence of the Holy Land against the Muslims. They would therefore be close to the Templars' interests and ideals even if they did not reflect them directly.

In this chapter, therefore, it is first necessary to consider the Templars' appearance in Wolfram von Eschenbach's *Parzival* and the later works based upon it, and other works in which knights guard a holy Temple, to establish what the appearance of the Templars is intended to achieve in these works. It is then necessary to consider Grail works or Grail-related works in which the Templars do not appear by name but in which the author may intend the audience to understand a connection between the fictional characters and the Templars. It is then necessary to examine the connection between the Grail romances and the Holy Land.

It is not the purpose of this study to discuss the mystical meanings of the Grail, but simply to identify the historical context of the composition of some of the Grail stories and to identify references to contemporary events, people and places within the narratives. This may help to explain why the authors composed as they did and elucidate any political significance which their work may have had for their immediate patron and audience. This is not intended to exclude the spiritual message of the story. It is assumed in this study that the Grail romances do describe the spiritual journey of the knight's soul to God and therefore it is legitimate to identify allusions to Biblical passages within them. Some authors, such as the author of the *Perlesvaus*, were clearly clerics and knew the Bible well; others, such as Wolfram von Eschenbach, were members of the laity but were very familiar with the Bible as a result of hearing it read and expounded in sermons.[6]

A few words of introduction to the Grail romances are required, as background to what follows. The form of the Grail and the nature of the quest for the Grail differ substantially in each of the many Grail romances. The Grail may be described generally as a large flat platter, big enough to hold a fish, or specifically identified as the dish used by Christ at the Last Supper. Uniquely, for Wolfram von Eschenbach the *Grâl* was a holy stone, brought by angels from heaven, which supplied all its guardians' wants and needs. The quest for the Grail involves finding the castle where the Grail is situated, but what happens there differs in different versions of the story. For Chrétien de Troyes, Wolfram von Eschenbach, Heinrich von dem Türlin and the anonymous

---

[6] For what follows, I am indebted to discussions with Peter Edbury, Karen Pratt and Kate Hamlyn. The conclusions which follow, however, are my own.

authors of the 'Didot' *Perceval* and *Perlesvaus* the quester must ask one or more questions: what is the infirmity of the king of the Grail Castle? And/or whom does the Grail serve? This done, the health of the king and the land will be restored, and the Grail knight may receive his inheritance, because he is the heir of the Grail king. In the Vulgate *Queste* and its later versions, there is more than one Grail knight, although one leads. Here, the aim of the quest is not to cure the king but to see the Grail clearly – which, it transpires, means to see God face-to-face.[7] There is no question to ask, although the leading Grail knight has a number of functions to fulfill: to end the evil enchantments which trouble Arthur's kingdom, and to cure a wounded king. This done, the Grail knights either return to normal life, to live as Christ's knights in the world, or sail to Sarraz to die.

The Grail romances differ from the works examined to date in that they quickly developed their own literary reality which was quite different from actual reality, and changed little in response to contemporary events. It will be suggested in Part Two of this study that one effect of this distinct literary reality was to eradicate the need to include the Military Orders within the plot. This said, it remains to be considered why the Templars do appear by name in one Grail romance, yet do not appear in other Grail romances.

1 *Legends of the Grail and associated romances which make specific reference to the Templars*

1.1 *Wolfram von Eschenbach's 'Parzival'*

Wolfram von Eschenbach probably wrote *Parzival* for Hermann I, landgrave of Thuringia (landgrave 1190–1217). He was writing in the first decade of the thirteenth century. Wolfram decided that the Grâl, too holy to be approached by sinners, should have a holy knighthood to guard it. The place where Wolfram's Grâl was housed is called 'the temple',[8] and the guardians of the holy stone are *Templeise*, normally translated as 'Templars'. Although in fact the medieval German name for the Templars was *Tempelherren*, not *Templeise*, the words *Templeise* and 'Templars' are so similar that Wolfram must have intended his audience to regard these men as at least having something in common with the actual Templars. Wolfram's *Templeise* serve

---

[7] On the object of the quest in the *Queste*, see Matarasso, *Redemption of Chivalry*, pp. 103, 180–200.

[8] Wolfram von Eschenbach, *Parzival*, ed. K. Lachmann and W. Spiewok, 2 vols (Stuttgart, 1981), 2, Bk 16, 816.15. I have also consulted the edition of Karl Bartsch (Leipzig, 1875). I am indebted to the excellent and readable translation by A.T. Hatto (Harmondsworth, 1980) for my initial impressions and first reading of *Parzival*. In particular, his summary of the relationships between the various characters (pp. 439–47) provided a starting point for my own study and greatly eased the task of analysis.

under a commander, patrol the area around the Grâl Castle to drive away intruders (including Parzivâl himself), and are chaste. From time to time, however, they may be sent away from the Grâl Castle to rule other lands, and in this case they may marry. They serve the Grâl in penance for their sins, and are called a 'Brotherhood', but it is not stated that they live under a monastic rule; and their badge is not a cross but a turtle dove, the symbol of pure and faithful love. They live from the Grâl stone, which heals the sick and confers eternal youth, and those who are to join them are chosen by God, not volunteers. Although they are guardians of sanctity and are allowed to gaze upon holy things barred from ordinary sinners, they do not act as spiritual advisers or guides to those seeking sanctity; as usual in romances, this role is taken by a hermit. The *Templeise* also appear briefly in the so-called *Titurel* fragments, which recount events before those in *Parzival*: here they appear alongside Titurel, guarding the Grâl.[9]

Wolfram's depiction of the Templars had a significant influence on the literary image of the Order of the Temple in German romances, and – if he was the originator of the image of the Templars as defenders of lovers, as suggested in Chapter 2 above – on their image in French romances also. Some other German authors who cited Wolfram's work, such as 'der Marner', referred to the *Templeise* as guardians of the Grâl.[10] Albrecht included *Templeise* in his description of the Grâl Castle in his *Jüngerer Titurel*, written between 1260 and 1276. In this work it is made clear that the Grâl is housed in a temple, and it is stated that the Master was an archbishop, with two prelates to help him. The *Templeise* are knights who fight the heathen daily to defend this temple, at the side of Titurel. They are the *werden bruderschaft*, the worthy brotherhood.[11] At the end of the thirteenth century, the author of *Reinfrid von Braunschweig*

---

[9] *Parzival*, 2, Bk 9: 443.6–445.30, 468.23–471.30, 473.1–11, 474.2–9, 494.1–14, 495.1–12, Bk 16: 792.20–30, 797.13–15, 802.11–20, 804.4–7, 805.22–3, 816.5–6, 16–17, 818. 24–32, 821.18–21; for the turtle dove, see Bk 9, 474.5–9; Wolfram von Eschenbach, *Willehalm, Titurel*, ed. Walter Johannes Schröder and Gisela Hollandt (Darmstadt, 1971): *Titurel*, p. 592, 11.2. On the similarities and differences between the historical Templars and Wolfram's *Templeise* see Jean Frappier, 'Le Graal et la Chevalerie', *Romania*, 75 (1954), 165–210: here 179. Frappier emphasises that Wolfram's *Templeise* are not the same as the actual religious Order, bound by lifetime vows.

[10] *Der Marner*, ed. P. Strauch (Strasbourg, 1876, reprinted Berlin, 1962), p. 127, XV 16: '*Ich sunge ouch wol wie Titurel/ templeise bi dem Grâle züge*'. The *Parzifal* of Claus Wisse and Philipp Colin, written between 1331 and 1336, used Wolfram, Chrétien de Troyes, and the continuations of Chrétien's Grail Romance: *Parzifal von Claus Wisse und Philipp Colin (1331–1336): eine Ergänzung der Dichtung Wolframs von Eschenbach zum ersten male herausgegeben*, ed. Karl Schorbach, Elsässische Litteraturdenkmäler aus den XIV–XVII Jahrhundert, ed. Ernst Martin and Erich Schmidt, vol. 5 (Strasburg, 1888; reprinted Berlin and New York, 1974), for instance, col. 582 lines 20–21, col. 845 lines 23–5, 33; see also *Elucidation*, pp. 13–15.

[11] Albrecht, *Jüngerer Titurel*, 1, pp. 106, 108, 114, 132, 138, 140, 154, 159, 168, 171: strophes 421, 431, Strophen des Marienlobs 21, 499, 517, 522, 581, 602, 638, 649; 2, p. 15, strophe 2012, (Anfortas as lord of the *Templeise* and the Gral); 3/1, p. 216, strophes 5255–6; 3/1, strophe 5259 (Sigune speaking to Parzival about the *Templeise*); 3/2, pp. 278, 279, strophes 5505–6.

observed that the *Templeise* were seen bearing the chaste turtle dove on many occasions in battle in defence of the Grâl.[12]

In the late fifteenth century, the Munich writer Ulrich Füetrer, composing his *Buch der Abenteuer* (possibly written in the 1480s for Duke Albrecht IV of Bavaria) began his book with the *Templeysen* and the setting up of the Grâl Castle. The *Templeysen* are bold and noble warriors, but the term 'templeyse' also covers the rulers of the Grâl, such as Frimontell, Parcival's grandfather, and clearly includes all the knights who live in the Grâl castle. This is not the case in Wolfram's poem, where the *Templeise* are a fellowship separate from and subordinate to the family who actually rule the castle. Apart from this, the role of the *Templeysen*, guarding the Grâl, is the same as in Wolfram, for Ulrich followed Wolfram, although he was also using Albrecht's work. In particular, Ulrich repeats Wolfram's humorous anecdote of Parcival's encounter with a *Templeis*, whom Parcival defeats and leaves clinging to a tree over a ravine. Ulrich, however, also mentions the *Templeysen* as Grâl guardians in the course of his retelling of the story of Lohengrin, although they do not appear in the thirteenth-century poem on which he based his account. Clearly interest in the *Templeise* as a dedicated band of crack fighters defending holiness was still very much alive in late fifteenth-century Bavaria.[13]

As Wolfram's work enjoyed great popularity among German speakers, it may also have been instrumental in encouraging patronage towards the Order of the Temple in the thirteenth century; but this can only be speculation. It does seems probable that it was a contributing influence on the very positive view of the Templars contained in the fictional-historical accounts of *Die Kreuzfahrt des Landgrafen Ludwigs* and Ottokar's *Reimchronik*, and may have contributed to German antipathy to the trial of the Temple.

Why did Wolfram include 'Templars' in his Grail romance when no other Grail writer (except some of those continuing or adapting his work) did so? This is not an easy question to answer. The 'meaning' of Wolfram's work has puzzled and intrigued generations of scholars. Wolfram himself warns his audience that the underlying message of *Parzival* is difficult to understand: its meaning will rush past them like a startled hare, '*rehte alsam ein schellec hase*'. He only emphasizes that resolution is essential; hearts should not be doubtful, or vacillating. He also refers to heaven and hell, black and white, reliability and unreliability.[14] This only tells the reader that the essence of Wolfram's story may be that resolute action is necessary, that there is a mixture

---

[12] *Reinfrid von Braunschweig*, lines 782–91; see also Schirok, *Parzivalrezeption*, p. 65ff.

[13] Ulrich Füetrer, *Das Buch der Abenteuer*, ed. Heinz Thoelen, with Bernd Bastert, 2 vols (Göppingen, 1997), 1, strophes 1–120, 1753.7–1757.5, 2479.6–7, 2490.3–4, 2625, 2665.6–7, 2994; 2, p. 533.

[14] *Parzival*, Bk 1: 1.1–2.22, esp. 1.19. For this translation see Wolfram von Eschenbach, *Parzival*, trans. A.T. Hatto (Harmondsworth, 1980), p. 15.

of opposites in it, and that the meaning of the story is likely to be very difficult to identify because it is full of contradictions and sweeps back and forth across itself, just as the fleeing hare zigzags across a field. However, Wolfram's own hints will be useful in the course of this investigation, for he himself indicates that if his story appears to contradict itself or cross one point twice, this is only to be expected; this is what the fleeing hare will do.

Certainly Wolfram's choice of Templars to guard his castle would have been influenced by the great interest which he and his patron Hermann had in the mysterious East, and Wolfram's own sympathetic interest in the Muslims, also demonstrated in his work *Willehalm*.[15] Hermann himself had taken the cross in 1195 and went on the German crusade of 1197–98. He was one of the leading lights in the promotion of the knightly ideal in the German society of his day and his court was a centre of pro-crusading culture.[16] In his interest in the East, Wolfram was far from being exceptional for his time,[17] and I shall return in Part Two to the increasing popularity of Muslim heroes in thirteenth-century literature. Wolfram also displays an interest in astrology, which was becoming increasingly popular at noble courts in western Europe following the influx from Spain during the twelfth century of Arab texts in Latin translation.[18] In holding such interests, Wolfram was very much the intelligent man of his age. These interests, therefore, cannot be the decisive factor which led him to include Templars in his Grail story when other authors omitted them.

Some commentators have supposed that Wolfram put the Templars into his Grail romance because they appeared in his source.[19] Wolfram claims a 'Kyôt of Provence' who translated his story from 'heathenish', or Arabic, as his source and accuses Chrétien de Troyes of getting the story wrong, but no Kyôt of Provence is known to have existed and no work of his survives. Hence this truth claim is probably no more than literary convention and a justification

---

[15] For general discussion of this subject see Hatto's translation, pp. 421–3, 424, 428, 438. For Wolfram's *Willehalm* as a crusading epic see Wentzlaff-Eggebert, *Kreuzzugsdichtung*, pp. 247–77.

[16] Claudia Naumann, *Der Kreuzzug Kaiser Heinrichs VI* (Frankfurt am Main, 1994), p. 116 and note 476, pp.122–4, 126, 251–2.

[17] For a general discussion see Willem Snelleman, *Das Haus Anjou und der Orient in Wolframs 'Parzival'* (Nijkerk, 1941), pp. 145–64; Malcolm Barber, *The Two Cities: Medieval Europe 1050–1320* (London, 1992), pp. 501–4.

[18] Jim Tester, *A History of Western Astrology* (Woodbridge, 1987), pp. 143–83; Jean Jolivet, 'The Arabic Inheritance', in *A History of Twelfth-Century Western Philosophy*, ed. Peter Dronke (Cambridge, 1988), pp. 113–48; Richard Kieckhefer, *Magic in the Middle Ages* (Cambridge, 1989), pp. 117–25; for Wolfram and astrology in particular, see Harald Haferland, 'Die Geheimnisse des Grals. Wolframs "Parzival" als Lesemysterium?', *Zeitscrift für deutsche Philologie*, 13 (1994), 23–57.

[19] See Joachim Bumke, *Wolfram von Eschenbach: Forschung seit 1945: Bericht und Bibliographie* (Munich, 1970), pp. 48, 114. This work supplies an extensive bibliography of studies of Wolfram's work published 1945–69.

for rewriting and altering another poet's work. In the same way, Wolfram's contemporary Manessier claimed to have found the Latin text of his Graal story at Salisbury in England; but the only definitely identified source for his work, and the most obvious source, is *La Queste del Saint Graal*.[20] It has been suggested that Wolfram's reference to 'Kyôt' is intended to refer to the knight-turned-Cluniac poet Guiot of Provins, but he is not known to have written a Grail romance. Certainly Guiot does praise the Templars' courage, but he also regards them as proud and rash, and states that he himself does not wish to join them because he does not wish to be a martyr.[21] Margaret Fitzgerald Richey suggested that Wolfram meant some other Guiot, now unknown.[22] This seems an unsatisfactory solution when other more satisfactory solutions are possible.

The theory popularised by Jessie Weston early in this century and still popular with conspiracy theorists and 'New Age' thinkers is that Wolfram put the Templars into his romance because of their secret heretical knowledge. However, modern scholarship has established beyond all reasonable doubt that the Templars were orthodox Catholics who, far from having any secret knowledge, were remarkably lacking in any form of learning, and who were destroyed by the king of France for political rather than religious reasons.[23] None of these theories, therefore, can hold water.

The work of Wolfram's successors, Albrecht and Ulrich Füetrer, may throw more light on Wolfram's intentions. They believed that Wolfram intended his audience to understand that his *Templeise* were in fact the equivalents of the actual Templars, and that the Grâl castle of which he wrote was the equivalent of Jerusalem. Wolfram's Grâl castle is a castle on a hill (like Mount Sion) with a wounded king (the king of Jerusalem 1174–85 was

---

[20] *Parzival*, Book 8, lines 416.17–30, Book 9, lines 453. 1–22, 455.2–24, Book 16, lines 827.1–14; *The continuations of the Old French 'Perceval' of Chrétien de Troyes*, ed. W. Roach et al., 5 vols in 6 (Philadelphia, 1949–83), 5: *The Third Continuation by Manessier*, lines 42658–68, and see pp. xiv–xv on the debate over Manessier's sources and the similarity of his work to the Queste.

[21] For a review of these theories see Bumke, *Wolfram von Eschenbach*, p. 211, pp. 248–9; Guiot de Provins, 'La Bible', in *Les Oeuvres de Guiot de Provins, poète lyrique et satirique*, ed. J. Orr (Manchester, 1915), lines 1695–788.

[22] Richey, *Studies*, pp. 144, 153–8.

[23] On some such theories see Bumke, *Wolfram von Eschenbach*, pp. 123, 162, 205, 222. Helen Adolf considered such a theory, but finally discarded it: *Visio Pacis: Holy City and Grail: an attempt at an Inner History of the Grail Legend* (Philadelphia, 1960), pp. 203–4, note 30. See also, for instance, Jessie Weston, *The Quest of the Holy Grail* (London, 1913, reprinted 1964), p. 136; Jessie Weston, *From Ritual to Romance* (Cambridge, 1920, reprinted New York, 1957), pp. 100 (and see 91–3), 187. On the Templars' orthodoxy, see Barber, *New Knighthood*, pp. 179–228; Forey, *Military Orders*, pp. 6–17, 148–203; Nicholson, *Templars, Hospitallers*, p. 77; Jonathan Riley-Smith, *Hospitallers: The History of the Order of St John* (London, 1999), pp. 51–4. On the Templars' lack of education, see Forey, 'Literacy', pp. 185–206. On the political motivation behind the destruction of the Order of the Temple, see Cohn, *Europe's Inner Demons*, pp. 79–101; Malcolm Barber, 'Propaganda in the Middle Ages: the Charges Against the Templars', *Nottingham Medieval Studies*, 17 (1973), 42–57; Kieckhefer, *Magic in the Middle Ages*, pp. 187–8.

a leper), awaiting the arrival of the heir, Parzivâl, who will heal the king and where, when all is restored to health, a Muslim (Feirefîz, Parzivâl's brother) will be welcomed and will readily convert to Christianity. The castle is called *Munsalvaesche* or *Munsalvatsche*. This could be taken to mean 'Mount Savage', or 'Wild Mountain', and many modern scholars have interpreted it in this way.[24] However, Wolfram's adaptors and rewriters did not interpret it as such. For them, the land of the Grâl is *Salva Terra*, the Land of Salvation or, in other words, the Holy Land; and the castle is *Montsalvatsche*, the Mount of Salvation – in other words, Sion, the hill of Jerusalem where the Temple stood.[25] Wolfram's medieval audience, therefore, certainly believed that Wolfram was writing about Jerusalem.

The interpretation that Wolfram's medieval audience put on his work may not have been Wolfram's own intention, although as they were close to Wolfram's own context they are more likely to have understood his intentions than modern readers living in a very different culture. However, the fact that Wolfram made his Grâl guardians 'Templars' strongly suggests that he did indeed intend his Grâl Castle to be Jerusalem. Just as Templars guarded Jerusalem and the Holy Sepulchre, where Christ, the cornerstone rejected by the builders (Ephesians ch. 2 v. 20), died and rose again, so Wolfram's 'Templars' guard the *Lapsit exillis*, the *lapis exilis* or little insignificant stone, the Grâl. As Wolfram's Grâl came down from Heaven, is the means of resurrection for the Phoenix (a symbol of the resurrected Christ) and its powers are renewed each Good Friday by a Dove (a symbol of the Holy Spirit) it seems reasonable to deduce that Wolfram's Grâl represents the presence of Christ or Christ's power among humanity. Again, just as the Templars served as an act of love the God of Love who laid down His life in love, so Wolfram's *Templeise* bear a symbol of faithful love, the turtle dove. By calling his Grâl guardians 'Templars', Wolfram signalled to his audience that he was writing of Jerusalem.

In the past it has been thought by some scholars that a German author would not write about Jerusalem because medieval Germans were not interested in the crusade to Jerusalem. It is now recognised that this view of German lack of involvement in the crusade is a misconception. The Rhinelanders and the Lotharingians under their duke, Godfrey of Bouillon, played an important role in the First Crusade; Conrad III, king of the Romans (emperor-elect), and his nephew Frederick Barbarossa took part in the Second Crusade, while as emperor Frederick Barbarossa was involved in the Third

---

[24] See, for instance, Hatto's translation of Wolfram, p. 431; the debate is summarised by Bumke, *Wolfram von Eschenbach*, pp. 115–16.
[25] See, for instance, Albrecht von Scharfenberg, *Jüngerer Titurel*, 3/1, pp. 192–3; 3/2, p. 577; Ulrich Füetrer, *Das Buch der Abenteuer*, 1, strophe 5.6–7, 34.4, 49.6–7, 102.4, 110.5, 2625.3, 2994.6.

Crusade. A German crusade took place in 1197–98, and Germans took part in the Fourth Crusade. The Germans continued to play an important role in crusading to the Holy Land throughout the thirteenth century. In short, the German peoples were enthusiastic crusaders to the Holy Land, and there would be nothing surprising in Wolfram and his successors focussing their work upon Jerusalem.[26]

It should be noted that there is one place name in *Parzival* which is clearly in the Holy Land: the land of Ascalûn, an obvious variation on the city of Ascalon. Jaffa-Ascalon had been a royal fief in the kingdom of Jerusalem before the fall of the kingdom to Saladin in 1187. It was held by Guy of Lusignan from 1180, after his marriage to Baldwin IV's sister Sybil. Guy inherited the kingdom of Jerusalem in right of his wife in 1186. The county was granted to Guy's brother Geoffrey in 1191 and then to Aimery of Lusignan, who went on to become king of Jerusalem with Hohenstaufen support in 1197. In *Parzival*, the landgrave of Schanpfanzûn, a city of many towers in Ascalûn (Wolfram's contemporaries reported that the city of Ascalon had fifty-three towers)[27] wishes to have control of the Grâl, and sends Gawân to win it for him.[28] Unlike Aimery and his Hohenstaufen supporters in their bid for Jerusalem, Gawân does not succeed. It will be argued below that in *Parzival* Gawân represents the Hohenstaufen Philip of Swabia; and that Wolfram, and his patron Hermann of Thuringia, did not support the Hohenstaufen bid for political control in the Holy Land.

The theory that Wolfram's Grâl castle is intended to be the city of Jerusalem was proposed in 1941 by Willem Snelleman. Other scholars, such as Helen Adolf, Margaret Fitzgerald Richey, Herbert Kolb and Stephen Knight have also deduced various connections between Wolfram's castle and Jerusalem. Adolf, developing her earlier theory on Chrétien's *Conte du Graal*, muddled the Church of the Holy Sepulchre (which appeared on the seal of the master of the Order of the Temple), the al-Aqsa mosque ('Temple of Solomon', the Templars' headquarters in Jerusalem) and the Dome of the Rock ('Templum Domini', home of the canons of the Temple), and proposed that Wolfram's Grâl stone was the Stone of the Dome of the Rock; but her confusion of the various holy sites does not lend credence to her theory.[29]

---

[26] For an overview of the subject, see Rudolf Hiestand, 'Kingship and Crusade in twelfth-century Germany', in *England and Germany in the High Middle Ages*, ed. Alfred Haverkamp and Hanna Vollrath (Oxford, 1996), pp. 235–65.

[27] *Itinerarium peregrinorum*, ed. Stubbs, Bk 5, ch. 6, p. 316; Denys Pringle, 'King Richard and the Walls of Ascalon', *Palestine Exploration Quarterly*, 116 (1984), 133–47, here 136; reprinted in his *Fortification and Settlement in Crusader Palestine* (Aldershot, 2000).

[28] Mayer, *The Crusades*, pp. 130–31; Riley-Smith, *Feudal Nobility*, pp. 117, 153–4; *Parzival*, Bk 8, lines 428.20–26.

[29] Willem Snelleman, *Das Haus Anjou und der Orient in Wolframs 'Parzival'* (Nijkerk, 1941); and see Bumke, *Wolfram von Eschenbach*, pp. 208, 214–17, 226–30; Herbert Kolb, *Munsalvaesche: Studien zum Kyot Problem* (Munich, 1963), for instance pp. 69, 178, cited by

In order to consider the possible Jerusalem connection of Wolfram's masterpiece in its contemporary context, it is necessary to consider the poem which most scholars acknowledge to have been Wolfram's true source: Chrétien de Troyes' *Conte du Graal*.

The 'Conte du Graal'. Chrétien's *Conte du Graal* has long been the subject of scholarly debate. It is the oldest surviving Grail romance, although a Grail romance may have been known before Chrétien began writing in the 1180s.[30] Despite Chrétien's reference in his prologue to a book which Philip of Alsace had lent him to use in writing his poem, his intentions in writing and the origins of his concept of the Grail, the bleeding lance, the wounded king and the Grail castle remain hotly debated. Chrétien's *graal* is actually a large plate or dish. Interpretation of the story is complicated by the fact that it is incomplete, and that the major character in at least half of it is not Perceval, the Grail-king's heir, but Lord Gauvain, King Arthur's nephew. The fact that Gawân is the Grail hero in another Grail romance, Henrich von dem Türlin's *Diu Crône*, would suggest that in the *Conte* Gauvain was intended to find the Grail and complete the adventure in which Perceval failed; but the preferred view of scholars has been that Gauvain was brought in as a contrast to Perceval, the worldly knight in contrast to Perceval's spiritual knight.[31]

In 1943 Helen Adolf published an article in which she set out to establish that Chrétien de Troye's Grail romance was in fact a '*roman à clef*'. She pointed out that the Graal Castle and the personalities involved there actually corresponded to actual places and actual people at the time Chrétien was writing, and that Philip of Alsace, count of Flanders, for whom Chrétien wrote the *Conte du Graal* and who lent him the book on which he based the story, was a central player in the actual events to which the *Conte* alludes. The Graal Castle, she argued, is the equivalent of Jerusalem. Perceval's relationship to the wounded king of the Graal Castle is exactly the same as Philip of Alsace's relationship to the Leper King of the kingdom of Jerusalem, Baldwin IV; they are first cousins (see fig. 4.1 for the rulers of Jerusalem and figs 4.2a and 4.2b for a comparison of Perceval and Philip's family relationships). Perceval's mother, whom he sets out to seek not realising that she is dead, is the equivalent of Philip's mother, Sybil of Anjou, who had travelled to Jerusalem

---

Bumke, p. 215; Richey, *Studies*, p. 133; Knight, 'From Jerusalem to Camelot', 228–9; Adolf, *Visio Pacis*, pp. 90–123, esp. 105–16. Medieval writers who did not know Jerusalem did tend to confuse the 'Templum Domini' with the 'Temple of Solomon', but Adolf does not seem to be aware of this; her confusion is all her own. On Adolf's original theory on the *Conte du Graal*, see below.

[30] The current scholarly view on this is summarised by Armel Diverres, 'The Grail and the Third Crusade: Thoughts on *Le Conte del Graal* by Chrétien de Troyes', *Arthurian Literature X*, ed. Richard Barber (Cambridge, 1990), pp. 13–109: here p. 16 and note 8.

[31] See, for example, Jean Frappier, 'Chrétien de Troyes', in *Arthurian Literature in the Middle Ages*, pp. 157–91, here pp. 189–90.

THE GRAIL

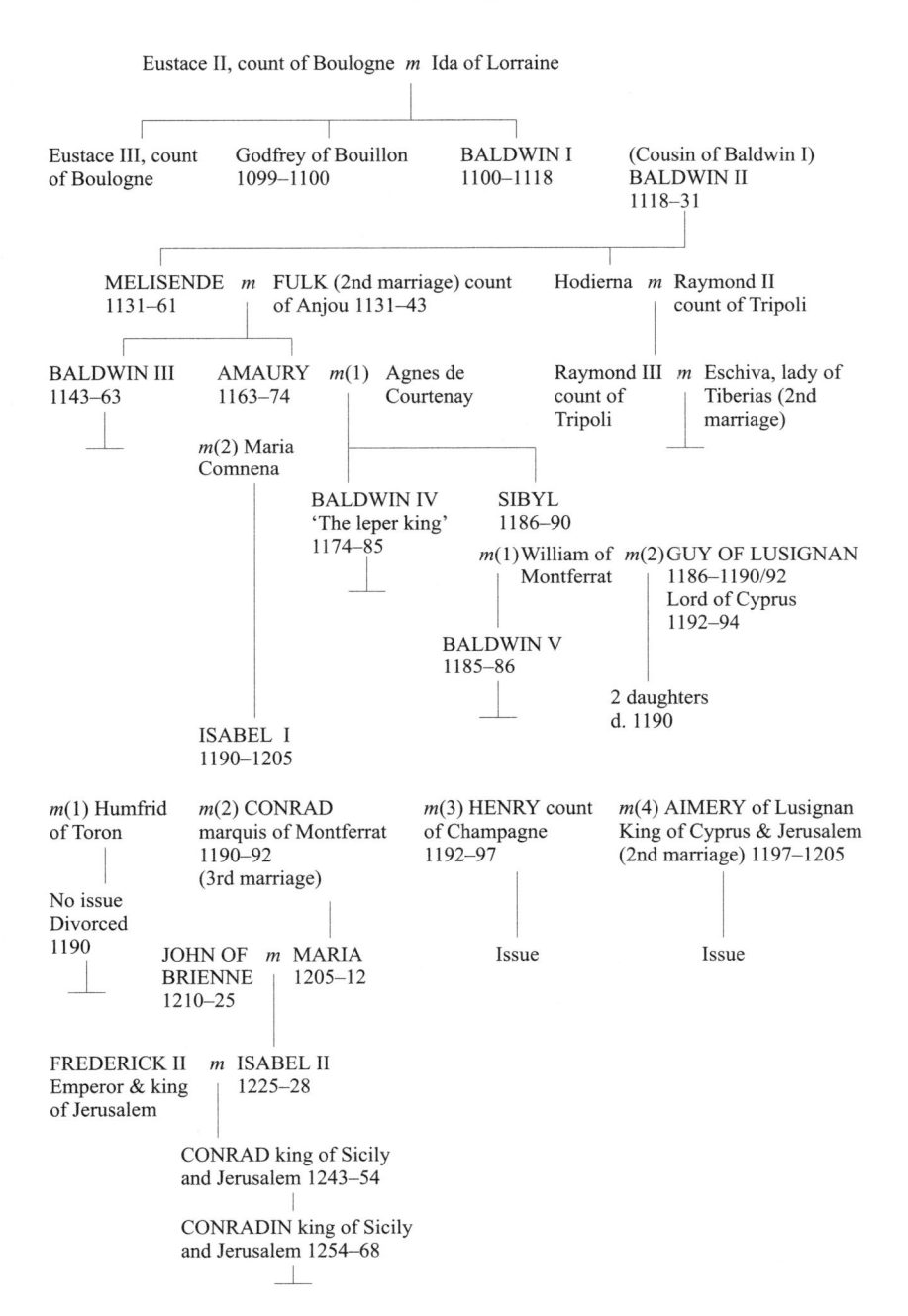

```
Eustace II, count of Boulogne  m  Ida of Lorraine
                                    |
   ┌──────────────┬──────────────┬──────────────┬──────────────┐
Eustace III, count  Godfrey of Bouillon  BALDWIN I   (Cousin of Baldwin I)
of Boulogne         1099–1100            1100–1118    BALDWIN II
                                                      1118–31
                                                         |
        ┌────────────────────────────────────┬──────────────────┐
   MELISENDE  m  FULK (2nd marriage) count          Hodierna  m  Raymond II
   1131–61       of Anjou 1131–43                                count of Tripoli
        |                                                            |
   ┌────┴─────────┐                                          ┌───────┴────────┐
BALDWIN III   AMAURY   m(1) Agnes de                     Raymond III  m  Eschiva, lady of
1143–63       1163–74       Courtenay                    count of        Tiberias (2nd
                                                         Tripoli         marriage)
              m(2) Maria
              Comnena
                    |
         ┌──────────┴────────┐
      BALDWIN IV          SIBYL
      'The leper king'    1186–90
      1174–85
                      m(1)William of  m(2)GUY OF LUSIGNAN
                          Montferrat      1186–1190/92
                                          Lord of Cyprus
                                          1192–94
                          |
                      BALDWIN V
                      1185–86
                                          2 daughters
                                          d. 1190
              ISABEL I
              1190–1205

m(1) Humfrid   m(2) CONRAD          m(3) HENRY count   m(4) AIMERY of Lusignan
of Toron       marquis of Montferrat of Champagne       King of Cyprus & Jerusalem
               1190–92                1192–97           (2nd marriage) 1197–1205
               (3rd marriage)
No issue
Divorced
1190
           JOHN OF   m  MARIA             Issue               Issue
           BRIENNE       1205–12
           1210–25

FREDERICK II    m   ISABEL II
Emperor & king      1225–28
of Jerusalem
                    |
           CONRAD king of Sicily
           and Jerusalem 1243–54
                    |
           CONRADIN king of Sicily
           and Jerusalem 1254–68
```

Fig. 4.1: The Rulers of the Kingdom of Jerusalem 1099–1268

```
                    'Best lineage of the Isles of the Sea'
      ┌──────────────────────┼──────────────────────┐
 Hidden recipient      Perceval's mother m      Hermit who
 whom Graal serves     a knight feared in the   advises Perceval
                       Isles of the Sea
      ┌──────┬──────┬──────┐         ┌──────┬──────┐
 Rich Fisher  Perceval's  Parent of   Two sons,  Perceval
 King, the    female      'Sore Pucele'  killed in
 wounded      cousin                  battle
 king of the  whose lover
 Graal Castle is dead
                         │
                    'Sore Pucele',
                    niece of Fisher
                    King, who sends
                    Perceval a sword
```

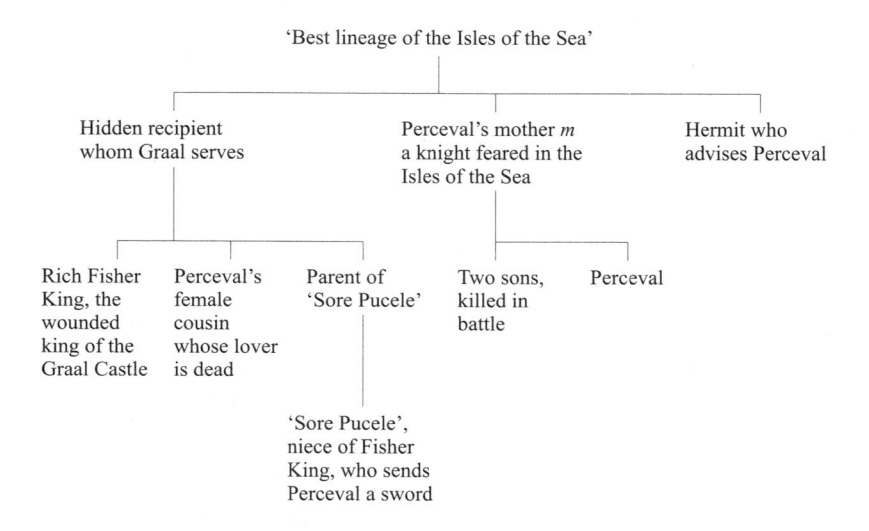

Fig. 4.2a: The maternal family relationships of Perceval in Chrétien's 'Conte du Graal'

in 1157 and died there, and whose grave Philip had visited in 1177. Perceval's bereaved cousin who berates him for failing to ask 'the question' in the Graal castle is the equivalent of Philip's recently bereaved cousin Sybil, heiress to the kingdom of Jerusalem; the cousin who sends Perceval a sword but does not appear before the Graal court may be the equivalent of Philip's cousin Isabel, who was a young child in 1177, too young to appear at court. Just as Perceval's first visit to the Graal Castle is a failure because he fails to ask 'the question' which will heal his cousin, so when Philip of Alsace had arrived the Holy Land in 1177, he had been expected by the lords of the realm to take over the regency on behalf of his sick cousin, but he had failed to do so. Now Philip was preparing to go again to the Holy Land, and Chrétien's story was to describe how, the second time, he fulfilled his duty. However, Chrétien never finished his book; either because of his own death, or because the count's death in 1191 and the failure of the Third Crusade to recapture Jerusalem made his message redundant. His continuators, therefore, either did not understand Chrétien's meaning or saw that it was no longer an attractive theme, and so 'what had been present history veiled by romance, became romance with a vague symbolic meaning'.[32] Adolf pointed out that her theory could not possibly

---

[32] Helen Adolf, 'An Historical Background for Chrétien's Perceval', *Publications of the Modern Language Association of America*, 58 (1943), 597–620. She later developed this theory

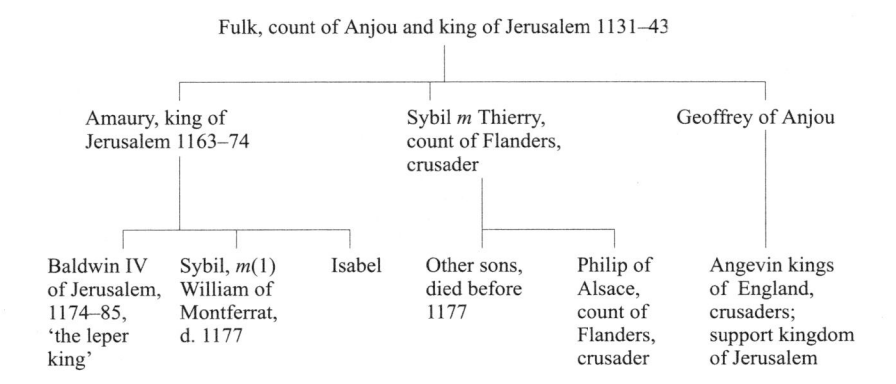

```
                    Fulk, count of Anjou and king of Jerusalem 1131-43
                                        |
      ┌─────────────────────────┬───────────────────────────┐
Amaury, king of            Sybil m Thierry,          Geoffrey of Anjou
Jerusalem 1163-74          count of Flanders,               |
      |                    crusader                         |
      |                         |                           |
  ┌───┬──────┬───────┐     ┌────┬──────────┐                |
Baldwin IV Sybil, m(1) Isabel Other sons, Philip of    Angevin kings
of Jerusalem, William of      died before Alsace,      of England,
1174-85,   Montferrat,        1177        count of     crusaders;
'the leper d. 1177                        Flanders,    support kingdom
king'                                     crusader     of Jerusalem
```

Fig. 4.2b: The maternal family relationships of Philip of Alsace, Count of Flanders (d. 1191)

explain the whole of Chrétien's story, because Chrétien had been following a book given to him by Philip of Alsace from which he drew some of his material; but it explained certain key events and references and gave a strong indication of date and Chrétien's purpose in writing.

Some scholars dismissed Adolf's theory out of hand: Eugène Vinaver wrote that nothing in the *Conte du Graal* and its later versions justified it.[33] Part of the problem was that scholars did not see the need for such a theory to understand Chrétien's poem; the problems which principally concerned them were the origins of the Grail as a Celtic or Christian symbol and the puzzling structure of the *Conte du Graal*, where Gauvain has almost as large a role as Perceval, and apparently replaces Perceval as hero after line 6292. Adolf's theory did not contribute to an elucidation of these problems.

Another problem may have been a reluctance among scholars to acknowledge the centrality of the physical city of Jerusalem to Christian faith and thought during this period, an attitude which has been rectified by the work of

---

further in her *Visio Pacis*. For the text of the *Conte du Graal*, see, for instance, *Les Romans de Chrétien de Troyes édités d'après la copie de Guiot (Bibl. nat., fr. 794), V: Le Conte du Graal (Perceval)*, ed. Félix Lecoy, 2 vols, CFMA 100, 103 (Paris, 1972-75). For Chrétien's continuators see Gerbert de Montreuil, *La Continuation de Perceval*, vols 1 and 2 ed. Mary Williams, vol. 3 ed. Marguerite Oswald, CFMA 28, 50, 107 (Paris, 1922-75); *The Continuations of the Old French Perceval of Chrétien de Troyes*, ed. W. Roach *et al.*, 5 vols in 6 (Philadelphia, 1949-83); *Elucidation*, ed. A.W. Thompson. On Philip of Alsace's pilgrimage to the East, see Phillips, *Defenders of the Holy Land*, pp. 232-9.

[33] Eugène Vinaver's notes to Leonardo Olschki, *The Grail Castle and its Mysteries*, trans. J.A. Scott (Manchester, 1966), p. 62.

many scholars in recent years.³⁴ But, even given the fact that Jerusalem was central to the Christian faith, Adolf did not fully explain why Chrétien should have transformed a Celtic symbol (assuming that this was the concept of the Grail which Chrétien found in Philip of Alsace's book and adapted) into a dish in the kingdom of Jerusalem. William of Tyre, writing in the 1180s, gave an account of an emerald dish at Caesarea which the Genoese took as their share of the booty after the capture of the city in 1101. From the second half of the thirteenth century, writers stated that this dish was the dish which Christ had used at the Last Supper and identified it with the Holy Grail. If Chrétien had heard this story in the 1180s it might have inspired him to place his Grail in the Holy Land. However, as James Douglas Bruce pointed out, William of Tyre made no mention of this dish being the Grail; and as Chrétien made no reference to Genoa in the *Conte du Graal*, there is no firm evidence that this was the inspiration for Chrétien's reinterpretation of the symbol.³⁵

A third problem was that previous attempts to attach the Grail romances to historical events had been discredited. J.S. Tunison suggested in a study published in 1904 that Galaad was intended as Henry the Young King, elder son of Henry II.³⁶ This theory was based on the assumption that the *Queste del Sainte Graal* was written by Walter Map, as its epilogue claims, a claim which modern scholarship has refuted.

Adolf's theory, however, was more firmly based both on the literary text and in historical events than Tunison's had been. Although her theory did not account for certain fundamental problems, it did explain other aspects of Chrétien's work which have long puzzled scholars. These include incidentals such as the comment at lines 3046–7, when Perceval first catches sight of the Grail Castle, that one would not see so fine a castle between here and Beirut. Ships sailing to the Holy Land from western Europe would sail to Cyprus, then – depending on the wind – generally sailed directly east until they came in sight of the Syrian coastline, then south to Tyre or Acre. This was the route which Richard the Lionheart took from Cyprus to Acre in June 1191. Philip's route to the Holy Land in 1177 is not recorded by the historian William of Tyre,

---

³⁴ For some recent scholarship see, for instance, J.G. Davis, 'Pilgrimage and Crusade Literature', in *Journeys Towards God*, ed. B.N. Sargent-Baur, pp. 1–30; Kaspar Elm, *Umbilicus mundi: Beiträge zur Geschichte Jerusalems, der Kreuzzüge, des Kapitels vom Hlg. Grab in Jerusalem und der Ritterorden* (Brugge, 1998); Bernard Hamilton, 'The Impact of Crusader Jerusalem on Western Christendom', *Catholic Historical Review*, 80 (1994), 695–713.

³⁵ Bruce, *Evolution*, pp. 360–62; William of Tyre, *Chronicon*, Bk 10, ch. 15 (16), 1, p. 471; Hans Mayer, *The Crusades*, trans. John Gillingham, 2nd edn (Oxford, 1988), pp. 68–9; see also for comparison Jessie Weston, 'Notes on the Grail romances: Caput Johannis = Corpus Christi', *Romania*, 49 (1923), 273–9: here 277.

³⁶ J.S. Tunison, *The Graal Problem – from Walter Map to Richard Wagner* (Cincinnati, 1904), pp. 18–30. For other such attempts see Diverres, 'The Grail and the Third Crusade', p. 22 note 27.

but as he landed at Acre it is likely that this was his route.[37] Beirut, as the most northerly city in the kingdom of Jerusalem, would be the first sight which the pilgrim would have of the kingdom. Hence, Chrétien is comparing Perceval's journey to a pilgrimage to the kingdom of Jerusalem; specifically, he is comparing it to Philip of Alsace's first pilgrimage to Jerusalem. It is also worth noting that as leprosy was regarded in the Middle Ages as an outward sign of sin, the leper-king, King Baldwin IV of Jerusalem, would have been literally *le roi Pescheor* in the sense of being a sinner king, as well as being represented in the *Conte du Graal* by *le roi Pescheor*, the fisher-king – as the old French word '*pescheor*' can mean both 'sinner' and 'fisher'.[38] Adolf's theory also explained major questions such as why Chrétien produced such a work for the count of Flanders; and why the work remained unfinished.

Other scholars took up or adapted Adolf's theory. In 1948 Urban Holmes suggested that the Graal Castle was 'a symbolical representation of the Temple of Solomon in Jerusalem' and that Philip of Alsace had commissioned Chrétien to develop in a popular romance the theme of the conversion of the Jewish people to Christianity.[39] In 1974 Claude Luttrell suggested that Chrétien's work was influenced by the preparations for the Third Crusade and that Chrétien accompanied Count Philip to the Holy Land.[40] In 1994 Stephen Knight surveyed Adolf's theory and agreed 'certainly it is clear that the *Conte du Graal* is written in the broad context of the crusades'.[41] In 1990 Armel Diverres published a substantial study taking up Adolf's theory and developing it in connection with the Third Crusade. After examining the historical background to the Third Crusade, especially the counts of Flanders' relations with the Holy Land, he went on to examine various details of the *Conte du*

---

[37] John H. Pryor, *Geography, Technology and War: Studies in the Maritime History of the Mediterranean, 649–1571* (Cambridge, 1988), pp. 95, 118. See also *Itinerarium peregrinorum*, ed. Stubbs, pp. 205, 210; Ambroise, *Estoire*, lines 2119–41; William of Tyre, *Chronicon*, Bk 21, ch. 13 (14), lines 1–3; 2, p. 979. In the early twelfth century, Saewulf went directly from Cyprus to Jaffa because of contrary winds: *Jerusalem Pilgrimage, 1099–1185*, ed. John Wilkinson with Joyce Hill and W.F. Ryan, Hakluyt Society, 2nd series, 167 (London, 1988), pp. 95–9; at the end of the fourteenth century, the lord of Anglure sailed from Cyprus directly to Beirut on his crusade to Jerusalem: *Le Saint Voyage de Jherusalem*, pp. 3–11.

[38] On leprosy as a sign of or metaphor for sin see, for instance, R.I. Moore, *The Formation of a Persecuting Society* (Oxford, 1987), pp. 60–65; on Baldwin IV's leprosy as a sign of sin see Edbury and Rowe, *William of Tyre*, p. 63.

[39] Urban T. Holmes, *A New Interpretation of Chrétien's Conte del Graal*, Studies in the Romance Languages and Literature, pamphlet no. 8 (1948), pp. 13, 29. He later developed this theory further: Urban T. Holmes and Sister M. Amelia Klenke, *Chrétien, Troyes and the Grail* (Chapel Hill, 1959).

[40] Claude A. Luttrell, *The Creation of the First Arthurian Romance: a Quest* (London, 1974), pp. 27–32; idem, 'The Prologue of Crestien's *Li Contes del Graal*', *Arthurian Literature III*, ed. Richard Barber (Cambridge, 1984), pp. 1–25: p. 11; cited by Diverres, 'The Grail and the Third Crusade', pp. 13–109: pp. 96–7, and note 192.

[41] Knight, 'From Jerusalem to Camelot', pp. 224–5.

Graal such as castles by the sea, placenames, the five years Perceval spends wandering without entering a church, various characters such as the loathly damsel, and episodes such as Perceval's visit to the Grail Castle, as well as Gauvain's adventures, drawing out the possible references to the Holy Land, the Muslims and the Third Crusade. He concluded by suggesting that Chrétien set out to write a 'family romance', embroidered around Philip of Flanders' family links with the ruling house of Jerusalem and underpinned by three important episodes in the life of the patron: his expedition to Jerusalem of 1177–78, the barons' revolt and his taking of the cross in January 1188.

However, after Philip died at the siege of Acre on 1 June 1191, Chrétien needed a new patron for the last portion of his incomplete romance. Diverres suggested that this was Henry of Champagne, son of Chrétien's former patron Marie of Champagne. Henry was a leading commander in the Third Crusade and went on to marry Isabel of Jerusalem, heiress to the kingdom, and to become ruler of the kingdom of Jerusalem (see fig. 4.1). Henry was also the nephew of both Richard I, king of England, and Philip II, king of France, both crusaders. Diverres suggested that when, in the *Conte*, Lord Gauvain replaces Perceval as the major figure, Gauvain is intended to represent Henry of Champagne, who historically replaced Philip of Alsace as potential ruler of the kingdom of Jerusalem. Diverres also suggested that the episode of Arthur holding court at Orquenie was supposed to represent Richard I's campaign in the Holy Land, June 1191 to October 1192, when he installed his nephew, Henry of Champagne, as *de facto* ruler of the kingdom of Jerusalem. This is certainly a plausible suggestion, given that Richard, as king of England and overlord of Scotland and Wales, was the successor to Arthur's throne, and that Richard was the owner of 'King Arthur's sword'.[42]

Diverre's theory had the great advantage that it also helped to account for one of the most difficult problems of the *Conte du Graal*: the intended role of Gauvain. The traditional view that he is intended to represent the worldly knight, concerned only with frivolity, is not supported by a careful analysis of Gauvain's journey to the *Roche de Champguin*. It seems odd, for instance, to dismiss his kindly goodness towards a little girl, the *Pucelle aux petites manches*, as misplaced courtliness inspired by the empty vanity of the court; surely his attitude towards her reveals a sensitivity and humanity lacking in the court and the world at large – and, one suspects, in the critics who have dismissed his kindness to a little girl. Rather, one is reminded of the words of Christ when He was explaining to His disciples the nature of true greatness:

> 'If any one would be first, he must be last of all and servant of all'. And he took a child, and put him in the midst of them; and taking him in his arms, he said to

---

[42] Diverres, 'The Grail and the Third Crusade', pp. 13–109, esp. pp. 97–100. Emma Mason, 'The Hero's Invincible Weapon', pp. 127–30.

them, 'Whoever receives one such child in my name receives me; and whoever receives me, receives the one who sent me'.[43]

There is more. Gauvain is himself good news to the poor (lines 8919–40); he takes under his escort l'Orguilleuse de Logres, who has seen her beloved murdered and is now vowed to destroy every man who comes her way, bears her insults patiently and obeys her commands, so that she is finally brought to peace of heart, and is welcomed into the Roche Champguin (lines 8649–732). The inhabitants of the Roche Champguin, meanwhile, were effectively prisoners there, waiting for the promised ruler who would see justice done to the disinherited women, find husbands for the maidens and knight the young men (lines 7313–52). This promised king is Gauvain. Gauvain, in fact, comes like Christ to 'bring good news to the poor, bind up the broken hearted, and to set the captives free'.[44]

This aspect of Gauvain's activity in the *Conte du Graal* was studied at length by Guy Vial. He demonstrated convincingly that there is a deliberate parallel between the adventures of Perceval and Gauvain, and that Gauvain is a Christ-figure, who comes to save, to serve, to suffer, be crucified and rise from the dead: 'the adventures of Gauvain ... allegorically recall the redemptive sacrifice of Jesus, who died to save us from the ties of sin'.[45]

If Gauvain plays such an important role in Chrétien's *Conte du Graal*, then any historical interpretation of the work must take Gauvain into account, as did Diverres' interpretation. Diverre's assessment of Gauvain concurred with Vial's: 'In no way can Gauvain be considered in these later adventures as a mere foil to Perceval ... On the contrary, he behaves with charity throughout and is considered free from all the vices'.[46] In fact Gauvain's Christly qualities support Diverre's interpretation of Gauvain as Henry of Champagne, a commander of the Third Crusade. It would be entirely reasonable for a crusading commander, leader of Christ's army on earth, and the future ruler of the earthly kingdom of Jerusalem, to be depicted as a saviour, Christ-like figure – since Christ is the commander of the hosts of Heaven and ruler of the heavenly Jerusalem (for instance, in Revelations ch. 19 vv. 11–16, and ch. 11 v. 15). Gauvain's actions also mirror the duties actually performed by crusading leaders: for instance, one of the responsibilities of Richard the Lionheart as a leader of the Third Crusade was to provide for the noble women dispossessed by Saladin's conquests.[47]

In short, although problems remained, the work of Adolf and Diverres indicated that Chrétien did intend his Graal Castle to represent the earthly

---

[43] Gospel of Mark, ch. 9 vv. 35–7: Revised Standard Version.
[44] Gospel of Luke, ch. 4 v. 18; Isaiah ch. 61 v. 1.
[45] Guy Vial, *Le Conte du Graal: sens et unité* (Geneva, 1987): here p. 97.
[46] Diverres, 'The Grail and the Third Crusade', p. 88.
[47] *Itinerarium peregrinorum et gesta regis Ricardi*, Bk 2, ch. 23, p. 172.

Jerusalem; yet his continuators did not obviously continue this theme. Perhaps they did not understand Chrétien's allegory, or perhaps – more likely – they or their patrons did not consider it to be useful. Diverres suggested that the 'Third Continuation' of Manessier, written for Joanna, countess of Flanders, in which Perceval is crowned Grail king, represents the Fourth Crusade, in which Baldwin of Flanders was crowned emperor of Constantinople.[48] The parallels with Chrétien's suggested theme, however, are not obvious. If Gauvain was intended by Chrétien to be Henry of Champagne, then this would be consonant with the only partial success of his visit to the Grail Castle in the First Continuation (as the Third Crusade did not recover Jerusalem), but does not explain Gauvain's subsequent adventures. It seems easier to assume that Chrétien's continuators did not set out to continue his biographical allegory, but only his spiritual allegory.

Wolfram, however, made the allegory explicit, by calling his Grâl guardians 'Templars'. His audience would know that the Templars guarded Jerusalem; so, clearly, the Grâl Castle *is* Jerusalem. The Templars, then, were included in order to give the story a vital connection with contemporary events which would aid the audience to understand the author's intention. To underline the point, he claimed that the story was originally written in *heidensch*, 'heathenish', that is, Arabic, an indication that it was based in Muslim lands.[49]

But why should Wolfram have been so anxious to identify his Grâl castle as Jerusalem, when Chrétien had been content to leave the identification ambiguous? It is also interesting that Wolfram went to the trouble of separating his work from Chrétien's by claiming an independent Provençal source and stating that Chrétien misinterpreted the story. This could simply mean that Chrétien was wrong in not identifying the Graal Castle clearly as Jerusalem. But why did it matter? Alternatively, if, as does appear possible, Chrétien had intended Gauvain to finally achieve the adventure of the Grail rather than Perceval, then Wolfram's comment could be interpreted as meaning that Chrétien was wrong in making the wrong knight complete the quest. But why should he care?

Did Wolfram also mean something more by his story than simply telling a tale? Whom do his Parzivâl and Gawân represent? This is a complex question, and it is necessary to discuss it at length in order to establish what Wolfram's fundamental purpose in writing may have been and thereby to appreciate the full significance of the Templars' role within his poem.

'Parzival' and the kingdom of Jerusalem. By the time that Wolfram wrote *Parzival*, there was no rivalry to the throne of the kingdom of Jerusalem. Henry of Champagne died in September 1197, but Aimery of Lusignan, king

---

[48] Diverres, 'The Grail and the Third Crusade', p. 100.
[49] *Parzival*, Bk 8, lines 416.25–7.

of Cyprus, was chosen as king by the barons of the kingdom and the leaders of the German crusade, headed by the imperial chancellor Conrad of Querfurt, bishop of Hildesheim. Aimery was already a vassal of the German emperor, Henry VI, who had bestowed his crown upon him; the chancellor Conrad had crowned him king of Cyprus in September 1197. The fact that Aimery was already an imperial vassal would have made him the imperial chancellor's obvious choice as king of Jerusalem. Having been chosen as king of Jerusalem, Aimery then married the heiress to the kingdom, Isabel of Jerusalem, as Henry of Champagne had done before him after having been chosen in a similar manner during the Third Crusade. Isabel and Aimery ruled until their deaths in 1205, when they were succeeded by Isabel's daughter Maria (see fig. 4.1). Maria's father was Conrad of Montferrat, whose mother, Giuletta, was the sister of Frederick and Conrad III of Hohenstaufen and thus the aunt of the emperor Frederick Barbarossa (see fig. 4.7b). At first glance, therefore, it does not seem likely that Wolfram was simply following Chrétien (as interpreted by Adolf and Diverres) and writing about the succession to the kingdom of Jerusalem.

Snelleman drew attention to the fact that Parzivâl's father, Gahmuret, was an Angevin, son of a king from Anjou. He suggested that Gahmuret represented Richard the Lionheart, Angevin king of England, son of Henry II, king of England, count of Anjou; and Gahmuret's long wanderings in the East, fighting and befriending Muslims, represents the Third Crusade. He went on to point out that Parzivâl, unlike Gahmuret, is not a man of courtly love and fighting for glory against the Muslims. Parzivâl is loyal in love and under his rule over the Grâl castle a Muslim warrior (Feirefîz) is welcomed in. Although the Muslim has to become a Christian, it is a new form of Christianity, a Grail Christianity, in which Muslims and Christians come together and live at peace. Therefore, according to Snelleman, Wolfram was proposing a new future of peace and co-operation between the two religions. He brought in the Templars as his Grâl-guardians to stress the connection with Richard the Lionheart, a patron of the Templars, and the crusading background to the story.[50]

Although Snelleman's historical argument can be faulted, its general lines are sound, and this interpretation at least holds water. Wolfram was writing at a time when the conversion, rather than the destruction, of Muslims had become an explicit aim of crusading, and his desire to convert the Muslims peacefully can be set alongside the writings of Joachim of Fiore or James of Vitry on the necessity of bringing about Muslim conversions.[51] The Templars, then, appear as a message to the reader that the story is about relations between Christians

---

[50] Snelleman, *Das Haus Anjou*, pp. 47–73, 75–144, especially 121–44, and 169, 195. Adolf suggested that Wolfram had a specific Angevin source for his poem, but gave no indication what sort of source she envisaged: *Visio Pacis*, p. 95.

[51] Benjamin Z. Kedar, *Crusade and Mission: European Approaches toward the Muslims* (Princeton, 1984), pp. 57–85, 112–35.

and Muslims, and perhaps to indicate that the new religion will be based in Jerusalem. Perhaps this Jerusalem represents an earthly paradise, or perhaps it indicates God and the centre of Christianity. In any case, the emphasis is on God's love, not God's violence; hence the 'Templars' bear a turtle dove, the sign of God's faithful love, not a cross, the sign of God's suffering and bloodshed.

Yet, much as this is the framework of the story, it does not account for the details. Once again we have the problem of Gawân. Is it sufficient to assume that he merely represents the courtly lifestyle and courtly love which Parzivâl, and the new religion, must pass through, but finally reject in favour of God's love? Gawân is clearly a doughty, honourable and good knight, kind to the little girl Obilôt, modest and humble, a healer, and a sufficiently outstanding example of knighthood to be a serious rival to Parzivâl as Grâl knight; and he, too, finally finds a permanent love in the form of Lady Orgelûse.[52] Bearing in mind Diverre's theory on the *Conte du Graal*, it would be reasonable to try to identify a stronger role for Gawân, and a more definite role for Parzivâl than being the hoped-for king of some yet-unseen future.

As Wolfram emphasizes that Chrétien misinterpreted the story of the Grail, this indicates that in order to find his meaning, it is necessary to consider what Wolfram changed from Chrétien's story. The first and most obvious change is that he begins with the history of Parzivâl's crusading father Gahmuret, who travels in the East, marries Belacâne, abandons her, and finally marries the beautiful Herzeloyde. Gahmuret is an Angevin. Parzivâl is the nephew, not the cousin of the Grâl king. Parzivâl's various family relationships on his fathers' and his mothers' side are set out in detail, with nearly all individuals given full names. There is a particular emphasis on loyal love. The *Templeise* are introduced as Grâl guardians, and the Grâl Castle is Munsalvâtsche, the mount of Salvation. Parzivâl has an encounter with one of the *Templeise* in a joust, defeats him and takes his horse, but is turned away from the Grâl Castle. Gawân marries Orgelûse, but is defeated by Parzivâl; he becomes a king, but not of the Grâl Castle. Parzivâl returns a second time to the Grâl Castle, asks 'the question', and becomes Grâl king. He marries his love Condwîrâmûrs. Parzivâl's Muslim brother, Feirefîz, fights with Parzivâl, comes to the Grâl Castle, is converted to Christianity and marries the Grâl maiden, Repanse de Schoye, who is Parzivâl's aunt. The story ends with a discussion of the heirs of these two couples, Prester John and Loherangrîn, who is identified with the Swan knight, and who marries a duchess of Brabant.

Some of these changes have been explained or partially explained by Snelleman. Snelleman's identification of Gahmuret with Richard the Lionheart of England seems to have a reasonable basis, and has won some

---

[52] See *Parzival*, Bk 14, line 695.2–7; *Parzival*, trans. Hatto, p. 347 note, p. 425.

acceptance from scholars.[53] The Grâl Castle is obviously Jerusalem, as it is on a hill, guarded by Templars, and Wolfram's successors clearly believed that it was intended as Jerusalem. Parzivâl's return to the Grâl Castle, asking of the question and marriage to his love is a reasonable ending to the story as begun by Chrétien. Feirefîz's conversion, as Snelleman argues, is what we would expect in the context of Wolfram's attitude towards the Muslims and his message. Likewise, the emphasis on faithful love is a characteristic of Wolfram. Snelleman explains both Wolfram's attitude to the Muslims and to love by deducing that Wolfram's 'message' is a depiction of a future Christianity which emphasises God's faithful love and into which Muslims and Christians are welcomed.

This leaves us with the problem of why it is so important that Parzivâl should be the son of an Angevin, why the relationship between the Grâl king and the hero has changed, why Parzivâl's family tree is given in such detail with nearly all individuals named (unlike Chrétien's story, in which only Perceval is given a name), whether the introduction of the *Templeise* does more than indicate a heavenly Jerusalem or earthly paradise of the future, and why Prester John and the Swan Knight are introduced.

Prester John first came to the attention of western Europeans in the work of Otto, bishop of Freising, who wrote that he had been told about him by Bishop Hugh of Jabala, in the crusader states, in 1145. Prester John was believed to be the priest-ruler of a rich kingdom in Asia. In about 1165 a letter began to circulate in western Europe which purported to be from Prester John to Manuel Comnenus, Byzantine emperor, and to have been forwarded by Manuel to the Emperor Frederick Barbarossa. 'Prester John' depicted his kingdom as an earthly paradise, except for the lack of horses; and explained that he, a priest, controlled both Church and State, including the Church leaders. In contrast, in western Europe the emperor and Pope Alexander III were battling over the question of whether the emperor could control the Church, or whether the Church should be above secular control. Modern scholarship has deduced that this letter from 'Prester John' was actually a forgery, commissioned by Rainald of Dassel, Frederick's chancellor, to demonstrate that the emperor's concept of Church-State relations produced harmony in the Christian world and allowed Christians to unite to fight the enemies of Christendom, in contrast to the papal concept, which led only to war.[54]

---

[53] For a survey see Martin H. Jones, 'Richard the Lionheart in German Literature of the Middle Ages', in *Richard Coeur de Lion in History and Myth*, ed. Janet L. Nelson (London, 1992), pp. 70–116, here 93–9 and notes.
[54] Bernard Hamilton, 'Prester John and the Three Kings of Cologne', in *Prester John, the Mongols and the Ten Lost Tribes*, ed. Charles F. Beckingham and Bernard Hamilton (Aldershot, 1996), pp. 171–85, here p. 177; previously published in *Studies in Medieval History presented to R.H.C. Davis*, ed. H. Mayr-Harting and R.I. Moore (London, 1985), pp. 177–91.

Whether or not Wolfram was aware that the letter was a forgery, he would have been well aware that Prester John's kingdom was an earthly paradise where Church and State were governed by one ruler, and that this paralleled the western imperial concept of the state. His reference to Prester John certainly indicates that he was interested in the expansion of Christianity – which is clear from elsewhere in his work – but it also suggests an interest in the role and authority of the emperor, for the emperors wished to govern Church and State in the same way as Prester John.

When Wolfram was writing, the imperial crown of western Europe was being fiercely disputed. As there was no obvious role for Parzivâl and Gawân in the Middle East while Wolfram was writing, and bearing in mind Wolfram's apparent interest in the imperial office, it is possible that these characters represent the rival parties in the politics of the Empire in the first decade of the thirteenth century. This may seem wildly fantastic, but as many theories on the meaning of the Grail romances seem wildly fantastic, it is at least worth considering the possibility.

The first question must be whether there was any connection between the western emperors and Jerusalem. In fact, the emperors had a considerable interest in the crusade and in Jerusalem. Successive emperors and emperors-elect had been involved in the crusade.[55] Conrad III of Hohenstaufen, king of the Romans, took part in the Second Crusade of 1147–48; Frederick I Barbarossa took part in the Second Crusade and set out on the Third Crusade but died tragically *en route*; his son, Duke Frederick of Swabia, played an important role in the siege of Acre before his death from disease in January 1191. The emperor Henry VI planned a crusade for 1197, but died before he was able to join it himself. The crusade, however, reached the Holy Land and recovered significant territory, including Beirut, although it lost Jaffa and failed to recapture Tîbnîn. Henry's chancellor Conrad also crowned Aimery of Lusignan as king of Cyprus, and Aimery did homage to the emperor; Aimery was then elected king of Jerusalem through the chancellor's influence. From 1197 to 1205, therefore, the kingdom of Jerusalem was ruled by a vassal of the emperor. In 1198 the chancellor Conrad, by the authority of the emperor Henry VI, granted Leon of Cilician Armenia a crown. Cilician Armenia was an Armenian Christian state to the north of the principality of Antioch and the kingdom of Jerusalem; through granting a crown to Leon, the chancellor made this kingdom an imperial vassal-state. In 1211 the emperor Otto IV sent a new crown to Leon of Armenia, and Leon publicly acknowledged his dependency on the emperor. Cyprus also remaned an imperial fief under Otto IV, although not until the emperor Frederick's crusade in 1228 did the emperors succeed

---

[55] For a general survey, see Hiestand, 'Kingship and Crusade in twelfth-century Germany'.

in re-enforcing their suzerainty over Cyprus.[56] Shortly before Wolfram wrote *Parzival*, Philip of Swabia, king of the Romans (that is, emperor-elect) played a decisive role in the lead-up to the Fourth Crusade; it was his support for the deposed emperor Isaac II of Constantinople and his son Alexius (father and brother of his wife Irene) which led to the diversion of the Fourth Crusade to Constantinople. In 1203 Philip promised Pope Innocent III that, if he were crowned emperor, he would lead a crusade to the East to unite the Eastern and Western churches.[57] Otto IV took the cross in 1209, with the intention of going to recover Jerusalem. He sent an embassy to the Latin East in July 1210, and received an embassy from al-'Adil, brother and successor of Saladin and overlord of the Ayyubid Empire, in September 1210. But his own political position quickly deteriorated, so that he was not able to set out on crusade.[58]

The emperors, as secular leaders of Latin Christendom, also had a vested interest in recovering and controlling Jerusalem, to reinforce their power and claim to spiritual authority as God's appointed rulers of the West. What is more, the old legend of the Last World Emperor – which originated in Byzantium and dated back to at least the seventh century AD – stressed the connection between the emperor and Jerusalem: the last great emperor would end his reign in Jerusalem, where he would hand over his imperial power to God.[59] Charlemagne, the first emperor of the West since the disintegration of the old Roman empire, was popularly believed to have led a crusade to Jerusalem, and during the First and Second Crusades there were expectations that a triumphal emperor would arise who would recover Jerusalem.[60] After Wolfram wrote, in 1225 Frederick II Hohenstaufen married Isabel II, heiress to the throne of Jerusalem, and became king of Jerusalem; and from then until the

---

[56] Edbury, *Kingdom of Cyprus and the Crusades*, pp. 31–3, 56; T.S.R. Boase, 'The History of the Kingdom', in *The Cilician Kingdom of Armenia*, ed. T.S.R. Boase (Edinburgh and London, 1978), pp. 1–33, here 18–19; Jonathan Riley-Smith, 'The Templars and the Teutonic Knights in Cilician Armenia', in *The Cilician Kingdom of Armenia*, pp. 92–117, here 111, 113; Naumann, *Kreuzzug Kaiser Heinrichs VI*, pp. 210, 223, 230. For Henry VI's political and dynastic motives in the crusade see Naumann, pp. 106–19. For Otto IV and Armenia see Bernd Ulrich Hucker, *Kaiser Otto IV*, MGH Schriften, 34 (Hanover, 1990), pp. 170–75.

[57] Donald E. Queller, *The Fourth Crusade: The Conquest of Constantinople, 1201–1204* (Leicester, 1978), pp. 30–34, 44, 45, 57, 69–70, 94. Queller added, p. 174, note 81: 'There is a little evidence that at an earlier date Philip had been invited by a Greek conspirator to take the Byzantine throne himself in the name of his wife'; see also p. 188, note 15. See now the second edition, Donald E. Queller and Thomas F. Madden, *The Fourth Crusade and the Conquest of Constantinople* (Philadelphia, 1997), pp. 33–7, 46, 64, 66–7, 82–8, 144, 310, 319. On Philip's proposed crusade see Hucker, *Kaiser Otto IV*, pp. 91–2, 126.

[58] Hucker, *Kaiser Otto IV*, pp. 127–31, 137–42.

[59] Marjorie Reeves, 'Originality and Influence of Joachim of Fiore', *Traditio*, 36 (1980), 269–316: here 274–5.

[60] See Norman Cohn, *The Pursuit of the Millenium: Revolutionary millenarians and mystical anarchists of the Middle Ages* (London, 1957; revised edn, 1993), pp. 71–4, 84.

death of the last Hohenstaufen heir in 1268, the Hohenstaufen candidate to the empire was also titular or absentee king of Jerusalem. Frederick II took the cross in 1215, although his crusade did not take place until 1228–29, when he succeeded in recovering Jerusalem by negotiation.

It is at least possible, then, that Wolfram's Grail king is intended to be the equivalent, not of the king of Jerusalem as in the suggested interpretation of Chrétien's *Conte du Graal*, but of the emperor; an emperor who also claims overlordship over Jerusalem.

At the time that Wolfram was writing, the rival candidates for the imperial crown were the Welf Otto of Brunswick, the Hohenstaufen Philip of Swabia (both elected in 1198), and the latter's nephew the Hohenstaufen Frederick of Sicily. Otto was a nephew of King Richard I and King John of England. His mother, Matilda, was daughter of Henry II, king of England, duke of Normandy and count of Anjou. Henry II himself was the son of Count Geoffrey of Anjou and grandson of Count Fulk of Anjou, who had become king of Jerusalem in 1131 after his marriage to Melisende of Jerusalem. Otto was crowned emperor on 4 October 1209, but after his invasion of Sicily in 1210 Pope Innocent III excommunicated him and transferred papal support to Frederick of Hohenstaufen. Otto had the support of King John of England and of some of the Rhineland, Saxon and Low Country princes, but after his defeat at the Battle of Bouvines on 27 July 1214 he was effectively deposed. He died on 19 May 1218 at Harzburg castle in Lower Saxony.

Philip of Swabia was the son of the emperor Frederick I and brother of Henry VI. He was crowned king of the Romans on 6 January 1205, but was assassinated on 21 June 1208. Frederick II was the son of Henry VI, and was crowned king of the Romans on 9 December 1212 at Mainz, recrowned in the proper place, Aachen, on 25 July 1215 – after the downfall of Otto IV – and crowned emperor on 22 November 1220.

So let us, then, suppose that to Wolfram, the king of the Grâl Castle is the emperor. The most obvious connection between the three candidates above and the characters in *Parzival* is Otto of Brunswick's connection with the Angevin dynasty of England, for Parzivâl's father was, as Snelleman reminds us, Gahmuret of Anjou. Like Parzivâl, Otto was the grandson of an Angevin monarch (see figs 4.3, 4.4a and 4.4b). Just as Parzivâl's connection with the Grâl Castle is through his mother, so Otto's connection with Jerusalem was through his mother, Matilda, daughter of Henry II of England; for Henry II had a claim to the kingdom of Jerusalem through his grandfather Fulk of Anjou, former king of Jerusalem. Henry was a cousin of Baldwin IV, the 'leper-king', and had been offered the crown of Jerusalem in 1185. Otto's uncle Richard I had claimed the kingdom of Jerusalem while he was in the Holy Land, and had given his consent to the election of his nephew Henry of Champagne as king;

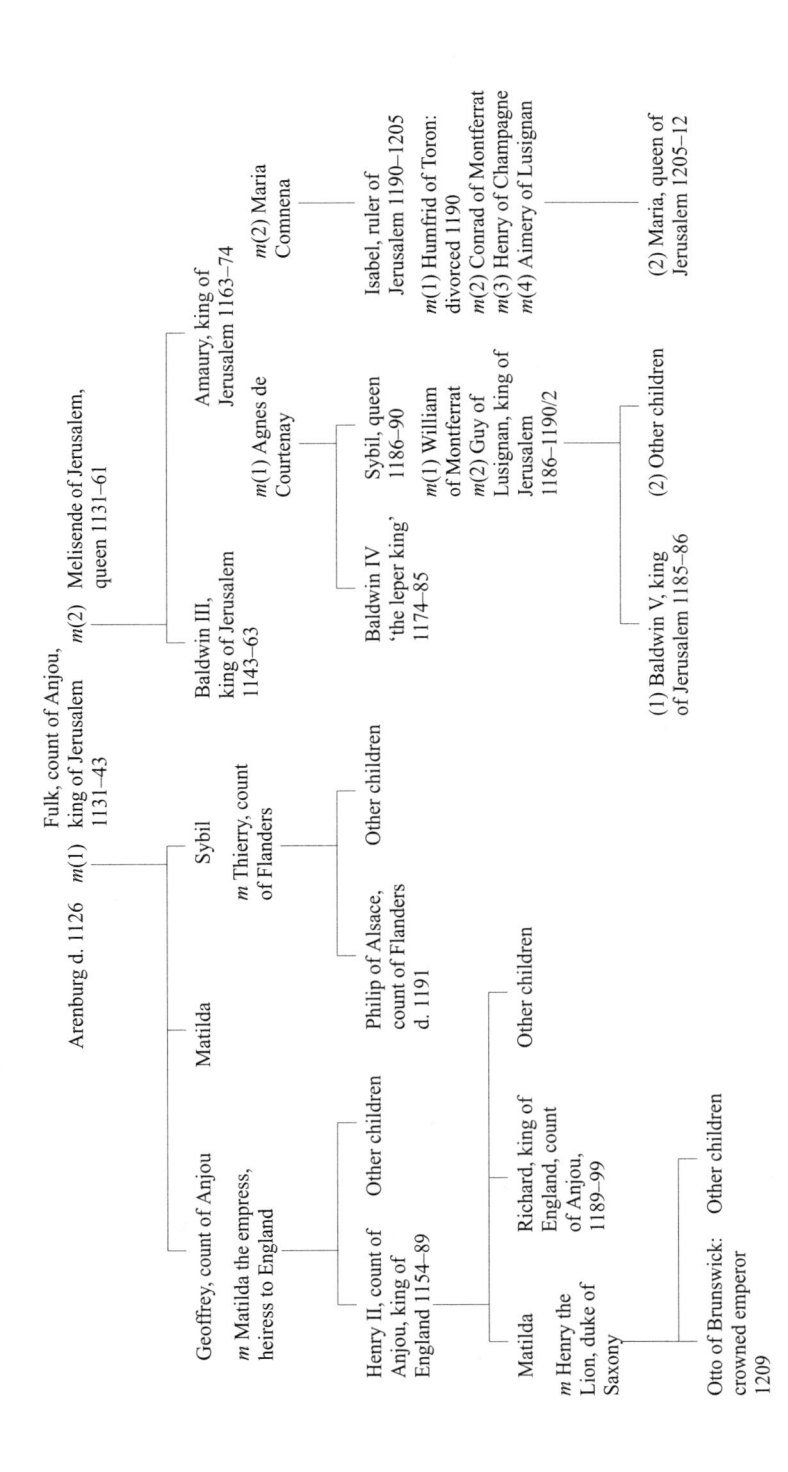

Fig. 4.3: The Relationship of the House of Anjou with the Rulers of Jerusalem, 1131–1212

128   CHAPTER FOUR

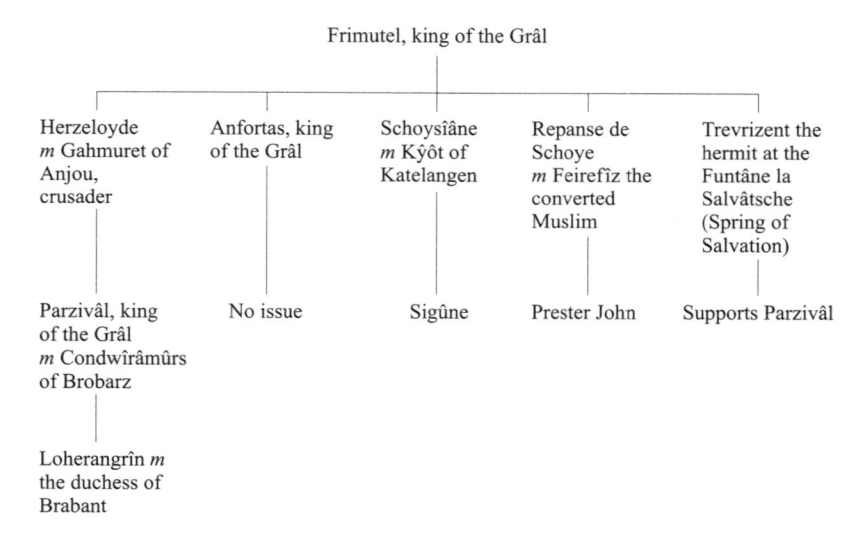

```
                          Frimutel, king of the Grâl
    ┌──────────────┬──────────────┬──────────────┬──────────────┐
Herzeloyde    Anfortas, king   Schoysîâne    Repanse de    Trevrizent the
m Gahmuret of   of the Grâl    m Kŷôt of     Schoye        hermit at the
Anjou,                         Katelangen    m Feirefîz the  Funtâne la
crusader                                     converted      Salvâtsche
                                             Muslim         (Spring of
                                                            Salvation)

Parzivâl, king   No issue       Sigûne       Prester John   Supports Parzivâl
of the Grâl
m Condwîrâmûrs
of Brobarz

Loherangrîn m
the duchess of
Brabant
```

Fig. 4.4a: The maternal family relationships of Parzivâl

in effect, Henry was made ruler of the kingdom of Jerusalem by Richard.[61] As John Gillingham remarks, 'at Richard's court the kingdom of Jerusalem was looked upon as a family inheritance'.[62] Or again, as the fifteenth-century English chronicler John Hardyng put it, 'King Richard gave Jerusalem and the kingdom of Syria to his sister's son Henry earl of Champagne ... but in his gift of Syria and Jerusalem he reserved the resort to him and to his heirs'.[63] Felix Fabri, writing in the 1480s, went further: he believed that King Richard had actually become king of Jerusalem in addition to being king of England, and wore two crowns.[64] Hardyng and Fabri are late sources, but they express the situation clearly.

---

[61] W.L. Warren, *Henry II* (London, 1973), pp. 604–7; Hans Eberhard Mayer, 'Henry II of England and the Holy Land', *English Historical Review*, 97 (1982), 721–39: here 731–4; on Richard I and the Holy Land, see *Itinerarium peregrinorum*, ed. Stubbs, Bk 4, ch. 31, p. 295 (for his claim to the kingdom), Bk 5, ch. 34, pp. 346–7 (for his confirmation of Henry's election); Ambroise, *Estoire*, lines 7371–84, 8987–9011.

[62] John Gillingham, 'Roger of Howden on crusade', in *Medieval Historical Writing in the Christian and Islamic Worlds*, ed. David O. Morgan (London, 1982), pp. 60–75: here p. 72 note 27. This was reprinted in his *Richard Coeur de Lion: Kingship, Chivalry and War in the Twelfth Century* (London and Rio Grande, 1994), pp. 141–53, here p. 146 note 27, and see p. 101. See also John Prestwich, 'Richard Coeur de Lion: *Rex Bellicosus*', in *Richard Coeur de Lion in History and Myth*, pp. 1–16, here pp. 6–7.

[63] *The Chronicle of Iohn Hardyng ... together with the Continuation by Richard Grafton*, ed. Henry Ellis (London, 1812), p. 266.

[64] Felix Fabri, *The Book of the Wanderings of Brother Felix Fabri*, trans. Aubrey Stewart, Palestine Pilgrims' Text Society, 9, part 3 (London, 1893), pp. 348–9.

THE GRAIL   129

Henry II, count of Anjou and king of England:
offered crown of Jerusalem 1185

Matilda m Henry the Lion, crusader	Richard, king of England: effective ruler of kingdom of Jerusalem 1191–1192	Eleanor m Alfonso, king of Castile	Joanna Refused marriage with al-'Adil, Saladin's brother, unless he converted from Islam to Christianity	John, king of England
Otto of Brunswick, emperor-elect (crowned as Otto IV 1209) betrothed to Marie of Brabant	No legitimate issue	Blanche of Castile		Supports Otto

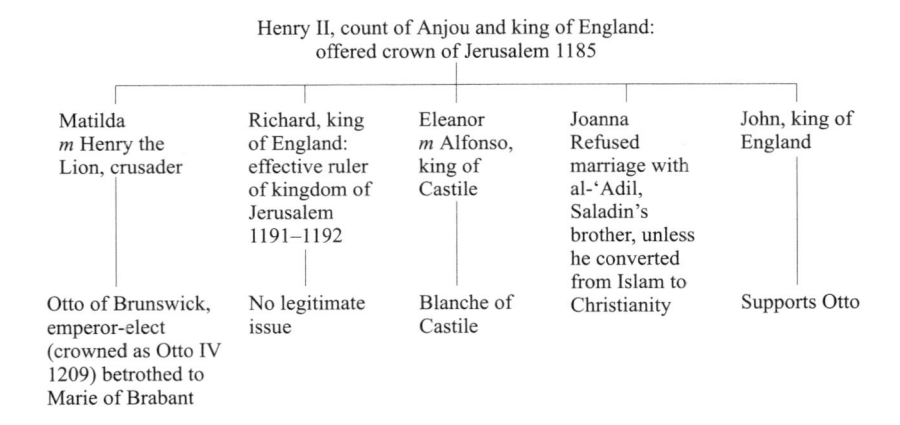

Fig. 4.4b: The maternal family relationships of Otto of Brunswick before June 1208

Like Parzivâl, Otto's father married twice; Henry the Lion divorced his first wife, Clementia of Zähringen, in 1162, and subsequently married Matilda of England. Like Parzivâl's mother, Otto's mother was a famous beauty, and again like Parzivâl's mother, Otto's mother died in sad circumstances. Matilda died in June 1189 when her husband and eldest son had been exiled from Germany by Emperor Frederick Barbarossa.

Like Parzivâl, Otto had a crusading father: Henry the Lion had been on pilgrimage to the Holy Land in 1172. Otto's elder brother, Henry count palatine of the Rhine, also went on crusade to the Holy Land in 1197. What was more, having spent much of his childhood at the English court, Otto was very close to his uncle, Richard I of England, for whom he had been a hostage during Richard's imprisonment in Germany, 1193–94. Richard had bestowed his own county of Poitou on this favoured nephew in 1194, and for a time he may have regarded him as his preferred heir. He promoted him vigorously as a candidate for the imperial throne after the death of Henry VI in 1197. On his death, Richard left Otto all his jewels and three quarters of his treasure.[65] In this respect, the crusading Angevin was effectively a second father to Otto.

---

[65] See, for instance, John T. Appleby, *England Without Richard, 1189–1199* (London, 1965), pp. 185–6, 211, 231. On Henry the Lion, Matilda of Anjou and Otto's childhood see Karl Jordan, *Henry the Lion: a biography* (Oxford, 1986), esp. pp. 150–54, 183–4, 188–9; Hucker, *Kaiser Otto IV*, pp. 4–9. On Henry's pilgrimage, see especially Einar Joranson, 'The Palestine Pilgrimage of Henry the Lion', in *Medieval and Historiographical Essays in Honor of James Westfall Thompson*, ed. James Lea Cate and Eugene N. Anderson (Port Washington, New York, 1966), pp. 146–225. On Richard and Otto, see Prestwich, '*Rex Bellicosus*', p. 5; Hucker, *Kaiser Otto IV*, pp. 9–21; John Gillingham, *Richard I* (New Haven and London, 1999), p. 248 note 94, p. 272 note 16, p. 279, p. 311–12, p. 335 note 1.

It is not impossible, then, that Parzivâl could be intended as Otto. However, there is an obvious problem with this comparison of Parzivâl's and Otto's family relationships. According to this interpretation, the fact that Parzivâl will rule Jerusalem implies that the imperial throne and government of Jerusalem go together, which at this time they did not; this did not become the case until 1225, when Frederick II of Hohenstaufen married Isabel II of Jerusalem. Again, the Angevin relationship, the crusading connections and the relationship with the monarchy of Jerusalem in *Parzival* do not tie up precisely with the corresponding relationships of Otto of Brunswick. Otto's dynastic claim to the imperial throne was through his father, not his mother, although his mother's family supported his claim and his claim to the kingdom of Jerusalem was through his mother. Parzivâl is the nephew of the Grâl king (rather than the cousin as in Chrétien's *Conte du Graal*); for Otto to be the nephew of the 'Grâl king', we would have to assume that Wolfram regarded Richard the Lionheart and his family as the true heirs to the throne of Jerusalem.

In fact, if Wolfram did believe this, he had good reason to do so. The succession of Maria of Montferrat to the kingdom of Jerusalem was irregular, for Maria had been born of a highly irregular marriage. Conrad of Montferrat had forced her mother Isabel of Jerusalem to go through with an illegal divorce in order to marry him, while he himself still had two wives living. The marriage had been condemned by most of the clergy present at the siege of Acre, where it took place, and Baldwin, archbishop of Canterbury, who was acting in place of the sick patriarch of Jerusalem, had placed the newlyweds under interdict. The repercussions of the case were still being worked out in the early decades of the thirteenth century.[66] It was therefore clear that Otto's claim to the throne of Jerusalem, via his mother and Henry II of England, was at least as good as Maria's. Otto was a legitimate first cousin twice removed of Isabel of Jerusalem and Baldwin IV, whereas Maria was arguably illegitimate. If Maria's claim was to be set aside, Otto and his brothers would have a strong claim to the kingdom.

In this context it should be noted that one of Otto's charters, dated by scholars to 27 October 1210, gives him the title of 'by the grace of God, emperor and forever Augustus, king of Jerusalem and Sicily'. Scholars have assumed that the reference to the crown of Jerusalem was a later copyist's slip

---

[66] On the marriage of Conrad and Isabel and its consequences, see *The Conquest of Jerusalem*, trans. Peter Edbury (Aldershot, 1996), pp. 95–7, 114–16, 168, 172–4; *Itinerarium peregrinorum*, ed. Stubbs, Bk 1, chs 63–77, pp. 119–34; *Itinerarium peregrinorum*, ed. Mayer, pp. 352–7; *Chronicle of the Third Crusade*, pp. 121–34 and notes 255–69; Ambroise, *Estoire*, lines 4111–412.

based on the claim of Emperor Frederick II to the crown of Jerusalem, but in view of the evidence just discussed it may in fact be genuine.[67]

So far it appears at least feasible that Wolfram intended Parzivâl to be the equivalent of Otto of Brunswick, and the succession to the Grâl Castle to parallel the succession to the imperial crown and to the kingdom of Jerusalem. However, there are many problems.

For example, who is represented by Anfortas, the wounded king of the Grâl castle? The obvious 'wounded king' is Baldwin IV, the 'leper king'; and, according to Helen Adolf's theory on Chrétien's *Conte du Graal*, Chrétien's wounded Graal king was intended as Baldwin IV.[68] Yet, while he was an obvious character for Chrétien to depict in his Grail romance, as Baldwin had died in 1185 he was a less obvious character for Wolfram to include in his story – except insofar as he 'inherited' him from Chrétien's romance. Again, Baldwin IV was not Otto's uncle, whereas Anfortas is Parzivâl's uncle. As Wolfram has deliberately altered the family relationship between his hero and the Grail ruler, it seems reasonable to assume that this relationship is significant.

It could be argued that Baldwin was the last valid, ruling king in the male line and that the next king of Jerusalem would effectively be his heir, as Parzivâl is the heir of Anfortas. Again, just as Anfortas' sister, Repanse de Schoye, actually guards the Grâl, so Baldwin's sister Sybil with her husband Guy became effective rulers of the kingdom of Jerusalem in 1183 when Guy was made regent for the ailing Baldwin. After the death of Baldwin, Sybil's son Baldwin, then Sybil herself, and finally Baldwin's and Sybil's sister Isabel, inherited the kingdom of Jerusalem. Hence the wounded king and his sister(s) guarding the Grâl have obvious parallels with Baldwin IV and his sisters. It is certainly possible that Chrétien had intended his Fisher King's niece to represent Isabel, and Perceval's cousin to represent Sybil.[69] Yet, again, while these parallels might have been obvious to audiences in the 1180s, they would not have been so obvious to Wolfram's audience in the first decade of the thirteenth century.

Although it is possible that Wolfram intended Anfortas and Repanse de Schoye to represent the same characters as the equivalent characters in Chrétien's work may have represented, this is not essential to the interpretation of the story. It is just as likely that the wounded king represents the monarchy

---

[67] '*Odo Dei gratia Romanorum imperator et semper augustus, Ierusalem et Sicilie rex*'. See Hucker, *Kaiser Otto IV*, pp. 151–3, for editions and discussion. On 14 September 1210 Maria of Montferrat had married John of Brienne, a French knight loyal to Otto's political enemy King Philip II of France. John became king of Jerusalem through his marriage. Otto's assumption of the title of king of Jerusalem at about the time when the marriage would have become known in Italy may have reflected his opposition to Maria and John's claim to the kingdom.

[68] Adolf, 'Historical Background', 605–7.

[69] Ibid., 603–5.

of Jerusalem as a whole, damaged by scandal of divorce and failure to produce heirs. Scholars are agreed that Anfortas's wound in the scrotum represents impotence, and an outstanding feature of the monarchy of the Latin kingdom of Jerusalem had been its failure to produce healthy, legitimate male heirs – or even any heirs at all. The figure of Anfortas, therefore, need not have any precise parallel in contemporary events; he may represent a situation more than an individual.

If this is the case, what is the importance of the uncle-nephew relationship? The most obvious parallel to the uncle-nephew relationship between Anfortas and Parzivâl is the uncle-nephew relationship between Richard the Lionheart and Otto of Brunswick. Richard the Lionheart was the 'king of the Grâl' in that he was effective rightful overlord of the kingdom of Jerusalem, but had failed to take over the kingdom, assigning it to another – his nephew Henry of Champagne – who had failed to solve its problems. In this respect, Richard, too, had been an 'impotent' Grâl king, lacking effective power to protect the Grâl Castle, Jerusalem. Yet, he was also an impotent king because he failed to produce a legitimate heir for his own kingdom of England. Like Anfortas, Richard had been renowned for his love for women; while Anfortas had loved a women not allowed to him by the writing on the Grâl stone, Richard had set aside his betrothed of long standing, Alice of France, in order to marry Berengaria of Navarre, and was also a notorious womaniser.[70] Like Anfortas, Richard was a proud and excellent knight who loved fighting. Anfortas received his wound from the hands of a Muslim; perhaps Richard was supposed to have become impotent as a result of his illness during his crusade. In any case, Richard of England is a clear parallel for Anfortas, the impotent Grail king.

It is interesting to consider other relatives of Parzivâl and to ask whether they also have similarities to Otto of Brunswick's maternal relations. The career of Repanse de Schoye, sister of Anfortas, bearer of the Grâl and aunt of Parzivâl, has an echo in the career of Joanna, queen of Sicily and countess of Toulouse, younger sister of Richard the Lionheart and aunt of Otto of Brunswick (see figs. 4.4a and 4.4b). At the end of *Parzival*, Parzivâl's Muslim brother Feirefîz falls in love with Repanse de Schoye, accepts Christianity, and the couple are married. There was a story in circulation after the Third Crusade, recorded by the contemporary Muslim historians Bahā' al-Dīn and 'Imād al-Dīn and by some Christian writers, that Richard had proposed to Saladin as part of their peace negotiations that Joanna (who had accompanied him on the Third Crusade) should marry al-'Adil, Saladin's brother. The only condition proposed was that al-'Adil should become a Christian. According to the Muslim sources, al-'Adil was in favour of the match, but the scheme fell

---

[70] John Gillingham, *Richard the Lionheart* (London, 1978), p. 162; Gillingham, *Richard Coeur de Lion*, p. 136 and note 83; Gillingham, *Richard I*, p. 263.

through because Joanna refused. This story also appears in two manuscripts of the Old French 'Ernoul' continuations of William of Tyre's 'History', written between 1220 and 1250.[71] It is possible that Wolfram knew the story and that it had caught his imagination. Pondering the implications of the marriage proposal, he could have wondered what would have happened if Joanna had accepted the hand of a converted Muslim, and what this would have meant for the expansion of Christianity.

Again, Parzivâl's other aunt, Schoysîane, has a parallel in Otto of Brunswick's aunt Eleanor (see figs 4.4a and 4.4b). Schoysîane married Duke Kyôt of Katelangen. 'Katelangen' sounds as if it may be intended as 'Catalonia', although there was no such figure as the duke of Catalonia when Wolfram was writing. Eleanor married Alfonso VIII of Castile. Schoysîane bore a daughter, Sigûne, who was brought up by Parzivâl's mother after Schoysîane's death in childbirth. Eleanor bore a daughter, Blanche, who was betrothed to King Philip II of France's son Louis in 1200, and, although she was still a young child, sent to live with her future father-in-law and husband in France. She was later mother of Louis IX, and regent of France after the death of her husband Louis VIII. Unlike Schoysîane, Eleanor did not die in her daughter's infancy, but like Schoysîane, her daughter was brought up away from her parents. Schoysîane, with her marriage to a far-off Iberian prince and famous daughter, echoes Eleanor's career, although it is far from being identical.[72]

The final member of Parzivâl's maternal family presents particular problems of interpretation: Trevrizent, the hermit, who first appears in Book Nine. This is a character very similar to the hermit uncle in Chrétien's *Conte du Graal*, and – unlike the Grail king – his relationship to Parzivâl is identical to the hermit's relationship to Perceval. This may indicate that he is not intended to parallel any one character in the contemporary world.

Otto of Brunwick had another uncle not so far accounted for: John, king of England. John supported Otto from 1206 with money, but certainly not with spiritual advice, as Trevrizent does Parzivâl.[73] In that John helped Otto when

---

[71] Bahā' al-Dīn, *The Life of Saladin*, trans. C.W. Wilson and C.R. Conder, Palestine Pilgrims Text Society (London, 1897), pp. 310, 324–5; 'Imād al-Dīn, *Conquête de la Syrie et de la Palestine par Saladin (al-Fath al qwsī fī l-fath al qudsī)*, trans. Henri Massé (Paris, 1972), pp. 350–51; *La Continuation de Guillaume de Tyr*, section 142, pp. 150 (Florence MS), 151 (Lyons MS); also published in *RHC Occ.*, 2, p. 198 (small print at bottom of page); for date, see Edbury, 'The Lyon *Eracles*', p. 143. The story of Joanna's proposed marriage to al-'Adil is accepted as true by modern scholars: Gillingham, *Richard the Lionheart*, pp. 196–7; Gillingham, *Richard Coeur de Lion*, p. 100; Gillingham, *Richard I*, pp. 22, 184–9. See also Prestwich, '*Rex Bellicosus*', p. 5.

[72] Prestwich, '*Rex Bellicosus*', pp. 5–6. The standard study on Blanche of Castile in English is Régine Pernoud, *Blanche of Castile*, trans Henry Noel (New York, 1975). For a short overview of her life see Elizabeth Hallam, *Capetian France, 987–1328* (London, 1980), pp. 130, 183, 207–13.

[73] It should be noted, however, that John's supposed impiety has been exaggerated. He was devoted to the Anglo-Saxon saint St Wulfstan; he founded the Cistercian monastery of Beaulieu and patronised various monastic houses and the Military Orders. The next-generation St Alban's

his career was at its lowest ebb, just as Trevrizent does Parzivâl, John could be seen as a sort of equivalent of Trevrizent. But the nature of his support was so different that further examination of this character is needed.

Harald Haferland has recently suggested that 'Trevrizent' is a garbled version of the French *Treble escient*, thrice-knowing, and is the equivalent of *Trismegistus*, that is, Hermes Trismegistus, Thrice-Great Hermes, the classical god and pagan prophet to whom many works of astrology, medicine and philosophy were attributed during the late Roman empire. These works were becoming well known to educated audiences in western Europe during the twelfth century in the form of Latin translations from the Arabic translations of Greek originals, found in the library at Toledo.[74]

Trevrizent's knowledge of planets and medicines in Book Nine certainly supports this interpretation, but it is notable that none of the attempted cures of Anfortas's wound succeed in doing more than limiting the pain – he cannot be cured until Parzivâl asks 'the question' – and hence Trevrizent's pagan knowledge is, in fact, ineffective. In fact Wolfram is making fun of Trevrizent's knowledge, which is so complex and extensive and yet does not work. Moreover, Trevrizent is a Christian, not a pagan as Hermes Trismegistus. Admittedly, Hermes Trismegistus had been regarded in classical times by some philosophers as the *Logos*, the creative word, and could therefore be seen as a parallel to Christ; but this was not known in the West at the time that Wolfram was writing. It is possible that Wolfram knew that some early Christian writers, notably Lactantius, believed that Hermes Trismegistus had foretold the coming of Christ, although St Augustine of Hippo had rejected this interpretation of the Hermetic writings. Twelfth-century western scholars regarded Hermes Trismegistus as a wise pagan, on a par with Aristotle and

---

chronicler Matthew Paris, who usually loses no opportunity to attack King John, informs us that he prevented heretics from entering the realm and so proved himself the upholder of orthodox Christianity. See W.L. Warren, *King John* (London, 1961), pp. 171–2, 255; Ralph V. Turner, *King John* (London, 1994), pp. 148–9; Nicholson, 'Military Orders and the Kings of England', pp. 204–7; Matthew Paris, *Historia Anglorum sive, ut dicitur, Historia Minor, item, eiusdem Abbreviatio Chronicorum Angliae*, ed. Frederic Madden, 3 vols, RS 44 (London, 1866–69), 2, p. 194; 3, p. 64. On King John and Otto see Natilie Fryde, 'King John and the Empire' in *King John: New Interpretations*, ed. S.D. Church (Woodbridge, 1999), pp. 335–46.

[74] Haferland, 'Die Geheimnisse des Grals', p. 39; for an example of works on astrology and medicine attributed to Hermes see 'les Cyranides' and 'le traité Hermetique de Quindecim Stellis' in *Textes latins et vieux français relatifs aux Cyranides*, ed. Louis Delatte (Liège and Paris, 1942), pp. 13, 241–75. For the god-prophet Hermes Trismegistus and the works attributed to him see Garth Fowden, *The Egyptian Hermes: A Historical Approach to the late Pagan Mind* (Cambridge, 1986; new edn Princeton, 1993), pp. 22–31; *Hermetica: the Greek Corpus Hermeticum and the Latin Asclepius in a new English translation with notes and introduction*, trans. Brian P. Copenhaver (Cambridge, 1992), pp. xiii–xlvii (esp. p. xlvii on the circulation of these works in the medieval West). For the circulation of works attributed to Hermes Trismegistus in the twelfth-century West see also, for instance, the references to the *Asclepius* and to Hermes Trismegistus in *A History of Twelfth-Century Philosophy*, ed. Dronke, esp. pp. 76–9.

Plato: philosophers who had received a divine revelation before the coming of Christ, and whose works could therefore be used beneficially by Christians.[75]

Trevrizent himself lives at the *Funtâne la Salvâtsche*, the fountain or spring of Salvation – which itself should mean Christ – and he gives Christian spiritual advice to Parzivâl, which Trismegistus could never have done. Wolfram may in fact have intended this figure to have more than one meaning – as if the hare he refers to in his opening lines were zig-zagging back and forth across its own tracks. The name Trevrizent also has echoes of *Treverensis*, that is, the ancient imperial city of Trier. The archbishop of Trier was one of the electors of the Empire, and therefore his support was essential for Otto. At the same time the cathedral of Trier was a cult centre, claiming to possess Christ's seamless robe. These spiritual and imperial connections would suggest that the archbishop of Trier would have been a more appropriate spiritual adviser for Parzivâl in this context than Hermes Trismegistus; but even he was not a close parallel to Wolfram's hermit, for he was not related by blood to Otto and his support for him was not consistent.[76]

A further problem is how to interpret of the various events in Parzivâl's career. Do they have any resemblance to the life of Otto of Brunswick, apart from the general points set out above? It could be argued that, just as Chrétien had built his story around Philip of Alsace's book as well as historical events,

---

[75] Fowden, *Egyptian Hermes*, pp. 24, 179–82, 206–7, 209; *Hermetica*, ed. Copenhaver, pp. xlii–xliii, 100, 102, 188. For the use of pagan philosophers by twelfth-century western scholars see, for instance, D.E. Luscombe, 'Peter Abelard', in *A History of Twelfth-Century Philosophy*, pp. 279–307, here pp. 299–302. For the fifteenth-century 'promotion' of Hermes Trismegistus to being the equal of Moses, see Frances A. Yates, *Giordano Bruno and the Hermetic Tradition* (Chicago and London, 1964), pp. 12–17, 42–3, 85, 116. It should be noted that Hermes Trismegistus was not so highly regarded as this in the early thirteenth century.

[76] Trier had been an imperial city in the fourth and fifth centuries AD, the capital of the emperor of Gaul and Britain, and it was seat of the oldest archbishopric in Germany. The cult of Christ's robe was celebrated there from 1197. Christ's robe was said to have been brought to the city by Saint Helena, discoverer of the true cross in Jerusalem and mother of the emperor Constantine the Great. The archbishop of Trier was one of the electors of the Empire. Hence Trier, with its imperial connections and sacred relic of Christ was an essential and valuable supporter for a would-be emperor. Archbishops of Trier had differed in their support for the Angevins. Folmar, elected archbishop in 1183, had never been able to take possession of his see and was deposed in 1189. He went into exile in England and was one of those participating in the coronation of King Richard. His successor Archbishop John of Trier (1189–1212) had been court chancellor to Emperor Frederick I, so his allegiances were more likely to be towards the Hohenstaufen than the Angevins or the Welfs. He promised to support Otto in 1198, but in fact he vacillated between support for Otto and for Philip. By 1202 he was negotiating with Philip of Swabia, and in 1203 Pope Innocent III excommunicated him for failing to support Otto when he had promised to do so. By 1206–7 he was supporting Otto against Philip: Helene Tillmann, *Innocent III*, trans. Walter Sax (Amsterdam, 1980), p. 122 and note 107 on p. 169, pp. 120–21, 132; and see Hucker, *Kaiser Otto IV*, p. 449, no. 97. On the archbishops of Trier see, for instance, Alfred Haverkamp, *Medieval Germany*, trans. Helga Braun and Richard Mortimer (Oxford, 1988), p. 275; on Archbishop Folmar or Fulmar see Roger of Howden, *Gesta regis Henrici secundi: the chronicle of the reigns of Henry II and Richard I*, ed. William Stubbs, 2 vols, RS 49 (London, 1867), 2, p. 79 and note 1; Roger of Howden, *Chronica*, 3, p. 8 and note 3.

so Wolfram was tied to the general lines of the Grail story as laid down by Chrétien. Although he could choose his own ending – as Chrétien's story was unfinished – he could not change the basic episodes within the central part of the story. Therefore it would be pointless to look in Otto's career, for example, for a previous failed visit to the Grail castle, like Parzivâl's failed visit in Book Five. For this theory to hold, Otto would have had to have made a previous, failed attempt at the imperial throne, or a previous, failed visit to the kingdom of Jerusalem.

In fact, if Wolfram was writing before the death of Philip of Swabia in 1208, Otto *had* made a previous, failed attempt at the imperial throne. Having been elected in 1198 at Aachen, his position was eroded by the death in 1199 of Richard I of England, his leading supporter, while his other supporters gradually deserted him for Philip of Swabia. In 1206 he went into exile to Denmark and England, seeking support for his cause, and he did not return until after the assassination of Philip of Swabia.

So Parzivâl's failure to achieve the Grâl at his first attempt could represent Otto's failure to win the imperial crown at the first attempt. However, it could also represent his family's failure to claim the crown of Jerusalem at the first attempt.

Otto's elder brother, Henry, count palatine of the Rhine, went on crusade in 1197 with his allies Henry, duke of Brabant and Lotharingia, and Archbishop Harwig II of Bremen. They did not travel with the imperial contingent but went by sea, via Portugal, and travelled at their own expense. Duke Henry of Brabant and Henry of the Rhine arrived in Acre shortly after the death of Henry of Champagne and before the rest of the crusade. Henry of Brabant replaced Henry of Champagne as leader of the army, and seems also to have been a claimant to the throne of Jerusalem. However, he was outflanked by the chancellor, and Aimery of Lusignan was elected king of Jerusalem instead. Claudia Naumann comments that Henry of Brabant could hardly have become king of Jerusalem, as he could not have married Isabel of Jerusalem, being married already.[77] But this is to overlook the nature of the duke of Brabant's claim.

Henry, duke of Brabant, was married to Matilda, great-granddaughter of Eustace III of Boulogne, the elder brother of Godfrey of Bouillon and Baldwin of Edessa, who were also the first two Latin rulers of Jerusalem after the capture of the city by the First Crusade (see fig. 4.5).[78] Matilda, therefore, had a claim to the throne of Jerusalem arguably better than Isabel of Jerusalem or even Henry of the Rhine. Yet Henry of Brabant failed to enforce his claim to the kingdom in right of his wife; and Henry of the Rhine failed to assert

---

[77] Naumann, *Der Kreuzzug Kaiser Heinrichs VI*, pp. 83, 136–7, 164 and note 272, pp. 176–7.
[78] *Lohengrin*, ed. Thomas Cramer (Munich, 1971), pp. 75–6.

THE GRAIL 137

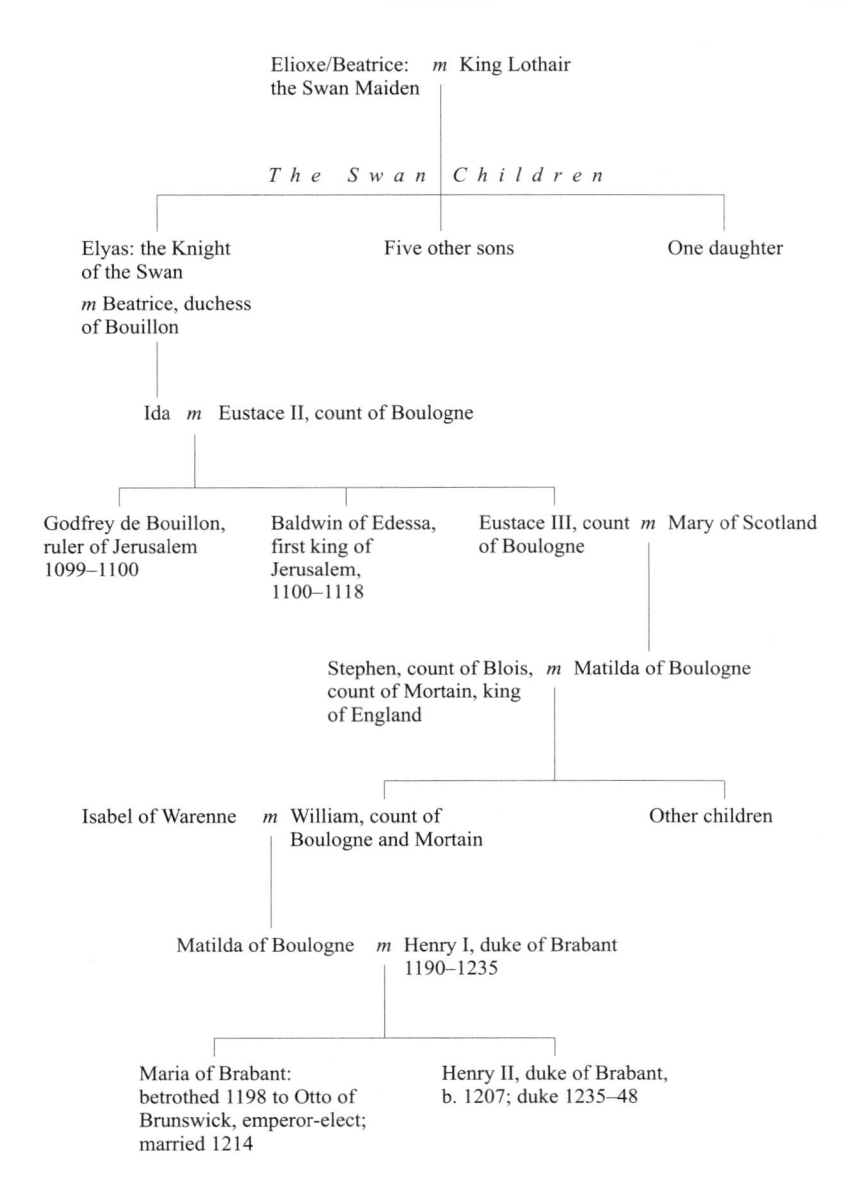

```
                    Elioxe/Beatrice:   m   King Lothair
                    the Swan Maiden


                    The   Swan  Children
        ┌─────────────────────┼─────────────────────┐
   Elyas: the Knight      Five other sons        One daughter
   of the Swan

   m Beatrice, duchess
   of Bouillon

        Ida   m   Eustace II, count of Boulogne
   ┌────────────────────┬────────────────────────┐
Godfrey de Bouillon,  Baldwin of Edessa,    Eustace III, count  m  Mary of Scotland
ruler of Jerusalem    first king of         of Boulogne
1099–1100             Jerusalem,
                      1100–1118

                          Stephen, count of Blois,   m   Matilda of Boulogne
                          count of Mortain, king
                          of England

                     ┌─────────────────────────────────┐
   Isabel of Warenne   m   William, count of          Other children
                           Boulogne and Mortain


           Matilda of Boulogne   m   Henry I, duke of Brabant
                                     1190–1235
                     ┌──────────────────────────────┐
           Maria of Brabant:               Henry II, duke of Brabant,
           betrothed 1198 to Otto of       b. 1207; duke 1235–48
           Brunswick, emperor-elect;
           married 1214
```

Fig. 4.5: The supposed descent of Maria of Brabant from the Knight of the Swan

his claim. Instead, the kingdom went to Aimery of Lusignan and Isabel of Jerusalem, half-sister of the leper king.

Again, Parzivâl's failure could be intended as a parallel to the failure of the German crusade in the Holy Land. Overall, in fact, the crusade was relatively successful; it recovered the coast between Tyre and Tripoli, notably Beirut and Jubail, enabling the Latin Christians to dominate the sea routes in the eastern Mediterranean. Yet the combined forces of the crusaders and the kingdom, under the leadership of Duke Henry of Brabant, were unable to recapture Tîbnîn, and some breach seems to have occurred with the Templars during the siege, as Otto of St Blasien later blamed the Templars for its failure. If one was to assume that Parzivâl's failed visit to the Grâl castle parallels the German Angevin's failure to claim the throne of Jerusalem in 1197, then one could interpret Parzivâl's clash with the *Templeis* in Book Nine as an echo of this clash between the crusaders and the actual Templars; Parzivâl wins his joust, but the *Templeis* successfully turns him away from the Grâl castle, which he is not yet worthy to approach.[79]

In any case, when Duke Henry of Brabant returned to Germany, he approved the betrothal of his seven-year-old daughter Maria, great-great-granddaughter of Eustace III and thus a (supposed) direct descendant of the legendary Swan Knight (see fig. 4.5), to Otto of Brunswick, emperor-elect.[80]

One of the details of Wolfram's *Parzival* which has puzzled scholars is his reference to the legend of the Swan knight at the end of the poem.[81] This version of the story is quite unlike any other version. Usually, the Swan knight is connected to Bouillon and Boulogne, is named Elias or Helias, is the son of a maiden whom a king meets by a fountain in the forest, and is the ancestor of Godfrey of Bouillon and Baldwin of Edessa. In Wolfram's poem he is Loherangrîn, son of Parzivâl and Condwîramûrs and is connected to Brabant. However, if it is assumed that Wolfram is attempting to establish a connection between Otto of Brunswick and the Grâl/Jerusalem and to strengthen Otto's claim to the imperial crown, then it would be reasonable for him to draw his audience's attention to the dynastic connections of Maria of Brabant and Lotharingia, Otto's betrothed, to the Swan Knight and the Grâl/Jerusalem family.

According to Roger of Howden, Otto married Maria when he was crowned king of the Romans at Aachen in 1198.[82] In fact Otto could not marry Maria at

---

[79] Naumann, *Kreuzzug Kaiser Heinrichs VI*, pp. 193–4; Otto of St Blasien, 'Continuatio Sanblasiana', ed. R. Wilmans, *MGHS*, 20, p. 327; Nicholson, *Templars, Hospitallers*, pp. 81–2 on this type of accusation against the Templars. For Parzivâl and the *Templeis* see *Parzival*, Bk 9, lines 443.6–445.30.

[80] On this betrothal and its aftermath see Naumann, *Kreuzzug Kaiser Heinrichs VI*, pp. 114, 200; see also Hatto's translation of Wolfram, p. 420.

[81] *Parzival*, Bk 16, lines 823.27–826.28; *Lohengrin*, pp. 48, 74–5, 124–8.

[82] Roger of Howden, *Chronica*, 4, p. 39.

once, as she was underage. The marriage was postponed until she was of age. In December 1203, Pope Innocent III, writing to urge her father to support Otto, referred to Otto as Maria's *sponsum*, her betrothed.[83] However, by 1204 her father was negotiating with Philip of Swabia to marry her to Frederick of Hohenstaufen, Philip's nephew. Pope Innocent III wrote in anger to forbid the marriage: Otto and Maria had been legitimately betrothed and their engagement should not be broken.[84] In November 1208, following the death of Philip of Swabia, Otto became formally betrothed to Philip's daughter Beatrice, in an attempt to win over the pro-Swabian princes. It is possible that this marriage had been arranged before Philip's death, as compensation for Otto's surrender of the imperial throne to Philip.[85] Otto married Beatrice in March 1212, when she was old enough to marry, but she died three weeks later. In May 1214 Otto finally married Maria of Brabant, thereby ensuring her father's support in his campaign against the French king Philip II in the following summer, which ended in disaster for Otto and his allies at Bouvines.

Yet, in the first decade of the thirteenth century, the disasters of Otto's later career were still in the future. When Wolfram was writing, he was still one of two or three candidates for the imperial throne. If Wolfram intended any contemporary parallels to actual people in his Grâl romance, the Otto-Parzivâl parallel is the most obvious parallel.

Turning to Otto's rivals, both Philip of Swabia and Frederick of Sicily were sons of emperors, Frederick being the nephew of Philip. In *Parzival*, Gawân is Parzivâl's rival. He is the son of the king of Norway and nephew of Arthur, high king of Britain – who is not quite an emperor, but not far away from being one. Wolfram describes Gawân winning glory and honour and true and faithful love, but not the Grâl Castle, for he has no dynastic right to it; and certainly the Hohenstaufen at this period had no dynastic claim to the throne of Jerusalem. Gawân and Parzivâl are descended from a common paternal ancestor, Mazadân; Otto and Philip were descended from a common paternal ancestor, Henry the Black, duke of Bavaria (d. 1126) (see figs 4.6a and 4.6b). Gawân could represent Philip or Frederick; given that he is an adult, while Frederick was still a child when Wolfram was writing, Philip is more likely. This would mean that Wolfram was writing before Philip's assassination in 1208, which fits the generally accepted chronology for Wolfram's work. It is worth noting here that the traditional descriptions of Philip of Swabia and Otto of Brunswick fit the characters of Gawân and Parzivâl: Philip was gentle,

---

[83] Augustus Potthast, *Regesta pontificum Romanorum inde ab a. post Christum natum MCXCVIII ad a. MCCCIV*, 2 vols (Graz, 1957), 1, p. 178, no. 2048; Innocent III, 'Liber registorum', vol. 3, col. 1104. For Otto's relations with Maria's father, see Hucker, *Kaiser Otto IV*, pp. 36–40.
[84] Potthast, 1, p. 199, no. 2312; Innocent III, 'Liber registorum', 3, cols. 1114–16.
[85] Tillmann, *Innocent III*, p. 134.

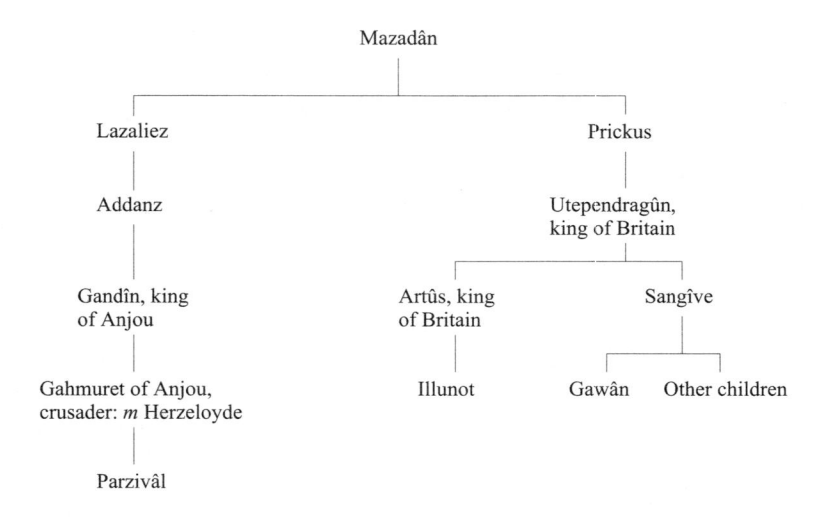

```
                            Mazadân
            ┌─────────────────┴─────────────────┐
         Lazaliez                            Prickus
            │                                   │
         Addanz                           Utependragûn,
            │                             king of Britain
            │                        ┌─────────┴─────────┐
      Gandîn, king              Artûs, king           Sangîve
       of Anjou                  of Britain              │
            │                         │          ┌──────┴──────┐
   Gahmuret of Anjou,             Illunot      Gawân      Other children
   crusader: m Herzeloyde
            │
         Parzivâl
```

Fig. 4.6a: The paternal ancestry of Parzivâl and Gawân

refined and courteous, a good description of Gawân, while Otto is regarded as lacking courtly polish, which would be appropriate for Parzivâl.[86]

The Hohenstaufen did have a connection by marriage to the throne of Jerusalem. Two sons of Giuletta, paternal great-aunt of Philip of Swabia, married the two heiresses of the kingdom of Jerusalem (see fig. 4.7b). Both died tragically; the elder, William of Montferrat, a few months after his wedding to Sybil of Jerusalem; the younger, Conrad, who had married Sybil's sister Isabel, was assassinated in April 1192. Hostile French and German commentators claimed that King Richard of England, Isabel's first cousin once removed, was behind Conrad's assassination; and this was one reason for the arrest of Richard by Leopold V of Austria in December 1192.[87] Interestingly enough, in *Parzival*, Gawân's paternal great-aunt was mother of Ithêr of Gaheviez, who is murdered by Parzivâl in Book Three (see fig. 4.7a). Only in Book Nine does Parzivâl discover from his hermit uncle Trevrizent that he was related to Ithêr through his father, Gahmuret. The exact nature of the relationship is not clear: Ithêr was Gahmuret's maternal nephew (line

---

[86] See Karl Hampe, *Germany under the Salian and Hohenstaufen Emperors*, trans. Ralph Bennett (Oxford, 1973), pp. 238–9.

[87] See, for instance, 'Historia de expeditione Friderici imperatoris', in *Quellen zur Geschichte des Kreuzzuges Kaiser Friedrichs I*, ed. A. Chroust, *MGHS rerum germanicarum, nova series*, 5 (Berlin, 1928), pp. 101–2, 105–6; *Itinerarium peregrinorum*, ed. Stubbs, Bk 5, ch. 27, Bk 6, ch. 35, pp. 341–2, 444–5; *Chronicle of the Third Crusade*, pp. 307–8 and note 55, pp. 383–5 and note 106.

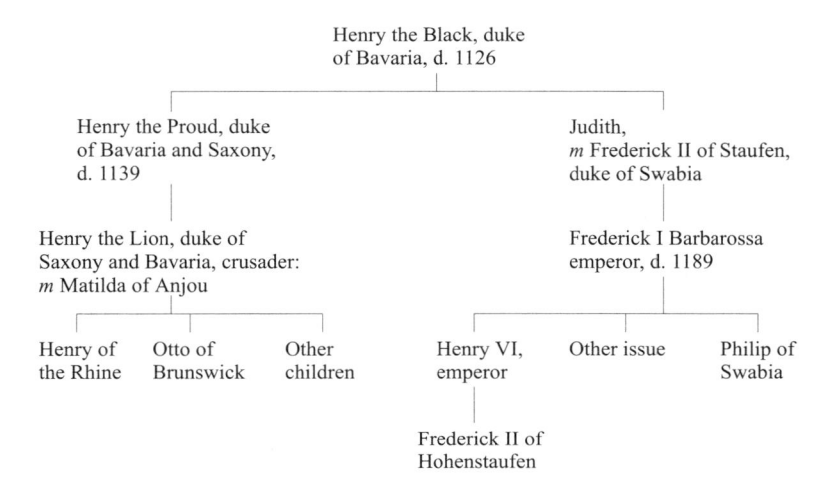

```
                    Henry the Black, duke
                      of Bavaria, d. 1126
         ┌──────────────────┴──────────────────┐
   Henry the Proud, duke                  Judith,
   of Bavaria and Saxony,                 m Frederick II of Staufen,
   d. 1139                                duke of Swabia
         │                                     │
   Henry the Lion, duke of                Frederick I Barbarossa
   Saxony and Bavaria, crusader:          emperor, d. 1189
   m Matilda of Anjou                           │
   ┌─────────┬──────────┐              ┌────────┼──────────┐
 Henry of   Otto of    Other        Henry VI,  Other issue  Philip of
 the Rhine  Brunswick  children     emperor                 Swabia
                                          │
                                    Frederick II of
                                    Hohenstaufen
```

Fig. 4.6b: The paternal ancestry of Otto of Brunswick, Philip of Swabia and Frederick of Hohenstaufen

498.13), but Ithêr's wife or beloved Lammîre was given her land of Styria by Gandîn, Gahmuret's father, which suggests that he was her father or grandfather (lines 499.4–6); and Lammîre was Parzivâl's aunt or cousin on his father's side (line 499.3). Whether Lammîre was Gandîn's daughter or granddaughter, assuming that her relationship with Ithêr was one of marriage, we find that Parzivâl's relationship to Ithêr – cousin-in-law – was similar to Richard of England's relationship to Conrad of Montferrat (see figs 4.7a and 4.7b). Like Richard's alleged murder of Conrad, Parzivâl's murder of Ithêr was a great sin which severely impeded his progress (line 499.20).[88]

In short, like Chrétien, Wolfram wove historical figures and events into the story which was his fundamental source, Chrétien's *Conte du Graal*. His message was different from Chrétien's; he was still writing about the succession to Jerusalem, but not of Philip of Alsace. He knew that contemporaries had not understood what Chrétien was writing about, and wanted to make his message clearer, while still retaining the fictional outline which made the Grail legend attractive to listeners. His German audience would be well aware that the emperor was the true overlord of Jerusalem. Therefore, to underline that he was in fact talking about Jerusalem and its lord the emperor, Wolfram called his Grail guardians 'Templars'.

This theory does account for a number of problems presented by Wolfram's *Parzival*. If Parzivâl is intended as a parallel to Otto of Brunswick, and Gawân

---

[88] For this aspect of Parzivâl's family tree, see Hatto's translation, p. 253.

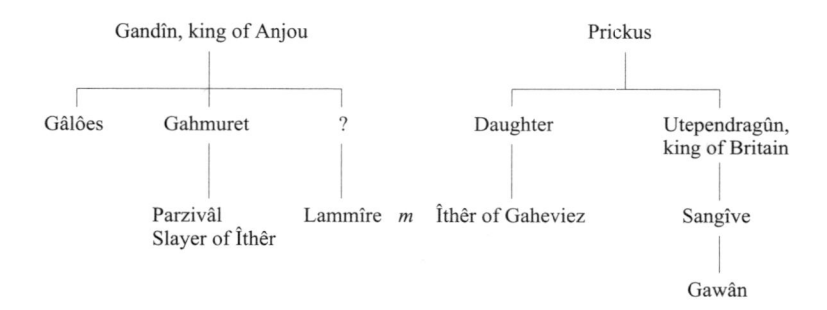

```
                Gandîn, king of Anjou                                    Prickus
        ┌───────────────┼───────────────┐                       ┌───────────┴───────────┐
    Gâlôes          Gahmuret            ?                    Daughter              Utependragûn,
                        │                                        │                  king of Britain
                        │                                        │                        │
                    Parzivâl        Lammîre   m   Îthêr of Gaheviez                   Sangîve
                  Slayer of Îthêr                                                         │
                                                                                       Gawân
```

Fig. 4.7a: The connection by marriage between Gawân and Parzivâl via the Angevin Dynasty

as a parallel of Philip of Swabia, this explains why Parzivâl is an Angevin, and accounts for the prominence yet ultimate failure of Gawân. The Grâl Castle is Jerusalem, guarded by 'Templars', 'Templars' whose emphasis is on their service of love rather than bloodshed. This is not simply a mystical Jerusalem, but the actual city of Jerusalem. As Parzivâl is nephew of Anfortas, the king of the Grail, so Otto of Brunswick was nephew of Richard I of England, who was by dynastic right king of Jerusalem. Parzivâl's tragic and lovely mother and his two aunts Schoysîâne, who married a Spanish prince, and Repanse de Schoye, who married a converted Muslim, had their parallels in real life in Otto's tragic and lovely mother Matilda of Anjou and her sisters Eleanor, who married a Spanish prince, and Joanna, who did not marry a Muslim because he refused to convert. The reference to Prester John points to the probability that Wolfram is talking about the emperor and the imperial concept of the state. Wolfram refers to the Swan Knight and Brabant at the end of the story because of Otto's betrothal to Maria of Brabant, and her relationship to the first Latin rulers of Jerusalem; he is also making Maria a descendant of Parzivâl. If this theory is correct, Wolfram was writing before Philip of Swabia's assassination in June 1208, at a time when Otto's only betrothed was still Marie of Brabant.

There are contradictions and duplication of identities in this interpretation: for instance, both Gahmuret, Parzivâl's father, and the Grâl king Anfortas, Parzivâl's uncle, can be interpreted as Richard the Lionheart, crusader and true heir to the kingdom of Jerusalem; but the wounded and impotent Grâl king can also be seen as representing the monarchy of Jerusalem, unable to produce strong male heirs. However, Wolfram has already warned his audience that his story will twist and turn back and forth like a hare, so these contradictions and duplications are not a fundamental obstacle to this interpretation. Wolfram was not setting out to reproduce recent events precisely in his work, because his story was set in the past and he also had to remain relatively close to

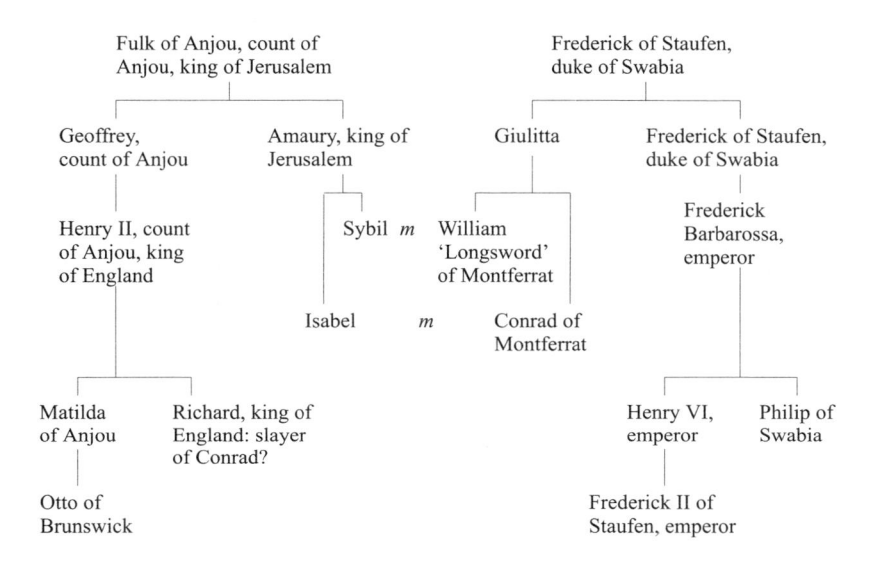

Fig. 4.7b: The connection by marriage between Philip of Swabia and Otto of Brunswick via the Angevin Dynasty

```
Fulk of Anjou, count of                    Frederick of Staufen,
Anjou, king of Jerusalem                   duke of Swabia
        |                                         |
   ┌────┴────┐                              ┌─────┴─────┐
Geoffrey,    Amaury, king of    Giulitta    Frederick of Staufen,
count of     Jerusalem             |        duke of Swabia
Anjou            |                 |              |
   |          ┌──┴──┐              |         Frederick
Henry II,    Sybil m William                 Barbarossa,
count of              'Longsword'            emperor
Anjou, king           of Montferrat
of England        |
   |           Isabel    m    Conrad of
   |                          Montferrat
   |
┌──┴──┐                                  ┌──────┴──────┐
Matilda  Richard, king of             Henry VI,    Philip of
of Anjou England: slayer              emperor      Swabia
  |      of Conrad?                      |
Otto of                              Frederick II of
Brunswick                            Staufen, emperor
```

the framework of the story as set out by Chrétien de Troyes. Instead he gave many hints and indications of his intended parallels with contemporary events, while remaining, like the dodging hare, just out of reach of his audience's immediate comprehension – although a little thought would have revealed his meaning. As for Wolfram's declaration in his opening lines that resolution is necessary and vacillation is to be avoided, this would certainly be an appropriate sentiment for Otto of Brunswick in 1206, when he was in exile, desperately trying to raise support for another attempt to secure the imperial throne.

However, this theory must remain more speculative than Diverre's or Adolf's theories on Chrétien's *Conte du Graal*. Chrétien's patrons and their crusading involvement can be identified with relative degree of certainty, but although it is generally believed that Wolfram's patron for *Parzival* was Hermann of Thuringia, Hermann's political allegiances were not clear-cut. It is certain that the landgraves of Thuringia were interested in the crusade and the recovery of Jerusalem. Landgrave Ludwig III had played an important role in the Third Crusade, while Hermann had played an active role in the German Crusade of 1197–98. Although his support for Otto was not consistent, it is certain that Hermann had not voted for Philip of Swabia in March 1198, because he was in Acre at the time. In 1202–1204 Hermann was recorded as being a supporter of Otto. It is clear that Hermann resisted Philip of Swabia when he invaded Thuringia in 1203; Otto drove Philip out of Thuringia with the help of his allies, including the Thuringians.[89] In 1204, however, Philip defeated Hermann of Thuringia and his ally Ottokar of Bohemia, and in September 1204 Hermann gave his support to Philip. He is later found supporting Otto, but in 1210 he deserted his cause and in April–June 1211 he was one of those who elected the young Frederick of Hohenstaufen as king of the Romans in place of the excommunicated Otto. In 1212 Otto waged war against Hermann, attempting to make him submit to his authority before setting out on his campaign against France. Ironically, Hermann may have changed sides again after the Battle of Bouvines and returned to support Otto.[90] Perhaps Wolfram's remarks about vacillation and unreliability in the opening sentences of his poem are a 'dig' at his notoriously unreliable patron.

But if Hermann was ambivalent in his support of Otto, he was certainly not pro-Hohenstaufen. He opposed Henry VI's attempts to enforce the inheritance of his son Frederick to the imperial throne and had maintained that he, unlike Henry VI, was going on crusade solely from a desire for divine reward. His political attitude was independent, contemptuous of the Hohenstaufen manipulation of the crusade for their own political ends, and determined to support only the imperial candidate who was prepared to grant him the concessions he required.

One of Hermann's major concerns was to ensure the rights of female heirs, for his only direct heir was his daughter; in light of this, it is interesting that inheritance in *Parzival* goes through the female line, while Otto of Brunswick's connection with the Angevins and the throne of Jerusalem was also through the female line. Hermann seems to have been the main pressure behind Henry VI's concession at the Hoftag in Würzburg in 1196 to allow female heirs to inherit to imperial fiefs. He was also a patron of the arts, and may have been accompanied on the crusade by the *Minnesinger* Count Otto of Henneburg-Botenlauben. All in all, none of this is inconsistent with *Parzival* having been written for Hermann and reflecting his interests, or inconsistent with support of Otto of Brunswick.[91]

It is possible to object that Wolfram himself never shows any overt support for Otto in his writings, and in fact makes a remark in *Willehalm* about Otto's ignominious retreat from Rome in October 1209, which could be interpreted

---

[89] Potthast, 1, p. 177, no. 2040; Innocent III, 'Liber registorum', 3, col. 1100: Hucker, *Kaiser Otto IV*, pp. 687–8.
[90] Hucker, *Kaiser Otto IV*, pp. 79, 687, 514, 298, 215, 227, 301, 329.
[91] For Hermann of Thuringia's relations with the Staufen, the crusade and for his cultural interests see, for instance, Naumann, *Kreuzzug Kaiser Heinrichs VI*, pp. 111–18, p. 116 and note 476, p. 126, 251–2. On Wolfram's *Parzival* as a pro-Welf work, see also Johns, 'Richard in German Literature', pp. 99–100.

as slighting.[92] Yet this remark could simply be an expression of regret and frustration at Otto's failures; Wolfram's comments do not imply that he opposes Otto, only that he regrets this event.

In fact, it is not necessary to believe that Wolfram did support Otto of Brunswick as an individual. Rather, he was writing a story for the benefit of a patron, Hermann of Thuringia, who had an active interest in crusading and the Holy Land. In this story, Wolfram proposed that the only solution for the problems of the Holy Land was for the legitimate dynasty to be installed as rulers of Jerusalem. Certainly, the Hohenstaufen had organised and taken part in crusades, but to date they had not succeeded in recovering Jerusalem. The fact that they had no dynastic claim to Jerusalem was against them, for God would not support them. In contrast, Otto of Brunswick held an indisputable claim to the throne of Jerusalem, shared by his elder brother Henry, count palatine, which Henry had failed to enforce when he was on crusade in 1197–98. Otto was also a claimant for the imperial throne, although by 1206 his claim seemed about to fail. Wolfram was arguing that if Hermann and those concerned for the future of the Holy Land would wholeheartedly and without vacillation or treachery support Otto in his bid for the imperial throne and in a crusade to recapture the Holy Land, installing Otto as rightful ruler of Jerusalem – as was his right by inheritance – then the political disputes which had torn the crusader states of the East apart would be ended, and under the emperor's strong and legitimate leadership, the future of the kingdom of Jerusalem would be assured. In arguing this, Wolfram would not have been alone among his contemporaries: the chronicler Arnold of Lubeck also depicted Otto as the rightful leader of the crusade that would recover the Jerusalem, while Caesarius of Heisterbach recorded a Saracen prophecy of 1190 that Jerusalem would be recovered for Christendom by an emperor named Otto. Otto himself seems to have claimed his right to the crown of Jerusalem in a charter of October 1210.[93]

It is worth asking why Wolfram put Templars in charge of his Grâl Castle and not Teutonic Knights, who, as a German Order which defended the Holy Places, might seem more appropriate. When Wolfram wrote, the Teutonic Order was a relatively young foundation; it had only become a Military Order in 1198. However, the Order was established in Thuringia at an early date, before 1200 and even before 1195, and must have been well known to

---

[92] Wolfram von Eschenbach, *Willehalm*, *Titurel*: *Willehalm*, Bk 8, 393.30–394.5. For discussion see, for instance, Wolfram von Eschenbach, *Willehalm*, trans. Marion E. Gibbs and Sidney M. Johnson (Harmondsworth, 1984), p. 191 note 82.

[93] Hucker, *Kaiser Otto IV*, pp. 131–3, 151–3; and see Caesarius of Heisterbach, *Dialogus miraculorum*, part 4, ch. 15, 1, pp. 187–8. The fact that these contemporaries saw Otto as a potential crusader reinforces the long-held historical interpretation of Walther von der Vogelweide's poems nos. 12,6 and 12,18 as being intended to urge Otto IV to go on crusade; for this, see Hucker, *Kaiser Otto IV*, pp. 134–5.

Wolfram's audience. Hermann of Thuringia, Henry of Brabant and Henry of the Rhine had all been present when the Teutonic Order was recognised as a Military Order.[94] On the other hand, the Templars had little property in German territories at the period when Wolfram was writing, and had no specific connections to the emperor (although Otto IV's Angevin uncles and ancestors were patrons of the Order).[95] In contrast, the Teutonic Order was associated with the Hohenstaufen family, although Otto IV protected and endowed the Order.[96]

In fact, Wolfram's main incentive for using the Templars in this role would have been that the Templars were the first Military Order set up to defend pilgrims and the Holy Places in the East, and could be regarded as epitomising all the Military Orders. They also represented the height of Christian love and devotion unto death. Like Sigûne, they died for love. They were therefore ideal for Wolfram's purpose.

Another possible motivation for Wolfram's choice of 'Templars' to guard his Grâl was that his hero was pro-Angevin and the Angevins were patrons of the Order. The Templars had been particularly close to Richard the Lionheart in the Holy Land; Robert de Sablé, Master of the Temple 1191–93, had been Richard's admiral before joining the Order and being elected Master; and the Richard initially sold the newly-conquered island of Cyprus to the Order. Richard was also said to have asked the Master of the Temple for an escort of Brothers for his journey back to England in autumn 1192, so that he could travel inconspicuously, disguised as a Templar.[97] The Templars were also very closely connected with the monarchy of Jerusalem; two Masters of the Order had been in royal service before entering the Order.[98] Hence, the inclusion of the Templars emphasized that Wolfram was writing about the crown of Jerusalem. In addition, the fact that the Templars were not involved in the political conflicts in Germany made them more suitable for his purpose than the Teutonic Order.

In brief, the appearance of the 'Templars' as Grail-guardians in *Parzival* is absolutely essential, for the 'Templars' act as an signpost to the audience

---

[94] Naumann, *Kreuzzug Kaiser Heinrichs VI*, p. 211; Wojtecki, *Studien zur Personengeschichte des Deutschen Ordens*, pp. 51–91.

[95] On the Templars in Germany, see Bulst-Thiele, *Sacrae domus*, pp. 211–13, 372–7; Schüpferling, *Der Tempelherren-Orden in Deutschland*, esp. pp. 240–41; on the Templars and the Angevin monarchy, see Bulst-Thiele, 'Templer in königlichen und päpstlichen Diensten', pp. 289–308, esp. 293–301; Nicholson, 'The Military Orders and the Kings of England', pp. 203–18; and the numerous works there cited.

[96] See Udo Arnold, 'Eight Hundred Years of the Teutonic Order', in *The Military Orders: Fighting for the Faith*, ed. Barber, pp. 223–35, here p. 224; Hucker, *Kaiser Otto IV*, pp. 287–90.

[97] Bulst-Thiele, *Sacrae domus*, pp. 125–7; Edbury, *Kingdom of Cyprus*, pp. 7–8; Peter Edbury, 'The Templars in Cyprus', in *The Military Orders: Fighting for the Faith*, ed. Barber, pp. 189–95, here pp. 189–90; *Chronique d'Ernoul*, pp. 296–7; see also Ralph of Coggeshall, *Chronicon anglicanum*, p. 54.

[98] Bulst-Thiele, *Sacrae domus*, 87–90, 106.

that in this story, the Grail Castle is Jerusalem. Should this be insufficient to convince the sceptical modern reader, Wolfram's successors also indicate that Wolfram's Grâl Castle is the Mount of Salvation, that is, Sion, meaning Jerusalem. Wolfram's Grail knight, Parzivâl, is descended from a crusader and from the heirs to the Grâl, and is the grandson of an Angevin monarch, so that if Parzivâl's family relationships are significant, then Parzivâl is intended as Otto of Brunswick – and the great care Wolfram takes to inform the audience of Parzivâl's family relationships indicates that they are very significant. Wolfram tells his crusading patron and his wider audience that Parzivâl the Angevin will achieve the Grâl Castle; so, in other words, Otto of Brunswick should become emperor, go on crusade, claim the throne of Jerusalem and restore the Holy Land. He is the only true legitimate heir, and therefore he alone will have God's support for this undertaking; but because he is the legitimate heir, he will be successful, provided he is faithful to God and to love. Under his government, peace will be restored to the Holy Land; the political factions will be reconciled and the kingdom will be prosperous.

When Wolfram was writing, Jerusalem itself was no longer in Christian hands, having been lost to Saladin in October 1187. Parzivâl's eventual success in reaching the Grâl castle, asking the all-important question which will heal his uncle and taking over the kingship of the Grâl community must in the real world involve the recovery of Jerusalem from the Muslims; presumably by peaceful means rather than warfare as Parzivâl does. This is in fact exactly what the emperor Frederick II of Hohenstaufen later endeavoured to achieve during his crusade of 1228–29.

Wolfram's 'Templars', however, also serve a further purpose, beyond simply informing the audience that his Grâl Castle represents Jerusalem. The fact that they bear a turtle dove, a symbol of peace and love, rather than a cross, a symbol of bloodshed and suffering, is an indication of what sort of kingdom the emperor is to rule. He is to convert the Muslims by love, and inaugurate a new era of Christian peace. This may appear to be an impossible dream in this world, a looking-forward to the heavenly Jerusalem rather than the physical one on earth. Yet, with his many allusions to the actual world and to an actual religious Military Order, Wolfram insists that it can exist in reality. The 'Templars', with their devotion to God and His love underlined by their turtle-dove shields, make the connection between the heavenly Jerusalem and the earthly Jerusalem, between mysticism and physical actuality.

1.2 *Perceforest: knights defending the temple*

Another romance should be considered here, which does not deal with the Grail itself by name but which does present an ideal knighthood and the search for the one true God, and which includes 'knights of the Temple'. This is *Perceforest*, written in French between *c.* 1335 and 1344 in the Low Countries and describing the supposed growth of chivalry in pre-Christian Britain. The purpose of the author was to connect the legend of King Alexander to the legend of the Grail and of King Arthur, and as such the romance is a 'prequel' to the prose *Estoire del Saint Graal*. Events in the romance reflect the fact that it was written against the background of the Anglo-Scottish war and the Hundred Years' War. While few manuscripts now survive, *Perceforest* was a well-known and influential work, and was also translated into Spanish and Italian. It has been argued that King Edward III of England's Round Table, in a hall 200 feet in diameter and with three hundred knights, is based on the 'Franc Palais' set up in Book Two of *Perceforest*, where an elite of English knighthood was, supposedly, first established, before the birth of Christ. Maurice Keen has pointed out that the chivalric 'Order of the Star' set up by King John II of France in 1350 seems also to have been based on the 'Franc Palais'. *Perceforest* may also have been used by the French knight Geoffrey de Charny when he was writing his *Livre de Chevalerie* in the early 1350s.[99] *Perceforest* is therefore a useful guide to the ideals of the highest nobility of England, the Low Countries and France at the time it was written and during the rest of the fourteenth century. The fact that all the surviving manuscripts date from the fifteenth century and that two French editions were published in the sixteenth century indicates its continuing popularity among the nobility.[100]

In Book One of *Perceforest*, the knights find a circular Temple to the Unknown God. Its shape echoes the round Church of the Holy Sepulchre in

---

[99] *Quatrième partie du roman de Perceforest*, ed. Gilles Roussineau, TLF 343 (Geneva, 1986), pp. ix–xiv (date), xxxv–xxxvi (translations). On the author of *Perceforest*'s purpose in writing, see Jeanne Lods, *Le Roman de Perceforest: origines – composition – charatères – valeur et influence* (Geneva, 1951), p. 37. On Edward III and *Perceforest*, see also Juliet Barker, *The Tournament in England, 1100–1400* (Woodbridge, 1986), pp. 93–4; Barber and Barker, *Tournaments*, p. 35. On King John II of France see Keen, *Chivalry*, p. 191. On the translations see also Ian Michael, 'The Spanish Perceforest: a recent discovery', *Studies in Medieval Literature and Languages in Memory of Frederick Whitehead*, ed. W. Rothwell, W.R.J. Barron, David Blamires and Lewis Thorpe (Manchester, 1973), pp. 209–18. One surviving French manuscript was copied for Philip the Good, duke of Burgundy: *Quatrième partie*, pp. xxvii–xxviii; for the *Perceforest* and Geoffrey de Charny, see: *The Book of Chivalry of Geoffroi de Charny*, pp. 74, 223–4, and p. 8 (for date). It is suggested that Geoffrey de Charny took the details of Caesar's assassination from *Perceforest*. There is no modern edition of this section of *Perceforest*: for the 1528 printed edition, see *Les Anciennes Cronicques Dangleterre faitz et gestes des roys Perceforest et Gadiffer descosse. Hystorie moult solatiense et delectable. Nouvellement Imprime a Paris* (1528), 6 vols in 2, vol. 5 ch. 4, fols. 13a–15d. Charny's version of events is also very similar to the details given by Martin the Pole in his *Chronicle*, which was widely used in the fourteenth century: 'Martinus Oppaviensis Chronicon', ed. Ludwig Weiland, in *MGHS*, 22, p. 406. Honoré Bonet's version of Caesar's assassination is also very similar to *Perceforest*, more so than Charny's account: *The Tree of Battles: an English Version with Introduction*, trans. G.W. Copeland (Liverpool, 1942), p. 112, (and see Copeland's introduction, pp. 47–52, for Martin the Pole). Although Charny may not have known *Perceforest*, Bonet probably did, so that the work was certainly known in France by the late fourteenth century.

[100] *Quatrième partie*, pp. xxi–xxxv.

Jerusalem, the most famous and important church in Christendom – although, in the story, there is as yet no Sepulchre. Perceforest takes up the worship of this God, names him 'the Sovereign God', and builds his own round Temple in His honour.[101] Like the Grail Castle, Perceforest's Temple is hidden, concealed deep in the forest which Perceforest conquered from the enchanter Darnant whose family are the enemies of right and good, law and order, and women.[102] Knights go to the Temple on pilgrimage to worship God. Two knights volunteer to guard the Temple for a year and a day; they both bear white arms and are called *'les chevaliers du Temple'*, 'the knights of the Temple', which was also the alternative name of the historical Templars. Like the Templars, these knights guard a round church which is central to the faith of those who visit it as pilgrims. Clearly these knights of the Temple are not Templars proper: they are not part of a religious order, they cannot bear a red cross because the cross has no significance in pre-Christian Britain, and they serve the king of England, not the pope; in *Perceforest* there are no priests, only hermits. However, these knights live in the Temple, entertain knights who visit it, and their purpose, like Wolfram von Eschenbach's *Templeise*, is to defend the Temple from the unworthy and to test the knightly skills of those who come to the Temple. In contrast, the genuine Templars fought alongside Christians rather than against them, but *Perceforest*'s knights of the Temple are performing a common task of Templars in literature: supporting and encouraging knights in their deeds of knighthood. When this round Temple is mentioned again, there are no longer any knights defending it. This indicates that the author only included his 'knights of the Temple', to underline to the reader that this round Temple is intended to foreshadow the Holy Sepulchre.[103]

The episode involving the Knights of the Temple takes place when Perceforest's kingdom of ancient English chivalry is at its peak. The knights who serve at the Temple are the son of King Alexander, that paragon of chivalry, and a Roman (here the equivalent of a Saracen), Lucius, 'the mute knight', a former spy. After visiting the Temple and jousting with the knights who guard it, Perceforest announces a festival of the Sovereign God. Here 'the

---

[101] *Le Roman de Perceforest, première partie*, ed. Jane Taylor, TLF 279 (Geneva, 1979), p. 244 lines 6411–12, p. 412 lines 12401–2; *Perceforest, troisième partie*, 2, p. 54.

[102] *Perceforest: troisième partie*, 3, p. 7, ch. 47, lines 232–5, p. 22, ch. 29, lines 135–7; p. 183, ch. 56, line 726.

[103] Ibid.: the two knights vow to defend the Temple: pp. 6–8, ch. 47 lines 180–208, 232–52; knights go on pilgrimage to the Temple: pp. 22, ch. 49 line 168; p. 27, ch. 49 lines 342–3; p. 29, ch. 49 lines 421–3; the two knights wear the same, white arms: p. 24, ch. 49, line 213, p. 25, ch. 49, line 251; knights go there to test their own skill in arms: p. 20, ch. 49, lines 66–73; they are 'the knights of the Temple', p. 28, ch. 49 , lines 367–8, p. 31, ch. 49, line 490, p. 32, ch. 49, line 508 (they are also called 'the knights who guarded the Temple'); they entertain knights: p. 31, ch. 49, lines 469–71; the king visits the Temple, but no knights now defend it: *Quatrième partie*, pp. 75–7, ch. 1 lines 2239–328.

mute knight' confesses his espionage to Perceforest, and expresses an ardent desire to become one of the knights of the 'Franc Palais'. So, as in *Parzival*, the Temple can be seen as a place where opposing religions come together and where the enemies of the one true faith are converted to truth. Yet it is also at this festival, by which time the knights of the Temple have served for their year and departed, that the seeds of destruction of the kingdom become evident. The young knights marry their ladies and leave the court to go to their own countries and castles; and Bethidés, Perceforest's son, announces his intention of marrying the Roman noblewoman Circe, who will later bring about the kingdom's destruction. The episode at the Temple is representative of Perceforest's knighthood at its apex; never again will Perceforest's kingdom rise to such heights of chivalry.

As the work was composed in the Low Countries, where both French and German were known, the author probably knew Wolfram's *Parzival*. However, the concept of knights guarding the Round Temple may well have been his own idea, derived from the historical Order of the Temple. Like Wolfram, the author of *Perceforest* took the most basic concept underlying the Templars – knights attached to a holy site, serving God – and developed it for his own purposes.

2 *Other Grail romances*

Numerous other Grail romances were written during the thirteenth century: Heinrich von der Türlin's *Diu Crône*, Robert de Boron's verse *Estoire dou Graal* or *Joseph*, the 'Didot' *Perceval*, the *Perlesvaus* or *Haut Livre du Graal*, the Vulgate *Queste del Saint Graal* and its 'prequel' the prose *Estoire del Saint Graal*, the post-Vulgate *Roman du Graal*, parts of which also appear in the prose *Tristan* and which was translated into Portuguese and Spanish as the *Demanda*, the Welsh *Peredur*, and later the English *Sir Perceval de Galles*, an adaptation of Chrétien's *Conte du Graal* which does not actually mention the Grail.[104] The Templars appear by name in none of these. However, it has been suggested by various scholars that they appear under another guise, and can be identified by the symbols associated with them. Alternatively, it can be

---

[104] See Chapter 1, note 64 above and Heinrich von dem Türlin, *Diu Crône*, ed. Gottlob Heinrich Friedrich Scholl, BLVS 27 (Stuttgart, 1852); Robert de Boron, *Le Roman de l'Estoire dou Graal*, ed. William A. Nitze, CFMA 57 (Paris, 1983); *The 'Didot' Perceval according to the manuscripts of Modena and Paris*, ed. W.H. Roach (Philadelphia, 1941); *Perlesvaus: Le Haut Livre du Graal*, ed. W.A. Nitze and J. Atkinson Jenkins, 2 vols (reprinted New York, 1972); *Historia Peredur vab Efrawc: Golygwyd gyda Rhagymadrodd Nodiadau*, ed. Glenys Witchard Goetinck (Cardiff, 1976); translated as 'Peredur son of Evrawg' in *The Mabinogion*, trans. Jeffrey Gantz (Harmondsworth, 1976), pp. 217–57; 'Sir Perceval of Galles' in *Middle English Metrical Romances*, ed. Walter Hoyt French and Charles Brockway Hale, 2 vols in 1 (New York, 1964), pp. 531–603.

suggested that the Grail hero Galaad represents the ideal Templar knight or that the Round Table represents the Templar Order. If the former is not the case, it could be argued that as the character of the figure of Galaad developed he became more like a Templar.

It could also be possible that the Templars had an indirect connection with the Grail romances, via the Order's connection with the Holy Land and Jerusalem. It is necessary to consider whether there is any connection between the Grail romances as a whole and the Holy Land; and whether any of the Grail romances were actually written in the Holy Land.

Recent scholarship has shown that Robert de Boron's *Estoire dou Graal* or *Joseph* was probably written in Cyprus. In 1970 Pierre Gallais noted that Robert de Boron's patron, Walter of Montbéliard, took the cross in 1199 but did not set out with the other crusaders for the Fourth Crusade. We find him next in Cyprus, where he was constable of Jerusalem by 1205. After the death of Aimery of Lusignan, king of Cyprus and Jerusalem, in 1205, he became regent for Aimery's son Hugh, and for the next five years he was one of the most powerful people in the Latin East. As soon as Hugh came of age, Walter fell from power and fled to Gastria, the Templar castle on Cyprus. He was unable to recover the royal favour and went to Acre, where he remained in the service of John of Brienne, his cousin and king of Jerusalem. He died in 1212, during a campaign against the Muslims.

Gallais pointed out that it would be far more likely that the Walter of Montbéliard who encouraged the literary arts was the man who was constable of Jerusalem and regent of Cyprus rather than the lord of no particular renown of the period before 1199. Therefore, it is likely that the *Estoire dou Graal* (or *Joseph*) and *Merlin* were written in Cyprus. It has often been noticed that Robert de Boron's works reflect certain oriental sources, which can more easily be accounted for if he was in the East while he was writing. Gallais argued that 'Robert perhaps did not learn Greek, but he certainly lived in a milieu wide open to Byzantine and Syriac influences'.[105]

---

[105] Pierre Gallais, 'Robert de Boron en Orient', in *Mélanges de Langue et de Littérature du Moyen Age et de la Renaissance offerts à Jean Frappier*, 2 vols (Geneva, 1970), 1, pp. 313–19. His theory has been developed by Krijnie Cigaar, 'Robert de Boron en Outremer? Le Culte de Joseph d'Arimathie dans le monde Byzantin et en Outremer', *Polyphonia Byzantina: Studies in Honour of Willem J. Aerts*, ed. Hero Hokwerda, Edmé R. Smits and Marinus M. Woesthuis (Groningen, 1993), pp. 145–159; Krijnie Cigaar, 'Le Royaume des Lusignans: Terre de littérature et de traditions échanges littéraires et culturels', *Actes du Colloque: Les Lusignans et L'Outre-Mer* (Poitiers, n.d. (1995)), pp. 89–98; Krijnie Cigaar, 'Flemish Counts and Emperors: Friends and foreigners in Byzantium', in *The Latin Empire: Some Contributions*, ed. V.D. Van Aalst and K.N. Cigaar (Hernen, 1990), pp. 33–62, esp. pp. 39–40. However, Alexandre Micha, *Étude sur le <Merlin> de Robert de Boron: Roman du XIIIe siècle* (Geneva, 1980), p. 7, assumes that Robert wrote in the West, before Walter of Montbéliard left for the East. Pierre le Gentil, 'The work of Robert de Boron and the *Didot Perceval*', in *Arthurian Literature in the Middle Ages*, pp. 251–62, also assumes that Robert de Boron wrote in the West (p. 255). See also Knight, 'From Jerusalem to Camelot', pp. 225–7, where he discusses Robert de Boron's work in connection with the Holy

There are also indications that the Latin Christians in the East had a particular interest in Arthurian romances: for instance, the first known 'Arthurian Round Table' tournament was organised in Cyprus by John of Ibelin to celebrate the dubbing to knighthood of his two eldest sons in 1223.[106] This was followed in 1286 by another at Acre to celebrate the coronation of Henry II of Cyprus as king of Jerusalem, in which knights dressed up as Lancelot, Tristan, Palamedes and many others.[107] Clearly, as Robert de Boron's work tells the story of the bringing of the Grail from the East by Joseph of Arimathea, the Latin Christians in the East would take a particular interest in his work; not only was it set in their local area, so to speak, but the *Estoire* also emphasizes the importance of the Latin East for Christendom, thereby raising its prestige and encouraging westerners to send aid and support to the East. However, there is no evidence of 'Templars' in this story, in disguise or otherwise. Joseph of Arimathea is a pious knight, but he is alone; he is not part of a religious order, and operates outside all forms of ecclesiastical organisation.

The *Perlesvaus* and *Queste del Saint Graal*, with the prose *Estoire* and the post-vulgate reworkings of the *Queste*, also give some indication that their Grail is connected with the Holy Land.

Perlesvaus, otherwise known as *Le Haut Livre du Graal*, is effectively a prose continuation of Chrétien's *Conte du Graal*. It was apparently written to establish a connection between Glastonbury Abbey in Somerset, England, and the Arthurian legend, and was therefore probably written by a writer with Benedictine connections, as Glastonbury was a Benedictine abbey. This is not inconsistent with the emphasis on holy war which pervades the whole work; among Benedictines, the Cluniacs had played a role in the 'peace movement' in the Church in the eleventh century which sought to encourage knights to fight for God and the Church rather than fighting between themselves and attacking the defenceless, and they had also supported the First Crusade. *Perlesvaus* certainly promotes such ideals.[108] Although not all scholars agree

---

Land, while maintaining that Robert wrote in France. I am indebted to Dr Peter Edbury for drawing my attention to Krijnie Cigaars' work.

[106] For the Round Table of 1223, see Philip of Novara: *Filippo da Novara, Guerra di Federico II*, p. 72, section 16 (112). This is identified as the earliest known instance of tourneying in Arthurian dress by Keen, *Chivalry*, p. 93. For the popularity of Arthurian romances in the Latin East see Jacoby, 'La littérature française dans les états latins'; and Jacoby, 'Knightly Values and Class Consciousness'.

[107] *Les Gestes des Chyprois, recueil de chroniques français écrites en orient en XIII et XIV siècles*, ed. Gaston Raynaud, Société de l'Orient Latin (Paris, 1887, reprinted Osnabrück, 1968), p. 220.

[108] *Perlesvaus*, 2, pp. 45–72, 86–99; on the Cluniacs, their attitudes to knighthood and their support for the First Crusade see H.E.J. Cowdrey, 'Cluny and the First Crusade', *Révue Benedictine*, 83 (1973), 285–311; reprinted in Cowdrey, *Popes, Monks and Crusaders* (London, 1984), XV; Riley-Smith, *The First Crusade*, pp. 4–5, 12, 31.

that it was written by a Benedictine, it is generally agreed that it was composed by a cleric.[109]

Perlesvaus may date from the first decade of the thirteenth century, or may be later, written after the first, non-cyclic version of *Lancelot*. Here the Grail Castle is clearly Jerusalem, both an earthly and heavenly Jerusalem. Like the earthly Jerusalem, it is captured by infidels when the wounded king dies; in this case the conqueror is the King of Castle Mortal (lines 5145–9). It is later recovered by Perlesvaus (lines 6133–240). This, then, is a post-1187 Jerusalem, held by the Muslims. Like the heavenly Jerusalem, the way in appears narrow (lines 2287–334; and see the Gospel of Matthew, ch. 7 vv. 13–14) although in fact it is not, and it is called 'Eden', 'Joy', and 'the castle of Souls' (lines 7204–6). Crusading parallels abound. Arthur is under attack from King Madaglans, king of Oriande (the Orient), a king of great power who has conquered a great deal of territory. This king is a relative of Arthur's, and claims the right to the Round Table (presumably, the right to excel in knighthood and to control all earthly knighthood). He does not follow the 'New Law' (Christianity) but the 'Old Law' (properly Judaism, but here clearly Islam); but he is eventually defeated by Lancelot, who converts his territories back to the New Law (lines 7842–52, 7860–63, 8500–552). The King of Castle Mortal is also a follower of the Old Law, and when Perlesvaus recaptures the Grail Castle he converts the inhabitants to the New Law (lines 5788–973). He also converts others to the New Law (lines 9037–256). During the course of the story, Perlesvaus travels over the sea to a mysterious island and 'the Castle of the Four Horns' where he encounters thirty-three men in white robes with red crosses on the chest (lines 9597–9). He is told that when he is summoned, he will return to be king in the castle (lines 9622–36).[110]

The Vulgate *Queste del Saint Graal* dates from around 1215. Albert Pauphilet argued that its author was connected with the Cistercian order, but not all modern scholars agree. It is, however, agreed that the author was connected to the monastic life in some respect.[111] In this romance the Grail quest is led by Galaad, who is a virgin and chaste, and descended from King Solomon. At a monastery of white brothers he receives a white shield with a red cross on it, which belonged to Joseph of Arimathea.[112] He and two other knights, Perceval and Bohort de Gaunes, eventually reach the Grail castle, which is in Britain and here named Corbenic, where they meet nine other

---

[109] Bruce, *Evolution*, 2, p. 17; Thomas Kelly, *Le Haut Livre du Graal: Perlesvaus. A Structural Study* (Geneva, 1974), p. 19.

[110] *Perlesvaus*, 1, p. 388, lines 9588–90. For *Perlesvaus* and the crusade, see Trotter, *Medieval French literature*, pp. 153–7; for date see *Perlesvaus*, 2, p. 89; for the Old and the New Law, see *Perlesvaus*, 2, pp. 259–60. For *Perlesvaus* and the Holy Land see also Knight, 'From Jerusalem to Camelot', pp. 229–30.

[111] Pauphilet, *Études*, pp. 53–84; Matarasso, *Redemption of Chivalry*, pp. 207–8; *Perlesvaus*, 2, pp. 83–5; Pratt, 'The Cistercians and the *Queste*', esp. pp. 87–8.

[112] *Queste*, p. 26, line 23–p. 35, line 12.

knights who have succeeded in the quest. They all take part in a communion service where Christ Himself is the priest, and are compared to the twelve apostles. The nine are then sent back into the world, but Galaad, Bohort and Perceval go with the Grail overseas to Sarraz, the city where Joseph of Arimathea was first made a bishop, and which is 'towards the parts of Jerusalem' and ruled by a king descended from pagans.[113] Pauphilet interpreted Sarraz as 'the transparent symbol of the Heavenly Jerusalem', and scholars have followed his interpretation; although it is a Jerusalem under Muslim rule, a post-1187 Jerusalem, as in *Perlesvaus*.[114] The king of Sarraz puts the Grail knights in prison, but eventually releases them and is converted by Galaad to Christianity. He then dies, and the people of Sarraz make Galaad king. Unlike events in *Perlesvaus*, therefore, 'Jerusalem' is recaptured and reconverted to Christianity by peaceful means. After seeing a vision of God Himself in the Graal, Galaad dies and is buried. Perceval dies as a hermit, and Bohort returns to King Arthur to tell the tale.[115] The post-vulgate reworkings of the 1230s and later repeat these basic episodes, although events at Corbenic are successively played down.

There is no evidence that the *Perlesvaus* or the *Queste* were written in the East. The Templars do not appear by name, yet it could be argued that they appear in a different guise. There are some similarities between the 'perfect knight' who wins the Grail, and the Templars and/or the Military Orders in general. Scholars have noted the parallel between the shield with the red cross on a white field which is borne by Galaad, the thirty-three holy men clothed in white with a red cross on the breast who meet Perlesvaus at the Castle of the Four Horns, and the red cross on white which was borne by the Templars, and have suggested that this symbolism indicates that Galaad and these thirty-three holy men are intended to be Templars.[116] Other symbolic connections between the Templars and the Grail Quest have also been suggested. However, in all cases these supposed symbolic connections do not stand up to informed and detailed historical investigation.

---

[113] *Queste*, p. 84 lines, 13–14, p. 276, lines 20–22.

[114] *Queste*, p. xiii; Frederick W. Locke, *The Quest for the Holy Grail: A Literary Study of a thirteenth-century Romance* (Stanford, California, 1960), pp. 86–101 and p. 118, note 10; see also Bruce, *Evolution*, 1, p. 423, note 155. On the *Queste* and the Holy Land, see Knight, 'From Jerusalem to Camelot', pp. 230–32.

[115] *Queste*, p. 265, line 12–p. 279, line 25.

[116] *Queste*, pp. 26–9, especially p. 28, line 9; Pauphilet, *Études*, pp. 70–1; Trotter, *Medieval French Literature*, p. 157; Bruce, *Evolution*, 1, p. 260, note 46 identifies the thirty-three holy men in *Perlesvaus* as hermits; Weston, *Quest of the Holy Grail*, p. 136, calls them hermits but says that they are Templars; see also Weston, 'Notes on the Grail Romances – *Sone de Nansai*, *Parzival* and *Perlesvaus*', 412–13, where she calls them monks but says that they are Templars – and, oddly, says that they have charge of the Grail, which is not in the text; see also on the suggested Templar connection with the *Queste*: Pratt, 'Cistercians and the *Queste*', p. 79; Knight, 'From Jerusalem to Camelot', p. 232.

2.1 *The 'red-cross shield': the Templars in a different guise?*

The first obstacle to the theory that a knight bearing a white shield with a red cross represents a Templar is that although the Templar knights did wear a red cross on their white mantles after this right was conceded to them by Pope Eugenius III (1145–53) in 1147, their shield and banner were actually black and white. The banner is usually seen depicted as having a black upper and a white lower section, although one depiction shows the banner with a white upper and black lower section, with a small red cross on the white section. The same picture shows the shield with a white upper and a black lower section, and with a small red cross on the white upper part.[117] Certainly the knight-Brothers' habit was white, but although a few Brothers testifying during the trial of the Templars claimed to have been given a completely new set of clothes when they were admitted to the Order, most only mentioned being given the mantle; and it is clear from the Rule and other evidence that it was the mantle which essentially formed 'the habit' of the Military Orders. The mantle of the knight-Brothers of the Order of the Temple was white with a red cross on the left-hand side; while sergeants, the non-knightly serving Brothers, wore a black mantle with a red cross. Contemporary illustrations indicate that the long tunic worn under the mantle was usually brown or black for both knights and serving Brothers.[118] The red cross on white was also borne by

---

[117] For the Templars' banner and shield, see: Luttrell, 'Earliest Templars', pp. 197–8 and notes 22, 27; and see *Templari e Ospitalieri in Italia: La chiesa di San Bevignate a Perugia*, ed. Mario Roncetti, Pietro Scarpellini and Francesco Tommasi (Milan, 1987), p. 133, fig. 92; Demurger, *Vie et mort*, fig. 18, between pp. 32 and 33; Nicholson, *Templars, Hospitallers*, p. 95. For the Order's black and white banner (black upper section, white lower section) see Nicholson, *Templars, Hospitallers*, p. 69 – the banner reversed in defeat – and Barber, *New Knighthood*, p. 146 – the right way up, carried by the *gonfanier*.

[118] For the Templars' habit, see: Bulst Thiele, *Sacrae domus*, p. 38 note 35; Demurger, *Vie et mort*, p. 79. For the equation of the mantle with the habit of the Order of the Temple, see *Règle du Temple*, pp. 247–8, sections 462–3, pp. 291–3, sections 557–60, p. 306, section 589, pp. 321–2, section 622; 'The *Tractatus de loci et statu sancte terre*', pp. 125–6; Anonymous Pilgrim V, 2, p. 30. For the significance of the mantle in the admission ceremony, see: *Règle du Temple*, p. 345, section 678; *Le Procès des Templiers*, ed. Jules Michelet, 2 vols (Paris, 1841–51, reprinted Paris, 1987), for instance, 1, pp. 193, 223, 325, 382, 417, 2, pp. 216, 296, 300, 305–6, 307–8, 310, 313; *Der Untergang des Templerordens mit urkundlichen und kritischen Beiträgen*, ed. Konrad Schottmüller, 2 vols (Berlin, 1887, reprinted Vaduz, Lichtenstein, 1991), 2, pp. 15, 20 (given new set of clothes), pp. 17, 18, 22, 24, 27, 28, 31, etc. (simply given mantle). Innocent III referred to the white mantle as the distinctive item of dress which formed the Templars' habit: Innocent III, 'Liber registrorum', Year 13, nos 125–6, *Pat. Lat.* 216, cols. 312–13; *Tabulae ordinis theutonici*, pp. 269–70, nos. 299–300. Contemporary pictures of the Templars show different colours of dress: a fresco on the west wall of the Orders' church of S. Bevignate at Perugia shows the Templars in white monastic dress, with hoods, but without red crosses on their habits: reproduced in Demurger, *Vie et mort*, plate 16 (between pp. 32–3); Barber, *New Knighthood*, p. 207; Nicholson, *Templars, Hospitallers*, p. 36; Alain Demurger, *A Brief History of Religious Military Orders: Hospitallers, Templars, Teutonic* ... , trans. Beryl Degans (Paris, 1997), p. 14 (originally published in French as *Brève Histoire des ordres religieux-militaires*, Paris, 1997). An illustration in a manuscript of Jacquemart Giélée's satirical poem *Renart le Nouvel* (1289), Bib. nat. MS fr. 25566 fol. 173, shows a Templar in a long dark tunic with white mantle; a white cross is placed on

other Military Orders and confraternities, while the Hospitallers bore the same colours in reverse, a white cross on a red field.[119]

The symbol of the cross was not the unique symbol of the Military Orders. Other, non-military religious orders also bore a cross: in 1393 the pope approved the foundation of a monastery of the Order of St Clare in Exeter diocese, whose canons were to wear cassocks with a small cross of red and white on the breast.[120] The cross was also the distinguishing mark of certain warrior saints. The red cross on a white field appears in Catholic iconography as part of the arms of St George, archetypal knight of Christ and helper of the crusaders, as early as 1170.[121] It is also the symbol on many national flags of Christian European countries. According to legend, the Danish national flag, a white cross on a blood red field, originally fell from heaven in 1219 when the Danes were fighting the heathen Estonians. Carrying this banner, the Danes won the victory.

Secondly, the red cross on a white field also appears elsewhere in literature where it is very unlikely to depict Templars. In the legend of the birth of the Knight of the Swan, the young Elias is sent by God a white shield bearing

---

the centre of the dark tunic: reproduced in Demurger, *Vie et mort*, plate 19; Nicholson, *Templars, Hospitallers*, p. 32. Another manuscript of *Renart le Nouvel*, Bib. nat. MS fr. 372 fol. 59, shows the masters of the Temple and Hospital doing homage to Renart the fox; it is not clear which is the Templar and which the Hospitaller. According to the text, the figure on the left of Renart should be the Templar: he wears red, with no cross. This is reproduced by Demurger, *Vie et mort*, plate 20; Nicholson, *Templars, Hospitallers*, p. 134. An illustration of two Templars playing chess in a manuscript of *The Book of Chess* composed by Alfonso X of Castile, in the Library of the Escorial, shows the Templars wearing long, dark tunics with hoods and white mantles, with the red cross on the left side: reproduced in *Libro de Ajedrez, Dados y Tablas de Alfonso X el Sabio* ed. Pilar Garcia Morencos (Madrid, 1977), fig. 6 and by Demurger, *A Brief History*, p. 8.

[119] The knights of Christ of Livonia bore a red cross on a white field, with a red sword, while the Prussian Order bore a red sword and star on a white field: Walter Kuhn, 'Ritterorden als Grenzhüter des Abendlandes gegen das östliche Heidentum', *Ostdeutsche Wissenschaft*, 6 (1959), 7–70: here 12, 27; the Militia of the Blessed Virgin Mary also bore a red cross: Norman Housley, 'Politics and Heresy in Italy: anti-heretical crusades, orders and confraternities, 1200–1500', *Journal of Ecclesiastical History*, 33 (1982), 193–208: here 206; for the Hospitallers' red banner with white cross see *Cartulaire général de l'ordre des Hospitaliers*, no. 627 (p. 426), no. 2928; Nicholson, *Templars, Hospitallers*, p. 69. This is now the national flag of the Sovereign Order of Malta and may be seen, for instance, outside their embassy in Malta. For various examples of the cross in Old French literature see, for example, Trotter, *Medieval French Literature*, pp. 58–69, 77–81, 114.

[120] *Calendar of the Papal Registers relating to Great Britain: Papal Letters*, vol. 4, AD 1362–1404, ed. W.H. Bliss and J.A. Twemlow (London, 1902), p. 462.

[121] See the image of St George on the Jerusalem map in Koninklijke Bibliotheek, The Hague, MS 69 (dating from *c*. 1170). Reproduced in black and white by Sophia Menache, *The Vox Dei: Communication in the Middle Ages* (Oxford, 1990), p. 118, plate 20. This image is sometimes erroneously identified as a Templar, although his name 'Sanctus Georgius' is clearly written behind his head. The red cross on white shield borne by this figure may be contrasted with the arms of the mysterious knight who guided the Christians in William of Tyre's account of the retreat from Bostrum in 1146: this knight was mounted on a white horse and bore a red standard. The French translation agrees with these details: William, archbishop of Tyre, *Chronicon*, 2, p. 733; Bk 16, ch. 12, lines 59–60; 'L'Estoire de Eracles Empereur', *RHC Occ.*, 1, p. 726.

a red cross, the white symbolising humility, the red justice, boldness and goodness.[122] When Elias' enemy Malquarés strikes the cross, flame leaps out and strikes him.[123] This shield, we are told, was passed down to Elias' grandson Godfrey of Bouillon, who became the first ruler of the Latin kingdom of Jerusalem.[124] However, in the later version of the 'Second Crusade Cycle', *Le Chevalier au Cygne et Godefroid de Bouillon*, Helyas' shield is mentioned only in passing during his fight with Mauquaret, where it is white with a red cross. Later it becomes white with a golden cross, but is seldom mentioned. Moreover, the shield is not kept for Godfrey's later use. The gold cross on a white field was in fact the arms of the kings of Jerusalem, Helyas' descendants. It seems that this author saw the significance of the cross primarily in heraldic, dynastic terms rather than in spiritual terms.[125]

Several red crosses on white appear in the 'prequel' to the *Queste*, the prose *Estoire del Saint Graal*. Scholars have generally assumed that this was written after the *Queste*, although the editor of the new edition of the text has argued that it was written before the *Queste*. In the prose *Estoire*, King Evalac of Sarraz is given a white shield on which a red cross is placed, and Josephus the bishop tells him: 'If anyone looks at this sign with pure heart no evil can come upon them'. Later, in a battle against the Egyptians, Evalac calls on Christ while regarding the shield, and Christ Himself, in the form of a knight with white arms and a red cross on his shield, comes to his aid. A maimed knight is cured by touching the shield. This shield is later kept for Galaad, the perfect knight of Christ. Again, a ship with a red cross on its white sail carries Christ Himself. Here the red cross on the white shield evidently depicts Christ, and those who carry it are carrying Christ with them.[126]

Elsewhere, the symbol indicates warriors of Christ, especially warriors with some spiritual aspect: in five manuscripts of the *Chanson de Jérusalem* the clergy who bless the attack on Jerusalem wear white with a red cross on their chests.[127] In the mid-thirteenth-century epic poem *Enfances Renier*, the knights of Renier's father Maillefer are clad in white with red crosses on their helmets, shields and pennants, and the poet states that they looked like angels –

---

[122] *Beatrix*, ed. Jan A. Nelson, lines 1228–35, 1242, 1252–3, 1297, 1390–91, 1448, 1550–54, 1563–70, 1585, 1687–704, 2553, 2609, 2695, esp. lines 1232–4, in *OFCC, I: La Naissance du Chevalier au Cygne*, ed. Emanuel J. Mickel and Jan A. Nelson (Alabama, 1977).

[123] Ibid., lines 1687–704; see also 1712–16.

[124] *La Fin d'Elias*, ed. Jan A. Nelson, lines 2300–3, in *OFCC, II: Le Chevalier au Cygne and La Fin d'Elias*, ed. Jan A. Nelson (Alabama, 1985).

[125] *Le Chevalier au Cygne et Godefroid de Bouillon*, 1, pp. 79–80 and note to line 1810, p. 98 and note to line 2285, p. 109; lines 1809–10 (red cross), 2284–5, 2589 (gold cross); for Helyas' last words to his wife and daughter, see 3405–8, 3425–9.

[126] *Lestoire del Saint Graal*, pp. 47–8, 55, 62–5, 72–3, 74, 93, 106, 285.

[127] *OFCC, VI: La Chanson de Jérusalem*, ed. Nigel R. Thorp (Alabama, 1991), pp. 271–2, lines 3–5.

although, despite these insignia, they are later all defeated by the Muslims.[128] In the fourteenth-century *Le Chevalier au Cygne et Godefroid de Bouillon*, the heavenly hosts who come to the assistance of the crusaders wear white, with a red cross; or white with a gold cross.[129] The *Prophecies de Merlin*, written in the 1270s, tell a story of a Christian woman of Frisia who, dressed as a knight, challenges the pagan king to battle, to prove that her god is better than his (and also, we later learn, to avenge the martyrdom of her husband). She bears a white pennant on her lance; Christ places a red cross on this as she rides against the king. The king breaks his lance on her shield, but she 'with the aid of Christ's virtue' puts her lancehead through his shield and hauberk and throws him off the back of his horse. She eventually dies a martyr in the ensuing battle.[130]

In the fourteenth-century prose romance *Perceforest* the Scottish knight Gallafur, grandson of the maimed king Gadifer, goes to the ruined Temple of the Sovereign God to receive guidance as to how he may destroy the evil enchantments in the forest of Darnant. Here he receives a vision of his learned grandmother the queen of Scotland, who gives him a white shield with a red cross by which he may protect himself against evil spirits and banish them in the name of the Virgin's Son. The symbol means nothing to the young knight because Christ has not yet come, but his grandmother explains that it represents virginity and love, and tells him how she herself saw the star which proclaimed the birth of the Virgin's Son. She also instructs Gallafur to build a castle and place the sign on it, and states that this will be the first place where the messengers of the Virgin's Son will come when they enter England. When built, this castle is Gallafort, which plays an important role in the conversion of Britain in the *Estoire del Saint Graal*. In *Perceforest* the inclusion of the red cross symbol underlines the author's intention to connect the legend of King Alexander to the legend of the Grail and of King Arthur.[131]

In fact, the tradition of Christian warriors placing a cross on their shield dated back to the Battle of Milvian Bridge of October 312, when (according to the historian Lactantius) Constantine the Great 'was advised in a dream to mark the heavenly sign of God on the shield of his soldiers and then to engage

---

[128] *Enfances Renier: canzone di gesta inedita del sec. XIII*, ed. Carla Cremonesi (Milan and Varese, 1957), 4353–9.

[129] *Le Chevalier au Cygne et Godefroid de Bouillon*, 2, pp. 235–6, 242, 250, 371, lines 9580–83, 9753–4, 9572, 10004–7, 13703–7, 3, pp. 163–4, lines 23883–7, 23906–12 (red cross), and 2, pp. 234–5, lines 9552–5 (gold cross).

[130] *Les Prophecies de Merlin*, ed. Paton, 1, pp. 257–9, chapters 219–20; *Les Prophesies de Merlin (Cod. Bodmer 116)*, ed. Anne Berthelot, Biblioteca Bodmeriana textes 6 (Cologny-Geneva, 1992), pp. 147–8, fols 60BVb–61Va.

[131] Lods, *Le Roman de Perceforest*, pp. 31–2, Bk 5 sections 58, 68, Book 6, section 71, pp. 44, 108–9, 110–11. There is no modern edition of the sections of *Perceforest* dealing with the red cross shield. See the 1528 printed edition, vol. 5 ch. 38 fols 98b-d, vol. 6 ch. 48 fol. 97a. For the palace of Gallafur and its strange sign, see also L.-F. Flutre, 'Études sur le roman de Perceforêt (huitième et dernier article)', *Romania*, 91 (1970), 189–226: here 208.

in battle ... armed with this sign, the army took up its weapons', and went on to destroy the pagan forces of the rival emperor Maxentius.[132]

According to Lactantius, the 'heavenly sign' was a cross with the top stroke bent over to form a 'P', a stamogram. This symbol for Christ could also be rendered as 'P' with 'X' superimposed, forming a monogram which was used by the early Christians as a symbol for Christ. The 'X' and 'P' represented the Greek letters 'chi' and 'rho', the first two letters of the word *christos*, christ. The 'chi-rho' appears on the shield of a soldier in the well-known depiction of the entourage of the emperor Justinian in the mosaic on the north-east wall of the presbyterium of S. Vitale, Ravenna (546–48).[133] Here again it is clearly intended to denote the Christian emperor who wages war to defend his Christian subjects. This version of the 'chi-rho' was multi-coloured, with gold, blue and green predominating, but red was the most obvious colour for a symbol that depicted self-sacrifice and suffering, and the 'chi-rho' also appeared in blood red.[134]

In short, it is evident that a knight bearing this symbol in a romance does not imply a connection with the Templars, but simply that he is a knight of Christ, warring against evil. The white symbolises purity, the red martyrdom, and the whole symbolises Christ Himself. In the case of Gallafur, the red-cross shield denotes that God has chosen Gallafur's lineage to serve Him in the future.

Turning to the *Queste del Saint Graal*, it is clear that Galaad's red-cross shield does not necessarily indicate that he is a Templar. It does, however, indicate a connection with Christ. Galaad is Christ himself, for the word 'Galaad' both in the Latin of the Vulgate Bible and in Old French means 'Gilead', one of the mystical names of Christ. Christ is the 'balm of Gilead' which heals God's people.[135] Galaad is also Christ's servant, and he is a holy knight. The red-cross shield may also indicate something more: for instance, symbolising Christ's sacrifice on the cross and the covenant between God and

---

[132] Lactantius, *De Mortibus Persecutorum*, ed. J.L. Creed, Oxford Early Christian Texts (Oxford, 1984), 44.4–6, pp. 64–5. This is the earliest reference to Constantine taking up the sign of the cross for this battle (p. 119, note).

[133] Often reproduced; see, for instance, Jean Lassus, *Landmarks of the World's Art: The Early Christian and Byzantine World* (London, 1966), p. 60, pl. 44.

[134] For instance, in a wall painting at Lullingstone, Kent: Robert Milburn, *Early Christian Art and Architecture* (Aldershot, 1988), p. 16.

[135] For the word 'Galaad' used to mean 'Gilead', see the Vulgate *Sacra Biblia*, Numeri XXXII, 1; Cantiam Canticorum IV, 1; Jeremias VIII, 22, XLVI, 11. For the use of the word 'Galaad' to mean 'Gilead' in the Latin of William of Tyre, see William, archbishop of Tyre, *Chronicon*, Bk 8, ch. 1, line 27; Bk 12, ch. 16, line 13; Bk 15, ch. 6, lines 10, 20; Bk 18, ch. 19, line 15; Bk 22, ch. 29 [was 28], line 6; compare the English of Babcock and Kray, *A History of Deeds Done Beyond the Sea*, 1, pp. 340, 538, 2, pp. 103, 269, 498. For the word 'Galaad' or 'Galaaz' used to mean 'Gilead' in the equivalent passages of the Old French translation of William of Tyre, 'L'Estoire de Eracles Empereur', see *RHC Occ.*, 1, pp. 536, 665, 652, 1124. For the balm of Gilead healing God's people, see Jeremiah, ch. 8 v. 22 and ch. 46 v. 11.

humanity.[136] In short, although he is a secular knight, Galaad is a knightly image of Christ; in stark contrast to the traditional view of the monk as an imitator of Christ. The figure of Galaad in the *Queste* was therefore a very significant development in the conception of knighthood, as is well expressed in the title of Pauline Matarasso's study of the *Queste*: 'The Redemption of Chivalry'. However, being or imitating Christ does not necessarily make Galaad a Templar. He represents for knights a development from the Templars. The concept of the Templars demanded that a knight must join a religious order in order to imitate Christ; Galaad shows that a knight can imitate Christ while remaining a lay person. Nevertheless, scholars have argued that Galaad acts like a Templar; this argument will be considered below.

Perceval carries a red cross shield in Gerbert of Montreuil's continuation of the *Conte du Graal*. This shield is presented to him by a maiden so that he can fight the knight of the dragon; the dragon represents the devil. As the dragon on the evil knight's shield is afraid of the cross on Perceval's shield, Perceval is able to vanquish the evil knight. He also needs the shield in order to recover the Graal and the bleeding lance and so to complete his quest. Here the red cross shield represents the power of Christ with Perceval. While Perceval is certainly warring against evil, there is no indication that the shield implies a connection with a specific religious order.[137]

2.2 *Perlesvaus and the sign of the red cross*

Perlesvaus is a complex work, exploiting many-layered symbolism to the full. The subtle and intricit symbolism is an important attraction of the work, which clearly aimed not only to instruct but also to intrigue. Yet as a result it is difficult to know how to interpret the thirty-three men, aged around thirty-two, wearing white with a red cross on the breast whom Perlesvaus encounters in the Castle of the Four Horns. As the interpretation of this passage is difficult, it is worth while quoting it at length. Perlesvaus has arrived on an island in the middle of the sea in a boat which he won from the pagans. He sees a fountain.

> Next to the fountain two men were sitting, their hair and beards whiter than fresh snow, and yet their faces seemed young. As soon as they saw Perlesvaus they rose to meet him ... they led him into a great hall, and he carried his shield with him. They were very joyful over the shield and honoured it. He saw that the hall was very rich, for he had never seen such a lovely one. It was all hung round with silken cloths and in the middle of the hall was a picture of the Saviour of the world, as He is in His majesty, and the apostles around Him. There were in that hall people who were very full of joy, and who seemed to be very holy; and so they were, for if they were not good men they could not have survived there.

---

[136] Matarasso, *Redemption of Chivalry*, pp. 18–54, especially pp. 26, 52 on the shield. See also Bruce, *Evolution*, 1, p. 421: Galaad is 'merely Christ in armour'.

[137] Gerbert de Montreuil, *La Continuation de Perceval*, 2, lines 8468–95, 8508–15, 8950–9037, 9295–7, 9555–67.

'Lord,' said the two masters to Perlesvaus, 'this house you see which is so rich is a royal hall' ... One of the masters blew a call of three blows, and thirty-three men came into the hall, all of one company. They were wearing white clothes and there was none who did not have a scarlet cross on the centre of his chest, and they all seemed to be of the age of thirty-two years. As soon as they came into the hall, they adored Our Lord with pure heart, and beat their chests; then they went to wash in a rich wash-basin of gold, and then went to sit at the tables. The masters made Perlesvaus sit at the highest table by himself. They were served in that hall very gloriously and in a very holy manner.

Perlesvaus was more interested in watching them than he was in eating. As he watched, he looked up and saw a golden chain descend, covered in many sweet precious stones, and in the middle a crown of gold. The chain descended ... as soon as the masters saw it descend, they opened a great wide vault which was in the centre of the hall, so that one could see the opening clearly. As soon as the entrance to the vault was uncovered, the greatest and most sorrowful cries anyone ever heard came out of it. When the good men of that place heard them, they held up their hands to Our Lord and all began to weep ... The masters covered the vault up again. It was very hideous to see and piteous to hear the voices which came out of it. The good men got up from the tables when they had eaten and gave their thanks sweetly to Our Lord. Afterwards, they went back to the place they came from.[138]

The white-haired men who appear to be young recall Saint John the Divine's vision of Christ in Revelations, ch. 1 v. 14; these are holy figures, of the heavenly realm. The fact that they are called 'masters' indicates that they are people in authority, but does not indicate a connection with any religious order; it could mean that they are learned, but in this context it may simply indicate that they are the people in charge of proceedings.

The symbolism of the castle is complex; it appears to be the otherworld, perhaps Paradise; it contains a place of punishment. On the basis that the Grail Castle is Jerusalem – as it was captured by the enemy and Perlesvaus recaptured it – the Castle of the Four Horns cannot be Jerusalem. Although it does have a wash-basin, which might suggest the Temple, unlike the Holy of Holies in Solomon's Temple it is not square and it is not lined with cedar but with silk.[139] In short, it does not appear to be intended as Jerusalem or as the Temple. The presence of the image of the Saviour suggests a church or cathedral rather than the Temple. In any case, it is a holy place, with an image of Christ enthroned at its centre.

The company of men in white with red crosses on their breasts, living together in the hall and served very gloriously at table, are at first glance very reminiscent of Templars. However, they wear the red cross on their breasts (*enmi son piz*), rather than on the left-hand side of their mantles as the Templars did. In the same way, in three manuscripts of *La Chanson*

---

[138] *Perlesvaus*, 1, pp. 387–9, lines 9557–9, 9576–84, 9587–98, 9599–605, 9608–12.
[139] On these aspects of Solomon's Temple see 1 Kings ch. 6 vv. 15–18, 20, ch. 7 vv. 23–6.

d'Antioche, the Christians who are killed in the Battle of Antioch are found to have 'crosses on their hearts and on their chests, scarlet like blood'. This sign, we are told, was placed on them by Christ in token of their trust in Him.[140] This suggests that the scarlet cross on the chest is an indication of martyrdom. It has been demonstrated above, in Chapter 2, that the Templars were particularly regarded as potential martyrs, but obviously they were not the only martyrs celebrated during the Middle Ages: the early Christian martyrs, warrior saints such as St George, St Demetrius, St Maurice and St Mercurius, who appear helping the crusaders in the *Chanson d'Antioche*,[141] Christians killed by non-Christians throughout the ages and the crusaders who were killed by Muslims during the crusade were all included within the ranks of the holy martyrs.

In addition, the company of the Castle of the Four Horns do not carry swords and, unlike in Wolfram's *Parzival*, we are not told that they are Templars; so even if we decide that they are intended as Templars we cannot be certain that this is how audiences at the time interpreted them.

The fact that there are thirty-three of them appears to be a symbol of the Trinity, or the years of Christ's ministry on Earth; the fact that they are aged around thirty-two echoes Christ's age when He was crucified (variously calculated at thirty-two or thirty-three). Again, Christ's earthly ancestor King David of Israel reigned thirty-three years in Jerusalem.[142] In short, these numbers indicate the centrality of Christ to their existence.

Their white robes recall the white of the angels and saints noted above and the martyrs seen in St John's vision in Revelations:

> They are those who have passed through the great ordeal: they have washed their robes and made them white in the blood of the Lamb. That is why they stand before the Throne of God and worship him night and day in his Temple; and he who sits on the Throne will protect them with his presence. Never again will they feel hunger or thirst ...
>
> (Revelations, ch. 6 vv. 13–16)

In short, Perlesvaus appears to have encountered the company of martyrs in Heaven, where Christ is enthroned. Their white robes with red crosses on the chest recall their martyrdom and Christ's sacrifice, and, like the martyrs in John's vision, they are gloriously fed by their lord.

In his study on this work, Thomas Kelly describes this company as a group of monks. The Castle of the Four Horns is Paradise, and Perlesvaus' journey

---

[140] *La Chanson d'Antioche*, ed. Suzanne Duparc-Quioc, (Paris, 1977), p. 475, lines 84–8, mss A, B, C.

[141] *La Chanson d'Antioche*, lines 5118–20, 9059–69.

[142] See 1 Chronicles ch. 29 v. 27. Thirty-three also symbolises perfection, as it is made up of ten threes plus three, and both ten and three were numbers of perfection: Ernst Robert Curtius, *European Literature and the Latin Middle Ages*, trans. Willard R. Trask, Bollingen Series 36 (Princeton, 1953), pp. 501–9, esp. p. 505; Christopher Butler, *Number Symbolism* (London, 1970), pp. 22–46.

there is part of the eschatological context which he suggests for the second half of Perlesvaus' career. If Kelly is correct in his eschatological interpretation, it is extremely likely that the thirty-three men are intended as the heavenly company of martyrs.[143]

However, the theme of holy war against unbelievers is so significant in *Perlesvaus* that medieval audiences may have seen a parallel with the Templars at this point, whose vocation was one of martyrdom; or they may have seen a parallel with other warriors of Christ, such as those listed above.

Perlesvaus himself carries a shield with a cross emblazoned on it, but this is not simply a red cross on a white field. It is *bendé* with silver and azur blue and has a scarlet cross with a golden border, all covered in valuable stones. It belonged to Joseph of Arimathea – as did Galaad's red-cross shield in the *Queste*.[144] On the Island of the Four Horns, Perlesvaus is given a snow-white shield in exchange for Joseph's shield. The replacement of the cross of suffering by the pure white of the redeemed and justified souls in Heaven apparently indicates Perlesvaus' promotion from the earthly level of suffering, torment and ordeal in holy war for the sake of the love of God to the heavenly level of eternal bliss, where all sin has been purged away; just as for the martyrs in Revelations.[145]

Perlesvaus is clearly a knight of Christ, but this does not make him a Templar. He has not taken religious vows and he is not a member of an ecclesiastical institution. Like the Joseph of Arimathea of the Grail romances, he is a godly warrior, a knight who wages holy war on God's enemies for the sake of Christendom and love of God. Like Galaad in the *Queste*, he informs the audience that knights may achieve a heavenly reward without becoming monks or joining a Military Order, but simply by remaining laity and serving God as knights.

2.3 Other Templar symbolism?

Various symbols have been suggested as being connected with the Templars, many more indicative of the writers' imagination than the historical evidence. Those discussed here are those which are best known.

The head. In 1888, Alfred Nutt suggested that the severed head was a symbol indicating the Templars. He stated:

> Wolfram's *Templeise* agree closely with the real Templars, one of the main charges against whom was their alleged worship of a head from which they expected riches and victuals, and to which they ascribed the power of making trees and flowers bloom ... The Grail myth in its oldest form is connected with

---

[143] Kelly, *Le Haut Livre du Graal*, pp. 41, 65, 83, 112–28.
[144] *Perlesvaus*, 1, p. 49, lines 610–11, 623.
[145] *Perlesvaus*, 1, p. 391, lines 9657–61.

John the Baptist. Thus in the Mabinogi the Grail is represented by a head in a platter; the head the Templars were accused of worshipping was probably the same form ...[146]

The theory that the Templars did worship a head and that this was the head referred to in the Grail legends was also taken up by Jessie Weston, who also connected it with the head of John the Baptist.[147] It has now passed into 'Grail' folklore. A recent work has taken the point a step further and stated that the piratical skull and crossbones were originally a Templar symbol, a novel if rather wild assumption presumably based upon the supposed connection of the Templars with the severed head.[148]

The Templars were not actually accused of worshipping a head. The charge was that they adored (*adhorabant*) or venerated (*venerabantur*) an idol in the form of a head.[149] There is an important difference between 'worship' and 'adoration' or 'veneration'. 'Adoration' and 'veneration' were the terms applied to the respect paid to saints' relics by Roman Catholic Christians. During the Middle Ages, many devout Catholics did believe that the intercession of the saints helped the trees and flowers bloom, and that if they did not treat the relics of the saints with veneration, disaster would follow.[150] In short, the accusations against the Templars in 1307 indicate that the supposed 'head' was actually some sort of saint's relic.

Scholars have not accepted the theory that the Templars' supposed head was the 'Grail head', although it regularly appears in non-academic works on the Grail. In fact the 'Grail head' only appears in the Welsh *Peredur*, where it is a man's head on a large platter.[151] In *Perlesvaus* a damsel, niece of the king of the Grail Castle, appears with a cart containing 150 heads of knights, some sealed in gold, some in silver and some in lead, very like the heads of medieval saints in their metal reliquaries. These heads have not come from the Grail Castle, although apparently their deaths were caused by Perlesvaus' failure to ask 'the question' on his first visit to the Grail Castle. They do not represent the Grail and are not, therefore, 'Grail heads'. We are later informed that the heads sealed in gold represent Christians, those sealed in silver represent the Jews, and those sealed in lead are the Saracens. Only those sealed in gold will come

---

[146] Alfred T. Nutt, *Studies in the Legends of the Holy Grail, with especial reference to the hypothesis of its Celtic origin* (London, 1888), p. 100.

[147] See Jessie Weston, 'Notes on the Grail romances: Caput Johannis = Corpus Christi', *Romania*, 49 (1923), 273–9, here note 1 on 278–9.

[148] Adrian Gilbert, Alan Wilson and Baram Blackett, *The Holy Kingdom* (London, New York, 1998), p. 211.

[149] *Procès des Templiers*, 1, p. 92.

[150] P. Geary, *Living with the Dead in the Middle Ages* (Ithaca, 1994), p. 171; *Cronica Jocelini de Brakelonda de rebus gestis Samsonis abbatis monasteri Sancti Edmundi*, ed. and trans. H.E. Butler (Edinburgh, 1949), pp. 106, 110–11. For the power of the saint to avenge himself, see pp. 68–71, 97; for the saint's 'ownership' of the lands and town belonging to the abbey, pp. 45–6, 50–53, 57.

[151] *Historia Peredur*, p. 20, lines 13–19; 'Peredur', trans. Gantz, p. 226.

to the paradise, to the Island of the Four Horns, with Perlesvaus; the others are in the *Isle Souffroitose* and it is not known whether they will ever leave it. The heads of the king and queen which are carried by the damsel and her companions are the heads of Adam and Eve, which are saved by Perlesvaus from the Black Hermit (Satan) to be carried to the Island of the Four Horns. The author of *Perlesvaus* has combined contemporary Roman Catholic symbolism of the saint's head in its metal reliquary and the three great world religions with the Grail story; but the episode of the heads has no connection with the Grail, except that the Grail king initially sends the damsel and her cart to Arthur's court.[152]

The Grail head is not mentioned by Wolfram, who describes the Grâl as a small stone. While modern scholarship may deduce the derivation of the Grail from the 'Grail head', it is unlikely that Wolfram knew of the distant origins of the Grail. His concern, as I have argued above, was the present state of the kingdom of Jerusalem and the western Empire, and he adapted his materials to that purpose, without worrying about the origins of the theme.

The head of St John the Baptist, the subject of the speculations of Alfred Nutt and Jessie Weston, was not connected with the Templars but with the Order of the Hospital, for the Hospital was dedicated to St John the Baptist. There is some evidence for a cult of the head of St John the Baptist among the Hospitallers. The head of St John the Baptist appeared on the seals of the English priory from the early thirteenth century until the dissolution of the Order in England: it is a bearded head, without a neck, surrounded by stars and with the sun on the left and the moon on the right. Some images of St John the Baptist appear in English churches of the Order of the Hospital, and the picture of a disembodied bearded head which has been connected with the church at Templecombe, Somerset, is probably an image of St John the Baptist, brought to the church by the Hospitallers when Templecombe passed into their hands after the dissolution of the Order of the Temple.[153]

The problem of the supposed 'Templars' head' has been studied by Malcolm Barber, who concluded that there was no satisfactory evidence

---

[152] *Perlesvaus*, 1, pp. 50–51, 109, 390, 402, lines 647–66, 2170–72, 9636–40, 9993–4, 2, pp. 231–2, on line 659.

[153] For descriptions and pictures of the seals of the English priory of the Hospital, see H.W. Fincham, *The Order of the Hospital of St. John of Jerusalem and its Grand Priory of England* (London, 1933), pp. 81–3, nos 10, 11, 13, 16, 18 and plate facing p. 83; *Catalogue of Seals in the Public Record Office. Monastic Seals* vol. 1, compiled by Roger H. Ellis (London, 1986), pp. 23–4, M212–25, and plates 32, 42: here M216; E.J. King, *The Seals of the Order of St John of Jerusalem* (London, 1932), pp. 97–100 and plate XVII; R. Gladstone, 'Early charters of the Knights Hospitallers relating to Much Woolton, nr Liverpool', *Transactions of the Historic Society of Lancashire and Cheshire*, 56 (1903), 1–24, here 16–21. Elsewhere the seal of the Order showed the lamb of God, the *Agnus Dei* – an image of Christ – or a figure lying on a bed, symbolising the Order's caring vocation. For images of St John the Baptist in the Hospital's churches and the painted head at Templecombe see Roberta Gilchrist, *Contemplation and Action*, pp. 95–6; Riley-Smith, *Hospitallers*, p. 53.

for the existence of a bearded head as described in the Templar trial proceedings.[154] However, Barber did admit that it appeared that those Templars who described having seen some sort of head – and no two descriptions agreed – were describing reliquaries of the sort that were common during the medieval period and which all religious orders would have owned to contain the relics of the saints venerated by the order. He did not attempt to identify any one relic which could have prompted the original accusations against the Order. Nevertheless, a number of Templars during the trial of the Order drew the inquisitors' attention to the Order's possession of various relics, heads of saints which would have been kept in silver reliquaries shaped like heads. In particular, the Order possessed the relics of St Euphemia of Chacedon (martyred 303) and of one of the eleven thousand virgins who were supposed to have died with St Ursula at Cologne early in the fourth century. The latter came with a certificate of validation: it was head no. 58 (*caput LVIIIm*, an abbreviation of *caput quinquagintaoctavum*). It is clear from the Templars' depositions that the Order was particularly proud of possessing the relics of St Euphemia, which in 1307 were in the Orders' treasury in Nicosia on Cyprus. Yet as the relics of St Ursula's maiden were brought out regularly for the Brothers in Paris to venerate, the latter is the head which is more likely to have come to their accusers' attention.[155] Why the Templars' accusers objected to the Brothers venerating the relics of a saint as all good Catholics did is another question, and may reflect changes in personal piety among the new literate class represented in the ministers of King Philip IV of France who framed the accusations against the Templars.[156] In any case, if the story of the 'Templars' head' had any basis in historical actuality, the most likely candidate was the head of one of these two young women. It could not, therefore, have corresponded with the Grail head, which was definitely male.

The only unquestionably genuine bearded male head which can be connected with the Order of the Temple is the head of Christ which briefly appeared on the seals of two of the provincial masters of the Order of the Temple in Germany, Brothers Widekind and Frederick Wildegrave, on documents of 1271, 1279 and 1289. Later provincial masters of Germany used a different seal. This head is bearded, with a clear neck, much as a monarch's

---

[154] Malcolm Barber, 'The Templars and the Turin Shroud', *Catholic Historical Review*, 68 (1982), 206–25; reprinted in Barber, *Crusaders and Heretics, 12th–14th Centuries* (Aldershot, 1995), VI. For the Turin Shroud, see also *The Book of Chivalry of Geoffroi de Charny*, pp. 39–41, where it is argued persuasively that the Shroud never belonged to the Templars, but that Geoffrey de Charny bought it when he was on crusade in the East in 1345–6, and regarded it as an icon rather than a relic of Christ.

[155] *Procès*, 1, pp. 143–4, 419; *Untergang des Templerordens*, 2, pp. 65, 93, 136.

[156] On this change, see Geary, *Living with the Dead*, pp. 175–6; on the new literate class and their role in the trial of the Templars see Malcolm Barber, 'The Trial of the Templars Revisited', in *The Military Orders*, vol. 2, ed. Nicholson, pp. 329–42: here pp. 340–42.

head appears on modern coins; it is not a decapitated head as are those which appear on the seals of the Hospital. It is surrounded by a halo with a star on the left and right. The implication is that the heavenly Christ is ruler of the Order of the Temple. Yet Christ's head did not appear on Templar seals outside Germany. In England the seal showed the *Agnus Dei*, the holy Lamb of God, another symbol of Christ.[157] In Aragon, seals showed the *Agnus Dei*, a cross, or military symbols such as a castle or a knight on horseback.[158] None of the Templars or other witnesses who testified during the trial referred to the symbol of Christ's head on the Order's seals, indicating that they did not imagine that this was the head under discussion.

The accusations that the Templars venerated a head were not so much based on the Templars' possession of these relics of women saints or on the symbolism on their seals but more on folk tradition, such as the story of the head in the Gulf of Satalia.[159] In that the head in *Peredur* is such a product of folk tradition, then the Templars' supposed head was indeed connected with the legendary head of this Grail romance. However, the historical Templars did not worship a head; the relics they actually venerated were of young women, not bearded men. To reiterate the point, the accusation against the Templars in 1307 that the Brothers venerated a head is not evidence that the Templars were actually worshipping the 'head' of the Grail legend – although it does tell us something about the attitudes of the Templars' accusers towards the cult of relics.

The pentagram. In an article published in 1982, Gregory Wilkin suggested that the reference to the pentagram or 'Solomon's star' on Gawain's shield in *Sir Gawain and the Green Knight* is an oblique reference to the Templars. He went on to argue that Gawain is intended as a 'failed Templar', trying to live up to a now-defunct ideal of knighthood.[160]

Wilkin argued a persuasive case, but there is no specific connection made in *Sir Gawain* between the Templars and Gawain. In epics and romances where the Templars are mentioned, the key symbol which invokes the Templars is the Temple of Solomon in Jerusalem, but there is no reference to the Temple of Solomon in *Sir Gawain*. The pentagram, or so-called Solomon's star, was a symbol of completeness, representing the number five because of its five points. The number five could symbolise the world, or more particularly men and women within the world. In the later Middle Ages, when *Sir Gawain* was written, the pentagram would also be a suitable symbol for

---

[157] The seals of the German provincial masters are reproduced in Bulst-Thiele, *Sacrae domus*, figs 2a–2c, following p. 416; see also pp. 372–4, 415; for the English master's seal see *Catalogue of Seals ... Monastic Seals*, 1, p. 56, M527, plate 34.
[158] Forey, *The Templars in the Corona de Aragón*, pp. 453–4.
[159] Malcolm Barber, *The Trial of the Templars* (Cambridge, 1978), p. 185.
[160] Wilkin, 'The dissolution of the Templar Ideal'. See *Sir Gawain and the Green Knight*, ed. J.R.R. Tolkein and E.V. Gordon, 2nd edn ed. Norman Davis (Oxford, 1967), lines 625–6.

representing the five wounds of Christ, a popular focus for devotion, as the *Gawain* poet uses it. It could also be used as a talismanic symbol and for magical purposes.[161] Its magical connections gave the symbol its connection with King Solomon, whose renowned wisdom was believed to have included knowledge of the magical arts. However, the *Gawain* poet does not use the pentagram to show Gawain's knowledge of the magical arts. He uses it to show his devotion to Christ, specifically to Christ's five wounds, and to the Blessed Virgin Mary. Therefore, while the mention of the name of Solomon by the *Gawain* poet may be intended to recall the Templars, as no more specific connection is made this remains unlikely. The reference to Solomon may recall his reputation as the wisest of kings, for Gawain himself is noted for his intelligence. However, it is far more likely to recall Solomon's reputation as a lover of women (based on 1 Kings ch. 11 vv. 1–8), a reputation shared by Gawain.

Wilkin attempted to make a connection between the Templars and the cult of the five wounds of Christ. It is true, as he points out, that the 'Jerusalem Cross' was depicted as one large golden cross with four smaller crosses at the corners to represent the five wounds of Christ, but the Templar's cross was not depicted in this fashion. It is also true that the Templars were devoted to the Blessed Virgin Mary, as is Gawain in *Sir Gawain*, and as were the Hospitallers and Teutonic Knights and the Cistercians – but as the cult of the Blessed Virgin Mary was extremely popular in Latin Christendom from the early twelfth century onwards, this is not sufficient grounds to suggest a specific and deliberate parallel between the Templars and Gawain. It only indicates that Gawain is a deeply, if conventionally, pious knight.

More suggestive are the grounds on which Bertilak condones Gawain's sin. Gawain broke his agreement with Bertilak to exchange all winnings by retaining the green girdle given to him by Bertilak's wife, but only because she had told him that he could not be killed while he was wearing it. Gawain's sin was to love his life too much (lines 2365–8). In this he certainly is acting in contravention of the Templars' ideal, which was one of martyrdom. However, yet again, while the modern critic can see an implicit connection with the Templars, the poet makes no specific connection with the defunct Order. In fact, no knight should love his life too much, for he will then be afraid to risk it in deeds of prowess.

---

[161] On the pentagram and the five wounds of Christ see *Sir Gawain*, pp. 92–6, notes on lines 620–56; on contemporary devotion to the five wounds of Christ and contemporary iconography see, for instance, Caroline Walker-Bynum, *Fragmentation and Redemption: Essays on Gender and the Human Body in Medieval Religion* (New York, 1992), pp. 271, 278–9; for the symbolism of the number five, see Curtius, *European Literature*, pp. 503–4; for the pentagram in magical texts, see Alexander Roob, *Alchemy and Mysticism: the Hermetic Museum* (Cologne, 1997), pp. 535, 536, 540.

In short, the pentagram was not a Templar symbol, and while it is possible to see connections and parallels between the ideal of knighthood in *Sir Gawain* and the ideal of the Templars, the *Gawain* poet offers only the vaguest of hints that this might be his intention. Gawain is an ideal knight, and he is pious; but he travels alone on his quest, and he is not in any way involved in a holy war. It is not necessary to assume that the *Gawain* poet was comparing Gawain and modern knighthood specifically with the Templar ideal. Gawain's virtues and failings are virtues and failings in any ideal of knighthood, not simply the Templar ideal.

2.4 *Galaad and the changing ideal of Christian knighthood*

Albert Pauphilet and James Douglas Bruce saw in Galaad the perfection of the ideal to which the Templars aspired, on the basis that in their view the *Queste* was clearly a Cistercian text and the Templars were an order close to the Cistercians and promoted by their great abbot, Bernard of Clairvaux. Moreover, it is possible to argue that Galaad, in destroying evil in Arthur's kingdom, is acting as Bernard envisaged the Templars acting against the Muslims. Yet Jean Frappier pointed out that although there were some parallels between the Grail-questers and the Templars, 'the assimilation is never total or explicit ... and the 'celestial' knighthood remains independent of all ecclesiastical organisation'.[162]

The *Queste del Saint Graal* does state a possible connection between the Order of the Temple and the perfect knight. The Templars' original headquarters was the Temple of Solomon in Jerusalem; the *Queste* states that Solomon knew of the coming of the perfect knight and prepared for it.[163] So, the *Queste* links the ideal monarch, the epitome of wisdom, and ancient patron (in a sense) of the Order of the Temple with the perfect knight. Yet the implication of the *Queste*'s statement is not that the Templars are perfect knights but that they fall short of perfection. It is not the Templars but Galaad who represents the fulfilment and completion of knighthood. The new knighthood of the *Queste* surpasses and replaces the old knighthood of the Templars: the new knighthood is based on a personal relationship between the knight and his God, without need for an Order, and the perfect knight does not kill his enemies but spares them to repent.[164]

Certainly Galaad does destroy evil, and at Château Carcelois he kills the knights who offended Christ. Yet these were not Muslims but Christians who had fallen away from the true path and were therefore, we are told, *worse* than

---

[162] Pauphilet, *Études*, pp. 69–71; Bruce, *Evolution*, 1, p. 421; see also the sources listed by Wilkin, 'The Dissolution of the Templar Ideal', 111, note 9; Matarasso, *Redemption of Chivalry*, p. 68; Frappier, 'Le Graal et la chevalerie', 179; Pratt, 'Cistercians and the *Queste*', esp. pp. 87–8.
[163] *Queste*, pp. 220–26.
[164] *Queste*, p. 54, but cf. pp. 229–33.

Muslims.¹⁶⁵ Rather than acting like Templars, Galaad and his companions are acting like knights such as Humbert of Beaujeu, who, having joined and then left the Order of the Temple, returned home, where he waged war on bandits and lawless knights. Peter the Venerable, abbot of Cluny, pleaded with the Master of the Temple and with Pope Eugenius III not to force Humbert to return to the Order, because in fighting bandits and lawless men in the neighbourhood of Cluny, men worse than Muslims, he was performing a far more useful task than he had as a Templar.¹⁶⁶ Not all commentators would have agreed with the abbot that fighting Christians who have turned to evil is even more important than fighting Muslims. The author of the *Queste*, however, was making the same point to his thirteenth-century audience as Peter the Venerable made to the pope in the late 1140s. By fighting evil knights who have offended Christ, Galaad is practising a form of knighthood even more perfect than the Templars'. In fact Galaad, Perceval and Bohort, the Grail companions of the *Queste*, never fight Muslims: in Sarraz the 'pagans' convert peacefully. Rather than going to Sarraz to fight, the three Grail companions go to encounter God and then die, as pilgrims went to Jerusalem.¹⁶⁷

It is striking that the *Queste* is aimed only at knights; not at non-knights, who are not mentioned, and not at women, who were excluded from the quest so that the men could concentrate on spiritual things. All the women in the *Queste* are either beyond redemption, like Guinevere, or already saved and showing the knights the way to God, as do Perceval's aunt and sister.¹⁶⁸ It is unusual for a romance to be so obviously aimed at one group to the exclusion of others, and this suggests that the author had a very specific message, for knights alone.

The author of the *Queste* was setting up a new ideal of knighthood, one that went deeper than the ideal of the Military Orders. The Military Orders had failed, for they had not reformed knighthood. According to the *Queste*, the way for a knight to win salvation is not by joining a religious order and

---

¹⁶⁵ *Queste*, p. 321, lines 30–33.

¹⁶⁶ *Letters of Peter the Venerable*, 1, pp. 407–13, nos 172–3.

¹⁶⁷ *Queste*, pp. 276–7, lines 16–30, 1–14; Riley-Smith, *The First Crusade*, p. 24; Benedicta Ward, *Miracles and the Medieval Mind* (London, 1982), pp. 124–5; Jonathon Riley-Smith, *The First Crusaders, 1095–1131* (Cambridge, 1997), pp. 19, 29, 36, 107.

¹⁶⁸ On Guinevere, see *Queste*, p. 125, lines 26–31; on Perceval's aunt, see p. 71, line 29–p. 81, line 16; on Perceval's sister, see especially p. 201, line 20–p. 210, line 7, p. 226, line 29–p. 228, line 28, p. 229, lines 12–16; for Perceval's sister as a saviour whose blood cleanses sinners (leprosy is a metaphor for sin), see the episode of the lepress, p. 236, line 29–p. 242, line 12; for Solomon's wife, who knows all about the future role of the holy ship although this is hidden from her husband, see p. 220, line 29–p. 226, line 7. In the prose *Estoire del Saint Graal* the natural godliness of women is even more marked: most of the women characters are already Christians, and the rest convert willingly – only the men cause any problems. See, for example, p. 15, Elyap (Joseph's wife); pp. 68–73, Sarrachinte (wife of Evalac-Mordrain), king of Sarraz; p. 154, Label's sister; pp. 132–4, Solomon's wife; pp. 184, 195, King Label's daughter, Sarracinte; pp. 270–72, 275–9, Camille; p. 294.

fighting Muslims but by living chastely, being humble and loving God.[169] The emphasis is not on fighting enemies outside Christendom but evil within Christendom and within oneself. Knights that live in this way will encounter God in their lives, and will win salvation. It was a more demanding ideal than that of the Military Order, for it was a path each knight must find alone; but on the other hand any knight could follow it, in whatever situation of life he might be; there was no need to go overseas or seek admission to an Order. Although as depicted in the *Queste* this was an ideal of knighthood which excluded all but those of the highest birth,[170] presumably Galaad and his companions were intended to show the way for lesser mortals to follow.

2.5 *Later reworkings of the 'Queste': a connection with the Templars or the Holy Land?*

The *Queste* remained popular throughout the Middle Ages. Around forty manuscripts survive from the thirteenth, fourteenth and fifteenth centuries. In addition, this was the version of the Grail legend translated by Thomas Malory for inclusion in his *Morte Darthur*.[171] However, not all contemporary audiences accepted the *Queste*'s vision for knighthood, for subsequent works altered and adapted its ideal.

The work which follows the *Queste* in manuscripts containing the Vulgate Cycle, although not necessarily composed after the *Queste*, was *La Mort le Roi Artu*. In this work Lord Gauvain, the knight who was condemned in the *Queste* as beyond salvation, goes straight to heaven on his death, saved by his charitable works; whereas Lancelot, who repented, and Bohort, one of the Grail knights, have to do penance as hermits in order to be saved.[172] Clearly this author, or the audience, would not have been impressed by the *Queste*'s rejection of Gauvain's virtues.

The *Queste* itself was also reworked in the Post-Vulgate *Queste* in the *Roman du Graal* and in later works. In these adaptations, Galaad became progressively more realistic and more like a member of a Military Order in that he fought Muslims and converted them to Christianity by force, although he remained a lone figure, outside ecclesiastical organisation. In later works, he became little more than a pious secular knight. His ultimate destination

---

[169] See Matarasso, *Redemption of Chivalry*, pp. 144–53; Pratt, 'Cistercians and the *Queste*, p. 79.

[170] Frappier, 'Le Graal et la chevalerie', 207.

[171] For a summary of the debate over Malory's use of the *Queste*, see Dhiva B. Mahoney, 'The Truest and Holiest Tale: Malory's Transformation of the *Queste del Saint Graal*', in *Studies in Malory*, ed. James W. Spisak (Kalamazoo, Michigan, 1985), pp. 109–28. An Italian translation of the *Queste* was made: see Fanni Bogdanow, 'The Italian Fragment of the *Queste del saint Graal* preserved in the Biblioteca Nazionale Centrale, Florence, and its French Source', *Medium Ævum*, 69 (2000), 92–5.

[172] *La Mort le Roi Artu*, p. 225, para. 176, pp. 258–9, para. 200, p. 263, para. 204.

became more clearly Jerusalem; thus begging the question of whether any of these later works on the Grail were written in the Latin East.

The Post-Vulgate *Queste* in the *Roman du Graal* has been dated by its editor to not later than 1235–40, that is, a generation after the composition of the original *Queste*. In this work, Galaad is depicted as rounded character, no longer simply a symbolic figure of Christ. We find him being propositioned by an amorous girl, whom he refuses; but when she picks up his sword and threatens to kill herself because he has refused to satisfy her desire he exclaims 'Ah, noble damsel! Calm down a bit and don't kill yourself like this, for I will do what you ask, as I see that I must.' In the fifteenth-century manuscript of the Portuguese translation, the *Demanda*, he is less begrudging, 'Ah, good damsel! Wait a moment and don't kill yourself like this, for I will do everything you ask.' Fortunately for the quest, she kills herself anyway; but the reader must wonder what would have happened to the quest for the Grail if Galaad had lost his virginity.[173]

The new Galaad wages holy war: he and his companions slaughter the 'pagans' of Chastel Felon without mercy, thereby encouraging the neighbouring pagans to convert to Christianity. In contrast, the original Galaad was not involved in conversion by force or fear. The new Galaad no longer stands aloof from ordinary sinners: we also find him talking in a friendly manner to Tristan, the adulterer. He is no longer unique, as Agravain declares that Galaad's name and his shield are far from being unusual. He is also allowed to appear ridiculous when he is unhorsed by Gauvain's son Guiglain; although, admittedly, he did not hear Guiglain's challenge. This is not the image of the perfect Christ-figure.[174]

This is still a religious account: Galaad is described as a holy man, and spends much time in prayer, wears a hair shirt, has taken a vow of lifelong virginity and declares that in killing herself for love, the damsel killed herself for no reason at all. Yet the work expresses lay piety rather than clerical piety, being far less mystical and far more reflective of contemporary actuality than the Vulgate *Queste*.[175]

---

[173] *La Version Post-Vulgate*, 2, pp. 151–2, section 116. For the date, see 1, p. 59. *Demanda*, 1 (1955), p. 151. For Galaad as a theological concept rather than a character conceived in the round in the *Queste*, see Matarasso, *Redemption of Chivalry*, p. 90.

[174] *Demanda*, 2 (1944), pp. 187–96, sections 496–509, esp. p. 193, section 505 and p. 196, section 509; *La Version Post-Vulgate*, 2, pp. 485–91, 494–5, 519–24 sections 364–8, 370, 381–4; *Demanda*, 2 (1944), pp. 44, section 365, pp. 61–3, sections 380–82, p. 175, section 486, p. 140, sections 458–9. On the decline of Galaad in the Post-Vulgate *Queste*, see also A. Pauphilet, 'La Queste du Saint Graal du MS Bibl Nat Fr. 343', *Romania*, 36 (1907), 591–609: here 607–8.

[175] See, for instance, *La Version Post-Vulgate*, 2, pp. 149–53, 491, 525–9, sections 113–17, 368, 384–7; see also Bogdanow, *The Romance of the Grail*, pp. 111–12, 203–12, 214–17. For the contrast between lay and clerical piety, see, for instance, *The Book of Geoffroi de Charny*, pp. 35–48; Keen, *Chivalry*, pp. 51–63.

The ideal knight of the Post-Vulgate *Roman du Graal*, therefore, is much closer to the Military Order ideal than the original Galaad, for he engages in war against non-Christians and wants to convert them to Christianity. However, he is not a Templar, for he is not a member of a religious order, but is working out his own salvation alone.

The author of the *Roman du Graal* does indicate that the knighthood of the Round Table itself is a kind of religious order, for the knights leave their families and homes to unite in a brotherhood around the Round Table. This was a concept adapted from Robert de Boron's *Merlin*, where the knights of the new fellowship of the Round Table send for their families to join them in Carduel because they cannot bear to leave the company of the other knights, whom they love like fathers. While Robert de Boron made more of the religious connotations of the Round Table, making it the third holy table after the table of the Last Supper and the table of the Holy Grail, the author of the *Roman du Graal* made his Round Table more monastic than Robert's, by forcing his knights to leave their families.[176] It has been suggested that the Round Table is based on the Templars' round churches, and the Templars' practice of sitting around in a circle when they had meetings.[177] However, the Templars' round naves were based on the church of the Holy Sepulchre, the ultimate Christian symbol on the site of Christ's empty tomb. If there is any connection between the Round Table and the Templars' round-naved churches, it is most probable that the Round Table was also based directly on the church of the Holy Sepulchre rather than on the Templars' churches – particularly as most Templar churches did not have round naves.[178] The Templars certainly sat in a circle when they held meetings, as did all religious orders: they sat on stone benches set against the walls of their chapter house. This only demonstrates again how like the knighthood of the Round Table is to a religious order.

Yet, the knighthood of the Round Table is not a religious order. The knights do take a vow, but it is far less restrictive than the vows taken by religious. They can marry, they travel individually, they are not bound by a vow of poverty, and their obedience is quite limited – they are subject to King Arthur, they must not attack each other, and they must give a true and full account of their adventures when they return to court. The knighthood of the Round Table might have been inspired in a general sense by the Templars' example to

---

[176] *La Version Post-Vulgate*, 1, p. 56; *Suite du Merlin*, 1, p. 202; Robert de Boron, *Merlin: Roman du XIII siècle*, ed. Alexandre Micha, TLF 176 (Geneva, 1979), pp. 185–196, section 48, line 75–section 51, line 28: esp. p. 189, section 49, lines 51–65. On the religious conception of the Round Table in Robert de Boron's *Merlin* see Micha, *Étude sur le <Merlin>*, pp. 106–10.

[177] Beate Schmolke-Hasselmann, 'The Round Table: Ideal, Fiction, Reality', in *Arthurian Literature*, 2, ed. Richard Barber (Cambridge, 1982), pp. 41–75, here p. 59.

[178] On the Military Orders' round-naved churches see Gilchrist, *Contemplation and Action*, p. 94.

become a 'new knighthood'; it can certainly be seen as an inspiration for secular Orders of knighthood such as the Order of the Garter in England, the Knights of the Band in Castile or the French Company of the Star.[179] Yet, like these secular Orders, the knighthood of the Round Table is not dedicated to holy war, members do not take the three vows of poverty, chastity and obedience, and they are not subject to ecclesiastical authority. Like the secular Orders, the concept of the Round Table was probably inspired by the lay confraternities of knights which are known to have existed from the eleventh century but became very common from the early thirteenth century.[180] The knights of the Round Table are free to travel alone to seek adventure with little restriction on their actions, in pursuit of individual honour and glory; unlike the Brothers of the Order of the Temple in the Holy Land, they do not expect to die on the battlefield to the glory of God.

The author of the second part of the prose *Tristan*, possibly writing in the 1240s,[181] used the Post-Vulgate *Roman du Graal* in the final stages of the

---

[179] On these secular Orders see D'Arcy Jonathan Dacre Boulton, *The Knights of the Crown: The Monarchial Orders of Knighthood in Europe, 1325–1520* (Woodbridge, 1987); Keen, *Chivalry*, pp. 179–99.

[180] On this difference between the secular Orders of knighthood and the Military Orders, and on lay confraternities, see Keen, *Chivalry*, pp. 180–82; see also on confraternities of knights: Forey, *Emergence*, 189.

[181] The date of the prose *Tristan* remains unclear. E. Löseth noted that the work falls into two parts: the first part, sections 1–183 of Löseth's summary (to vol. 3, p. 198, section 158, line 25 in *Tristan*, ed. Ménard) is the same in all versions, but the rest of the story appears in a long and a short version: Löseth, *Roman en prose de Tristan*, p. v, and note 1, p. vi. Emmanuel Baumgartner dated the first part to the period 1235–40, and the rest to after 1240 (see Emmanuel Baumgartner, *Le 'Tristan en Prose', essai d'intérpretation d'un roman médieval* (Geneva, 1975), pp. 36–62; cited in *Tristan*, ed. Ménard, 9, ed. Laurence Harf-Laucner, pp. 36–7). The version of the second half of the story published by Philippe Ménard is the long version, or 'Vulgate' (1, p. 10). It seems clear that the second part of the prose *Tristan* has close similarities with the Post-Vulgate *Queste*, and probably used that version of the *Queste* for the section of the *Tristan* dealing with the quest for the Grail (see F. Bogdanow, *Romance of the Grail*, pp. 106–9, 118; *La Version Post-Vulgate*, 1, pp. 44, 60–97, 295–416). This indicates a date for the prose *Tristan* after 1240. However, the author of *Meliadus-Gyron* seems to have known the prose *Tristan*, making various references to the characters which appear in it, and some copyists identified the author of *Meliadus-Gyron* with the author of the prose *Tristan*, identifying the *Tristan* as his earlier work the *Bret*: see Lathuillère, *Guiron*, pp. 23–30. *Meliadus-Gyron* apparently dates from before 5 February 1240, probably from around 1235 (Lathuillère, *Guiron*, pp. 31–4; *La Version Post-Vulgate*, 1, p. 59). With its skilful development of character and subtle use of humour it is certainly a more mature work than the prose *Tristan*, which suggests that it was a later work. It is clear that the author of the Post-Vulgate *Roman du Graal* also knew a version of the *Tristan* story. It has been suggested, therefore, that there were two versions of the prose *Tristan*; a first, shorter one, written 1225–30, used by the Post-Vulgate *Roman du Graal* and *Meliadus-Gyron*, and a second, longer one, written after the Post-Vulgate *Roman du Graal* and *Meliadus-Gyron*, which incorporated the Post-Vulgate *Queste* (see Eugène Vinaver, *Études sur le Tristan en Prose* (Paris, 1925), pp. 23, 28–30; E. Vinaver, 'The Prose *Tristan*', in *Arthurian Literature in the Middle Ages*, p. 339; cited by *La Version Post-Vulgate*, 1, pp. 36–7 and note 19 and also pp. 59, 60–97). However, this theory has its problems, as certain episodes in the Post-Vulgate *Queste* only make sense in the context of the long version of the prose *Tristan* (see Laurence Harf-Laucner in *Tristan*, 9, p. 37). The problem is complicated by the fact that the prose *Tristan* was reworked and added to by later redactors. The difficulty could

book but adapted it still further to reflect an almost wholly secular viewpoint. Here Galaad is no longer all-conquering, and is depicted as little more than another wandering knight, although a pious one. Not only is he unhorsed by Guiglain, but also by Dinadan, and he is captured by Brehus sans Pitié and has to be rescued from death by Engennés. Again Agravain denies Galaad's uniqueness.[182] Löseth's summary indicates that in later redactions of the *Tristan* Palamedes, the courteous and wise Muslim, denounces Galaad as less good a knight than Tristan. It is perhaps not surprising that the Muslim should see the chaste knight, representing Christ, as being no better a knight than the adulterous but doughty knight; but as in other respects Palamedes is seen as a sympathetic character and the epitome of knighthood, perhaps we should pay attention to what the redactor has him say.[183]

The basic plot of the French prose version of the Grail romances became fixed by 1250, as did the basic plots of other French Arthurian prose romances. However, the character and status of Galaad continued to undergo subtle changes. In the *Prophecies de Merlin*, written in the 1270s, Galaad appears as the excellent knight, king of Sarraz. He is cited alongside Segurades le Brun, who becomes king of Babylon and Abiron.[184] Segurades is clearly the equal of the Christ-figure; he spends most of the romance pursuing the dragon, a symbol of Satan. Doughty, gracious and valiant, we are told that he will have the 'los de chevalerie', the greatest reputation for knighthood. In contrast, Galaad represents the peak of spiritual knighthood, which appears to give him less status in the physical world. Like Galaad, Segurades brings an end to the evil enchantments in Arthur's kingdom. Yet there is nothing in Segurades' character or piety which would suggest the person of Christ; he appears to

---

be somewhat resolved if we assumed that the author of the second part of the prose *Tristan* was actually who and what he claims to be, the author who wrote *Meliadus-Gyron* and a companion-in-arms of the author of the Post-Vulgate *Queste* (see the epilogue in Löseth, pp. 402–5, especially p. 404; and the author of the Post-Vulgate *Roman du Graal* in *La Suite du Roman de Merlin*, 1, p. 194, section 239 lines 31–5) and that these two authors knew each other's texts and exchanged their work. It has long been assumed that the supposed names and relationship between the two authors are false, but even if the names are pseudonyms, how can we be certain that they did not know each other? On this problem, see below, pp. 177–80.

[182] *Tristan*, ed. Ménard, 9, p. 82 (Guiglain); 6, p. 139 (Dinadan); 7, pp. 212–16 (Engannés); 9, p. 115 (Agravain); and 9, pp. 127–37 (Chastel Felon).

[183] Löseth, *Roman en prose de Tristan*, pp. 349–50 para. 495, where Palamedes declares that Tristan is a better knight than Galaad; p. 308–12 para. 449, where Palamedes praises Tristan over Galaad. Neither of these speeches occur in the 'Vulgate' published by Philippe Ménard and his collaborators: the equivalent passages appear in *Tristan*, ed. Ménard, 7 pp. 223–33, sections 111–19; 8, p. 78, section 10 lines 39–43 (where Palamedes praises Galaad). See also Löseth p. 297, section 430, where Erec is seen as a better knight than Galaad. For the character of Palamedes in Arthurian romance, see below, pp. 207–11.

[184] *Prophecies de Merlin*, ed. Paton, 1, p. 143, ch. 87, also p. 165, ch. 132, p. 206, ch. 158; *Prophesies de Merlin*, ed. Berthelot, p. 82, fol. 25Ra, p. 93, fols 30Vb–31Ra, and see also p. 335 fol. 165Va. On the Brun family, see Löseth, *Roman en prose de Tristan*, p. 434, note 3, pp. 487–8, note on p. 434.

be simply a hard-bitten, hard-fighting warrior. His surname 'le Brun' seems to have implications of strength and efficiency in battle. The Christ-figure of Galaad, then, has become no more than an excellent knight, a king, the equal of any good Christian warrior.

In John Hardyng's English verse chronicle, written in the fifteenth century down to 1461, Galaad appears as an historical figure, who, having found the Grail in Wales,

> Then rode he forth unto the Holy Lande,
> Through God and holy inspiracyon,
> To God he gaue his seruyce, and hym bonde
> To chastyte, and greate contemplacyon;
> And kyng was made, by hole coronacyon,
> Of Garras [Sarras in one version of the text] then, and duke of Orboryk,
> Of whome the people full well [dyd theym] lyke.[185]

Galaad goes on to make Bors and Perceval 'and other moo of the table round' knights of the Holy Grail:

> Whiche order he so ordeyned then and founde
> Att Sarras, that to Egypt lande doth bounde;
> To lyve chaste and maynteyne Christentye,
> Lyke as Ioseph dyd of Armathye.[186]

This sounds like a Military Order; but it transpires that there were only twelve of them, and that they represented the table founded by Joseph of Arimathea and the twelve disciples. This is the brotherhood of the Graal which was created at Corbenic in the *Queste del Saint Graal*, and Hardyng has simply 'glossed' the story a little.[187]

Hardyng, then, makes Galaad a holy knight, but rather than a mystical figure he is very much historical, and the king of a real place – real, that is, as far as Hardyng knew. In the following century, writing in 1549, the civil servant John Coke, following Hardyng, reduced Galaad to the level of 'a noble knight' of North Wales who went on crusade:

> The noble knyght Galahad, borne in Northwales, dyd great actes in the Holy Lande, who for the hygh enterpryses atcheved by hym, was crowned kynge of Garras and duke of Orborycke besydes Egypte. He dyed at Garras aforesaid...[188]

This Galahad is a holy and valiant knight, and for Coke he is important evidence of England's historic involvement in the crusade; but he is certainly not Christ. He is a hero, no more.

---

[185] *The Chronicle of Iohn Hardyng*, p. 135.
[186] Ibid.
[187] Ibid., p. 136.
[188] *Le Débat des hérauts d'armes de France et d'Angleterre, suivi de The Debate between the Heralds of England and France by John Coke*, ed. Léopold Pannier and Paul Meyer, SATF (Paris, 1877), p. 73, section 53.

Thus the character of Galaad, and the nature of Sarraz, the city of the Grail, changed considerably during the course of the Middle Ages. Galaad was demoted from a 'type' of Christ who tries to avoid killing sinners to a pious, doughty crusading knight who converts Muslims, and Sarraz became the real, earthly, historical Jerusalem. It is worth asking why this change took place.

The author of the *Queste* had a very monastic outlook, and his vision for chivalry, although secular, was monastic in tone. Clearly the authors of the *Roman du Graal* and the prose *Tristan* and their prospective audiences did not agree with the *Queste*'s vision for knighthood and wished to amend it, making the perfect knight closer to actuality, more concerned to fight non-Christians and forcibly convert them to Christianity, but also anxious to convert doughty and courageous Muslims by peaceful means. It is interesting, therefore, that the author of the *Roman du Graal* claims to be 'Lord Robert de Boron', companion in arms of one Helie de Boron, while the epilogue to some manuscript of the prose *Tristan* states that this work was completed by Helie de Boron, companion-in-arms of Robert de Boron.[189] In other words, these authors are claiming to be, respectively, the same as the author of the verse *Estoire ou Saint Graal* (*Joseph*) and *Merlin*, and his companion-in-arms. It seems extremely likely that Pierre Gallais is correct in his contention that the real Robert de Boron wrote his works in Cyprus; and anyone describing himself as Robert's companion-in-arms would certainly have travelled to Cyprus with him. Thus, if these authors' claim is true, then the whole of the *Roman du Graal* and the second part of the prose *Tristan* could have been written in the Latin East.

The claim that the author of the *Roman du Graal* was Robert de Boron was firmly rejected by Gaston Paris, on the basis of the difference in material (the *Estoire* is religious and mystical, the *Roman du Graal* much more secular) form (prose rather than verse), language, and a number of major inconsistencies between the two works.[190] There was also a difference in date, although this is not an insurmountable problem, as an author writing in Cyprus *c*. 1210 could still have been writing in the 1230s. The lapse in time could account for the other inconsistencies, such as the alteration in the concept of the Round Table from a religious symbol to the focus of a semi-monastic knightly order. It is not clear whether the original Robert de Boron was a knight or a cleric: James Douglas Bruce judged that he was a knight, but Pierre

---

[189] *La Suite du Roman de Merlin*, 1, p. 194, section 239, lines 31–5 (for the author of the *Roman du Graal*); the epilogue in Löseth, pp. 402–5, especially p. 404 (for the author of *Tristan*); Renée Curtis, 'The Problems of the Authorship of the Prose *Tristan*', Romania, 79 (1958), 314–35, here 326, 335.

[190] *Merlin: roman en prose du XIIIe siècle, publié avec la mise en prose de poème de Merlin de Robert de Boron d'après le manuscrit appartenant à M. Alfred H. Huth*, ed. Gaston Paris and Jacob Ulrich, 2 vols, SATF (Paris, 1886), 1, pp. xxv–xxviii on Robert, pp. xxviii–xxxvii on Helie.

Gallais decided that he must have been a cleric.[191] The authors of the *Roman du Graal* and the prose *Tristan* claim to be knights.

If the author of the *Roman du Graal* was the original Robert de Boron, still writing in the East, this would explain why he was more enthusiastic about holy war than the author of the Vulgate *Queste*. It would also explain his anxiety to convert the Muslims, and his extremely sympathetic view of some Muslims, represented in the character of Palamedes. The nobility of the Latin East were more aware of Muslims as doughty warriors than were the nobility of the West, and more aware of the need to fight and to convert them. Moreover, if he were writing in the East, it would be possible that his ideals of knighthood, different from those of the Vulgate *Queste*, were in some ways influenced by the ideals of the Military Orders, whom he would have seen at first hand in operation in the field against the Muslims.

It was noted above that the nobility of the Latin East, in common with their relatives in the West, appear to have been very enthusiastic about the Arthurian legend. Their enthusiasm was not dampened by the fact that it is set in Britain, at the other end of Europe from the Holy Land, or the fact that holy war against Muslims plays little part in most stories of Arthur and his knights.[192] If the *Roman du Graal* was written in the East, by Robert de Boron in later life, or by another writer who took his name to indicate that he was writing in the same location and in the same tradition as Robert de Boron, this would help to account for the popularity of the Arthurian legend in the East.

There is a hint that Robert's supposed companion-in-arms, Helie de Boron, was – or was thought to have been – connected with the East Mediterranean. In some manuscripts of the prose *Tristan* his epilogue states that he, 'Helie de Berron' is descended from the noble blood of the family of Barres, 'which has always been commander and lord of Outres in Romanie, which is now called France'. 'Romanie', or 'Romania', was the name for the territories in the north-eastern Mediterranean which had formed part of the Byzantine Empire when it was conquered by the Fourth Crusade in 1204. These territories subsequently passed under the control of the various French nobles who had been involved in the crusade. 'Helie' is therefore claiming to be a member of one of these noble families which held land in Frankish Greece, which was now French and not 'Roman' or Byzantine. Although, obviously, this was not the same as holding land in the crusader kingdoms in the Holy Land, it still gives 'Helie' a crusading connection; crusades continued in this area until the sixteenth century. The identity of 'Outres' is unclear: no place with this name has been identified. The word means 'beyond', and is usually found in connection with the Holy Land, as in the name commonly used by

---

[191] Bruce, *Evolution*, 2, p. 114; Gallais, 'Robert de Boron', p. 317.
[192] On the incidence of holy war against Muslims in the stories of Arthur, see below, pp. 211–15.

medieval European writers to refer to the Holy Land, 'Outremer' – the land overseas. It looks as if 'Helie' is claiming to rule a lordship overseas in Frankish Greece, or even to be a commander in Frankish Greece. The des Barres were a French noble family which was famous for its involvement in the Third Crusade; William des Barres role in the crusade is commemorated in the fifteenth-century romance *Saladin*. However, no member of the family appeared in the Fourth Crusade, and I know of no evidence that they did hold land in Frankish Greece, or even in the Holy Land. Hence the information in this epilogue is almost certainly spurious, but indicates that at least one redactor of the prose *Tristan* imagined the 'Boron' or 'Berron' family having a connection with the East, either Frankish Greece or the Holy Land.[193]

The most conclusive evidence that the prose works attributed to Robert and Helie de Boron were written in the Latin East would be if a substantial number of the manuscripts originated from that area. Unfortunately it is not easy to distinguish manuscripts which originated in the Latin East from those which originated in the West. Although Jaroslav Folda has identified a number of manuscripts which were either the product of the Acre scriptoria in the late thirteenth century or influenced by the style of one particular illuminator, none of these manuscripts contain the *Roman du Graal*, although one, British Library Royal MS 20.D.II, contains the prose *Tristan*. Folda deduced that this was written in Paris between 1287 and 1291. Unlike many other manuscripts of the prose *Tristan*, it does not contain any reference to Helie de Boron. This does not seem very convincing evidence for its having been composed in the Holy Land.[194]

At present, therefore, there is no direct evidence that 'Robert de Boron's' *Roman du Graal* was written in the Latin East. There is very slight evidence that the author calling himself 'Helie de Boron' may have written in the East. Yet as the first author of the prose *Tristan*, Luce de Gat, claims to be an English knight living near Salisbury, Wiltshire, it seems rather unlikely that the *Tristan* was begun in England and completed in the East. Therefore, there is not sufficient evidence to state that any of the figures of Galaad definitely reflects the particular viewpoint of the Crusader States. There is certainly no evidence that the figure of Galaad was influenced by any direct, first-hand knowledge of the Military Orders. We may only be certain that the nobility of the Latin East

---

[193] Epilogue printed by Löseth, *Roman en prose de Tristan*, p. 404; also by Curtis, 'Problems of the Authorship', 322–3, and note 1 to p. 323; for the crusade in 'Romania', see Housley, *Later Crusades*, pp. 49–150. For an overview of Frankish settlement in the area see Peter Lock, *The Franks in the Aegean, 1204–1500* (London, 1995). For participants in the Fourth Crusade see Jean Longnon, *Les Companions de Villehardouin: recherches sur les croisiés de la quatrième croisade* (Geneva, 1979). For the des Barres' participation on the Third Crusade, see *Chronicle of the Third Crusade*, pp. 203 and note 11, 238 and note 24, 247, 256; Ambroise, *Estoire*, pp. 532, 545.

[194] Jaroslav Folda, *Crusader Manuscript Illumination at Saint-Jean d'Acre, 1275–1291* (Princeton, 1976), pp. ix–xviii, esp. xv, pp. 121–2; Curtis, 'Problems of the Authorship', 325.

enjoyed Arthurian romance for the same reasons as their counterparts in western Europe, who were also their close relatives. Nevertheless, as no scholar has as yet made a systematic examination of the surviving manuscripts of the *Roman du Graal* and the prose *Tristan* with the possibility of a Latin Syrian or Cypriot provenance in mind, the question cannot yet be said to be completely closed.

If the character of Galaad was not changed to suit the viewpoint of the nobility of the Crusader States, then it must have been changed to suit the viewpoints of the nobility of Western Europe. They did not totally reject the ideal knighthood of the *Queste*, but some authors and audiences wished to amend it to be more practical and to reflect the demands of their own situations. The character of Galaad was therefore changed so that he no longer stood completely apart from the world and sinners, took part in holy war against non-Christians, and, finally, travelled to a real Holy Land, fought the Saracens and died there. He became a character whose life could feasibly be emulated by modern knights.

In conclusion, it is clear that although the *Queste del Saint Graal* circulated widely throughout the later Middle Ages, its ideals were not accepted by all knights. Successive authors rewrote the theme introduced by the *Queste del Saint Graal* to express their own opinions or audience demand. However, while their view of knighthood differed from that of the *Queste*, it was not identical with the ideal of the Military Orders. It was a lay, even secular, ideal which concentrated on the individual rather than the group, each knight working out his own salvation without the guidance of a religious rule. Although they operate within the constraints of the Round Table, this is a secular fraternity, not a religious order. Originally the Grail knights and the Grail ended their wanderings in the Holy Land, and went from there straight to Paradise; but this was a mystical Holy Land rather than the real one. With successive developments of the story, it became the real Holy Land and real cities which the Grail knights visited, while the mystical element was lost. Instead, the history of Galaad and his Grail knights was used to demonstrate that knights of the past had served God by fighting in the Holy Land, and that this was the greatest act a knight could perform for God: an example to knights of the present day to follow their path.

3 *The Grail romances: tales of mystery*

The various Grail romances and associated works which have been examined above all have some relationship with the Holy Land. Although many scholars disagree with this interpretation of these works, a careful examination of the Grail romances of Wolfram von Eschenbach and Chrétien de Troyes indicate that they intended their Grail Castles to be identified as Jerusalem. This identification may not be essential to an appreciation of the spiritual and mystical meaning of their work, but is essential to an understanding of why they wrote as they did. The author of the *Perlesvaus* also regarded the Grail Castle as Jerusalem, whereas the author of the *Queste del Saint Graal* sent his Grail knights to Jerusalem with the Grail at the end of their quest. However, although the *Perlesvaus* promotes holy war, the *Queste* repudiates it, preferring peaceful conversion. The author of *Perceforest* included an echo of the Church of the Holy Sepulchre in his round temple to the Sovereign God. Robert de Boron's *Estoire dou Graal* or *Joseph* begins in Jerusalem, and was probably written in Cyprus. None of the other Grail romances originated in the East.

It is only to be expected that the Grail, the symbol of God on Earth, should be associated with Jerusalem, because Jerusalem was the centre of medieval Catholic Christianity. Many people from the West visited the East during the twelfth and thirteenth centuries – more, probably, than the number of Latin Christians actually resident in the East. The fact that the attitudes towards knighthood and towards the Muslims in the post-Vulgate Grail romance mirror the attitudes which we would expect to find among Latin Christian knights in the East, even though this work was apparently written in western Europe, underlines the essential cultural unity between the Latin East and West.

Neither Chrétien nor Robert de Boron, nor the authors of the *Perlesvaus*, the *Queste* and its Post-Vulgate reworkings specifically refer to the Templars or to any Military Order. These works are all concerned with secular knights on a spiritual quest for God, not religious knights. The author of *Perceforest* has two knights defending his round temple for a year and a day, and their title of 'knights of the Temple' recalls the Templars; but there is no 'Grail' in this Temple, so these are not Grail knights. The *Queste del Saint Graal* is promoting a route of salvation for knights completely different from that of the Templars. The *Perlesvaus* certainly does not exclude the Templars, and it is tempting to see the Military Orders among the company of martyrs in the Castle of the Four Horns; but the author did not link the symbolic meaning of the holy war within his work to any specific group of knights.

The works of Chrétien and Robert de Boron do not include any group of knights who guard the Grail. Perceval does not encounter any knights guarding the Grail Castle. Robert's 'Graal' is guarded by Joseph of Arimathea, who is a pious knight in the employment of Pontius Pilate. Nor is there any group of knights guarding the Grail in *Perlesvaus*, the *Queste* or its Post-Vulgate reworkings. Perlesvaus meets his white-clad martyrs in a cathedral-like hall which may be heaven, not at the Grail Castle, and they bear no weapons. The *Elucidation*, the later prologue to Chrétien's *Conte du Graal*, mentions 'seven guards' of the story, but these guards are not knights guarding the Grail; they are a narrative device and represent the seven parts of the story to come.[195] In the *Queste* and its Post-Vulgate reworkings the Grail knights are the knights who reach the Grail Castle, see the Grail and (in the *Queste*) take part in the communion service there. They depart immediately afterwards, except for the three central figures who escort the Grail back to Sarraz/Jerusalem. These are not an organised or permanent group of Grail guardians, but three comrades selected by God for the task.

None of the heroes of these stories are comparable with the Templars. In each of these stories, the emphasis is on the secular knight's individual search for God, outside the constraints of the established Church and of society. This is completely different from the knighthood of the Military Orders, where the emphasis was on the religious community, constrained by the three monastic vows, and subject to ecclesiastical authority. The Brothers of the Military Orders, epitomised by the Templars, expected to die a martyr's death in battle against the Muslims. The Templars' devotion to martyrdom is emphasized by many contemporary sources. While Galaad dies when he has had a vision of God face-to-face, this is in the church of the Grail, before the altar, not on the battlefield. The other Grail knights do not die in the course of their search; success consists in possessing or seeing the Grail. Certainly, both Grail knights and the Brothers of the Military Orders were seeking God, but they were doing so in very different ways.

This difference was a result of the fact that the Military Orders represented the Church's ideal of knighthood in the early twelfth century, whereas the Grail romances represented later developments in the concept of knighthood: some apparently originating from monastic ideals, such as *La Queste del Saint Graal*, while others seem to express the ideals of the knights themselves, such as Chrétien de Troyes' *Conte du Graal* and the Post-Vulgate *Roman du Graal*. This does not mean that knights or the Church had rejected the Military Orders' ideal of knighthood, but that they did not believe it offered all knights a means of salvation. The Grail romances suggest that a knight does not need to leave the world and join a religious order in order to find God; he may remain a secular knight, and seek God through the exercise of knightly deeds. It must be admitted, however, that some Grail heroes – Perceval in the Third Continuation of *Perceval* by Manessier, and Bohort in the *Queste* – nevertheless end their lives withdrawing from the world, albeit remaining outside organised monastic life, to live as hermits doing penance for their sins. Writers were not in agreement over how knights could best win salvation. This divergence of ideals will be considered further in Chapter 5, part 6, below.

Given the undeniable connections between certain Grail romances and the Holy Land, it may seem puzzling that only Wolfram von Eschenbach

---

[195] *Elucidation*, lines 17–19, 339–82; and see p. 107 on line 318, pp. 67–78.

specifically mentioned the Templars in connection with the Grail. This seems to have been because the Templars were included in literature for a specific purpose: in this case to identify the Grâl Castle as Jerusalem, to show that Wolfram was writing about the inheritance to the kingdom of Jerusalem, and to emphasize Wolfram's own particular message of God's love. Other writers achieved this identification without mentioning the Templars, by giving other indications that the Grail Castle was Jerusalem. This could be done by referring to a lame king and Beirut, as in Chrétien's *Conte du Graal*, or by describing how the castle has recently been captured by the enemy of Christendom, as in *Perlesvaus*. The failure to mention the Templars does not necessarily indicate hostility to the Templars, but rather an unwillingness to make the meaning of the mystery too obvious. It must be remembered that one of the great attractions of the Grail legends is their mystery, which seems to promise great knowledge and insights if only it can be understood. Certainly medieval writers must have been aware that the mystery was at least as important as the message in attracting an audience. Hence, the writer of *Perlesvaus* combines many layers of meaning and symbolism – the Grail Castle is both the earthly and heavenly Jerusalem, while the Island of the Four Horns is an otherworld paradise, yet it is also a place where Perlesvaus will be king. In the same way, Wolfram von Eschenbach delights in making his story race back and forth 'like a hare', as he warns the audience in his opening lines. Unfortunately, allusions which would have been relatively simple, intriguing and amusing for the original audience to decipher have proved difficult for modern scholars to interpret.

PART TWO

ANALYSIS

CHAPTER FIVE

THE APPEARANCES OF THE MILITARY ORDERS IN MEDIEVAL FICTIONAL LITERATURE

1 *Their roles*

The Military Orders appeared in a wide variety of epic and romance works in French, German, Occitan and English during the period 1150–1500, in a variety of different roles. The Brothers are religious, giving hospitality and providing a place of penance or a place of refuge, especially for lovers; they are also military, fighting the infidel and giving military advice to rulers, and defending the holy places against the unworthy. Their spirituality is taken for granted, but they are seldom depicted as giving spiritual leadership.

All these roles were realistic, although conventualised. The Temple was indeed a place of penance for murderers, and the Order of the Temple was a place of retirement for knights; the Military Orders did practise hospitality, ransom prisoners and bury the dead, act as messengers for kings, call the West to aid the Holy Land and fight alongside crusaders during crusades against the Muslims and the pagans of north-eastern Europe. In addition, in actuality the members of Military Orders seldom held positions of spiritual leadership. The fact that the Military Orders appeared in more 'monastic' than 'military' roles reflected the demands of literary plots, but also what the writers and audiences of these works saw of the Military Orders in the West. In western Europe, the Military Orders gave hospitality, acted as a place of retirement from the world, buried the dead and acted as messengers for kings, and these were therefore the roles in which they were most familiar to the people of western Europe in their everyday lives.

The works in which the Military Orders appeared continued to be popular throughout the Middle Ages. Some, such as *Renaut de Montalban* and Jean d'Arras' *Mélusine*, were translated into other languages; others were rewritten and adapted from verse to prose. Sometimes their role changed as a result, as in *Renaut*, where what was initially a reference to the headquarters of the Order of the Temple became more and more simply a synonym for Jerusalem, or in *La Fille du Comte de Ponthieu*, where the fifteenth-century version depicts the people at the Temple as priests rather than Brothers of a Military Order. In other cases, as in the alliterative *Morte Arthure* and *Esclarmonde*, the later version omitted the reference to a Military Order. But elsewhere they remained in their original role, as in Albrecht's and Ulrich Füetrer's reworkings of Wolfram von Eschenbach's *Parzival*, in the translations of Jean d'Arras' *Mélusine*, and the reworkings of *Theséus de Cologne*.

Some of the works in which the Military Orders appeared were extremely popular. The most popular work was Wolfram von Eschenbach's *Parzival*, followed by Albrecht's *Jüngerer Titurel*, but Antoine de la Sale's *Jehan de Saintré* was also popular, as, clearly, was Jean d'Arras' *Mélusine*. Other works, such as *Sone de Nansay* and *Claris et Laris*, appear to have been less well known, as only single manuscripts survive; but the number of surviving manuscripts is not an entirely reliable guide to the popularity of a work of literature.[1] Taking all their various appearances into account, it is safe to say that, overall, the Military Orders were well known in literature of the Middle Ages.

The continued appearances of the Military Orders in literature throughout the Middle Ages indicates that their vocation continued to arouse interest and sympathy and that the war against the Saracens and pagans continued to be seen as important to Christendom. The latter point is already established from recent historical scholarship, but the evidence of literature confirms it.

It is significant that the Brothers are always depicted taking a supporting role. In most of their appearances, the Brothers of the Orders are not even given personal names. Very seldom does a member of a Military Order emerge as a personality, and hardly ever do they attain a crucial role in the course of events. Certainly Tirant lo Blanc and Mélusine's sons would have been disappointed if they had had no Hospitallers to assist them in their adventures against the infidel, but secular knights might have done just as well. The Hospitallers, Templars and Teutonic Knights in semi-historical works such as *Du Bon William Longespee*, *Die Kreuzfahrt des Landgrafen Ludwigs* and Ottokar's *Reimchronik* have names and play important supporting roles, but are only of secondary importance to the story. Margon the Templar in *Sone de Nansay* has a more crucial role, and both he and Brother Simon de Far in *Tirant lo Blanc* emerge as strong personalities. Perhaps only Harpin de Bourges in the 'Third State' of the First Crusade Cycle can be said to have achieved hero status, and even here he was a hero before he became a Templar.

This was inevitable, for the Orders' strength lay in the group and in trust and cooperation between members of the group, not in the individual. The discipline so praised by their contemporaries depended on the group working together, and no one Brother seeking his own glory. No one member should be singled out for special praise; for instance, by becoming canonised after their death. It is notable that not one of the active warriors within the Military Orders who died in the field against the Muslims received canonisation or

---

[1] Lachet, *Sone de Nansay*, pp. 4–5.

even beatification.[2] All members were of equal importance in the line of battle; all were potential martyrs. This was essential for the military effectiveness of the Orders, but made bad material for literature, where the emphasis was not on good fighting tactics but on the individual hero. The Military Orders were the best supporting fighting force a hero could have; but they could only be a supporting force.

The appearances of the Military Orders in literature were conventionalised, but not wholly so. Their roles do reflect current events, although they are not a strict guide to contemporary actuality. If they were, we might expect that the Order of the Temple would have ceased to appear in literature after the Order was annulled in 1312 by Pope Clement V at the Council of Vienne. However, even after the destruction of the Order of the Temple the Order continued to appear in new literature, albeit in less significant roles. It appears fleetingly in *Le Chevalier au Cygne et Godefroid de Bouillon* and is referred to in *Baudouin de Sebourc* and *Saladin*. A Templar appears in a brief but effective role in *Le Livre de Baudoyn, conte de Flandre* and the alliterative *Morte Arthure*. Templar-Hospitallers appear in *Theséus de Cologne*, Templars appear in *Orendal*, and Ulrich Füetrer began his *Buch der Abenteuer* with the *Templeysen*.

Nevertheless, these are works set in the past, when the Order still existed, or could be assumed to have existed. In works set in a time nearer to the present, or in no particular time, such as *Tirant lo Blanc* or *Jehan de Saintré*, the Hospitallers or Teutonic Knights appear instead. Hence, authors do appear to have taken contemporary actuality into consideration when composing their works.

In addition, it is clear that later authors did not know much about the Templars. They no longer used the Templars in the multiplicity of roles they performed in literature before 1312. They must have known about these roles, for many of the manuscripts in which the Templars appear in these multiple roles were copied in the fourteenth or fifteenth centuries; for instance, thirty-two manuscripts of Wolfram von Eschenbach's *Parzival* survive from the fourteenth century and ten from the fifteenth, and the work of Ulrich Füetrer demonstrates the continued attraction of Wolfram's work. Even in cases where the only manuscript dates from before the abolition of the Order, the fact that the manuscript has survived to the present day indicates that it was still valued, and therefore probably still being read. In particular, the redactor of the later version of *Baudouin de Sebourc*, preserved in a fifteenth-century manuscript, put in a reference to the Temple as a place of penance which was not in his original, although similar references appeared in different, older works – indicating that he was familiar with these older works. However, other

---

[2] For details see Nicholson, *Templars, Hospitallers*, pp. 118–20.

redactors working after 1312 removed or diminished the role of the Templars. In general after 1312 the Templars' literary roles were simple and straightforward: they were either depicted as simple clergy who pray and care for pilgrims, as in *Le Chevalier au Cygne et Godefroid de Bouillon*, *Theséus de Cologne* and the fifteenth-century *La Fille du Comte de Ponthieu*, or they were involved in the promotion of holy war.

It could be argued that the Military Orders were included in literature because of the exotic location of their activities and the exceptional nature of their devotion and prowess, and that the suppression of the Templars actually enhanced the exotic image of the Order in the perception of writers, patrons and audiences; hence the Order continued to appear in literature. However, this argument fails to take two factors into account.

Firstly, the Military Orders do not appear in all works where modern readers would expect them to appear if they were included to add an exotic atmosphere to a work of literature. They do not appear in many works which include the crusade, nor in most of the Arthurian prose romances, notably the Vulgate and Post-Vulgate cycles. While it is impossible to identify all the factors which would lead a writer to include the Military Orders in a work or to exclude them, their appearances are too erratic to be explained simply by the need to add an exotic touch.

Secondly, this argument does not account for the change in the nature of the Templars' appearances in literature after 1312. They appeared less often in literature, and their appearances became far less exotic, rather than more so. Their roles are limited to uncontroversial activities such as looking after pilgrims or promoting holy war. These were activities which anyone who had heard of the Templars would have known were associated with that Order, and which were doctrinally irreproachable. In contrast, the Hospitallers and the Teutonic Order appeared more often in literature, but, again, their roles strictly reflected contemporary actuality and were doctrinally irreproachable.

These changes after 1312 suggest that the appearance of the Military Orders in a work of literature was intended to give that work a firm grounding in actuality: either contemporary or past. When the Order of the Temple no longer existed, there was no reason to include the Templars, unless the story was known to be set in a time when the Order existed and the Brothers were given a straightforward role which everyone would know they had performed. Rather than including the Hospitallers or Teutonic Knights to give a work an exotic setting, the presence of these Orders brought the story out of a non-existant literary context into an historic or contemporary actuality. In short, adding the Hospitallers made even such an unlikely tale as the story of Mélusine appear more credible.

2 Realism and the truth assertion

While it is true that much medieval fictional literature does not appear to modern readers to have much connection with actuality, it is evident that from the early thirteenth century onwards, when the Military Orders began to appear frequently in literature, realism – that is, contemporary or past actuality – played an important role in fictional literature. It became extremely important in the fifteenth century, as evidenced by works such as *Tirant lo Blanc* and *Jehan de Saintré*. It is necessary to stress that there does appear to have been a change in attitudes towards 'fictional' literature towards the end of the twelfth century. D.H. Green has argued persuasively that in the second half of the twelfth century and at the beginning of the thirteenth century 'fictional' literature in Germany was openly fictional, and avowedly separate from historical 'truth'. However, there was then a reaction, and German literature written after around 1220 was given a firm historical orientation and context.[3] This was also true, although to a lesser extent, in France, where the writers of epic and romance literature were careful to state that they had a Latin source and where they had found it, while the authors of the great Arthurian prose romances went to enormous lengths to describe how the material which was included in the romances was originally recorded by Blaise and various other scribes, while Arthur's reign was fixed precisely in time to the early fifth century – in fact, a century before the 'real' Arthur appears to have lived.

While it is clear that the 'truth assertion' in literature was a *topos* that was not necessarily taken at face value by the audience and could be little more than a joke, it is important to remember the cultural context of these stories. The twelfth-century renaissance had brought a growth in literacy. As a result, noble audiences now began to expect written history rather than the oral tradition represented by the epics and verse romances. In the seventh century, Isidore of Seville had defined history in his *Eymologiae* (Book 1, 41–4): history had to be eyewitness in order to be accepted as true, and should be written down. Epics and verse romances, being based on oral tradition, were therefore inherently untrue, although epic was 'truer' than romance because it was necessarily based on historical events, whereas romance, such as the romances of King Arthur, could be based on oral legend and did not necessarily have any basis in recorded history.[4]

Works in Latin and Greek, as classical languages of education, were regarded as more authoritative than the vernacular. Writers of prose Latin,

---

[3] Green, *Medieval Listening and Reading*, pp. 237–69, 275: esp. p. 265.
[4] Green, *Medieval Listening and Reading*, p. 266; André Moisan, 'Les traditions rolandienne et turpinienne dans les croniques et conquestes de Charlemaine de David Aubert', in *Aspects de l'épopée romane*, pp. 399–408: here p. 406 n. 277.

even those translating Latin into the vernacular for lay readers, could be very dismissive of anything we would now regard as romantic and epic literature.[5] Thus, Helinand of Froidmont, writing in the early thirteenth century, dismissed the prose *Estoire del Saint Graal* as unworthy of discussion because he had not been able to find its supposed Latin source: he preferred to turn to works for which he had Latin sources, which were more likely to be true and useful: *verisimiliora et utiliora.*[6]

Works in verse were particularly open to criticism, as writers of verse had to manipulate their material in order to make it scan or rhyme.[7] It was agreed that poetry can have moral value when it depicts virtuous actions which audiences should imitate, and certainly the pleasure of reading or listening could be profitable, but some writers considered that poetry which had no moral value should be avoided.[8]

Yet verse remained a valuable literary form; for example, after Jean de Meun translated Vegetius' *De Re Militari* from Latin prose into French prose in 1284, Jean Priorat translated it into French verse, probably in the late 1280s.[9] Verse epic and romance was still being produced in France in the late fourteenth century, and in England and Germany in the fifteenth century. It has even been suggested that English writers deliberately composed Arthurian romance in verse to distinguish it from the anti-English French prose Arthurian romances.[10] Verse was clearly the medium of choice for works to be recited to a large audience, as verse is able to keep the attention of a

---

[5] See, for example, *The Chivalric Vision of Alfonso de Cartagena*, pp. 12–14.

[6] Helinand of Froidmont, *Chronicon*, in *Pat. Lat.* 212, cols. 814–15; Bruce, *Evolution*, 1, pp. 247, 284–5, 450–51 n. 2; Jill Mann, 'Malory and the Grail Legend', in *A Companion to Malory*, ed. E. Archibald and A.S.G. Edwards, pp. 203–20, here pp. 203–4, 208. Helinand was writing before 1216, but his discussion of the Grail legend may be a late thirteenth-century interpolation.

[7] Much has been written on the increasing distrust of verse as a literary medium during the twelfth and thirteenth centuries. See, for instance, Brian Woledge and H.P. Clive, *Répertoire des plus anciens textes en prose française depuis 842 jusqu'aux premières années du XIII siècle* (Geneva, 1964), pp. 27–31; Tyson, 'Patronage of French vernacular history writers', 186–7; Emmanuel Baumgartner, 'Les techniques narratives dans le roman en prose', in *The Legacy of Chrétien de Troyes*, ed. N.J. Lacy, D. Kelly and K. Busby, 2 vols (Amsterdam, 1987), 1, pp. 167–8.

[8] On this debate see *Medieval Literary Theory and Criticism, c. 1100–c. 1375: The Commentary Tradition*, ed. A.J. Minnis and A.B. Scott (Oxford, 1988), pp. 113–26; Glending Olson, *Literature as Recreation in the Later Middle Ages* (Ithaca and London, 1982), pp. 20–38, 128–63, esp. pp. 149–55 on writers hostile to reading poetry purely for pleasure. Yet not all writers dismissed fiction as worthless; William Caxton recommended that knights should read Arthurian romance to learn about knighthood, *The Book of the Ordre of Chyvalry translated and printed by William Caxton from a French version of Ramon Lull's 'Le Libre del orde de Cavayleria'*, ed. Alfred T. P. Hyles, EETS 168 (London, 1926), p. 123; cited by Fallows, *The Chivalric Vision of Alfronso de Cartagena*, p. 15.

[9] *L'Art de Chevalerie: Traduction de Du Re Militari de Végèce par Jeun de Meun, publié avec une étude sur cette traduction et sur Li Abrejance de l'ordre de chevalerie de Jean Priorat*, ed. Ulysse Robert, SATF (Paris, 1897), pp. viii, x–xii, and note 2 on p. xi; *Li Abrejance de l'ordre de Chevalerie mise en vers de la traduction de Végèce de Jean de Meun par Jean Priorat de Besançon*, ed. Ulysse Robert, SATF (Paris, 1897), lines 10544–67.

[10] Morris, 'King Arthur and the Growth of French Nationalism', p. 128.

large audience better than prose. It must be remembered that many of the great playwrights of the early modern period – such as Shakespeare, Racine, Corneille and Schiller – composed in verse. Verse, therefore, was not an invalid medium *per se*; it was not the medium alone which made it necessary to demonstrate that literature was true.

Even more important than the move from oral to written history in the emphasis on 'truth' in literature were the philosophical developments of the twelfth-century renaissance, which encouraged rational thought and discouraged fantasy. The concern of twelfth-century scholars, both in the growing universities and in the Church as a whole, was to restore humanity's knowledge of God, through reason and faith. They believed that God, and nature as God's creation, are intelligible to human thought, and therefore sought to find rational explanations for everything, both in matters of faith and in the material world. One manifestation of this was an attempt to define what 'truth' is, as shown, for instance, in the works of Anselm, Abelard and Bernard of Clairvaux. Scholars redefined more strictly the divisions between the natural and the supernatural, and redefined the nature of the supernatural. There was also a determination to codify and harmonize law, manifested in Gratian's *Digest* of canon law. Classical authorities played an important role in these developments: in particular, Aristotle's works on logic stimulated debate on the application of reason to problems. In the thirteenth century, the influence of Aristotle became paramount: prompted by his writings, scholars attempted to produce a natural theology which harmonised reason and faith. Scholars disagreed over how far reason and faith could be reconciled and whether complete knowledge could be obtained through reason alone or whether reason must eventually give way to faith; but all agreed that reason was an essential part of the search for knowledge.[11]

Anything which did not have an obvious rational explanation must either be fitted into the new philosophical system – so that magic was regarded as the manipulation of the natural forces of the physical universe – or, if this was not possible, it was liable to be rejected as theologically questionable. One result of this was that the traditional trial by ordeal to establish guilt or innocence, which could not be accounted for by natural events or canon law, was forbidden in 1215 by the Fourth Lateran Council, and replaced in ecclesiastical proceedings by formal legal investigation. This change was not

---

[11] For the development of thought and rational enquiry from the eleventh century onwards see, for example, *A History of Twelfth-Century Philosophy*, ed. Dronke, esp. p. 2; Gordon Leff, *Medieval Thought from Saint Augustine to Ockham* (Harmondsworth, 1958), pp. 92–140, 168–71; Alexander Murray, *Reason and Society in the Middle Ages* (Oxford, 1978), pp. 213–33; R.W. Southern, *Scholastic Humanism and the Unification of Europe*, vol. 1: *Foundations* (Oxford, 1995), esp. pp. 17–51; Brian Stock, *The Implications of Literacy: Written Language and Models of Interpretation in the Eleventh and Twelfth Centuries* (Princeton, 1983), pp. 326–454.

simply due to changes in beliefs about how the physical world operated; it was also due to the Council's determination to prevent clerics being involved in the shedding of blood in the course of judicial processes. However, the change in the intellectual climate was a contribution to this reform.[12]

Belief continued to be given to matters now generally regarded as non-existent, notably miracles and magic, but such events were only accepted within a rationalistic context. Sanctity no longer rested upon local acclamation; saints must be approved by the central authority of the Church, with their miracles properly recorded and attested. Nature was seen as operating according to rules.[13] It is for this reason that some of the fantasy of romance – such as spinning islands or spinning castles – became unacceptable, as is obvious from the lengthy efforts of the author of *Le Livre d'Artus* to provide a rationalist explanation for a spinning island.[14] The author states that it is essential to show the correct reason for this phenomenon – *droite raison monstrer* – and only to tell what is known to be true.

In short, to be 'true' and philosophically and theologically irreproachable, a literary work had to firstly demonstrate that it was by an eye-witness or based on a written eye-witness account, preferably in Latin, and, secondly, be firmly based in the rational and actual. Works which could not demonstrate this were lies and fables. Such works were regarded as dangerous to the mind and soul, because they were contrary to the new understanding of the Christian faith.

The prologue to a prose translation of the 'Lives of the Fathers' for Blanca of Navarre, countess of Champagne (1199–1229), put the problem succinctly: the verse romances of Cligès and Perceval are lies which darken the heart and corrupt the clarity of the soul.[15] Caesarius of Heisterbach, in his *Dialogus miraculorum*, told a story of Gevard, a past abbot of his abbey, who rebuked his monks for dozing through his sermons, but waking up to hear a 'fable of Arthur' (*fabulam Arcturi*). The tale of Arthur was *verba levitatis*, trivial words, while the monks who dozed in his sermons but woke up to hear about Arthur were being tempted by the devil.[16] Jehan Maillart, beginning his *Roman du comte d'Anjou* in around the year 1316, stressed that he was writing a true story, not a lie, which would be beneficial to the readers and encourage them to live better and to avoid hell – unlike the *gens malades*, the sick

---

[12] On clerical attitudes towards the ordeal by fire and water from the twelfth century see Robert Bartlett, *Trial by Fire and Water: the Medieval Judicial Ordea* (Oxford, 1986), pp. 70–71, 81–90, 98. For the concern among the new *literati* of the twelfth-century renaissance to abolish superstitious practices see Moore, *Formation of a Persecuting Society*, esp. p. 138.

[13] Murray, *Reason and Society*, pp. 6–14; Moore, *Formation of a Persecuting Society*, p. 138.

[14] *Le Livre d'Artus*, p. 299 line 20–p. 301 line 22.

[15] Old French quoted by Woledge and Clive, *Répertoire des plus anciens textes en prose française*; also by Kennedy, 'Knight as reader', p. 86; see also Bruce, *Evolution*, 1, p. 253 n. 1 (from p. 251).

[16] Caesarius of Heisterbach, *Dialogus miraculorum*, 1, p. 205: Dist. 4, ch. 36.

people who listened to works which only amuse and have no moral benefit.[17] The Knight of La Tour Landry, writing 1371–72, instructed his daughters to read lives of the saints, which are profitable to souls and bodies, and not to read invented stories and fables which do not increase knowledge and are unprofitable to the soul.[18] Jean Germain (died 1460) stated that those who read romances and fables and false doctrines – as if the three categories of writing were equivalent to each other – were out of their senses and sick with the malady of bad belief: *tous degectez et malades et enfumés de la maladie de mauvaise foy*.[19] Jean thus equated romances with false doctrine, virtually stating that they were heretical. Christians should seek to read and hear only truth.[20]

The descriptions used to describe these dubious writings were very close to those used to describe heretical writings, which Roman Catholic writers described as *errores*, *fabulae*, *falsa*, and *frivola*: errors, fables, false and frivolous. For instance, Bernard, abbot of Clairvaux, referred to the doctrines of heretics as 'absurdities'.[21] A person under interrogation by the investigator of heresy in Quercy told his interrogator that he:

> had received from the hands of heretics two quires of their errors which he held for eight days and more ...[22]

by which he meant that he had been in possession of two quires of heretical writings. The author of a treatise on the beliefs of the Italian Cathars described these heretics' beliefs as 'errors and fatuities'.[23] Bernard Gui, a Dominican friar and investigator of heresy during the first three decades of the fourteenth century, wrote at length on the 'errors' of the Waldensian heretics, for instance:

> Now, the principal error of the aforesaid Waldensians was and still continues to be contempt of ecclesiastical authority. Then, having been excommunicated for this and given over to Satan, they were plunged by him into countless errors, and they combined with their own fantasies the errors of heretics of an earlier day.[24]

---

[17] Jehan Maillart, *Roman du comte d'Anjou*, ed. Mario Rocques, CFMA 67 (Paris, 1931), lines 1–47; for date, see p. vi.

[18] *The Book of the Knight of La Tour =Landry, compiled for the instruction of his daughters*, ed. Thomas Wright, EETS 33 (London, 1868), p. 118; translated from Geoffrey, Chevalier de la Tour Landry, *Le Livre du Chevalier de la Tour Landry pour l'enseignement de ses filles*, ed. Antoine de Montaiglon (Paris, 1854).

[19] French quoted by Geneviève Hasenhoir, 'Religious reading amongst the laity in France in the fifteenth century', in *Heresy and Literacy, 1000–1530*, ed. Peter Biller and Anne Hudson (Cambridge, 1994), pp. 205–21, here p. 218.

[20] Thomas Aquinas, *Summa theologiae*, Blackfriars edn. (London, 1963), 46, p. 25: 2a2ae 180, 3–4: Blackfriars' translation.

[21] Translated in *Heresies of the High Middle Ages*, ed. Walter L. Wakefield and Austin P. Evans (New York, 1969, 1991), p. 138.

[22] Peter Biller, 'The Cathars of Languedoc and written materials', in *Heresy and Literacy*, pp. 61–82: here p. 77; my translation.

[23] Translated in *Heresies of the High Middle Ages*, p. 352.

[24] Ibid., p. 388.

As well as being absurdity, error, fatuity and fantasy, heresy was also represented as a disease of the soul, which could manifest itself as a physical disease such as leprosy. It was often described as an infection.[25]

Heresy was regarded as a danger to the Church and to society as a whole. It was believed that heresy would bring down the punishment of God upon society for its failure to correct wrong belief. What was more, as the Church supported the secular authorities, heresy was viewed as a direct threat to the secular authorities because it denied the 'truths' preached by the Church. As a result, the twelfth century saw increasing legislation against heresy, and active persecution of heretics.[26] Heretical writing was regarded as a considerable danger. Many of the new heresies were literate and based on the study of vernacular translations of the Bible. What was more, from the twelfth century onwards, European heretics produced many writings of their own.

Potentially, then, a literary work which was not based on an eye-witness authority in Latin or firmly based in actuality could be at least a danger to the soul and could even be heretical. Clearly it would not have been beneficial for the writers of epic and romance for their work to be regarded as spiritually dangerous. Some writers within the epic-romance tradition certainly encountered problems from the religious authorities as a result of the new emphasis on 'truth', and the need to demonstrate authority for one's statements and that what one was writing was firmly based in actuality. The works of both Mechtild of Magdeburg and Marguerite Porete, who wrote in the romance tradition, were accused of being heretical. Mechtild escaped into the convent at Helfta (c.1270), but Marguerite and her book were burned for heresy at Paris in 1310. Their works were regarded as spiritually dangerous because they wrote on religious subjects without reference to recognised literary authorities who could give their work authenticity, and they wrote in the vernacular, rather than Latin, the recognised language of scholarship. Wolfram von Eschenbach altered his description of the neutral angels at a late stage in *Parzival*, apologising for having misled his hero and his audience earlier on. Presumably he had been taken to task by a theologian for spreading religious misconceptions.[27] The author of the first part of the prose *Tristan* indicates that there was a problem for writers of chivalric works intended for entertainment when writing of religious matters: he states that he has been forbidden by the archbishop of Canterbury to say anything about 'the Divinity', although

---

[25] *The Birth of Popular Heresy*, ed. R. Moore (London, 1975), pp. 5, 7, 135; translations in *Heresies of the High Middle Ages*, pp. 210, 227, 237, 245, 268, 306 ('malady of error'), 332, 436; see also James of Vitry, Sermon 28, p. 419: 'infected with the heretical poison'.

[26] For the increasing persecution of heretics as a result of the rise of the new literate class and the increasing powers of secular government, developments which were also stimulated by the twelfth-century renaissance, see Moore, *Formation of a Persecuting Society*.

[27] See A.T. Hatto's translation of Wolfram's *Parzival*, p. 436; and see Wolfram von Eschenbach, *Parzival*, Bk 9, 471.15–30, Bk 16, 798.6–22.

he considered himself well able to write on such subjects.[28] Whatever the accuracy of this statement, it indicates that secular writers could incur the wrath of the ecclesiastical authorities if they wrote on religious matters in works intended for entertainment.

Nevertheless, some writers of secular works intended for entertainment did discuss religion with overtly heretical overtones; yet their work was not burnt, and no action was taken against them. The otherwise orthodox and ascetic Catholic work *La Queste del Saint Graal* contains an odd passage where Perceval is told by a good and holy man that the devil took Enoch and Elijah. In fact, the Old Testament states clearly that God took Enoch and Elijah. The same good man also states that the first Law came from the devil, whereas it is clear from the Old Testament Book of Exodus that the first Law came from God.[29] This passage is repeated in the prose *Tristan*.[30] The concept that the God of the Old Testament was the devil was a belief of the Cathar heretics. According to the repentant heretic Bonacursus, writing between 1176 and 1190 about the Italian Cathars:

> They assert that whatever things were said or done by Abraham, Isaac or Jacob were said and done by a demon. They also aver that it was the devil who appeared to Moses in the bush and spoke to him. Moreover, the miracles performed by Moses in Pharaoh's presence, the fact that the children of Israel passed through the Red Sea and were led into the Promised Land, God's speaking to Moses, and the Law which God gave to him – all these, they say and believe were the work of this same devil, their master.[31]

Again, according to an account of the Italian Cathars, written between 1200 and 1214:

> The common belief of all Cathars is that all things recounted in Genesis – namely, about the flood, the deliverance of Noah, God's speaking to Abraham, the destruction of Sodom and Gomorrah – were done by the devil, who is there called god. And likewise this very god led the people out of Egypt, and gave them the Law in the desert, and led them into the Promised Land.[32]

The author of *Perlesvaus* also equates the Old Law, the Law of the Old Testament, with the devil, but here it is firmly associated with Islam.[33] In fact, the idea that the Old Law was the work of the devil was a logical conclusion from the Epistles in the New Testament, where it is depicted as binding people

---

[28] *Tristan*, ed. Curtis, 1, pp. 105–6, 171 lines 2–14.
[29] *Queste*, p. 102, lines 13–21; see the Book of Genesis, ch. 5 v. 24; 2 Kings ch. 2 vv. 11–12; Exodus, chs 20–31.
[30] *Tristan*, ed. Ménard, 8, p. 123, 56 lines 39–45, 59–65.
[31] Translated in *Heresies of the High Middle Ages*, p. 172.
[32] Ibid., p. 166. On the devil and the Old Testament, see also, for example, ibid, pp. 47, 237–8, 308–9, 312, 322, 355; Malcolm Lambert, *The Cathars* (Oxford, 1998), p. 30; Bernard Hamilton, *The Albigensian Crusade*, Historical Association Pamphlet no. 85 (London, 1974), pp. 5–6.
[33] For example, see *Perlesvaus*, lines 5788–973, 7842–52.

up, whereas the New Law of Christ sets them free.[34] In other words, the statements about the Old Law in the *Queste*, prose *Tristan* and *Perlesvaus* need not be heretical, but could simply derive from Catholic doctrine. Nevertheless, the comments in the *Queste* about the devil taking Enoch and Elijah are certainly heretical, although probably not deliberately so.

Yet these works were not, apparently, accused of being heretical during the Middle Ages. This was because their writers had taken precautions to avoid being accused of heresy.

In order to demonstrate that a 'fictional' work was based on actuality it was necessary either to show a proper authenticated source for one's material or to fit one's work firmly into an irreproachable actuality. The writers of the *Perlesvaus* and the *Queste* claimed an historical authority, a Latin manuscript which they had translated, complete with an explanation of the circumstances in which this translation came about; and they set their stories firmly into a well-established literary reality (the 'Arthurian legend') which was already fully familiar to their noble audience. These were normal procedures for such writers. A writer could then insist that their work rested on a firm historical basis, and had proper authority because it did not express their own opinions but only reproduced what was in their written source. These claims to have translated an historical Latin source are not now taken seriously by scholars. However, they were taken seriously by contemporaries. Helinand de Froidmont went to great lengths to find the Latin source for the prose *Estoire del Saint Graal*: although he failed to find it and concluded that the existence of the Latin source was doubtful, he would not even have attempted the search had it been generally accepted that such claims were only conventional.[35]

However, while these procedures were effective for stories written within well-established literary cycles such as the stories of Charlemagne, Guillaume d'Orange or Arthur, non-cyclical stories, especially those in verse, had more of a problem in demonstrating that they reflected a genuine actuality and were not dangerous fables. They could claim to be translating a Latin manuscript, but if they were writing a non-cyclical work this claim was unlikely to seem credible. The best way to demonstrate actuality was for the writer to include details and characters from either contemporary or past actuality.

It is in such non-cyclical stories that the Military Orders were most likely to appear. In a work with some crusading connection, the Military Orders were an obvious example of indisputable actuality. Depending on the setting of the plot, their role could be to give contemporary colour, or historicity. The need for historicity ensured the continuing appearance of the Order of the Temple in literature even after its abolition. The Order's many roles might have been forgotten, but the Order was known to have existed and audiences

---

[34] See, for example, Galatians ch. 3 James ch. 1 v. 25.
[35] Helinand de Froidmont, cols 814–15.

knew something about its past activities. Therefore, if the Order appeared in a story, the audience would know that this story reflected actuality; it was not a complete invention, an 'error' or a fable, and it would not endanger the soul.

3 *The origins of realism; the sources of the Military Orders' roles*

Where did the writers of literature find their information on the Military Orders, in order to make their work reflect actuality?

Some writers were obviously writing against a background of current events. Jean d'Arras' description of the Hospitallers of Rhodes is clearly based on the Order's actual work in the East, and he may have had information on the Order's participation in the crusades of Peter I of Cyprus. His exact source of information is unknown, but it has been suggested that he was identical with the Jean d'Arras who was a tenant of the Hospitallers at Arras in 1382.[36] Joanot Martorell's description of the Hospitallers of Rhodes being threatened by the Genoese and involved in the defence of Constantinople reflects the Order's activities in the Eastern Mediterranean in the fourteenth and fifteenth centuries, and Genoese expansionism in this area. He may have used a contemporary Catalan or Valencian poem on the siege of Rhodes by the Mamluks in 1444, *Romanç de l'armada del Soldà contra Rodes*, or had information from his friend Jaume de Vilaragut, who was on the island during the siege. His depiction of Genoese hostility towards the Hospital reflects the actual Genoese attitude during the siege of 1444.[37]

Many of the literary images of the Military Orders reflected current actualities. In particular, the depiction of the Order of the Temple as a place of penance and as a place of retirement for knights certainly reflects actual practice in the society for which the literature was composed.

Depictions of the Military Orders' involvement in crusading warfare would originally have been based on eye-witness accounts from pilgrims returning from the Holy Land, as well as on the preaching of the Orders' own almscollectors in the West, and the letters sent by the Orders to the West to publicise their deeds in the East and ask for aid.[38] Even when the Crusader states had been finally lost to the Muslims, the activities of the Military Orders in the East were preserved in the 'History' written by William, archbishop of Tyre, up to 1184. Although this work had a relatively small circulation

---

[36] See Luttrell, 'The Hospitallers in Cyprus after 1386', p. 135.

[37] *Tirant lo Blanc*, pp. 7–9, 12; David H. Rosenthal, *Tirant lo Blanc* (London, 1984), pp. xii–xiii; Housley, *Later Crusades*, pp. 92–3, 100, 191–7, 222–5, 227.

[38] On these letters, see Nicholson, *Templars, Hospitallers*, pp. 105–7; Smail, 'Latin Syria and the West, 1149–1187'; Lloyd, *English Society and the Crusade*, pp. 24–31, 36–41, 248–52, 256–61; Phillips, *Defenders of the Holy Land*; Cook, 'The Transmission of Knowledge about the Holy Land through Europe, 1271–1314', unpublished PhD, pp. 402ff., esp. pp. 419ff., 453ff., 477–88, 490ff.

in Latin, it was translated into French by the early thirteenth century and continuations were added to it. These were extremely popular and widely read, so that it has been calculated that the French translation of William of Tyre and its continuations 'must have been known in nearly every town and considerable city in Europe'.[39] While the Military Orders' literary image is far more positive than their image in William's work and its continuations, the continuing popularity of his 'History' would have ensured that writers and patrons remembered the importance of the Military Orders in the defence of the Holy Land, and included them in their literature. In particular, the composer of *Saladin* seems to have used the continuation attributed to Ernoul for his description of Saladin's capture of Jerusalem, including the role of the Templars in ransoming the Christian captives.[40]

Presumably, writers also drew their concepts of the Military Orders from earlier literature. This is particularly likely with the continuing use of the image of the 'Temple' as a place of penance, even when it is quite obvious that the writer does not realise that the 'Temple' was originally the Order of the Temple, rather than simply a building in Jerusalem.

4 *Crusading as an influence on the Military Orders' appearances in fictional literature*

The obvious category of fiction in which the inclusion of the Military Orders would strengthen a claim to reflect actuality would be stories involving crusades or holy war. They certainly do appear in a number of such works, including *L'Histoire de Gilles de Chyn, L'Escoufle, Esclarmonde* and so on.

However, if Military Orders appeared in fictional literature in order to tie it more closely to actuality, we must ask why the Orders did not appear in most crusading epics: they do not, for example, appear in *Gui de Warwick*, in *Pontus et Sidoine* or its fifteenth-century German translation, in *Le Lion de Bourges* or *La Belle Hélène de Constantinople*. Their role in the Crusade Cycle is small: Galaan (Wayland the Smith) appears as often as they do.[41] In the case of the First Crusade Cycle, the explanation obviously is that the Military Orders were not founded until after the First Crusade, and so they should not appear before the story reaches this stage: hence the Hospital is the first of the Military Orders to appear, still unmilitarised, in the 'Second State' of the First Crusade Cycle, followed by the Order of the Temple in the 'Third State' of the Cycle. By the time the 'Second Cycle' was composed, the authors were not so sure about when the Orders were founded, and the Templars appear briefly before

---

[39] Babcock and Krey, *A History of the Deeds Done Beyond the Sea*, 1, p. 43; Davis, 'William of Tyre', p. 71.
[40] See above, 66–7.
[41] See the relevant entries in Moisan, *Répertoire*.

the First Crusade and are referred to in passing occasionally thereafter. In this case, as the Order of the Temple had been abolished, it is not very surprising that it is given so small a role. What is surprising is that the Hospital does not receive a larger role. This was probably because by the time the 'Second Crusade Cycle' was written the Hospital was established on Rhodes, and contemporary audiences were not fully aware of its earlier involvement in the Holy Land. Including the Hospital in the story would not make it appear more reflective of actuality; so it was left out. Writers knew that the Temple had been involved in the Holy Land, but the Temple no longer existed, so they did not include that Order either.

Arguably, other writers failed to include Military Orders in a story where we would expect to find them because their inclusion would not make the story more reflective of actuality. This could be because the story had some other basis for its 'realism'. As noted above, works which formed part of a cycle with a set of familiar characters needed little other background detail to carry audience belief: so the Arthurian romances, especially those in prose, and the epics of Charlemagne contain few references to the Military Orders. There are no references to the Military Orders at all in the cycle of Guillaume d'Orange and his illustrious family, where the stories and the characters were so familiar that the author of *Aliscans* could drop the audience straight into the middle of a battle scene and know that there was no need to introduce either the situation or the characters. According to the legal expert and contemporary commentator Philip of Novara, in 1231 John, lord of Beirut, came into King Henry of Cyprus's court to seek help for his besieged castle of Beirut. In his request he compared the relations between Guillaume d'Orange and his liege-lord Louis the Pious to his own relations with the king of Cyprus. The king of Cyprus took the hint and granted him the necessary aid. Philip may have embellished this account, but his use of this reference indicates that he expected his audience to be so familiar with the legends of Guillaume that they would understand the allusion without further explanation.[42] Such well-established works, therefore, did not require the addition of the Military Orders to make them more 'real'.

The Military Orders appear very occasionally in Arthurian romance and Charlemagne epic. Yet they appeared far more often in non-cyclic works, where the author obviously had a more difficult task to convince the audience of the credibility and non-heretical nature of these works. This then begs that question of why they do not appear in certain non-cyclic works which involve the crusade and where their appearance would improve the 'realism' of the story for the modern reader.

---

[42] See Filippo da Novara, *Guerra di Federico II in Oriente*, 64 (160), p. 150; Edbury, *Kingdom of Cyprus*, pp. 62–3.

For instance, *La Belle Hélène de Constantinople* (written in the mid-fourteenth century) is a form of the familiar story of 'the girl with the cut-off hands' – the girl who ran away from her would-be incestuous father, married a stranger who went away to the wars, and was betrayed by her mother-in-law. It is interwoven with a crusade to the Holy Land by Hélène's husband King Henry of England. One would expect that the inclusion of the Military Orders in the crusade would give a necessary realistic detail to the familiar folktale; yet, they do not appear. Instead, the crusading hero, the king of England, is given the name Henry, the name borne by three reigning kings of England by the mid-fourteenth century, when this poem was written. No King Henry of England had yet been on crusade, but all the Henrys had shown an interest in the crusade, so clearly Henry was an appropriate name for a crusading king of England. A crusading king of Scotland is named Amaury; no king of Scotland bore that name, but it was the name of a king of Jerusalem, and in this story the newly-converted Muslim king of Jerusalem is baptised Amaury after the Scottish king. Overall, then, *La Belle Hélène* was such a collection of familiar motifs from folklore, epic and history that it contained sufficient 'realism' and credibility without introducing the Military Orders. The writer may also have had other, personal or circumstantial reasons for not including them. The exact date of composition of this story is not known; perhaps it was written so soon after the abolition of the Order of the Temple (1312) and the move of the Hospital to Rhodes (by 1310) that the inclusion of the Military Orders would have seemed inappropriate and would have confused the audience. In any case, the story certainly enjoyed a long period of popularity without any need to include them.[43]

It could also be suggested that by the fourteenth century audiences did not expect stories of the crusades to reflect actuality. In her study of the continuations of the chronicle of William of Tyre, Ruth Morgan noted that from the mid-thirteenth century onwards writers on the Holy Land tended to move away from giving information towards pure entertainment.

> The nature of their work, compared with that of their predecessors, suggests that their readers were not taking the crusades as seriously as an earlier generation had done. What had been formerly an aspect of current events became a literary topos, a central thread around which to weave multi-coloured patterns ... in

---

[43] *La Belle Hélène de Constantinople, chanson de geste du XIV siècle*, ed. Claude Roussel, TLF 454 (Geneva, 1995), p. 95 (date). See also Claude Roussel, *Conter de Geste au XIV siècle: inspiration folklorique et écriture épique dans La Belle Hélène de Constantinople*, (Geneva, 1998), esp. pp. 7–8 on the story's long popularity and pp. 425–7 on its attractiveness to listeners and readers. The central theme, the princess betrayed by her midwife, appears in many other epics and romances such as the story of the birth of the Knight of the Swan, Osane in *Theséus de Cologne*, and the story of the Two Sisters who Envied their Younger Sister in *Arabian Nights Entertainments*, ed. Robert L. Mack (Oxford, 1995), pp. 860–92.

Europe stories of the crusades and the East were being drawn into the ever more attractive orbit of a thriving vernacular adventure literature.[44]

Certainly, there is much fantasy in the later continuations of the First Crusade Cycle: for example, in the London-Turin continuation Baldwin of Edessa rides a unicorn.[45] The fictional literature of the crusade by the mid-thirteenth century contains a considerable element of wishful thinking, for the Christians are depicted winning battles against the Muslims whereas in actuality they were losing ground. Yet, overall, the fictional literature of the crusades reflects actual events. The London-Turin continuation of the *Chanson de Jérusalem* does not deny the rise of Saladin and the forthcoming disaster for the Christians; in the 'Second Crusade Cycle', although Saladin is depicted as a knight and a chivalric warrior on the western pattern, he remains a Muslim until his deathbed and he conquers the whole of the kingdom of Jerusalem (whereas, in fact, the coast remained in Christian hands). Literature certainly attempted to soften the blow of Christian defeat, but it did not deny the fundamental actualities of the situation, and it certainly claimed to be historical – so that we might reasonably expect to find the Military Orders fighting alongside the crusaders as they did in actuality. The fact that we do not find them in some crusading epics, although they are present in others, is probably not due to any general trend towards fantasy. Rather, it shows that crusades and the Military Orders were not inextricably linked in the minds of writers and their audiences; they knew that there had been crusades before there had been Military Orders, and if one were composing a crusade epic set long ago, it could have been before the Military Orders were founded.

Another consideration in whether or not the Military Orders appeared in a work must have been whether the writer or the patron of the work had an interest in the crusades. In a number of works in which the Military Orders appear it is clear that the writer did have an interest in the Holy Land or the crusade, or that the patron of the work had an interest in the Holy Land or the crusade. For instance, Jean Renart's patron for his work *La Roman de la Rose* or *Guillaume de Dole*, Milon de Nanteuil, went on the Fifth Crusade, while his patron for *L'Escoufle*, Baldwin VI of Flanders and Hainault, was one of the leaders of the Fourth Crusade and first Latin emperor of Constantinople.

---

[44] M. Ruth Morgan, 'The Rothelin Continuation of William of Tyre', in *Outremer: Studies in the History of the Crusading Kingdom of Jerusalem presented to Joshua Prawer*, ed. Benjamin Z. Kedar, Hans E. Mayer and R.C. Smail (Jerusalem, 1982), pp. 244–57: here p. 254. See also Karl-Heinz Bender, 'Retour à l'histoire: les dernières épopées du premier cycle de la croisade', *Les Épopées de la croisade. Premier colloque international (Trèves, 6–11 août, 1984)*, ed. Karl-Heinz Bender and Hermann Kleber. *Zeitschrift für französische Sprache und Literatur, Beiheft*, neue Folge Helf 11 (Stuttgart, 1987), pp. 98–104. For the Crusade Cycle as fantasy literature see also Jacoby, 'La littérature française dans les états latins', p. 636.

[45] *OFCC, VIII: The London-Turin Version*, lines 12846–8, 16057–8, 18056–7, 18026, 18215, 18438, 18544–5.

Wolfram von Eschenbach clearly had an interest in Christian–Muslim relations, as evidenced by his work *Willehalm*, and his patron Hermann of Thuringia had a personal interest in the crusade to the Holy Land; the writer of *Claris et Laris* refers to the crisis in the Holy Land in the introduction to the work; the writer of *Sone de Nansay* had some sort of interest in the lordship of Beirut. The writer of the *Roman de Laurin* had an interest in the Holy Land;[46] this is reasonable for, as a part of the cycle of the Seven Sages of Rome, the work has its origins in the Levant, and other works in the cycle (*Les Sept Sages de Rome* and *Cassiodorus*) preserve much folktale material of oriental origin – although *Laurin* itself is more western in concept and content. Duke Philip the Good of Burgundy, who was either the patron or intended reader of several of the works noted in Part One, took the cross in 1453 and made detailed preparations for a crusade, although he never set out.[47]

Nevertheless, other works which definitely had an interest in the Middle East – such Robert de Boron's *Estoire dou Graal* – make no mention of Military Orders. It could be objected that the *Estoire* is set in a period long before the Military Orders were founded, but that did not prevent the author of *Orendal*, for example, including the Templars, and the Hospitallers certainly claimed that their Order dated from at least as early as the second century BC.[48] In addition, many appearances of the Military Orders in literature cannot be explained by a known interest of the author or patron, simply because the author and the patron of the text are unknown. So, while an interest in the crusades may have been a factor which led a writer to include the Military Orders in a work, it was not the only factor, and it cannot account for all their appearances.

5 *Changing views of knighthood as an influence on the Military Orders' appearances in fictional literature*

One reason for excluding Military Orders from a story would be that their form of knighthood did not fit the ideal of knighthood promoted in the story. I have argued above that this was certainly the case in the Vulgate version of the *Queste del Saint Graal*. The great Arthurian prose romances had built up their own reality in successive works, forming a complete pseudo-geography and history, which could stand on its own and did not require any specific, unambiguous reference to actual religious orders to support it. There was

---

[46] *Le Roman de Laurin*, pp. 153–5.
[47] Housley, *Later Crusades*, pp. 101, 106–9.
[48] *The Hospitallers' Riwle*, lines 1–112, and to line 368 on the Hospital during the time of Christ.

no single ideal of knighthood propounded in the Arthurian prose romances; each author had their own ideas, and it is likely that successive developments reflect audience reaction to previous works. None of these multiple ideals necessarily reflected the Military Orders' ideal of chastity, poverty and obedience to a superior with the purpose of self-sacrifice to God for the defence of Christendom.

This is not surprising, for by the early thirteenth century contemporary views of knighthood were different from the assumptions which underpinned the Military Orders. The Military Orders were founded on the basis that worldly knighthood had failed in its purpose in society, and that knights must join a Military Order and become monk-knights if they were to achieve salvation. Yet this is not at all the view of Raoul de Hodenc in his *Roman des Eles*, written in around 1210. He believed that knighthood itself was created to serve God.[49] Therefore, there was no need for knights to join a Military Order. The author of *L'Ordene de Chevalerie*, writing *c.* 1220, wrote that if knights acted as they should nothing could prevent them going straight to Paradise on death. There was no need for a knight to join a Military Order to win salvation, and certainly no need for him to die a martyr. He need only act as a responsible knight, guarding the Church and the defenceless.[50]

The ideal knight of the Vulgate *Queste* is quite different from the Templar, as if the author of the Vulgate *Queste* was setting up a new knightly ideal to supercede that of the Templars. Although later writers did not accept this ideal in full and adapted it considerably, the ideals that they proposed were if anything further from the Military Orders' ideal. Tristan and Lancelot are the best knights in the world largely because they are inspired by their adulterous loves for Queens Iseut and Guinevere. This ideal of knighthood was certainly attractive and retained its popularity for a long period: in Antoine de la Sale's *Jehan de Saintré*, the hero's lady 'Madame' declares that the great and valiant deeds of Lancelot, Gauvain, Tristan, Guiron le Courtois and also of Pontus (as in *Pontus et Sidoine*) were inspired by their service of love.[51] Some heroes, however, could stand apart from even the courtly ideal. King Meliadus was declared a greater knight than his son Tristan, because Tristan only achieved his great deeds of arms through force of love (his love for Iseut), but Meliadus achieved his great deeds through force of arms alone and through his own skill, with no help from love.[52] Guiron le Cortois rejects the love of the lady of Maloanc/Malohaut, reckoning his honour and his comradeship with Danain le

---

[49] Raoul de Hodenc, *Le Roman des Eles*, pp. 38–9, lines 280–83.
[50] *L'Ordene de Chevalerie*, in ibid., lines 473–5.
[51] Antoine de la Sale, *Jehan de Saintré*, p. 9, lines 11–18.
[52] *Meliadus*, fol. 176d; Lathuillère, *Guiron*, p. 234, section 48. 31 manuscripts of *Meliadus-Guiron* survive: Lathuillère, *Guiron*, p. 35, and it was translated into Italian and was well known to the French, Italian and Spanish nobility (ibid., pp. 170–71).

Roux, the lady's husband, to be more important than love.[53] For these authors, love was less important than deeds of arms and honour for the perfect knight.

Other authors felt that even deeds of arms were not enough for the perfect knight without good sense and self control. One of the versions of the first continuation of Chrétien de Troye's *Perceval* depicts Gauvain stating that the wise knight should not fight voluntarily, but only when he is forced to do so.[54] In the prose *Tristan*, first Kahedin and then Dinadan jeer at the customs of the Arthurian knights. It is senseless that knights should attack each other without good reason, and fighting to win honour is not a good reason, for (as Kahedin says) 'If you happen by some chance to throw me dead to the ground at the first blow, what honour will you do me then?' Fighting is not glorious, it is painful: while Tristan rejoices over a successful battle, Dinadan complains that he cannot regard it as successful, as his whole body is in pain from the battering he has received. Fighting simply for honour, rather than in self-defence, is foolishness.[55] There is more, then, to knighthood than simply fighting. Yet this attitude attacked the concept of the Military Orders at its very heart, for the Brothers had to be prepared to die unquestioningly as martyrs on the battlefield, in obedience to their commanders. As Guiot of Provins wrote in the early thirteenth century, mulling over the Order of the Temple: the Brothers were brave and much admired, but 'I would rather be a coward, and alive, than dead and the most admired man in the world'.[56] It must be said, however, that the old adage that death with honour was better than life with shame still had support; Alfonso de Cartagena, bishop of Burgos, repeated this in his *Doctrinal de los cavalleros* in c. 1444.[57] He was a cleric, whose vocation did not involve fighting; Guiot de Provins was a disillusioned and retired knight. Clearly neither of these writers is truly representative of the warriors of their day, and both views of knighthood remained current throughout the Middle Ages.

Yet, being the best knight in the world did not automatically win one salvation, and Lancelot, for instance, has to become a hermit in the final years of his life in order to earn forgiveness of this sins. In the Vulgate *Mort Artu*, Gauvain achieved salvation through his charity to the poor and his help for women.[58] For other knights, however, service of God or conventional pious deeds were not essential for salvation, for romantic love alone was sufficient. Love alone ensured the salvation of Tristan and Iseut in the prose *Tristan*. In *Gyron*, Brehus sans Pitié finds in an underground cavern the bodies of the

---

[53] *Gyron le Courtoys*, fol. 48a–c, 80b–81a; Lathuillère, *Guiron*, p. 254 section 65, pp. 261–2, section 73.
[54] *The Continuations of the Old French Perceval*, 2, lines 1529–31.
[55] *Tristan*, ed. Ménard, 1, p. 194; 2, pp. 121–3, and see also 4, pp. 200–203.
[56] Guiot de Provins, 'La Bible', lines 1722–3.
[57] *Doctrinal de los cavelleros*, pp. 224–5 and note 4.
[58] *La Mort le Roi Artu*, p. 225 para. 176.

knights Phebus and his lady-love laid out in splendour and still incorrupt after generations, as if they were the bodies of saints; but these two died for love of each other, rather than love of God.[59] Religious difference is not important: Phebus was a Christian and the king of Northumberland's daughter was a pagan, but that did not matter, and she was at fault in believing that it did matter.[60] This episode of *Gyron* was so attractive to thirteenth- and fourteenth-century audiences that it was translated into Italian and formed the basis of an Italian poem, *Febus-el-Forte*.[61] In a fourteenth-century addition to *Gyron*, it is possible to be a martyr for love, so that love for the lady was as important for the knight as love of God. Love was certainly sufficient for salvation.[62]

The Military Orders served God from love of God, and the papacy promoted the Templars as the epitome of self-sacrificing Christian love. Wolfram von Eschenbach depicted them bearing the badge of faithful love, the turtle dove. Yet, in actuality, the concept of finding salvation through romantic love alone was foreign to the Military Order's ideal of celibacy. It is therefore not surprising that the Military Orders do not appear in the Arthurian prose romances which espouse this means of knightly salvation.

6 *Did religious belief matter?*

Gyron le Courtoys also suggests that differences in religious belief are not important. If religious belief is not important in defining the ideal knight, then the Military Orders are irrelevant to the conception of knighthood. The Military Orders existed to protect Christians and Christendom from other, hostile religions; once those religions were reconciled, then the Military Orders would no longer be necessary. The ideal of the Military Orders was also based on the assumption that it was possible to win merit in God's eyes and honour and glory in secular society by fighting against knights of a different religion, because of their different religion. If there was no merit or glory to be gained in this because religious difference did not matter, then the Military Orders were superfluous.

Palamedes the pagan. The concept that religious difference was of little or no importance finds its clearest expression in the figure of Palamedes. As there is

---

[59] *Gyron le Courtoys*, fols 234a–235d; Lathuillère, *Guiron*, pp. 307–8, section 110.
[60] *Gyron le Courtoys*, fols 242c–266a; Lathuillère, *Guiron*, pp. 310–14, sections 112–14.
[61] The Italian versions are printed in *Dal Roman de Palamedés al Cantari di Febus-el-Forte*, ed. Alberto Limentani (Bologna, 1962).
[62] *Gyron le Courtoys*, fol. 107c; Lathuillère, *Guiron*, pp. 365–6, section 159 (MS BN f. fr. 355): 'The martyrs who died for Jesus Christ never received death as willingly as I receive it for love ... so I say that after my death I ought to be called a martyr for love.' See also Madame in Antoine de la Sale's *Jehan le Saintré*, declaring that whoever loves a lady and serves her will be saved in soul and body: p. 17, lines 15–24; she expands this on pp. 18–34.

no full scholarly study of this figure who is so prominent in the Post-Vulgate *Roman du Graal* and the prose *Tristan* and apparently so popular with the audiences of Arthurian literature in the Middle Ages, it is necessary to discuss him here. I will argue that because Palamedes, a Muslim, became a hero of prose Arthurian romance, the appearance of the Military Orders in these romances was inappropriate.

Palamedes appears to have made his first appearance in Arthurian romance in the Post-Vulgate quest in the *Roman du Graal*, where he appears as a mysterious knight who is pursuing the *Beste Glatissante*, who will not allow any other knight to pursue it, and who is more doughty than all of Arthur's knights. Not until he has encountered and unhorsed most of the knights of the quest does he finally declare himself to be 'Palamedes the Saracen, the knight of the *Beste Glatissante*'.[63] Galaad praises his prowess to Tristan, but says that he has to regard the man with something like hatred because he is a Muslim. Later he amends this to state that he is amazed by Palamedes' prowess and courtesy, for he came to Tristan's assistance even though he knows that Tristan hates him; but he still wishes that Palamedes would become a Christian.[64] This leads Galaad to tell Palamedes that he is not 'of our company' and may not fight with the Christian knights, which greatly distresses Palamedes.[65] Eventually, Palamedes, afraid at the prospect of fighting Galaad to defend himself against the charge of killing Lionel, Galaad's first cousin once removed, decides to become a Christian. Galaad urges him to be baptised.[66] Once baptised, Palamedes joins the quest for the Holy Grail with Galaad and Perceval, kills the *Beste Glatissante* and is one of those knights privileged to reach Corbenic, who are hailed as knights full of faith and belief who are raised above all other knights. They receive the eucharist in the presence of the Grail, and are then sent back into the world to seek to do good. Galaad, Perceval and Bohort depart with the Grail for Sarraz, and Palamedes, setting off alone, encounters Gauvain and is killed. He dies a martyr's death, with the words 'Lord Father Jesus Christ! Have mercy on my soul' on his lips.[67]

It is possible that Palamedes had appeared in an earlier, short version of the prose *Tristan*, but the slow and careful development of the character in the Post-Vulgate quest indicates that the main facets of the character were the invention of the author of the latter. He appears first as anonymous and threatening, but then we, with Galaad and Bohort, learn detail of his family,

---

[63] *La Version Post-Vulgate*, 2, pp. 111–14, sections 82–6, pp. 127–36, sections 97–102, pp. 160–68, sections 122–8, pp. 186–90, sections 142–4, pp. 221–3, sections 163–5, pp. 263–6, sections 193–5, pp. 486–7, 488–509, sections 365–77; esp. p. 504, section 375.
[64] *La Version Post-Vulgate*, 2, p. 487, section 365, pp. 521–2, section 382.
[65] *Demanda*, 2, p. 151, section 468.
[66] Ibid., pp. 243–55, sections 554–67.
[67] Ibid., pp. 257–83, sections 568–94, pp. 285–92, sections 595–9.

and discover that he is an obdurate Muslim.[68] Later – in a night-time lament in a lonely place, overheard by chance by Galaad and Tristan – we learn of his new-found love for Queen Iseut, at which Tristan is most indignant to learn that he has a rival.[69] Tristan pursues the mysterious knight and fights him, but is prevented by the knight's own courtesy and the intervention of Blioberis from killing him.[70] Later on, Palamedes intervenes in a battle when Tristan is heavily outnumbered and saves his life.[71]

If this was a familiar figure, this mystery would be nonsensical; and in fact, when the author of the second part of the prose *Tristan* copied this section into the 'quest' section of the work it is strikingly out of place.[72] The audience already know Palamedes, know that he is the knight of the *Beste Glatissant* and a Muslim, and that he has loved Iseut for as long as Tristan has loved her. The night-time lament has become a standing joke at Palamedes' expense, and Tristan and Palamedes have many times fought over their rivalry. Palamedes and Tristan have saved each other's lives on various occasions, they are long-standing comrades, and Palamedes' wisdom and courtesy is well-established.[73] It seems, therefore, that the author of the *Roman du Graal* invented the figure of Palamedes, and the author or authors of the prose *Tristan* developed it, following the pointers in the *Roman du Graal*.

---

[68] *La Version Post-Vulgate*, 2, pp. 163–8, sections 123–8.
[69] Ibid., pp. 488–91, sections 366–8.
[70] Ibid., pp. 491–509, sections 368–77.
[71] Ibid., pp. 517–19, sections 380–81.
[72] See, for instance, *Tristan*, ed. Ménard, 8, pp. 214–16 (138–9), 217 (140, lines 18–24: some later mss of the *Tristan* changed this passage to make sense in the context of the longer story: *La Version Post-Vulgate*, 4.1, pp. 314–15, note on section 369(^{2*})), and p. 224 (147), where Tristan resents having a rival for Iseut, which seems very odd after 11 volumes of Tristan and Palamedes' rivalry for Iseut in the prose *Tristan*. The prose *Tristan*'s earliest references to Palamedes all derive from the Post-Vulgate quest in the *Roman du Graal* and do not presuppose any earlier existence of the character: *Tristan*, ed. Curtis, 2, p. 146, 284 lines 18–19 refers to Palamedes in the quest for the Grail; ibid., 1, p. 162, 323 lines 6–7 refers to Palamedes who loved Lady Iseut, as he does in the *Roman du Graal*; ibid., 2, p. 164 lines 17–22 state that Palamedes was a Saracen who had never been a Christian, but all around him thought that he was, which again is consonant with the *Roman du Graal* – as is the information that his father was Esclabor the *Mesconëuz* (the unknown) and that Palamedes had eleven brothers, all good knights.
[73] Palamedes and the *Beste Glatissant: Tristan*, ed. Curtis, 2, p. 216, 636 lines 17–18, and p. 237; *Tristan*, ed. Ménard, 5, p. 80, 11 lines 14–15. Palamedes falls in love with Iseut before Tristan: *Tristan*, ed. Curtis, 1, p. 164, 328 lines 10–17, pp. 164–5, 329. Palamedes and the night-time lament: *Tristan*, ed. Curtis, 3, pp. 198–202; *Tristan*, ed. Ménard, 1, pp. 165–72 (Kahedin laments and Palamedes overhears him), 2, pp. 306–10; 4, pp. 149–53; 6, pp. 95–6, pp. 98–104; 7, pp. 114–25. Palamedes and Tristan in single combat: *Tristan*, ed. Ménard, 2, pp. 141–5, pp. 313–28 (in tournament); 3, pp. 231–42, and 6, pp. 104–10 (arranging single combats which do not take place). Palamedes and Tristan save each others' lives: *Tristan*, ed. Ménard, 3, pp. 231–8; 7, p. 195–204. Palamedes and Tristan as comrades: *Tristan*, ed. Ménard, 3, pp. 242–51; 5, pp. 150–52, 75 lines 21–2, pp. 160–61; 7, pp. 167–88 (adversaries yet allies); 7, pp. 223–79. Palamedes as courteous and wise: *Tristan*, ed. Ménard, 2, pp. 364–5; 3, pp. 238–41; 6, pp. 229–34; 7, pp. 236–7, 122 lines 26–7, 39–45.

Before 1240, Palamedes had also appeared in *Meliadus-Gyron*, which, if modern scholarly dating of these texts is correct, was written before the second part of the prose *Tristan* but after the *Roman du Graal*. The author begins by declaring that the subject of this romance is courtesy:

> And as courtesy is the basis of my book, it is sensible and right that I begin my subject with a courteous knight, and so I will, if I can. With whom shall I begin? Not Lancelot, because Master Walter Map has said enough about him in his book; Lord Tristan? Not in this book, because I have said enough about him in the *Brut*, and I have written a whole book about him already. What name can I give this book? – something that will please King Henry. He wishes that this book of mine which is to be about courtesy should begin with Palamedes, because there was no more courteous knight than Palamedes, nor any such knight so doughty, as history bears witness. So, as it pleases my lord that I should begin this book in the name of the good knight Palamedes, I wish to begin just as it pleases the noble lord King Henry, my lord. So I beg my lord Jesus Christ to give me grace so that this work of mine, which is begun in the name of Palamedes, should be completed to my honour.[74]

He then begins by describing how Palamedes' father and uncle, both Muslims, came to Britain with their families. Although they were Muslims, no one realised this, and they were treated with great honour, just as if they were Christians.[75] In *Gyron li Cortois*, only Palamedes, 'the powerful pagan', is able to defeat Guiron's son Galinan the White, after Galinan has defeated all the knights of Arthur's court.[76]

Despite the introduction to the work, *Meliadus-Gyron* says nothing about Palamedes which is not in the *Roman du Graal* or the early part of the prose *Tristan*. The author of the prose *Tristan*, however, developed the character far beyond the paragon of prowess and courtesy of these other works, who – when he has been baptised – is the equal of the best Christian knights, except Galaad. In the prose *Tristan*, Palamedes the Muslim became a personality, a three-dimensional character, far more sympathetic and convincing than almost any other in Arthurian prose romance. He is doughty, courteous, sensible and determined, but he is also prone to fits of temper and black depression; he is humorous, and has a sense of humour. Whereas Tristan hardly progresses beyond the figure of perfect prowess or the archetypal romance hero, Palamedes is interesting. He is, in fact, the true hero of the story. His position is tragic; he will never win the affection of his idol, Iseut; but he has the sympathy of author and, presumably, audience, for his predicament. Eventually he agrees to be baptised, so suddenly that it seems almost a spur of the moment decision. He joins the quest and arrives at Corbenic, but he and the other

---

[74] *Meliadus*, fol. 1d; Lathuillère, *Guiron*, p. 180 (slightly different).

[75] *Meliadus*, fols. 2b–10b; Lathuillère, *Guiron*, pp. 187–9, sections 2–4, p. 191 section 4.

[76] *Gyron le Courtoys*, fols. 340d–339(sic, should be 342)d. In some other versions of the story he is Calinan the Black; Lathuillère, *Guiron*, pp. 189–90 chapter 4.

knights do nothing there; only Galaad performs the necessary healings, and then departs with Perceval, Bohort and the Grail.[77] The author of the prose *Tristan* was not really interested in Palamedes as a Christian; his conversion was necessary because he had converted in the *Roman du Graal*, and literary convention demanded that he should convert. But he was far more interesting, romantic and credible as a Muslim.

Palamedes the Muslim remained a popular character in Arthurian prose romance.[78] Writers had different views on his religion. Whereas the author of the *Roman du Graal* depicted him as initially refusing to convert to Christianity, and the author of *Meliadus* and of the prose *Tristan* seem not to have been worried about the religious difference, some manuscripts of the *Prophecies de Merlin* reflect a version of the Arthurian romances where Palamedes decided very early in his career that he would become a Christian but that he was not yet ready for baptism.[79] The Middle Dutch poem *Morien* includes a black Moorish hero, but makes him a Christian.[80]

Holy war in Arthurian literature. Given the popularity of Palamedes, it is not surprising that little Arthurian literature after the appearance of Palamedes includes references to holy war or crusading against Muslims in the Holy Land.[81] Next to the figure of Palamedes, who is a better knight than most of the Christians even before he converts to Christianity, holy war seems inappropriate. Earlier in the thirteenth-century *Perlesvaus* had been based on the concept of holy war against the followers of 'the Old Law', but, unlike Chrétien's *Conte du Graal*, Wolfram's *Parzival* and the *Queste del Saint Graal*, this version of the Perceval legend found no adaptors or successors. There are a few references to holy war against Muslims in the Holy Land

---

[77] *Tristan*, ed. Ménard, 9, pp. 248–50 (XIII, 118 lines 1–22), pp. 250–51 (119, lines 1–31), p. 252 (120 lines 1–11), p. 259 (126, lines 1–10).

[78] Apart from the appearances cited here, he also appears in Ernoul d'Amiens' interpolation into the vulgate *Lancelot*, Oxford Bodleian Rawlinson Q. B. 6, fols 168d–185r: here fols 168d–175d, 181b, but as an enemy of the hero, Gauvain. In the latter part of the fourteenth century, one Palamedes Giovanni was admiral of the Hospital of St John on Rhodes and the Order's prior of Venice: Malta, National Library, Archives of Malta 321, fol. 160 (new 169); Jean Delaville le Roulx, *Les Hospitaliers à Rhodes (1310–1421)* (Paris, 1913, reprinted London, 1974), pp. 212–13, 225, 229, 272, 278. Admittedly, it is possible that he was named after the character Palamedes in the *Roman de Troie*: e.g., Benoit de Sainte-Maure, *Le Roman de Troie*, ed. Léopold Constans, 4 vols, SATF (Paris, 1904), lines 6957–78; but the Arthurian character was the more outstanding hero.

[79] *Prophecies de Merlin*, ed. Paton, 1, p. 384 (5g); *Prophesies de Merlin*, ed. Berthelot, p. 195, fol. 87Vb.

[80] *The Romance of Morien, a metrical romance rendered into English prose from the Medieval Dutch*, by Jessie Weston (London, 1901), pp. 44–5, 50, 93. I am grateful to Dr Kari Maund for drawing my attention to this work. The figure of Morien, who is Perceval's nephew, is based on Feirefîz in *Parzival*; see Hendricus Sparnaay, 'The Dutch Romances', in *Arthurian Literature in the Middle Ages*, pp. 443–61, here pp. 450–51.

[81] On Arthurian literature and the Crusades up to the 1220s see Knight, 'From Jerusalem to Camelot'. This does not consider literature written after 1230.

in later Arthurian romances. Two late-thirteenth- or early-fourteenth-century manuscripts of the 'Group I' version of *Les Prophecies de Merlin* describe Arthur financing a crusade for the assistance of Jerusalem. The crusade is also used as a means of forcing political rivals to leave the country.[82] A later redaction of the prose *Tristan* included a sequence where King Mark tries to send Tristan to Jerusalem on crusade, and claims to be about to go on crusade himself.[83] The Latin *De ortu Walwanii*, composed in England in the thirteenth century, has the young Gawain going on a rescue-mission to the land of Jerusalem, in imitation of the crusade of Richard the Lionheart.[84] The alliterative *Morte Arthure* makes various allusions to the crusade and holy war.[85] Thomas Malory ended his *Morte Darthur* by sending Sir Bors, Sir Ector, Sir Blamor and Sir Blioberis to the Holy Land, on Sir Lancelot's instructions, to fight the unbelievers and Turks for God's sake; but although he stated that he had this information out of his French source, this is not in either the Vulgate or the Post Vulgate *Mort Artu*.[86] Yet these are exceptions.

Holy war did continue to appear in Arthurian romance in the conflict between Arthur and the pagan Saxons. This part of the Arthurian story rested on a quasi-historical foundation, as it played an important part in Geoffrey of Monmouth's *Historia regum Britanniae*. Geoffrey placed great emphasis on the fact that the Saxons were pagans, and informs us that at the battle of Mount Badon, where Arthur won a great victory over the Saxons, Arthur had an image of the Blessed Virgin Mary painted on his shield. In addition, he depicts the archbishop of Caerleon describing the war against the Saxons as a holy war, as well as a war *pro patria vestra*: for the homeland. Clearly Geoffrey regarded Arthur as a knight of Christ who fought God's wars against the pagans.[87]

---

[82] *Prophecies de Merlin*, ed. Paton, 1, pp. 407–9, 412–13, pp. 421–2 n. 4; London BL Add. MS 25434, fols 150a–155c, 164c–165b; *Prophesies*, ed. Berthelot, pp. 300–309, 323–5, 370–74; and *Prophecies*, ed. Paton, 1, p. 421; *Prophesies*, ed. Berthelot, p. 353, fol. 177Rb.

[83] Löseth, *Le Roman en prose de Tristan*, pp. 202–3, section 282e–f, Paris, MS BN fr. 99; *Prophecies*, ed. Paton, 1, pp. 417–18; *Prophesies*, ed. Berthelot, fols 170Va–171Rb; this episode also appears in Thomas Malory's *Morte Darthur*, Bk 10, ch. 51: 'The Tale of King Arthur', ed. Vinaver, 2, pp. 677–8.

[84] For the text, see *Historia Meriadoci and De ortu Waluuanii, two Arthurian prose romances of the XIIIth century in Latin Prose*, ed. J. Douglas Bruce, Hesperia, Ergänzungsreihe: Schriften zur englischen Philologie, 2 (Göttingen and Baltimore, 1913), pp. 54–93; *The Rise of Gawain, Nephew of Arthur (De ortu Waluuanii nepotis Arturi)*, ed. and trans. Mildred Leake Day (New York and London, 1984). For the relation of the text with the Third Crusade, see Helen Nicholson, 'Following the path of the Lionheart: the *De ortu Walwanii* and the *Itinerarium peregrinorum et gesta regis Ricardi*', *Medium Ævum*, 69 (2000), 21–33.

[85] See above, and Matthews, *The Tragedy of Arthur*, pp. 63, 184, 128–9, 145–6, 169.

[86] 'The Tale of King Arthur', ed. Vinaver, 3, p. 1260: Bk 21 ch. 13; see also Kennedy, *Knighthood in the Morte Darthur*, pp. 347, 351; see Tyerman, *England and the Crusades*, p. 304.

[87] *The Historia regum Britanniae of Geoffrey of Monmouth, I: Bern Burgerbibliothek, MS 568*, ed. Neil Wright (Cambridge, 1984), pp. 65–6 section 98 (Saxons as pagans), pp. 103–4 section 147 on Arthur and holy war against the Saxons.

Geoffrey's successors Wace and Layamon, who translated and reworked his material, continued to emphasise the Saxons' paganism and the importance of the holy war in Arthur's reign. Wace, while making it clear that the Saxons were pagans, depicted the war against them more as a national war of defence than a religious war. In contrast, Layamon laid stress on the paganism of the Saxons, even depicting Arthur as calling them 'heathen hounds'.[88] The Saxons were also depicted as pagans in the French prose works of the early thirteenth century. In the Vulgate *Merlin* and its sequel, it is stated that the Saxons are not Christian. At one point Gauvain states that he wishes that one of the Saxon leaders would become a Christian because he is such a good knight; but the Saxon refuses with scorn, so Gauvain kills him.[89] However, while the religious difference is significant, it is not as significant as the fact that Arthur is fighting for control of territory; this is war *pro patria vestra* more than it is holy war. It may be indicative of English attitudes towards non-Christians that in the late-fifteenth-century English translation of the Vulgate *Merlin*, just as in Layamon's version of the *Brut*, the paganism of the Saxons is given more emphasis than in the earlier French version.[90]

In the sequel to the *Merlin* known as the *Livre d'Artus* (written before 1250), there is far more emphasis placed on the religious difference between the two sides. This is most emphatically a holy war: in fact, it is a crusade, for the Christian knights fight for love of God and to save their souls and to aid in upholding holy Christianity and to exalt the love of God; and they call on the Holy Sepulchre to aid them in their fight, as the crusaders did.[91]

The *Prophecies de Merlin* also depict Saxons invading England as pagans. The war is not depicted as a holy war so much as a war over territory, although it is stated that God gives the Christians victory. The pagans do not convert to Christianity.[92]

However, the majority of Arthurian prose romances give holy war far less emphasis. In the non-cyclic *Lancelot do Lac*, written before 1226, although the Saxons and Irish invade Scotland and destroy Arthur's land, there is no statement that they are pagans. In contrast, we are told that the Turks came 'from many lands of paganism' to Arthur's court and became Christian

---

[88] Wace, *Le Roman de Brut de Wace*, ed. Ivor Arnold, SATF, 2 vols (Paris, 1938–40), lines 6764–96, 9293–6, 9316–36; Layamon, *Brut, edited from British Museum MS. Cotton Caligula A. IX and British Museum MS. Cotton Otho C. XIII*, by G.L. Brook and R.F. Leslie, 2 vols, EETS 250, 277 (London, 1963, 1978), lines 6935–69, 10553–99, esp. line 10564.

[89] *Merlin*, in *The Vulgate Version*, 2, p. 195 lines 29–39, p. 224 line 24, p. 397 lines 22, 31, p. 394 lines 5–23.

[90] *Merlin: the Early History of King Arthur*, pp. 316 (Saracen), 325–6 (the giants are 'Saracens'), 531 (Saracens), 592 (Christian versus heathen), 596 (Gawain versus the pagan Saxon who refuses to convert to Christianity).

[91] *Le Livre d'Artus*, pp. 3–21, esp. p. 6 lines 19–20; p. 13, line 47; see also *Itinerarium peregrinorum*, ed. Stubbs, Bk 4 ch. 12, p. 253.

[92] *Prophesies de Merlin*, ed. Berthelot, pp. 172, 173, 199, 202, 212, 221, 230–31, 237–8, 245, 249, 250, 252, 253–7, 264–8, 278–81, 294–5, 299–300.

because they were so impressed by Arthur; and that they subsequently performed many great deeds of prowess. The fact that we are not told that the Saxons and Irish are pagans indicates either that they are not or that their paganism is not significant in the context of Arthur's wars against them. Again, in the later Vulgate *Lancelot*, Arthur's excellence is sufficient to draw the pagan Turks to his court and cause them to convert without any need for war. Arthur's enemies are the Saxons and Irish, but there is no mention of any religious difference between them and Arthur's people. This is purely a war over territory.[93]

In the Post-Vulgate *Queste*, preserved in the Portuguese *Demanda*, the Saxons who invade Arthur's kingdom in alliance with King Mark of Cornwall are not portrayed as religious enemies. Galaad prays to God to help the kingdom of Logres, but not because it is threatened by pagans. His prayer is based on the fact that Logres is the kingdom where God is most honoured and in the whole world there are not as many good knights as there are there. This again indicates that this is not a holy war, but a war over territory.[94]

Galaad's prayer appears again in the prose *Tristan*, in exactly the same context. Here, however, the author has already introduced the Saxons at an earlier stage of the story, when they invaded Cornwall. These Saxons are apparently Christians; they give thanks to God for their good fortune, call on God for aid and refer to 'Father Sovereign God' (*Dieus peres souverains*). From pagans we would expect references to Mahom, Tervagant, Apollin, Jupiter and/or Cahu. Possibly the author decided not to portray them as polytheists while still regarding them as pagans; yet the lack of emphasis on the Saxons' faith indicates that they are not religious enemies.[95] Hence, this is not holy war, but a war over territory between equal nations.

In other words, although there was a tradition of holy war within Arthurian tradition, this had become less important by the 1230s. In most works, the pagan Saxons of Geoffrey of Monmouth's *Historia* became an aggressive rival Christian or secular nation. Holy war survived in the sequels to the *Merlin*, but was only significant in the version which seems to have been least widely known, the version now known as the *Livre d'Artus*. Therefore, it is fair to say that overall there is little emphasis on holy war or religious difference in

---

[93] *Lancelot do Lac: the Non-Cyclic Old French Prose Romance*, ed. Elspeth Kennedy, 2 vols (Oxford, 1980), 1, p. 33, lines 26–7, p. 506 line 14, p. 525 lines 16–17, pp. 41–2 for date; *Lancelot*, ed. Micha, 7, p. 60, VIIIa, 9; 8, p. 408, LVI a, 2; p. 431, LXXa, 8; p. 436, LXXa, 24; p. 440, LXXa, 30; p. 449, LXXa, 43; p. 464, LXXIa, 18; p. 469, LXXIa, 24; p. 470, LXXIa, 25; p. 471, LXXIa, 26; p. 472, LXXIa, 27.

[94] *Demanda*, 2, pp. 127–33, pp. 139, 147–9; sections 445–52, 457, 4645–83. For Galaad's prayer, see pp. 149–50, section 467.

[95] *Tristan*, ed. Ménard, 4, pp. 281–339, sections 187–241, esp. p. 293, section 197 lines 15–16; p. 319, section 221 line 21; p. 330, section 233 lines 22–5; 9, pp. 70–75, 81, 114–19, sections 1–5, 9, 88–96: for Galaad's prayer, see 9, p. 91, section 15, lines 12–22.

Arthurian prose romance from the 1230s onwards. Knightly skill in arms and honourable conduct are depicted as being more important than religious belief in determining the best knights in the world.

In general, then, the knightly ideal in the prose Arthurian romance from the 1230s onwards did not place much emphasis on religious difference, was ready to praise knights who were not Christians, and did not exalt warfare against non-Christians for religious reasons. This was a view of knighthood which had little to do with the ideal of the Military Orders. It is true that the Military Orders, just as Ottokar depicted them in his *Reimchronik*, made truces and alliances with the Muslims, and that friendships existed between Muslims and Christians in the Holy Land. However, the Muslims also admired and feared the Military Orders and regarded them as their greatest foes among the Christians; it was for good reason that Saladin had all the Templars and Hospitallers that were captured at the Battle of Hattin on 4 July 1187 executed, and considered that he was performing a pious deed in so doing.[96] Holy war was the fundamental reason for the Military Orders' existence, and if the Muslims were no longer to be fought on religious grounds, then the Military Orders had no reason to exist. In this context it is worth reiterating that although Wolfram von Eschenbach called his Grail guardians *Templeise*, they do not bear a cross but a turtle dove; this was a new sort of Templar, based on love rather than war.

The Military Orders' ideal continued to be admired; but other views of knighthood were at least as influential as theirs. The other views of knighthood were not hostile to the Military Orders; these were simply worlds in which they had no particular relevance. Therefore it is not surprising that the Military Orders did not appear in the great Arthurian prose romances.

Positive images of the Muslims in other medieval literature. The positive view of Muslim warriors in the Arthurian prose romances is not unique to them; it not only mirrors Wolfram von Eschenbach's view of Muslims, itself taken up by writers such as Wirnt von Grafenberg, Johannes von Würzburg and

---

[96] On friendships and alliances between Christians and Muslims, see *An Arab-Syrian Gentleman and Warrior in the Period of the Crusades: Memoirs of Usāmah ibn-Munqidh*, ed. Philip K. Hitti (Princeton, 1929, 1987), pp. 161, 163–4, 169–70; Walter Map, *De nugis curialium*, ed. M.R. James, C.N.L. Brooke and R.A.B. Mynors (Oxford, 1983), pp. 374–6 on Salius, son of a Muslim emir, who converted to Christianity and became a Templar. For the Battle of Hattin, see: 'Imād al-Dīn, *Conquête de la Syrie*, p. 31. For other alliances, see: Peter Jackson, 'The Crusades of 1239–41 and their Aftermath', *Bulletin of the School of Oriental and African Studies*, 50 (1987), 32–60; Riley-Smith, *Knights of St John*, pp. 78 n. 1, 139–44, 162 on the Hospitallers and the Assassins, and other Muslim princes; Bulst-Thiele, *Sacrae domus*, pp. 200, 221, 276; Nicholson, *Templars, Hospitallers*, p. 78. For an extensive survey of Muslim attitudes towards Christians, see Carole Hillenbrand, *The Crusades: Islamic Perspectives* (Edinburgh, 1999), especially pp. 257–327.

Ulrich von dem Türlin,[97] but also the favourable image of Saladin found in the work of the 'Minstrel of Reims' and in the chronicle attributed to Ernoul and its derivations.[98] Descriptions of Muslims in twelfth-century epic literature including remarks such as 'God! What a warrior, if only he were a Christian',[99] indicate that admiration for Muslims by Christians was not new, and it was only natural to exalt the enemy, as this increased the achievement of defeating them and lessened the ignominy of being defeated by them. Yet with increasing contact between the two cultures, especially during the crusades, the admiration of western nobles for their Middle Eastern counterparts increased. In fact, the difference in religion became less important than knightly prowess, and western nobles came to see Muslims as their equals in this respect.[100] Antoine de la Sale represents his knights, who travel around Europe practising deeds of arms against other knights, also wishing to go to the Saracens and only deciding not to do so because the Saracens are too fierce and proud. Nevertheless, Jehan de Saintré travels to Cairo with other knights and squires later in his career, fights renegade Christian knights before the sultan, and defeats them.[101] The Muslims, then appear as fully the equals of Christian knights, and worthy to be part of European knightly culture – if only they were not so proud.

This respect was not a literary invention, but mirrored actuality. For instance, in the late twelfth century, Usāmah ibn Munqidh, an Arab Syrian nobleman, recalled his friendship with a Christian crusading knight: 'He was of my intimate friendship and kept such constant company with me that he began to call me "my brother". Between us were mutual bonds of amity and friendship.'[102]

---

[97] Wirnt von Grafenberg, *Wigalois: the Knight of Fortune's Wheel*, trans. J. W. Thomas (Lincoln and London, 1977), esp. pp. 186–92; Johannes von Würzburg, *Wilhelm von Osterreich*, ed. Ernst Regel, Deutsche Texte des Mittelalters 3 (1903, reprinted Dublin and Zurich, 1970), and see study in Wentzlaff-Eggebert, *Kreuzzugsdichtung*, pp. 290–93; Ulrich von dem Türlin's *Arabel* is discussed by Danielle Buschinger, 'Deux témoins de la réception des *Aliscans* en Allemagne au moyen âge tardif: l'*Arabel* d'Ulrich von dem Türlin et *Die Schlacht von Alischanz*', in *Aspects de l'épopée romane*, pp. 339–44.

[98] For instance, *Ménestrel de Reims*, pp. 104–9, 112, sections 198–208, 213; *Continuation de Guillaume de Tyr*, section 52; *Estoires d'Outremer*, pp. 109–14, 174–5, 217–20, 235.

[99] *La Chanson de Roland*, ed. F.Whitehead (Oxford, 1942), line 3164.

[100] For recent studies and discussion of this, see François Suard, 'Les héroes Chrétiens face au monde Sarracin', Margaret A. Jubb, 'Enemies in Holy War, but brothers in chivalry; the crusaders' view of their Saracen opponents', Sarah Kay, 'Le Problème de l'ennemi dans les chansons de geste', Huguette Legros, 'Entre Chrétiens et Sarrasins, des amités paradoxales: liberté de l'imaginaire ou rêve d'un monde réconcilé', Wolfgang Spiewok, 'L'importance de la croisade pour l'évolution de l'idéologie courtoise et le développement de la littérature médiévale allemandes – du dogme à la tolérance', and others in *Aspects de l'épopée romane*.

[101] *Jehan de Saintré*, p. 182, lines 26–8, p. 308.

[102] *An Arab-Syrian Gentleman and Warrior*, p. 161. Despite this friendship, however, Usāmah regarded the western Europeans in the East as essentially barbarians: see Hillenbrand, *The Crusades*, pp. 276–82, and pp. 259–62.

In literature, however, Christian convention demanded that good, heroic Muslims should convert to Christianity in order to achieve salvation. One writer, the composer of the 'Second State' of the First Crusade Cycle, represented in Paris BN f.fr. 12569, actually allowed the Muslim Dodequin of Damascus to remain a valiant warrior without having to convert to Christianity. Dodequin dies at the hand of Baldwin of Edessa. In the same way, the redoubtable Queen Calabre was depicted dying as a Muslim, by her own hand.[103] However, audiences clearly were not happy with this end for these valiant Muslims, for in the 'Third State' of the cycle, represented by the London-Turin continuation, they were both 'allowed' to convert; Calabre becomes a pious nun, while Dodequin becomes one of the leading Christian heroes.[104] Another leading hero of the First Crusade Cycle is Corbaran, the doughty and honourable Muslim who converts to Christianity in the first continuation of the *Chanson de Jérusalem*; in the London-Turin continuation he is joined by the converted Dodequin, who is baptised Hugh and later lord of Tiberias. Hugh Dodekin is also a leading character in the 'Second Crusade Cycle'. Other converts are Abilan of Damascus, seen above in prison with Brother Harpin of the Temple, Calabre's daughter Queen Florie, who marries Godfrey of Bouillon and, after his death, Tancred, and Margalie, who marries Baldwin I. So, although in general the composers of the Crusade Cycle believed that Muslims had to convert to Christianity in order to fulfill their potential as human beings, once converted these Muslims are the best of all knights and ladies.

The figure of Saladin remained ambiguous. Writers were not sure whether he had converted to Christianity at the end of his life, or even whether it was necessary for him to have done so in order to have been the best knight in the world. The story of the historical Hugh of Tiberias – that is, the historical Christian noble (d. after 1204), not the fictional converted Muslim – explaining knighthood to Saladin seems to have appeared for the first time in the poem *L'Ordene de Chevalerie*, written *c.* 1220, but there was an older story that Saladin was knighted by Humfrey II of Toron, which appears in the original version of the *Itinerarium Peregrinorum*, written during the Third Crusade, around 1191–92.[105] In the *Ordene* it is stated that only Christians can become

---

[103] *OFCC, VII, part 2: The Jérusalem Continuations, part 2*, lines 4592–5, 1719–44; see also François Suard, 'Les héros chrétien face au monde Sarrasin', in *Aspects de l'épopée romane*, p. 204.

[104] *OFCC, VIII: The London-Turin Version*, lines 3220–28, 13272–3.

[105] For the text of *L'Ordene de Chevalerie* see *Le Roman des Eles by Raoul de Hodenc and L'Ordene de Chevalerie*, ed. Keith Busby, pp. 105–19, translated pp. 170–75 (Saladin is not actually knighted; see lines 241–55); see also Maurice Keen, *Chivalry* (New Haven and London, 1984), pp. 6–8; *Estoires d'Outremer*, p. 10; for the prose version included in the *Estoires*, see ibid., pp. 109–14 (here Saladin is knighted); for date, p. 8. On Humfrey II of Toron, see *Itinerarium peregrinorum*, ed. Stubbs, Bk 1 ch. 3, p. 9; *Itinerarium peregrinorum*, ed. Mayer, p. 251, line 4; and Nicholson, *Chronicle of the Third Crusade*, p. 27 and note 8; for date, see

knights, and therefore although Hugh of Tiberias demonstrates knighthood to Saladin he does not actually knight him. However, in the version of this story in the later *Estoires d'Outremer*, Hugh does knight Saladin.

The legend of Saladin as a paragon of chivalry was evidently very popular by the fourteenth century. In his account of the Battle of Poitiers (1356) Froissart describes the lord of Englure, on the French side, as wearing the arms of Saladin and using the warcry: 'Damascus!'[106] In *Saladin*, the last part of the 'Second Crusade Cycle', it is clear that Christian society still believes that only Christians should become knights, and Christians should not love Muslims. However, as in the earlier *Ordene*, these conventions are broken for Saladin, whom the converted Muslim Hugh Dodekin of Tiberias knights, and who is loved by the Aragonese lady who is here the wife of Philip II of France.[107] In this work Saladin is clearly a better knight than the Christians, with or without a deathbed conversion. The Military Orders do appear in *Saladin*, but only in passing. As the story was about the Third Crusade, the author could hardly leave them out altogether, but they were only depicted ransoming captives and, in one manuscript, lodging a fugitive; they did not fight the Muslims.

So, as we would expect, Military Orders were not included in a story where they did not fit the conception of knighthood described. More puzzlingly at first sight, the Military Orders do not appear at all in *Le Bastard de Bouillon*, an early poem in the 'Second Crusade Cycle' written in the mid-fourteenth century, although here holy war is a major theme. The theme of the bastard as courtly hero was familiar from medieval romance: in the Vulgate cycle of Arthurian romance, Lancelot's brother Hector is illegitimate, as is Galaad himself. Yet in *Le Bastard de Bouillon* the illegitimate hero is no longer courtly. This is holy war gone mad: the Bastard does not fight chivalrously like the knights of previous ages, but slays women and children rather than giving them a chance to repent and be baptised as is usual in the First Crusade Cycle.[108] Love becomes a justification for the Bastard's murderous deeds, but again this is a love without reason, a love which instead of bringing the hero honour only brings him shame.[109] Hugh Dodekin of Tiberias, the converted Muslim and courteous comrade of Tancred from the London-Turin continuation of the *Chanson de Jérusalem*, now becomes the accessory to the Bastard's irrationality and lack of chivalry, declaring that women are nothing

---

pp. 9–10. For the legendary Saladin, see Margaret Jubb, *The Legend of Saladin in Western Historiography and Literature* (forthcoming, 2000).

[106] Froissart, *Chroniques: manuscrit d'Amiens*, 3 (1992), p. 111, ch. 559.

[107] *Saladin*, pp. 73–7, especially lines 124, 157; p. 109, lines 52–6.

[108] *Le Bâtard de Bouillon: chanson de geste*, ed. Robert Francis Cook, TLF (Geneva, 1972), lines 5392–4, 5416–18, 5608.

[109] *Bâtard*, lines 5436–9, 5444, 5549, 5838–9, 5854–5, 5915–41. For the element of farce in the poem, see pp. xxx–xxxii.

but trouble, and burning the Bastard's wife Ludie at the stake when her only crime is to have remained faithful to her first true love.[110] Several times we are told that a man should not listen to a woman (contrary to the chivalric knighthood of, say, *Perceforest*, where women are respected); but in each instance the woman is either telling the truth, or being entirely reasonable.[111] This is a world where the traditional values of knighthood (epitomized by Tancred, who is treacherously slain at the end of the poem[112]) have no place; and so it is not surprising that the Military Orders do not appear.

It is interesting that on Tancred's death we are told: 'There was none more noble than him in the Temple of Solomon' (lines 6508–9). In this poem the Temple of Solomon is the royal palace; but the audience would probably have thought of the recently destroyed Order of the Temple of Solomon. There is another hint of this in the writer's remark in the final lines of the poem (lines 6139–42) that he will take the story down to the time of King Philip IV, who destroyed the Flemish. He does not say, but no doubt the audience realised his implication, that Philip as the successor to Louis VII, Philip II and Saint Louis should have been fighting Muslims instead of Christians; and he does not observe that Philip, rather than help fight the war against the Muslims, also destroyed the Templars – but presumably it went unsaid. In the author's own day, rather than being involved in war against the Muslims the French nobility were fighting against the English and had suffered an humiliating defeat at Crécy in 1346. *Le Bastard de Bouillon* may even have been written in the aftermath of the Battle of Poitiers in 1356, where French chivalry failed utterly against an apparently inferior foe. The author had good reason to be bitter about the quality of modern knighthood. It is possible to see *Le Bastard de Bouillon*, with its ridiculously bloodthirsty hero and element of farce, as a satirical attack on the standards of knighthood of the mid-fourteenth century, and a lament for the glorious knighthood of the past, now destroyed.

7 Conclusions

The most significant influence on the appearance of the Military Orders in medieval literature was the need to give a work a context in actuality. The story as a whole need not reflect total actuality, but in order to show that a story was based on truth and not lies or heresy, it needed some grounding in actuality. The inclusion of the Military Orders helped to provide such grounding in *Le Livre du tres chevalereux conte d'Artois et de sa femme, fille du conte de Boulogne*, as well as *Gilles de Chyn, Esclarmonde, Jehan de Saintré*, Jean

---

[110] Ibid., lines 5874–90, 6228–45, and lines 4627–35, 4912–14, 5546–7, 5436–9.
[111] Ibid., lines 2089–95, 4243–9.
[112] Ibid., lines 6403–17, 6452–9, 6497, 6508–9 on Tancred as the epitome of the noble knight, and lines 6515–17 on his death.

d'Arras' *Mélusine* and Joanot Martorell's *Tirant lo Blanc*, among others. In works of fictionalised history such as *Du Bon William Longespee*, Ottokar's *Reimchronik* and *Richard Coeur de Lion* the Military Orders' appearances underpinned the essentially historical foundations of the account.

Writers also included references to Military Orders in their works in order to make a point clear: for instance, to indicate that a work or an episode within a work was about holy war, as in the alliterative *Morte Arthure*. Again, Wolfram von Eschenbach included *Templeise* in his *Parzival* to show that he was writing about Jerusalem, although he changed the design on their shields from a black and white field with a red cross to a turtle dove in order to emphasize that God is love and the Muslims should be converted by love, not violence. Hence the Military Orders appear in some works which include crusading, although not all.

Writers might also include the Military Orders if they or their patron had a particular interest in them or in crusading, as in the case of Jean Renart's works *L'Escoufle* and *Guillaume de Dole*, as well as *Claris et Laris* and *Sone de Nansay*.

Writers excluded the Military Orders, or gave them the briefest of mentions, even when their subject matter might be expected to demand their appearance, when their own view of knighthood was quite different from the ideal of knighthood of the Military Orders. This was particularly the case in *La Queste del Sainte Graal*, but also applied to most of the great Arthurian prose romances. If knights could achieve salvation through romantic love, or if religious belief was irrelevant in determining the ideal knight (as in the case of Palamedes), then the Military Orders were completely out of place.

The Military Orders might be left out of a story which involved crusading or holy war because events were set in a period before the foundation of the Military Orders – as in most of the poems of the Crusade Cycle. This did not worry all writers, however, and in some stories, such as *Orendal*, *Theséus de Cologne* and *Parzival* the Military Orders appear centuries before they were actually founded. Yet this could be justified, as the Military Orders, in particular the Hospital of St John, claimed lengthy histories stretching back into biblical times.[113]

Writers would also have excluded the Military Orders from a work involving crusading or holy war if at the time of writing their presence did not seem appropriate, as it might not have been in French works written just after the dissolution of the Templars. The Order's positive literary roles were completely at variance with the crimes of which the Order had been accused, and whether audiences believed in these crimes or not, as both the pope and King Philip IV of France had accepted them it would be dangerous to question

---

[113] See especially *The Hospitallers' Riwle*, lines 1–368; see also Borchardt, 'Two Forged Thirteenth-Century Alms-Raising Letters'; and Nicholson, *Templars, Hospitallers*, pp. 112–15.

their accuracy. At the same time, the Teutonic Order in Livonia was also under investigation for heresy, while the Hospital of St John was trying to establish itself in a new base on Rhodes in the face of a volley of demands for its root and branch reform, and it was unclear what the Order's future would be. Against such a background, it would have been quite reasonable for writers to leave these dangerously controversial Orders out of their works.

Arguably, writers would also exclude the Military Orders from a work in which they might otherwise have been expected to appear in order to make a point clear. For instance, in *Le Bastard de Bouillon* the reference to the murdered Tancred as the noblest knight in the Temple of Solomon may be intended to recall the audience's minds to the murdered Templars. Written a generation after the dissolution of the Order of the Temple, the writer could safely look back and mourn the passing away of true knighthood, and regret that King Philip IV fought the Flemish instead of the Muslims.

Overall, however, it is clear that many writers did not include the Military Orders in situations where their inclusion would seem appropriate to modern readers simply because their narratives did not require it. If a significant influence on the inclusion of the Military Orders in a work of fictional literature was the need to give that work a context in actuality, then where that context was already provided by some other means a writer would not include them unless some other factor required their inclusion: such as a patron's interest in the Military Orders.

CHAPTER SIX

SERVANTS OF CHRISTIAN KNIGHTS

It was pointed out at the beginning of this study that the authors, patrons and audiences of literary works are generally unknown. The images of the Military Orders in literature are, however, so consistent that this lack of information is not a significant problem. Where we do know the patron or audience of a literary work – such as the count of Hainaut or the duke of Burgundy – they were from the highest nobility. These works were, then, written for the same class which provided most of the patronage for the Military Orders, and on the basis that literature must reflect the views of the intended audience, these works presumably reflect the view which these nobles held of the Military Orders.

With a very few exceptions, such as Harpin de Bourges, the Military Orders only appear in literature to serve and support knights. They may even appear to be lacking initiative when left to themselves – as Tirant lo Blanc takes the initiative in saving the Hospitallers of Rhodes, when they are unable to defeat their enemies by their own efforts. It is therefore reasonable to ask whether this is how the actual Military Orders were seen by their patrons. Unfortunately for the Orders, there is considerable evidence that an important factor in patrons' relations with the Military Orders – as with all religious orders – was the use that could be made of the Orders and their members by the patron.

The service of the Military Orders for kings and popes has been extensively studied by historians.[1] It was not unusual for officials of the Military Orders to

---

[1] See, for instance, B. Bromberg, 'The Financial and Administrative Importance of the Knights Hospitaller to the English Crown', *Economic History*, 4 no. 15 (Feb. 1940), 307–11; Bulst-Thiele, 'Templer in königlichen und päpstlichen Diensten'; L. Delisle, 'Mémoire sur les opérations financières des Templiers', *Mémoires de l'Institut National de France, Académie des Inscriptions et Belles-Lettres*, 33, 2 (1889); A. Luttrell, 'The Aragonese Crown and the Hospitallers of Rhodes, 1314–1332', in his *The Hospitallers in Cyprus, Rhodes, Greece and the West (1291–1440)* (London, 1978); J. Piquet, *Des banquiers au moyen âge: Les Templiers: Étude sur leur opérations financières* (Paris, 1939); A. Sandys, 'The Financial and Administrative Importance of the London Temple in the Thirteenth Century', in *Essays in Medieval History presented to Thomas Frederick Tout*, ed. A.G. Little and F.M. Powicke (Manchester, 1925), pp. 147–62; Jürgen Sarnowsky, 'Kings and Priors. The Hospitaller Priory of England in the Later Fifteenth Century', in his *Mendicants, Military Orders and Regionalism*, pp. 83–102; H. Nicholson, 'The Knights Hospitaller on the frontiers of the British Isles', in ibid., pp. 47–57; Nicholson, 'The Military Orders and the Kings of England'. On lay patrons and religious orders in general see, for instance, C.B. Bouchard, *Sword, Miter and Cloister: Nobility and the Church in Burgundy, 980–1198* (Ithaca and London, 1987); Emma Mason, 'Timeo barones et dona ferentes',

be so occupied by their duties in the service of a monarch that their service to their Order suffered. In 1213 Philip II of France made Brother Garin, his vicechancellor and a Hospitaller, bishop of Senlis. In the service of Philip and his son Louis VIII, Brother Garin was rebuked by the pope for promoting falsehoods rather than following right and was criticised by onlookers for making jokes about the French army's destruction of Flemish towns – remarks felt to be unseemly for a religious man.[2] In 1264, Pope Urban IV wrote to the Order of the Temple on behalf of King Louis IX of France, instructing the Order to appoint Brother Amaury de la Roche to the position of preceptor of the Temple in France, because Louis wanted Amaury to serve him in France. When the Order refused because Amaury was needed in the Holy Land, the pope threatened the Brothers with ecclesiastical censure if they did not comply. Later, Amaury was seconded on the instructions of Pope Clement IV to assist Louis' brother Charles of Anjou in his campaign in Sicily. In the event, Amaury's role on behalf of Charles of Anjou during Louis' Tunisian crusade prevented the crusade from achieving anything.[3] In a similar way, the Hospital of St John was ordered to send Brother Philip d'Eglis to assist Charles of Anjou in his Sicilian campaign. Philip and the Hospitallers were given papal permission to take up arms on Charles' behalf, but this won them the hatred of the Sicilians – who destroyed the Order's property; and also criticism for forgetting their vows – which bound them to fight Muslims, not Christians.[4] Brother Joseph of Chauncy, formerly treasurer of the Hospital of St John, served King Edward I of England for several years, 1273–80, as royal treasurer, until he was recalled to the East by the Master of the Order, who needed his services in the Order.[5] For some Brothers of the Orders, royal service turned out to be fatal to their service for their Order: the Grand Prior

---

in *Religious Motivation: Biographical and Sociological Problems for the Church Historian*, ed. Derek Baker, Studies in Church History, 15 (1978), pp. 61–75.

[2] On Brother Garin, see Petit-Dutaillis, *L'Étude sur la vie et le règne de Louis VIII*, p. 335; for these incidents, see Innocent III, 'Liber registrorum', vol. 3 (*Pat. Lat*. 216), cols. 618–19, register 15, no. 107; The Anonymous of Béthune, in *RHGF*, 24 pp. 764, 766.

[3] Bulst-Thiele, *Sacrae domus*, pp. 245–76; see also *Les Registres d'Urbain IV*, 1 nos. 760, 765, 771; *Cartulaire général de l'ordre des Hospitaliers*, no. 3228; Primat, 'Chronique', trans. Jean du Vignay, *RHGF*, 23, pp. 50–51, 55, 56.

[4] Bulst-Thiele, *Sacrae domus*, p. 247; see also *Cartulaire général de l'ordre des Hospitaliers*, nos 3221; 3279, 3308 (vol. 4); Bartholomeo de Neocastro, 'Historia sicula', ed. G. Paladino, *Rerum Italicarum Scriptores: Raccolta degli storici Italiani dal cinquecento ad millecinquento*, ed. L. Muratori: new edition ed. G. Carducci, V. Fiorini, P. Fedele (Citta di Castello, Bologna, 1900ff.), 13.3, p. 7.

[5] His career is summarised by Riley-Smith, *Knights of St John*, p. 312. He became English royal treasurer on 2 October 1273: *Cartulaire général de l'ordre des Hospitaliers*, no. 3518. He appears as royal treasurer in the Close Rolls at 15 November 1279: *Calendar of the Close Rolls Preserved in the Public Record Office. Prepared under the Superintendence of the Deputy Keeper of the Rolls, Edward I, AD 1272–1279* (London, 1900), p. 583. By 10 June 1280 he was no longer royal treasurer: *Calendar of the Patent Rolls, Edward 1, 1272–1281* (London, 1901), p. 381. He seems to have left his office in 1280, as he is still treasurer on p. 353.

of the Hospital of France was killed at the battle of Crécy, 1346, while Brother Robert Hales, prior of the Hospital in England and royal treasurer, was beheaded on Tower Hill by the rebels during the Peasants' Revolt of 1381.[6]

In addition, the Military Orders performed administrative services for nobles. For instance, at his death in 1219 William Marshal, earl of Striguil and Pembroke, was employing a Templar, Brother Geoffrey, as his almoner.[7] One of the executors of Petrona, countess of Bigorre, following her death in 1251 was the lord commander of the Knighthood of the Temple of Bordères.[8] Alphonse of Poitiers, brother of King Louis IX of France, employed two Templars, Brothers Jean de Kays and Gui de Buci, to organise his crusade in 1269. He called them his friends, his faithful men and his *familiers*.[9] Hubert de Burgh, justiciar of England (d. 1243), deposited his valuables at the New Temple in London, as did Geoffrey of Lusignan, half-brother of King Henry III.[10] The Military Orders in the epics and romances perform the same sort of tasks; they serve and support the hero, but do not take the initiative themselves.

It is clear that the sympathetic but rather exploitative attitude towards the Military Orders in literature reflects the nobility's attitude towards them on a day-to-day basis in actual life. In actual life, the Military Orders could be trusted with difficult financial and organisational matters. In literature, they were given the same sort of roles, and in French romances, especially *Sone de Nansay*, their organisational role was expanded slightly to depict them as supporters of nobles in their love affairs also. The fact that German writers were less exploitative was probably due to the greater influence of Wolfram von Eschenbach on German literature.

This does not mean that knights were completely self-interested and irreligious. Knights were certainly pious, although it was a piety which stood apart from the piety of the Church.[11] This is clear from epic and romantic literature, such as the *Roman du Graal*, *Perceforest*, the *Chanson de Roland* and the Guillaume epics, and also 'factual' works on the nature of knighthood by knights, such as Raoul de Hodenc's *Roman des Eles*, written in the early thirteenth century, Alfonso XI of Castile's *Libro de la Vanda*, written in 1330,

---

[6] Froissart, *Chroniques: manuscrit d'Amiens*, 3, p. 26, 514 line 55; Froissart, *Chroniques. Dernière rédaction*, CCXXVII, lines 105–20, pp. 737–8. For the execution of Robert Hales, the best and most detailed study of the Peasant's Revolt remains André Reville, *Le Soulèvement des Travailleurs d'Angleterre en 1381, études et documents publiés avec un introduction historique par Charles Petit-Dutaillis*, Mémoires et Documents Publiés par la Société de l'école des Chartes, vol. 2 (Paris, 1898), p. xc, with a complete list of primary sources.

[7] *L'histoire de Guillaume le Maréchal*, lines 18317–20.

[8] *Layettes du trésor des chartes*, ed. A. Teulet *et al.*, 5 vols (Paris, 1863–1909), 3 no. 3966.

[9] *Correspondence administrative d'Alfonse de Poitiers*, ed. Auguste Molinier, 2 vols (Paris, 1894–1900), 2 no. 1779, 1796, 1801, 1755, 1808, 1809, 1814, 1815, 1832, 1134.

[10] Hubert: Roger of Wendover, *Flores historiarum*, ed. Henry Hewlett, 3 vols RS 84 (London, 1886–89), 3 pp. 31, 41 (under 1232); Geoffrey of Lusignan: *Close Rolls of the Reign of Henry III, 1261–1264* (London, 1936), p. 118 (under 1262).

[11] See Keen, *Chivalry*, pp. 51–63.

and Geoffroi de Charny's *Livre de Chevalerie*, written in the mid-fourteenth century. Raoul states that knights were first created to protect the Church, and they are the fountain of courtesy, which has its source in God.[12] Alfonso XI of Castile, drawing up the regulations for his secular order of knighthood, the Order of the Band, states that 'The highest and most precious order God has made in the world is knighthood', and stressed that knights' duty was to defend the faith and the other two orders of society, the clergy and the workers.[13] Charny urges the warrior to honour Christ and His Mother, but is emphatic that knighthood is a higher calling than the religious life, because, while knights also serve God, their work is more dangerous than the work of religious and priests. Yet, in return for serving God, the knights expect not only to save their souls but also to win honour and glory: '*Certes, en ceste ordre de chevalerie, peut l'on tres bien les aumes sauver et les corps tres bien honorer*'.[14]

Moreover, knights also expected the Church to serve them in return for their serving God. The author of the *Ordene de Chevalerie* wrote that because knights protect the Church the Church should honour them; in fact, knights deserve to be honoured more than any social group except priests.[15] The author of the *Lancelot*, probably writing within a decade before or after the *Ordene*, depicts Ninian, the damsel of the Lake, teaching the young Lancelot that just as the knight must uphold the Church so the Church must uphold the knight:

> In the same way, the holy Church must uphold him spiritually and purchase for him the life which never ends with orisons and with prayers and almsgiving, so that God will be his saviour to eternity, just as he is the protector and defender of the holy Church on earth.[16]

Therefore, when knights were serving Christendom, it was the duty of all religious people to help them. European writers and their patrons believed that the Military Orders had a duty to serve the nobles who came to the East to fight the Muslims; in serving them, they were fulfilling their vocation of defending Christendom. This was more important than defending Christendom on their own initiative. It must then be asked whether this was also how potential crusaders regarded crusades – whether crusades, too, existed as a means of assisting knights to win honour and glory as well as a means of serving God in penance and self-sacrifice.

---

[12] *Roman des Eles*, lines 282–3, 12–15. For the writer's identity, see pp. 14–15.

[13] Quoted by Alfonso de Cartagena, *Doctrinal de los cavalleros*, p. 293, and see p. 31.

[14] *The Book of Chivalry of Geoffroi de Charny*, pp. 35–48, 148, 156–70, 174–90, 192–8, and *passim*; here, p. 176 lines 32–3.

[15] *Ordene de Chevalerie*, lines 425–80.

[16] *Lancelot do Lac*, 1, p. 144 line 36–p. 145 line 1; *Lancelot*, ed. Micha, 7, p. 253, XXIa, 16. For the date of the non-cyclic version of the story, see Kennedy in *Lancelot do Lac*, pp. 41–2. Micha dated the vulgate cycle to 1215–25 or 1225–30: Alexandre Micha, *Essais sur le cycle du Lancelot-Graal* (Geneva, 1987), p. 12.

Epic literature in particular indicates that winning renown was always an important motivation for going on crusade, but writers such as Froissart and Antoine de la Sale indicate that by the fourteenth and fifteenth centuries the crusade had become a distinctive part of the knight's formation and career.[17] Antoine de la Sale's Jehan de Saintré goes on crusade to Prussia on his lady's command at a distinct stage in his career (just after he has succeeded to his inheritance) to win salvation, but also to increase his honour and establish his reputation as a knight worthy of the title of lord of Saintré. Froissart recounts under 1346 how when the English captured the Norman town of Caen, the constable, the chamberlain of France and other knights and squires were trapped on the city gate, but then saw Sir Thomas of Holland approaching; they recognised him because they had been companions and had seen each other in Granada, Prussia, in the East and in several other places where good knights meet. They therefore surrendered to him.[18] For these knights, the crusade was almost the equivalent of the later 'Grand Tour'.

The nature of knightly piety is also illustrated in the biographies written of leading members of the noble class. The biographer of Marshal Boucicaut tells us that in August 1407 Boucicaut, then governor of Genoa, sent a squire and a Hospitaller to Janus of Lusignan, king of Cyprus, to urge a campaign against the Muslims of Alexandria. Boucicaut's first justification for the attack was that it was 'for pure love of our Lord, wishing to employ ourselves in His service, and for the good and exaltation of Christianity', and the second was 'to acquire merit for our soul'. However, his third justification was that all knights should use their youth and strength in doing good from which they will acquire praise forever, and the fourth was that all knights and gentlemen should unceasingly employ their bodies in the pursuit of arms to acquire honour and renown.[19]

Clearly an essential part of knighthood was piety and service for God; but it was only a part of the crusade experience. Knights expected to receive some return for their service in the honour of God; they expected honour and glory. And, because they believed that their warfare was in the service of God, they expected the Military Orders to assist them in their battles; for, in assisting the crusaders from western Europe to serve God, the Military Orders were also serving God. In practice this could seriously restrict or complicate the Military Orders' military operations, for crusaders were unwilling to take their advice, and expected the Military Orders to fall in with their own plans, irrespective of considerations of strategy.

---

[17] On knights and crusading after 1291, see Housley, *Later Crusades*, pp. 394–403; Keen, *Chivalry*, pp. 170–74; Keen, 'Chaucer's Knight'.

[18] Froissart, *Chroniques: manuscrit d'Amiens*, 2, p. 384, ch. 494.

[19] *Le Livre des fais du bon Messire Jehan le Maingre, dit Bouciquaut, marechal de France et gouverneur de Jennes*, ed. Denis Lalande, TLF 331 (Geneva, 1985), Bk 3 ch. 15, p. 351.

CHAPTER SEVEN

THE PREDOMINANCE OF THE TEMPLARS

Of the three major Military Orders, the Templars predominate in epics and romances written before 1312, not only those written by French authors but also those in German. Even after the abolition of the Order of the Temple in 1312, it still continued to appear, although in less significant roles. There is no evidence that the Order of the Temple appeared more often in epic and romance than other Military Orders because it was more popular. This was clearly not the case in Germany, for example, where the Teutonic Order was the most widely patronised of the three major Military Orders, yet, in German romances, the Temple usually received more attention than the Teutonic Order.

The Order of the Temple had evidently captured the imagination of writers, patrons and audiences to a far greater extent than the other Orders. This may have been partly because the Order of the Temple was the first Military Order, but also because it was the only international Military Order which had not developed from being a hospital. Other Military Orders shared its exotic location in the Holy Land and its religious aura, but because the Order of the Temple had a purely military vocation it was set apart from the colourless respectability of conventional monasticism. Its distinctiveness made it ideal for inclusion in a story which required additional realistic detail drawn from actuality: it was immediately recognisable and its various functions were well known. It was also more adaptable than other religious orders to the requirements of knightly epic and romance: it was involved in fighting, its Brothers travelled around Europe collecting alms and carrying news of the East, and the Order also performed religious roles such as hospitality.

It is clear that the Order of the Temple came to be viewed as the Order most responsible for the defence of the Holy Land. In 1289 the satirist Jacquemart Giélée, writing in Lille, depicted a Templar declaring: 'It is common knowledge that we are defenders of, and fighters for, the Holy Church'. His rival Hospitaller argues that it is the Hospital which is actually responsible for defending Christendom, and it is clear that Giélée believes neither of them,[1] but the Templar's assertion is supported by other evidence. In 1277 the Parisian poet Rutebuef wrote 'La Nouvelle complainte d'Outremer', a lament

---

[1] Jacquemart Giélée, *Renart le Nouvel*, ed. H. Roussel, SATF (Paris, 1961), lines 7549–666: esp. 7549–85.

for the failure of the knights of the West to go on Crusade, addressed to William of Beaujeu, master of the Order of the Temple, as the man chiefly responsible for the defence of the Holy Land.[2] Many contemporary and later accounts of the loss of Acre in 1291 gave the Templars prominence in the final defence of the city, and indeed the Templars' headquarters was the last part of the city to fall. The chronicler of Erfurt depicted the Templars fighting to the last man; Thaddeo of Naples recorded that the Saracens knew that as long as the master of the Temple lived, the city could not be taken, a sentiment echoed by the later accounts of Bar Hebraeus' continuator and Giovanni Villani, both writing towards the mid-fourteenth century. The Dominican Ricoldo of Monte Cruce was not at all sure about William of Beaujeu's credentials as a pious leader of a religious order, but he agreed that the city of Acre would not have fallen had he lived.[3]

How did the Templars achieve this position of being viewed as the leading crusading order, the Military Order *par excellence*? During the existence of the Order of the Temple the Order certainly sent newsletters regularly from the East to the West, to the pope and bishops, kings and princes, keeping them informed of events and the Order's own role in these events, and asking for aid. The Order also went to various lengths to ensure that the image which western patrons received of it and its activities was positive. Yet this was not what gave the Order its special prominence in literature, for the Hospital of St John and the Teutonic Order pursued the same policies.[4] In fact, in the long run the Hospital was arguably the most successful Order at public relations, as it convinced Pope Clement V to give it the properties of the dissolved Order of the Temple in 1312.

Nevertheless, propaganda and public relations could not achieve a great deal in a society where there was no system of mass communication and opinion was more likely to be founded on rumour than factual reports. Whatever they reported to their patrons in the West and no matter how they tried to justify their deeds, the Military Orders were never without their critics, and the Hospitallers' acquisition of the Templars' properties did not win them any

---

[2] *Oeuvres complètes de Rutebuef*, ed. Edmond Faral and Julia Bastin, 2 vols (Paris, 1959–60), 1, p. 508, lines 327–37.

[3] 'Cronica S. Petri Erfordiensis Moderna', ed. O. Holder-Egger, *MGHS*, 30, pp. 424–5; Thaddeo of Naples, *Historia de desolacione et conculcacione civitatis Acconensis et tocius terre sancte in AD MCCXCI*, ed. Paul Riant (Geneva, 1873), p. 19; Bar Hebraeus: *The chronography of Gregory Abû' l-Faraq (1225–1286), the son of Aaron, the Hebrew Physician, commonly known as Bar Hebraeus, being the first part of his history of the world*, trans. E.A.W. Budge, 2 vols (London, 1932, reprinted Amsterdam, 1976), 1, pp. 492–3; Giovanni Villani, *Cronica di Giovanni Villani*, ed. G. Antonelli, 4 vols (Firenze, 1823), 2, pp. 353–4; 'Lettres de Ricoldo de Monte Cruce', ed. R. Röhricht, *Archives de l'Orient Latin*, 2 (1884), 292; see also Nicholson, *Templars, Hospitallers*, pp. 125–8.

[4] See Nicholson, *Templars, Hospitallers*, pp. 102–24. For general discussion of newsletters sent between the crusader states and the West, see Smail, 'Latin Syria and the West, 1149–1187'; Phillips, *Defenders of the Holy Land*; Lloyd, *English Society*, pp. 24–31, 36–41, 248–52, 256–61.

friends. Adam of Murimuth accused them of bribing the pope to give them the Templars' properties, an accusation reiterated late in the fourteenth century by Thomas Walsingham.[5] In around 1320 Geoffrey of Paris remarked on their great possessions and asked when they were going to use them to do something pleasing to God.[6] Jean Dupin, author of *Les Mélancholies*, writing between 1323 and 1340 and who may have been a monk at St-Martin-des-Champs in Paris, was not convinced that the Templars had been guilty as charged, and did not think that the Hospitallers were discharging their vocation. They had lost the Holy Land, they were not hospitable to the poor, few of them were priests, they were not pious and they had too many possessions.[7] Later in the century, the warrior and administrator Eustace Deschamps wrote his *Chartre des Fumeux*, dated 9 December 1368, in which he complained about the foolishness, arrogance and ignorance of the clergy, both secular and regular: 'abbots, priors, simple monks, cantors, deans, princes and canons ... and many Hospitallers, Carmelites, Jacobins, Cordeliers, Austin Friars, and male and female lay associates of these orders', as well as nobles, bourgeois, knights and all sorts of other people.[8] The Hospitallers' suffering during the English Peasants' Revolt of 1381 was partly due to their reputation for acquisitiveness: the attack on the former Templar house at Cressing in Essex was apparently prompted by one of the rebels, Thomas Farndon or Faringdon of London, who claimed that he had been disinherited by the Hospital of St John of Jerusalem in England, a claim his fellow rebels accepted without question.[9] Meanwhile,

---

[5] *Adae Murimuth, Continuatio Chronicarum, and Robertus de Avesbury, de Gestis Mirabilis regis Edwardi*, ed. Edmund Maunde Thompson, RS 93 (London, 1889), p. 17; *Chronica Monasterii S. Albani. Thomas Walsingham, quondam monachi S. Albani, Historia Anglicana*, ed. Henry Thomas Riley, 2 vols, RS 28 (London, 1863–64), 1, p. 127.

[6] Geoffrey of Paris, 'Le dit des Paternostres', in *Nouveau Recueil de contes, dits, fabliaux et autres pièces inédits*, ed. Achille Jubinal, pp. 238–49: here 242. See also his 'Le dit des Mais', p. 189.

[7] *Les Mélancholies de Jean Dupin*, ed. Lauri Lindgren (Turku, 1965), pp. 7–8, and lines 457–522. Sixteen manuscripts survive, mostly fifteenth-century, and two printed editions, one of 1485 and one of around 1500.

[8] *Oeuvres Complètes de Eustache Deschamps*, ed. Gaston Raynaud, vol. 7 (Paris, 1891), pp. 312–20, line 155 for the Hospitallers.

[9] PRO KB 145/3/6/1 (unnumbered membranes); this is printed in Reville, *Soulèvement*, pp. 194–5; Charles Oman, *The Great Revolt of 1381*, new edn with introduction by E.B. Fryde (Oxford, 1969), pp. 211–12; and translated in R.B. Dobson, *The Peasants' Revolt of 1381* (Basingstoke, 1970, 1983), pp. 218–19. Thomas Farndon or Faryngdon was also accused of being the man chiefly responsible for the murder of Robert Hales, Prior of the Hospital in England: PRO KB27/484 rex 3r. For the damage suffered by the English Hospital during the Peasant's Revolt, see, for instance, Thomas Walsingham's *Chronica monasterii S. Albani*, pp. 456–62; Reville, *Soulèvement*, pp. lxxii, lxxvi, lxxxv–lxxxvi, lxxxvi–lxxxix, xc, c, p. 9, pp. 119–200 no. 13, pp. 201–4, nos 18–25, p. 205, nos 30–31, p. 210 nos 37–8, p. 211 nos 42–5; and see also Andrew John Prescott, 'Judicial Records of the Rising of 1381', unpublished PhD thesis, Bedford College, University of London, 1984, pp. 14–15 (the death of the prior of the Hospital, Robert Hales), 32, 37–8 (sacking of the Hositallers' priory of Clerkenwell), 108–9, 112, 115, 116; for the Military Orders' reputation for acquisitiveness, see Nicholson, *Templars, Hospitallers*, pp. 44–5, 50,

the Templars' post-mortem reputation remained diverse. While the Franciscan friar Nicole Bozon was writing in the 1320s of the priest and Templar pensioner who had saved up all his money for the Templars and had nothing left to live on – thus illustrating the Brothers' miserliness – by 1364–75 John of Hildesheim was writing of the pious master and Brothers of the Temple who used their wealth to buy valuable relics such as the diadem of Melchior. The work of John of Hildesheim was very popular, with many manuscripts surviving, and was translated into many languages. [10]

All in all, it could be argued that the two leading Military Orders came out fairly equal in the 'propaganda battle'. Although the Templars were dissolved and the Hospitallers survived, there remained a body of opinion which was convinced that the Templars were innocent, and the Hospitallers did not inherit the Templars' reputation as the crusading Order *par excellence*. Rather than the Hospital replacing the Temple in literature, the Military Orders' role in literature changed. They appeared in a smaller variety of roles, so that instead of being a place of penance and retirement and helping and lodging lovers, for instance, they simply pray, lodge pilgrims, promote holy war and participate in it. On the other hand, more Orders appeared – the Spanish Orders as well as the Hospital, Temple and Teutonic Order – and they appeared in crusades over a wider arena, in Spain and Prussia as well as the East. This development in the Orders' literary roles reflected the actual state of patronal and audience interests; there had been holy war in Spain since the eleventh century and in Prussia since the thirteenth, but it was not until the fifteenth century that writers began to send their heroes to crusade in these areas with the support of Military Orders, just as actual knights, as described by Froissart, were going crusading in Spain and Prussia as well as the East.

This expansion in literary images of the crusade was good for the Military Orders, which would benefit from patrons in the West realising that the war against the infidel was being fought on many fronts. However, unfortunately for the Hospital of St John, writers were unsure of the relationship between the former Order of the Temple and the Hospital of St John, and even after 1312 some writers gave the Order of the Temple primacy over the Hospital. The confusion probably arose from the fact that the Hospital received the Temple's property after the dissolution of the latter in 1312: although the former

---

77, 80–84, 129–30. One of the accusations brought against the Templars in 1307 was that the Brothers did not consider it a sin to acquire property by illegal means: *Procès*, 1, p. 94: '*quod non reputabant peccatum in dicto ordine per fas aut nephas jura acquirere aliena*'.

[10] *Les contes moralisés de Nicole Bozon, Frère Mineur*, ed. Lucy Toulmin Smith and Paul Meyer, SATF (Paris, 1889), pp. 181–2; two manuscripts survive. *The Three Kings of Cologne, an Early English Translation of the Historia Trium Regum by John of Hildesheim*, ed. C. Horstmann, Early English Texts Society 85 (London, 1886), ch. 4, p. 215 and p. 11; on the popularity of this work, see pp. ix–x.

Templars did not become Hospitallers, their houses became Hospitaller houses. So the redactor of the Paris manuscript of *Theséus de Cologne*, writing after 1361, referred to the same men as both 'Hospitallers' and 'Templars', and apparently thought that they were the same; religious men attached to the Temple of Solomon and serving pilgrims at a nearby hospice. The writers who produced the prose versions of the work tried to sort out the confusion, either by removing most of the references to 'Hospitallers' and all references to 'Templars' (as in the short prose version) or by changing most of the references to 'Hospitallers' into 'Templars', so that the Templars were now attached to a Hospital in Jerusalem (as in the long prose version). The confusion reached its logical conclusion in the eighteenth-century summary of *Theséus* by André Guillaume Contant d'Orville, who depicts Queen Osane giving her hospice in Jerusalem to the Templars 'and this was the first property possessed by the Order, which became so famous later' – as though the Hospital of St John was founded by the Templars.[11] At least one earlier writer, however, had believed that the Hospital arose from the Order of the Temple. Joanot Martorell, writing *Tirant lo Blanc* in the 1460s, thought that the Order of St John was founded after the dissolution of the Temple:

> When the Templars were dead and destroyed, another Order was set up, which is called 'of Saint John of Jerusalem'; and as Jerusalem was lost, it has settled the island of Rhodes, and restored the Temple of Solomon.[12]

Did he think that the Templars were dead because the pope had dissolved the Order, or because the Templars had all died at the loss of Acre in 1291 – as some contemporaries had believed?[13] The remark that the Hospital had restored the Temple of Solomon is particularly odd – did he mean that the Hospital had restored all that the Templars had been? or that they had rebuilt the Temple? – which they certainly had not, although they had built a new infirmary, to replace those lost in Jerusalem and Acre. However, this was not a momentary slip of the pen, for Joanot Martorell went on to depict the Master of Rhodes declaring that Tirant had liberated 'Our house of Jerusalem at the Temple of Solomon'.[14]

The great historian of the fourteenth century, Jean Froissart, was also confused about the Military Orders. Writing the first version of his chronicle, preserved in the Amiens manuscript, he described Philip VI of France's plans for a crusade in 1336, adding: 'and the King of France provisioned the island of Rhodes, and sent there the Grand Prior of France, whom the Templars

---

[11] Contant d'Orville, *Mélanges*, p. 213; see also Rosenthal, 'Theséus de Cologne', pp. 1625, 1717, notes 510 and 511.
[12] *Tirant lo Blanc*, chapter 98, 1, pp. 159–60.
[13] 'Cronica S. Petri Erfordiensis', p. 424.
[14] *Tirant lo Blanc*, chapter 107b, 1, p. 191.

obeyed.'[15] Presumably, he was trying to explain who exactly the Grand Prior of France was, but confused the two Orders, writing 'Templars' instead of 'Hospitallers'. In the second version of his chronicle he seemed to have realised his mistake, and removed the reference to the Templars.

Froissart also referred to commanderies of the Hospital which had formerly belonged to the Templars as Templar houses, even though the Templars had been abolished more than half a century before he began to write. In this he was following common custom.[16] In the first version of his chronicle, under 1369, he recorded how the earl of Pembroke, Lord Thomas Percy, Lord Baldwin of Franville, the seneschal of Saintonge, Lord Thomas the Despenser and other knights came under attack from a superior French force and took refuge in *une maison des Templiers* – a house of the Templars – in Purnon in Anjou. He eventually admitted that this was *l'hospital de Puirenon* – the Hospital of Purnon – as clearly it must have been, as the Templars had been abolished more than fifty years before; but obviously Froissart and his informant regarded the house as a Templar house even though the Order no longer existed and its property had passed to the Hospitallers.

Froissart continued to follow this practice in the last version of his chronicle. In the version preserved in the Amiens manuscript, he recorded that in 1346, before the Battle of Crécy, Edward III of England and his men lodged at the Hospital of Oisemont. By the time he came to write the last version of his chronicle, this had become the Temple of Oisemont – although by this time the Hospital had held the house for almost a century.[17]

This confusion in the minds of writers indicates that there was confusion in society as a whole. When the Hospital of St John was alms-collecting in the West, or trying to drum up support for a campaign against the Muslims, this confusion must have discouraged donations and support. To express the problem in modern terms, the Hospital of St John after 1312 lacked a clear-cut public image, and this deficiency would have undermined its attempts to

---

[15] Froissart, *Chroniques: manuscrit d'Amiens*, 1, p. 166, ch. 130 lines 12–14. For this manuscript as the first redaction, see 1, pp. ix–xxiii, esp. p. xix. For the altered text in the second redaction, see *Chroniques de Jean Froissart publiées pour la Société de l'histoire de France*, ed. Siméon Luce, Gaston Raynaud, Léon Mirot and Albert Mirot, 15 vols (Paris, 1869–1975), 1, p. 118.

[16] See Dominic Selwood, *Knights of the Cloister: Templars and Hospitallers in Central-Southern Occitania 1100–1300* (Woodbridge, 1999), p. 5 and note 13: 'John of Ypres, abbot of Saint-Bertin (d. 1383) wrote that the people (*vulgus*) called the Hospitallers "Templars" in those places where there had been a Templar commandery which the Hospital had taken over after the suppression of the Temple'.

[17] Froissart, *Chroniques: manuscrit d'Amiens*, 3, pp. 1, 3, 501 lines 22–3, 502 lines 1–2; Froissart, *Chroniques. Dernière Rédaction*, p. 709, CLXVII, lines 16–21. The papal inquest of 1373 into the Hospital of St John indicates that this had indeed been a Templar house before the dissolution of that Order: *L'Enquête Pontificale de 1373 sur l'ordre des Hospitaliers de Saint-Jean de Jérusalem*, publiée sous la direction de Jean Glénisson, vol. 1: *L'Enquête dans le prieuré de France*, ed. Anne-Marie Legras and Robert Favreau (Paris, 1987), p. 93.

publicize its work to potential supporters and donors in the West. The Order's repeated financial crises and problems in launching effective military efforts during the fourteenth and fifteenth centuries must have been partly due to this confusion in the West over what the Order was and what it actually did.[18] Even after its dissolution, therefore, the Order of the Temple retained in literature and in real life the vestiges of its former predominance.

---

[18] There is no modern single-volume history of the Order of the Hospital of St John in the fourteenth and fifteenth centuries. See Jean Delaville le Roulx, *Les Hospitaliers à Rhodes (1310–1421)*; Anthony Luttrell's articles republished in his *The Hospitallers in Cyprus, Rhodes, Greece and the West, 1291–1440* (London, 1979), *Latin Greece, the Hospitallers and the Crusades, 1291–1440* (Aldershot, 1982), *The Hospitallers of Rhodes and their Mediterranean World* (Aldershot, 1992), *The Hospitaller State on Rhodes and its Western Provinces, 1306–1462* (Aldershot, 1999), and his 'The Military Orders, 1312–1798', in *The Oxford Illustrated History of the Crusades*, pp. 338–42. Housley, *Later Crusades*, pp. 212–29.

CHAPTER EIGHT

SOME CONCLUSIONS

The Military Orders' appearances in medieval literature reflect both convention and actuality, and changed and developed over time. Certain conventions built up around the appearances of the Orders, particularly the Order of the Temple, from the late twelfth century to the early fourteenth century: in particular, that the Order of the Temple (occasionally the Hospital) was a suitable place of penance for a knight who had committed murder, and a suitable place of retirement for a knight; and that the Order of the Temple (very occasionally the Hospital) helped and assisted lovers. These conventions did reflect actuality, but were exaggerated beyond actuality. The Templars, for example, were promoted by the papacy as an outstanding example of sacrificial Christian love; but their common literary role of helping lovers owed more to Wolfram von Eschenbach's *Templeise* and the romantic interests of literary patrons. The Military Orders' conventionalised roles largely vanished from fictional writing after the Order of the Temple was annulled by papal provision in 1312. Their strictly realistic roles and particular vocation, promoting the defence of Christians, fighting in the defence of Christendom against non-Christians and caring for pilgrims to the holy places, remained their major literary roles for the rest of the Middle Ages. The Military Orders appeared in literature throughout the Middle Ages in France, Germany, Aragon and England; the works in which they appeared continued to be popular and were sometimes translated into other languages (although sometimes a later redactor removed the Military Orders from a story); and in fifteenth-century literature the Military Orders were depicted fighting in new crusading arenas, in Spain and Prussia, as well as the Holy Land. These appearances mirrored the continued interest in crusading of the western European nobility throughout the Middle Ages, and the increasing popularity of crusades in Spain and Prussia in the fourteenth and fifteenth centuries. In short, literary convention was important but not all-controlling in shaping literary roles, and became less important in the later Middle Ages with the increasing emphasis on truth and actuality in literature. Hence it may be surmised that literature does reflect actual views of the Military Orders, the views held by the authors, patrons and audiences of this literature. These patrons and audiences were primarily the knightly nobility, the same class who supported the Military Orders with donations and who supported the crusade.

The Military Orders' appearances in literature appear to have been partly governed by the interest of the writer or patron (if any) of the work in actual crusading, but their major function was to give credibility to a work by giving it a context in actuality. While literature from the late twelfth century onwards was not wholly reflective of actuality, because, like modern literature, it was governed by certain conventions, it was certainly based on actuality; and the appearance of the Military Orders in one of their conventional roles could serve to add the appearance of actuality. This was essential to demonstrate the fundamental truth of a work, to prove that it was beneficial to its audience and not heretical. In other words, the 'truth assertion' was not purely a topos; it was essential to the viability of a work of literature in an age in which fantasy had not only become unacceptable for its irrationality, but even spiritually dangerous.

The Military Orders were not needed to perform this function and therefore did not generally appear in works which had their own framework of literary reality, notably the great Arthurian prose romances and the Guillaume d'Orange epic cycle. This framework was presented as being set in actual historical events, and by the mid-thirteenth century was essentially unchangeable; stories told against the backdrop of this 'fictional history' might still be regarded as dubious, but were generally accepted as not being dangerous. The Military Orders were most likely to appear in non-cyclical works which had no such authenticating framework of fictionalised history to support them. Their appearance particularly indicated a connection with holy war. They did not generally appear in works which were antipathetic to holy war, such as the *Queste del Saint Graal*, nor in works where the Muslim hero Palamedes was prominent. The Templars did appear in an altered form in Wolfram von Eschenbach's *Parzival* and works based upon it, as knights bearing the symbol of faithful love rather than the cross. In this case they were included to tie the story into the real world, indicating that the centre of Wolfram's story was Jerusalem, and also to convey a deliberate message, Wolfram's desire to convert Muslims through love rather than by force. Yet, although the Military Orders were put into a story to provide a link with actuality, it is clear that many writers, especially those writing after 1312, did not know a great deal about the Military Orders, and that some writers were vague as to their origins and confused the Order of the Temple and Hospital with each other.

The Military Orders did not appear in literature as a model of chivalry. They supported and encouraged knights, but very seldom did they indicate to a knight how he should behave. They are sometimes found as an example of Christian knighthood for converted Muslims; in this respect they represent Christian knighthood to outsiders. In later works they urge knights to take part in holy war. It is clear that the Military Orders' ideal of knighthood was not the only ideal of knighthood in the period, and that many authors and audiences had completely different priorities for knightly behaviour, although the Military Orders' ideal continued to be attractive. By the thirteenth century knights preferred to believe that lay knighthood was created by God and was pleasing to Him in itself, and that they could serve God better as lay knights than as monks or religious. There was therefore no need to join a military religious order to serve God, and arguably religious orders were of lower spiritual status than knights, for their lifestyle was less dangerous than knights', and they suffered less than knights in God's service. If religious orders were of lower spiritual status than lay knights, then it followed that the Military Orders themselves were also of lower spiritual status than lay knights. This would explain why patrons and audiences did not expect the Military Orders to take the initiative in holy war, but to follow the lead of the knightly crusaders and serve them. They believed that the Military Orders existed to serve knightly interests; as knighthood was created by God and served God, this was also service for God. It is interesting that the Military Orders' appearances were not always directly linked to crusading, and that in many works involving the crusade they did not appear.

In that these literary works were part of the 'invented tradition' of knighthood, what do they tell us about the knights themselves? It is clear from this literature that knights continued to believe throughout the Middle Ages that crusading was an important activity, both pleasing to God and a valuable means of obtaining experience of war and winning honour and glory. These works also reveal the intensity of lay piety: they indicate that knights regarded themselves as servants of God and believed that an important part of the Military Orders' vocation lay in aiding them in their service for God, even to the extent of assisting them in their day-to-day lives, including their love affairs. These views of knights' own function in God's service and the Military Orders' function remained constant from the late twelfth century to the start of the sixteenth century and beyond. It is also obvious that knights wanted their literature to appear realistic – quite apart from the philosophical and religious need for truth, if literature was not realistic it was of no value as invented tradition.

Finally, there is little evidence of criticism of the Military Orders in romance and epic literature, and no indication of the blasphemy and immorality of which the Templars were accused in 1307. A few writers depicted them as excessively cautious, lacking in courage or in spiritual understanding, but only *La délivrance Ogier le Danois* refers to treachery. While chronicles and satires contained criticism, romances and epics generally gave a positive view of the Military Orders and their vocation. The criticism of the Military Orders which was expressed outside western and central Europe – for instance, of the Teutonic Order in eastern Europe – found little echo in the western European literature. This lack of criticism within literature indicates that although the nobility of western Europe found fault with certain actions of the Military Orders, they continued throughout the Middle Ages to believe in their ideal and continued to believe that Military Orders were necessary for Christendom, if only to support them when they chose to set out themselves to seek honour, glory and God's approval in the crusade.

BIBLIOGRAPHY

This is a list of the works referred to in the notes, as well as other works consulted in the preparation of this study. Translations used in the course of preparing this study have their own individual entries. For the convenience of readers I have also noted other relevant translations with the editions of original texts. These translations may differ from my own.

Unpublished sources

British Library, London, Additional Manuscript 25434 (*Les Prophecies de Merlin*)
Bibliothèque nationale, Paris, nouveau acquisition français 10060 (*Theséus de Cologne*)
Bibliothèque nationale, Paris, manuscrit français 1473 (*Le roman de Theséus de Cologne et de Gadifer*)
Malta, National Library, Archives of Malta 321
Oxford Bodleian Rawlinson Q. B. 6, fols. 169r–185r (Ernoul d'Amien's *Lancelot*)

Primary sources

These are listed under first name of author, if known. If no author is named, then they are listed under the first word of the title (excluding 'the', 'a', 'de', 'ex'). Works on Bueve of Hampton, Perceforest and Theséus of Cologne are grouped together for convenience of reference.

Adam of Murimuth, *Adae Murimuth, continuatio chronicarum, and Robertus de Avesbury, de gestis mirabilis regis Edwardi*, ed. Edmund Maund Thompson, RS 93 (London, 1889)
Albrecht von Scharfenberg, *Jüngerer Titurel*, ed. Werner Wolf, Deutsche Texte des Mittelalters, 45 (1955), 55 (1964), 61 (1968), 73 (1984), 77 (1992)
Alfonse de Poitiers, *Correspondence administrative d'Alfonse de Poitiers*, ed. Auguste Molinier, 2 vols (Paris, 1894–1900)
Alfonso de Cartagena, *The Chivalric Vision of Alfonso de Cartagena: Study and Edition of the Doctrinal de los cavalleros*, by Noel Fallows (Newark, Delaware, 1995)
The Alliterative Morte Arthure: A Critical Edition, ed. Valerie Krishna (New York, 1976)
Ambroise, *Estoire de la Guerre Sainte: Histoire en vers de la troisième croisade*, ed. Gaston Paris (Paris, 1897). An English translation is available: M.J. Hubert and J.L. La Monte, *The Crusade of Richard Lion-heart by Ambroise* (reprinted New York, 1976)
Anglo-Norman Political Songs, ed. Isabel S.T. Aspin, Anglo-Norman Texts 11 (Oxford, 1953)
Annals of Dunstable, *Annales monastici*, ed. H.R. Luard, 5 vols, RS 36 (London, 1864–69), 3
The Anonymous of Béthune, in *RHGF* 24
Anonymous Pilgrim V,2 in *Anonymous Pilgrims I–VIII (11th and 12th Centuries)*, trans. Aubrey Stewart, Palestine Pilgrims' Text Society 6 (London, 1894)
Antoine de la Sale, *Le Paradis de la reine Sibylle*, ed. Fernand Desonay (Geneva, 1930)
——, *Jehan de Saintré*, ed. J. Misrabi and C.A. Knudson, TLF (Geneva, 1967)
Aucassin et Nicolette, ed. Jean Dufornet (Paris, 1984)

Bahā' al-Dīn, *The Life of Saladin*, trans. C.W. Wilson and C.R. Conder, Palestine Pilgrims Text Society (London, 1897)

Bar Hebraeus: *The Chronography of Gregory Abū' l-Faraq (1225–1286), the son of Aaron, the Hebrew Physician, commonly known as Bar Hebraeus, being the first part of his History of the World*, trans. E.A.W. Budge, 2 vols (London, 1932, reprinted Amsterdam, 1976)

Bartholomeo de Neocastro, 'Historia sicula', ed. G. Paladino, *Rerum Italicarum Scriptores: Raccolta degli storici Italiani dal cinquecento ad millecinquento*, ed. L. Muratori: new edition ed. G. Carducci, V. Fiorini, P. Fedele (Citta di Castello, Bologna, 1900ff.), 13.3

Le Bâtard de Bouillon: chanson de geste, ed. Robert Francis Cook, TLF (Geneva, 1972)

Beatrix, *see Old French Crusade Cycle*

La Belle Hélène de Constantinople, chanson de geste du XIV siècle, ed. Claude Roussel, TLF 454 (Geneva, 1995)

Benoit de Sainte-Maure, *Le Roman de Troie*, ed. Léopold Constans, 4 vols, SATF (Paris, 1904)

Bernard, abbot of Clairvaux, *Liber ad milites Templi de laude novae militiae*, in *S. Bernardi Opera*, ed. Jean Leclercq, C.H. Talbot and H.M. Rochais, 8 vols (Rome, 1957–77), 3 pp. 213–39. There is an English translation available, *The Works of Bernard of Clairvaux, 7: Treatises III: On Grace and Free Choice*, trans. Daniel O'Donovan; *In Praise of the New Knighthood* trans. Conrad Greenia (Kalamazoo, Michigan, 1997), pp. 115–171

Beroul, *The Romance of Tristan by Beroul, a poem of the twelfth century*, ed. A. Ewert (Oxford, 1977)

The Birth of Popular Heresy, ed. R.I. Moore (London, 1975)

The Book of the Ordre of Chyvalry translated and printed by William Caxton from a French version of Ramon Lull's 'Le Libre del orde de Cavayleria', ed. Alfred T.P. Hyles, EETS 168 (London, 1926)

Bueve de Hanton:

Der Anglonomannische Boeve de Hauntone, ed. Albert Stimming (Halle, 1899)

Der festländische Bueve de Hantone, Fassung I, ed. A. Stimming, GRL 25 (Dresden, 1911)

Der festländische Bueve de Hantone, Fassung II, ed. A. Stimming, 2 vols, GRL 30, 41 (Dresden, 1912–1918)

Der festländische Bueve de Hantone, Fassung III, ed. A. Stimming, 2 vols, GRL 34, 42 (Dresden, 1914–1920)

Caesarius of Heisterbach, *Caesarii Heisterbachensis monachi ordinis Cisterciensis dialogus miraculorum*, ed. J. Strange, 2 vols (Cologne, Bonn and Brussels, 1851)

Calendar of Documents Relating to Ireland Preserved in Her Majesty's Public Record Office, London, ed. W.S. Sweetman, 5 vols (London, 1875–86)

Calendar of the Close Rolls Preserved in the Public Record Office. Prepared under the Superintendence of the Deputy Keeper of the Rolls, Edward I, AD 1272–1307, 5 vols (London, 1900–1908)

Calendar of the Papal Registers relating to Great Britain: Papal Letters, vol. 4, AD 1362–1404, ed. W.H. Bliss and J.A. Twemlow (London, 1902)

Calendar of the Patent Rolls Preserved in the Public Record Office, Henry III, AD 1266–1272 (London, 1913)

Calendar of the Patent Rolls Preserved in the Public Record Office, Edward 1, 1272–1281 (London, 1901)

Cartulaire général de l'ordre des Hospitaliers de S. Jean de Jérusalem, ed. J. Delaville le Roulx, 4 vols (Paris, 1894–1905)

Cartulaire général de l'ordre du Temple, 1119?–1150, ed. le marquis d'Albon (Paris, 1913)

Catalogue of Seals in the Public Record Office. Monastic Seals, vol. 1, complied by Roger H. Ellis (London, 1986)

Les Cent Nouvelles Nouvelles, ed. Franklin P. Sweetser, TLF (Geneva, 1966)

Chandos Herald, *Life of the Black Prince by the herald of Sir John Chandos. Edited from the manuscript in Worcester College with linguistic and historical notes*, by Mildred K. Pope and Eleanor C. Lodge (Oxford, 1910)

La Chanson d'Antioch, ed. Suzanne Duparc Quioc (Paris, 1977)

La Chanson de Floovant: Étude critique et édition, ed. F.H. Bateson (Loughborough, 1938)

La Chanson des quatre fils Aymon, d'après le manuscrit la Vallière, ed. Ferdinand Castet (Montpellier, 1909, reprinted Geneva, 1974)
La Chanson de Roland, ed. F.Whitehead (Oxford, 1942)
Les Chansons de Jaufré Rudel, ed. A. Jeanroy, CFMA 15 (Paris, 1924)
La Chastelaine de Vergi, poème du XIII siècle, ed. G. Raynaud, 2nd edn revue par L. Foulet, CFMA 1 (Paris, 1912)
La Chastelaine de Vergi. Edition critique du ms. B.N. f. fr. 375 avec introduction, notes, glossaire et index, suivie de l'edition diplomatique de tous les manuscrits connus du XIIIe et du XIVe siècle, ed. René Ernst Victor Stuip (The Hague and Paris, 1970)
La Chevalerie Ogier de Danemarche, ed. M. Eusebi (Milan and Varese, 1953)
Le Chevalier au Cygne et Godefroid de Bouillon, ed. Frederic A.F.T. Baron de Reiffenberg and A. Borgnet, 3 vols (Paris, 1846–54)
Chrétien de Troyes, *Les Romans de Chrétien de Troyes édités d'après la copie de Guiot (Bibl. nat., fr. 794), V: Le Conte du Graal (Perceval)*, ed. Félix Lecoy, 2 vols, CFMA 100, 103 (Paris, 1972–75). An English translation of *Perceval* is available: *Perceval: the Story of the Grail*, trans. Nigel Bryant (Cambridge, 1982)
Chronica Albrici monachi Trium Fontium, ed. Paul Scheffer-Boichorst, in *MGHS* 23
Chronicle of the Third Crusade: a translation of the Itinerarium peregrinorum et gesta regis Ricardi, trans. Helen Nicholson (Aldershot, 1997)
Chronique d'Ernoul et de Bernard le trésorier, ed. L. de Mas Latrie, SHF (Paris, 1871)
Chronique latine de Guillaume de Nangis, 1113 à 1300 avec les continuations de cette chronique de 1300 à 1368, nouvelle édition, ed. H. Géraud, 2 vols SATF (Paris, 1843, reprinted New York and London, 1965
Claus Wisse and Philipp Colin, *Parsifal von Claus Wisse und Philipp Colin (1331–1336): eine Ergängzung der Dichtung Wolframs von Eschenbach zum ersten male herausgegeben*, ed. Karl Schorbach, Elsässische Litteraturdenkmäler aus den XIV–XVII Jahrhundert, ed. Ernst Martin and Erich Schmidt, vol. 5 (Stuttgart, 1888: reprinted Berlin and New York, 1974)
Close Rolls of the Reign of Henry III preserved in the Public Record Office, 1227–72, 14 vols (London, 1902–38)
The Conquest of Jerusalem, trans. Peter W. Edbury (Aldershot, 1996)
La Continuation de Guillaume de Tyr (1184–97), ed. M.R. Morgan (Paris, 1982)
The Continuations of the Old French 'Perceval' of Chrétien de Troyes, ed. W. Roach et al., 5 vols in 6 (Philadelphia, 1949–83)
Correspondance administrative d'Alfonse de Poitiers, ed. Auguste Molinier, 2 vols (Paris, 1894–1900)
Cronica Jocelini de Brakelonda de rebus gestis Samsonis abbatis monasteri Sancti Edmundi, ed. and trans. H.E. Butler (Edinburgh, 1949)
'Cronica S. Petri Erfordiensis Moderna', ed. O. Holder-Egger, *MGHS*, 30
Cyranides, in *Textes latins et vieux français relatifs aux Cyranides*, ed. Louis Delate (Liège and Paris, 1942)
Le Débat des hérauts d'armes de France et d'Angleterre, suivi de The Debate between the Heralds of England and France by John Coke, ed. Léopold Pannier and Paul Meyer, SATF (Paris, 1877)
'De constructione castri Saphet', in 'Un nouveau texte du traité "de constructione castri Saphet"', ed. R.B.C. Huygens, *Studi Medievali*, 4 (1965), 355–87
'La Déliverance Ogier le Danois, fragment d'un chanson de geste', ed. Adrien de Longpérier, *Journal des Savants* (April, 1876), 219–33
A Demanda do Santo Graal, ed. Augusto Magne, 3 vols and 1 vol. (Rio de Janeiro, 1944–49, 1955)
The 'Didot' Perceval according to the manuscripts of Modena and Paris, ed. W.H. Roach (Philadelphia, 1941)
'Le Dis dou chevalier à la mance', *see* Jean de Condé
Le Dossier de l'affaire des Templiers, ed. Georges Lizerand (Paris, 1923)
The Elucidation: a Prologue to the Conte del Graal, ed. Albert Wilder Thompson (New York, 1931)
Enfances Renier: canzone di gesta inedita del sec. XIII, ed. Carla Cremonesi (Milan and Varese, 1957)

The English Charlemagne Romances: The Boke of Duke Huon of Burdeux, done into English by Sir John Bauchier, Lord Berners, and printed by Wynkyn de Wade about 1534 A.D., ed. S.L. Lee, Early English Text Society Extra Series, 4 vols bound as two, nos. 40–41, 43–50 (London, 1882–87)

The English Charlemagne Romances: parts X, XI: The Right Plesaunt and Goodly Historie of the Foure Sonnes of Aymon, Englisht from the French by William Caxton, and printed by him about 1489, ed. Octavia Richardson, EETS Extra Series 44/45 (London, 1885)

L'Enquête pontificale de 1373 sur l'ordre des Hospitaliers de Saint-Jean de Jérusalem, publiée sous la direction de Jean Glénisson, vol. 1: *L'Enquête dans le prieuré de France*, ed. Anne-Marie Legras and Robert Favreau (Paris, 1987)

Ernoul, *see Chronique d'Ernoul*

Esclarmonde, Clarisse et Florent, Yde et Olive, drei Fortsetzungen der chanson von Hugh de Bordeaux, ed. M. Schweigel, Ausgaben und Abhandlungen aus dem Gebiete der romanischen Philologie, 83 (Marburg, 1889)

'Estoire de Eracles empereur et la conqueste de la Terre d'Outremer', in *RHC Occ*, 1–2

Lestoire del Saint Graal, in *The Vulgate Version of the Arthurian Romances, edited from Manuscripts in the British Museum*, ed. H. Oskar Sommer, 8 vols (Washington, 1908–16), 1

A Critical Edition of the Estoires d'Outremer et de la Naissance Saladin, ed. Margaret A. Jubb (London, 1990)

Eustace Deschamps, *Oeuvres complètes de Eustache Deschamps*, ed. Gaston Raynaud (Paris, 1891)

'Excerpta e codice ms^{to} Lansdowniano', in *Materials for the History of Thomas Becket*, ed. J.C. Robertson, 7 vols, RS 67 (London, 1875–85)

Felix Fabri, *The Book of the Wanderings of Brother Felix Fabri*, trans. Aubrey Stewart, Palestine Pilgrims' Text Society, 9–10 (London, 1893)

Filippo da Novara, *Guerra di Federico II in Oriente (1223–1242)*, ed. Silvio Melani (Naples, 1994)

La Fille du Comte de Ponthieu: nouvelle du XIIIe siècle, ed. C. Brunel, CFMA 52 (Paris, 1926)

La Fille du Comte du Ponthieu, conte en prose, versions du XIIIe et du XVe siècle, ed. Clovis Brunel, SATF (Paris, 1923, reprinted New York and London, 1968)

Fin d'Elias, see Old French Crusade Cycle

Florent et Octavien. Chanson de geste du XVI siècle, ed. Noëlle Laborderie, Nouvelle Bibliothèque du Moyen Age, 17, 2 vols (Paris, 1991)

Gaufrey, chanson de geste publié pour la première fois d'après le manuscrit unique de Montpellier, ed. F. Guessard and P. Chabaille (Paris, 1859)

Geoffrey Chaucer, *The Canterbury Tales*, General Prologue, lines 49–67, in *The Riverside Chaucer*, 3rd edn, ed. Larry D. Benson (Oxford, 1987)

Geoffrey de Villehardouin, *La Conquête de Constantinople*, ed. Edmond Faral, 2 vols, (Paris, 1973)

Geoffrey of Charney, *The Book of Chivalry of Geoffroi de Charny: Text, Context and Translation*, ed. Richard W. Kaeuper and Elspeth Kennedy (Philadelphia, 1996)

Geoffrey of Paris, 'Le dit des Patenostres', in *Nouveau recueil de contes, dits, fabliaux et autres pièces inédits*, ed. Achille Jubinal, pp. 238–49

Gerbert de Montreuil, *La Continuation de Perceval*, vols 1 and 2 ed. Mary Williams, vol. 3 ed. Marguerite Oswald, CFMA 28, 50, 107 (Paris, 1922–1975)

Les Gestes des Chyprois, recueil de chroniques français écrites en orient en XIII et XIV siècles, ed. Gaston Raynaud, Société de l'Orient Latin (Paris, 1887, reprinted Osnabrück, 1968)

Giovanni Boccaccio, *The Decameron*, trans. G.H. McWilliam, 2nd edn (Harmondsworth, 1995)

Giovanni Villani, *Cronica di Giovanni Villani*, ed. G. Antonelli, 4 vols (Firenze, 1823)

Girart d'Amiens, *Escanor. Roman arthurien en vers de la fin du XIIIe siècle*, ed. Richard Trachsler, TLF (Geneva, 1994)

Gontier de Soignies, *Gontier de Soignies: il canzoniere*, ed. L. Formisano (Milan and Naples, 1980)

Guiot de Provins, 'La Bible', in *Les Oeuvres de Guiot de Provins, poète lyrique et satirique*, ed. J. Orr (Manchester, 1915)

Gyron le Courtoys, with an introductory note by C.E. Pickford (London, 1979)
Hans Sachs, 'Tragedie mit 25 personen zu agiern, die Melusina, und trat 7 actus', in *Hans Sachs*, ed. Adelbert von Keller, vol. 12, BLVS 140 (Tübingen, 1879), pp. 526–64
Heldris de Cornuälle, *Le Roman de Silence: A Thirteenth-century Arthurian verse-romance by Heldris de Cornuälle*, ed. Lewis Thorpe (Cambridge, 1972)
Heldris de Cornualle, *Silence: A Thirteenth-century French Romance*, ed. and trans. Sarah Roche-Mahdi (Michigan, 1992)
Helinand of Froidmont, *Chronicon*, in *Pat. Lat.* 212.
Heinrich von dem Türlin, *Diu Crône*, ed. Gottlob Heinrich Friedrich Scholl, BLVS 27 (Stuttgart, 1852)
'Henri d'Arci: the Shorter Works', ed. R.C.D. Perman, in *Studies in Medieval French Presented to Alfred Ewert in Honour of his Seventieth Birthday* (Oxford, 1984), pp. 279–321
Henry of Livonia, *Chronicon Livoniae*, 2nd edn, ed. Leonid Arbusow and Albert Bauer, MGH Scriptores rerum Germanicarum in usum scholarum separatim editi (Hanover, 1955)
——, *The Chronicle of Henry of Livonia*, translated with an introduction and notes by James A. Brundage (Madison, 1961)
Heresies of the High Middle Ages, trans. Walter L.Wakefield and Austin P. Evans (New York, 1969, 1991)
Hermetica: the Greek Corpus Hermeticum and the Latin Asclepius in a new English translation with notes and introduction, trans. Brian P. Copenhaver (Cambridge, 1992)
Histoire des ducs de Normandie et des rois d'Angleterre, ed. Francisque Michel, SHF no 18 (Paris, 1840, reprinted New York, 1965)
L'Histoire de Gille de Chyn by Gautier de Tournay, ed. Edwin B. Place, Northwestern University Studies in the Humanities no.7 (Evanston and Chicago, 1941)
L'Histoire de Guillaume le Maréchal, comte de Striguil et de Pembroke, ed. Paul Meyer, 3 vols, SHF (Paris, 1891–1901)
Historia de expeditione Friderici imperatoris, in *Quellen zur Geschichte des Kreuzzuges Kaiser Friedrichs I*, ed. A. Chroust, *MGHS rerum Germanicarum*, nova series, 5 (Berlin, 1928)
Historia de la linda Melosina, ed. I.A. Corfis (Madison, 1986)
Historia Meriadoci and De ortu Waluuanii, two Arthurian prose romances of the XIIIth century in Latin Prose, ed. J. Douglas Bruce, Hesperia, Ergänzungsreihe: Schriften zur englischen Philologie, 2 (Göttingen and Baltimore, 1913)
Historia Peredur vab Efrawc: Golygwyd gyda Rhagymadrodd Nodiadau, ed. Glenys Witchard Goetinck (Cardiff, 1976)
The Historia regum Britanniae of Geoffrey of Monmouth, I: Bern Burgerbibliothek, MS 568, ed. Neil Wright (Cambridge, 1984)
'Ex historia regum Franciae continuatione Parisiensi', ed. O. Holder-Egger, *MGHS*, 26
Honoré Bonet, *The Tree of Battles: an English Version with Introduction*, trans. G.W. Copeland (Liverpool, 1942)
Honorius III, *Regesta Honorii papae III*, ed. Petrus Pressutti, 2 vols (Rome, 1888, reprinted Hildesheim, 1978)
The Hospitallers' Riwle: Miracula et regula Hospitalis Sancti Johannis Jerosolymitani, ed. K.V. Sinclair, Anglo-Norman Texts Society 42 (Oxford, 1984)
Hugues Capet: Chanson de geste du XIV siècle, ed. Noëlle Laborderie, CFMA 122 (Paris, 1997)
Hugh, lord of Berzé, *La 'Bible' au seigneur de Berzé*, ed. Félix Lecoy (Paris, 1938)
Hystoire Tresrecreative: see *Theséus de Cologne*
'Imād al-Dīn al-Isfahānī, *Conquête de la Syrie et de la Palestine par Saladin (al-Fath al-qwsī l-fath al qudsī)*, trans. Henri Massé (Paris, 1972)
Innocent III, *Die Register Innocenz' III*, ed. Othmar Hageneder and Anton Haidacher, vol. 1 (Graz and Cologne, 1964)
——, 'Liber registorum sive epistolarum', 3 vols, *Pat. Lat.* 214–16
Innocent IV, *Les Registres d'Innocent IV*, ed. Élie Berger, 4 vols, BEFAR (Paris, 1884–1921)
Itinerarium peregrinorum et gesta regis Ricardi, in *Chronicles and Memorials of the reign of Richard I*, ed. William Stubbs, 2 vols, RS 38 (London, 1864–65)
Das Itinerarium peregrinorum. Eine zeitgenössische englische Chronik zum dritten Kreuzzug in ursprünglicher Gestalt, ed. Hans E. Mayer, MGH Schriften, 18 (Stuttgart, 1962)

Jacquemart Giélée, *Renart le Nouvel*, ed. H. Roussel, SATF (Paris, 1961)
James of Vitry, 'Sermones', in *Analecta novissima spicilegii solesmensis: altera continuatio* 2, *Tusculana*, ed. J.B. Pitra (Paris, 1888)
Jean d'Arras, *Mélusine: Roman du XIVe siècle*, ed. Louis Stouff (Dijon, 1932, reprinted Geneva, 1974)
Jean de Condé, 'Le Dis dou chevalier à la mance', in *Dits et contes de Baudouin de Condé et de son fils Jean de Condé, publiés d'après les manuscrits de Bruxelles, Turin, Rome. Paris et Vienne et accompagnés de variantes et de notes explicatives*, ed. Auguste Scheler, 3 vols: vol. 2, *Jean de Condé, première partie* (Brussels, 1886)
Jean de Meun, *L'Art de chevalerie: Traduction de De Re Militari de Végèce par Jean de Meun, publié avec une étude sur cette traduction et sur Li Abrejance de l'ordre de chevalerie de Jean Priorat*, ed. Ulysse Robert, SATF (Paris, 1897)
Jean Dupin, *Les Mélancholies de Jean Dupin*, ed. Lauri Lindgren (Turku, 1965)
Jean Froissart, *Chroniques, Livre 1: Le manuscrit d'Amiens, Bibliothèque municipal no. 486*, ed. George T. Diller, 5 vols, TLF 407, 415, 424, 429, 499 (Geneva, 1991–98)
——, *Chroniques de Jean Froissart publiées pour la Société de l'histoire de France*, ed. Siméon Luce, Gaston Raynaud, Léon Mirot and Albert Mirot, 15 vols (Paris, 1869–1975)
——, *Chroniques. Dernière rédaction du premier livre. Édition du manuscrit de Rome, Reg. lat. 869*, ed. George T. Diller, T.L.F. 194 (Geneva, 1972)
Jean Priorat, *Li Abrejance de l'ordre de Chevalerie mise en vers de la traduction de Végèce de Jean de Meun par Jean Priorat de Besançon*, ed. Ulysse Robert, SATF (Paris, 1897)
Jean Renart, *L'Escoufle, roman d'aventure*, ed. F. Sweetser, TLF 211 (Geneva, 1974)
——, *Le Roman de la Rose ou Guillaume de Dole*, ed. Félix Lecoy, CFMA 91 (Paris, 1962)
Jehan Maillart, *Le Roman du comte d'Anjou*, ed. Mario Roques, CFMA 67 (Paris, 1931)
Jerusalem Pilgrimage, 1099–1185, ed. John Wilkinson with Joyce Hill and W.F. Ryan, Hakuyt Society, 2nd series, vol. 167 (London, 1988)
Joanot Martorell, Martí Joan de Galba, *Tirant lo Blanc*, ed. Marti de Riquer and Maria Josepa Gallofré, 2 vols, 2nd edn. (Barcelona, 1985). There is an English translation available: *Tirant lo Blanc*, trans. David H. Rosendal (London, 1984)
Johannes von Würzburg, *Wilhelm von Osterreich*, ed. Ernst Regel, Deutsche Texte des Mittelalters 3 (1903, reprinted Dublin and Zurich, 1970)
John Harding, *The Chronicle of Iohn Hardyng ... together with the Continuation by Richard Grafton*, ed. Henry Ellis (London, 1812)
John of Hildesheim, *The Three Kings of Cologne, an Early English Translation of the Historia Trium Regum by John of Hildesheim*, ed. C. Horstmann, EETS 85 (London, 1886)
Knight of La Tour, *The Book of the Knight of La Tour =Landry, compiled for the instruction of his daughters*, ed. Thomas Wright, EETS 33 (London, 1868)
Die Kreuzfahrt des Landgrafen Ludwigs des Frommen von Thüringen, ed. Hans Naumann, *MGH: Deutsche Chroniken (scriptores qui vernacula lingua usi sunt)*, 4, 2 (Berlin, 1923; Munich, 1993)
Lancelot do Lac: the Non-Cyclic Old French Prose Romance, ed. Elspeth Kennedy, 2 vols (Oxford, 1980)
Lancelot, roman en prose du XIII siècle, ed. Alexandre Micha, 9 vols, TLF 247 etc. (Geneva, 1978–83)
Lactantius, *De mortibus persecutorum*, ed. J.L. Creed, Oxford Early Christian Texts (Oxford, 1984)
Layamon, *Brut, edited from British Museum MS. Cotton Caligula A. IX and British Museum MS. Cotton Otho C. XIII*, by G.L. Brook and R.F. Leslie, 2 vols, EETS 250, 277 (London, 1963–78)
Layettes du trésor des chartes, ed. A. Teulet *et al.*, 5 vols (Paris, 1863–1909)
Livländische Reimchronik, ed. F. Pfeiffer, BLVS 7B (Stuttgart, 1844)
Le Livre d'Artus, in *The Vulgate Version of the Arthurian Romances, edited from Manuscripts in the British Museum*, ed. H. Oskar Sommer, 8 vols (Washington, 1908–16), 7
Le Livre de Baudoyn, conte de Flandre, ed. C.P. Serrure and A. Voisin (Brussels, 1836)
Le Livre des fais du bon Messire Jehan le Maingre, dit Bouciquaut, marechal de France et gouverneur de Jennes, ed. Denis Lalande, TLF 331 (Geneva, 1985)

Le Livre des Juges. Les cinq textes de la version française faite au XII siècle pour les chevaliers du Temple, ed. le Marquis d'Albon (Lyon, 1913)
Lohengrin, ed. Thomas Cramer (Munich, 1971)
Marguerite Porete, *The Mirror of Simple Souls*, trans. Ellen Babinsky (New York, 1993); original Old French text, *Le Miroir des simples âmes anéanties*, ed. Romana Guarnieri and Paul Verdeyen, in *CCCM*, 69 (Turnholt, 1986)
Der Marner, ed. P. Strauch (Strasbourg, 1876, reprinted Berlin, 1962)
Martin the Pole, 'Martinus Oppaviensis chronicon', ed. Ludwig Weiland in *MGHS*, 22
Matthew Paris, *Chronica majora*, ed. H.R. Luard, 7 vols, RS 57 (London, 1872–83)
——, *Historia Anglorum sive, ut dicitur, Historia minor, item, eiusdem Abbreviatio chronicorum Angliae*, ed. Frederic Madden, 3 vols, RS 44 (London, 1866–69)
Mechtild of Magdeburg, *The Flowing Light of the Godhead*, trans. Frank Tobin (New York, 1998); German text in *Das fliessende Licht der Gottheit. Nach der Einsiedler Handschrift in kritischem Vergleich mit der gesamten Überlieferung*, ed. Hans Neumann, 2 vols (Munich, 1990)
Meliadus de Leonnoys, 1532, introduction by C. E. Pickford (London, 1980)
Melusine, compiled (1382–1394 AD) by Jean d'Arras, englisht about 1500, edited from a unique manscript in the library of the British Museum, by A.K. Donald, Early English Text Society 68 (London, 1895)
Merlin: roman en prose du XIII siècle, publié avec la mise en prose de poème de Merlin de Robert de Boron d'après le manuscrit appartenant à M. Alfred H. Huth, ed. Gaston Paris and Jacob Ulrich, 2 vols, SATF (Paris, 1886)
Merlin, in *The Vulgate Version of the Arthurian Romances, edited from Manuscripts in the British Museum*, ed. H. Oskar Sommer, 8 vols (Washington, 1908–16), 2
Merlin: the Early History of King Arthur: a prose romance about 1450–1460 AD, edited from the unique manuscript in the University Library Cambridge, ed. Henry B. Wheatley, 2 vols, EETS (London, 1899)
'Minstrel of Reims', *Récits d'un ménestrel de Reims au treizième siècle*, ed. Natalis de Wailly, SHF (Paris, 1876), and in *MGHS*, 26
Der mittelenglische Versroman über Richard Löwenherz: kritische Ausgabe nach allen Handschriften mit Einleitung, Anmerkungen und deutscher Übersetzung, ed. Karl Brunner, Weiner Beiträge zur englischen Philologie, ed. J. Schipper, vol. 42 (Vienna and Leipzig, 1913)
La Mort le Roi Artu, roman du XIII siècle, ed. J. Frappier, TLF 58 (Geneva, 1964)
Nicole Bozon, *Les contes moralisés de Nicole Bozon, Frère Mineur*, ed. Lucy Toulmin Smith and Paul Meyer, SATF (Paris, 1889)
Nigel Wireker, *Speculum stultorum*, ed. Thomas Wright, 2 vols, RS 59 (London, 1872)
Nouveau recueil complet des fabliaux, ed. W. Noomen and N. von den Boorgaard, 9 vols (Assen and Maastricht, 1983–96)
Odo of Deuil, *De profectione Ludovici VII in orientem*, ed. and trans. Virginia G. Berry (New York, 1948)
The Old French Crusade Cycle: La Naissance du Chevalier au Cygne, ed. Emanuel J. Mickel and Jan A. Nelson (Alabama, 1977)
The Old French Crusade Cycle, II: Le Chevalier au Cygne and La Fin d'Elias, ed. Jan A. Nelson (Alabama, 1985)
The Old French Crusade Cycle, V: Les Chétifs, ed. G.M. Myers (Alabama, 1981)
The Old French Crusade Cycle, VI: La Chanson de Jérusalem, ed. Nigel R. Thorp (Alabama, 1991)
The Old French Crusade Cycle, VII: The Jérusalem Continuations, part 1: *La Chrétienté Corbaran*, ed. Peter R. Grillo (Alabama, 1984)
The Old French Crusade Cycle, VII: The Jérusalem Continuations, part 2: *La Prise d'Acre, La Mort Godefroi, and La Chanson des Rois Baudouin*, ed. Peter R. Grillo (Tuscaloosa and London, 1987)
The Old French Crusade Cycle, VIII: The Jérusalem Continuations: the London-Turin Version, ed. Peter R. Grillo (Tuscaloosa, 1994)
Oliver the Templar, 'Estat aurai lonc temps en pessamen', in *Choix des poésies originales des troubadours*, ed. M. Raynouard, 6 vols (Paris, 1816–21), 5, p. 272

L'Ordene de Chevalerie, in Raoul de Hodenc, *Le Roman des Eles* and The Anonymous *Ordene de Chevalerie*, ed. Keith Busby, Utrecht Publications in General and Comparative Literature no. 17 (Amsterdam, 1983)
Orendal, ed. H. Steinger, Altdeutsches Textbibliothek 36 (Halle, 1935)
Orson de Beauvais, chanson de geste du XIIe siècle, ed. G. Paris, SATF (Paris, 1899)
Ortnit und die Wolfdietriche nach Müllenhofs vorarbeiten, ed. A. Amelung and O. Jänicke, 2 vols, Deutsches Heldenbuch 3, 4 (reprinted Dublin and Zurich, 1968)
Otto of St Blasien, 'Continuatio Sanblasiana', ed. R. Wilmans, *MGHS*, 20
Ottokars Österreichische Reimchronik nach den Abschriften Franz Lichtensteins, ed. Joseph Seemüller, 2 vols, *MGH Deutsche Chroniken (scriptores qui vernacula lingua usi sunt)*, 5 parts 1 and 2 (Dublin and Zurich, 1974).
Papsturkunden für Templer und Johanniter, Archivberichte und Texte, ed. Rudolf Hiestand, Abhandlungen der Akademie der Wissenschaften in Göttingen, phil-hist Klasse, dritte Folge, no. 77 (Göttingen, 1972)
Papsturkunden für Templer und Johanniter, neue Folge, ed. Rudolf Hiestand, Abhandlungen der Akademie der Wissenschaften in Göttingen, phil-hist Klasse, dritte Folge, no. 135 (Göttingen, 1984)
Parsifal, *see* Claus Wisse
Patrologus cursus completus, series latina, ed. J.P. Migne, 217 vols and 4 vols of indexes (Paris, 1834–64)
Paul von der Aelst, *Die vier Heymons Kindern*, Bibliotheca Anastatica Germanica (Berne, Frankfurt am Main, New York, 1986; reprint of 1618 edition)
Peter von Dusberg, *Chronik des Preussenlandes*, ed. K. Scholz and D. Wojtecki (Darmstadt, 1984)
Perceforest:
Les Anciennes Cronicques Dangleterre faitz et gestes des roys Perceforest et Gadiffer descosse. Hystoire moult solatiense et delectable. Nouvellement imprimé, 6 vols in 2 (Paris, 1528)
Perceforest: deuxième partie, ed. Gilles Roussineau, vol. 1, TLF 506 (Geneva, 1999)
Perceforest: troisième partie, ed. Gilles Roussineau, 3 vols, TLF 365, 409, 434 (Geneva, 1988–93)
Le Roman de Perceforest, première partie, ed. Jane Taylor, TLF 279 (Geneva, 1979)
Quatrième partie du roman de Perceforest, ed. Gilles Roussineau, TLF 343 (Geneva, 1986)
'Perceval of Galles' *see* 'Sir Perceval of Galles'
'Peredur son of Evrawg' in *The Mabinogion*, trans. Jeffrey Gantz (Harmondsworth, 1976), pp. 217–57
Perlesvaus: Le Haut Livre du Graal, ed. W.A. Nitze and J. Atkinson Jenkins, 2 vols (reprinted New York, 1972). An English translation is available: *The High Book of the Grail: a translation of the thirteenth-century romance of 'Perlesvaus'* trans. Nigel Bryant (Cambridge, 1978)
Peter the Venerable, 'Miracula', Bk 1 ch. 27, in *Pat. Lat.*
——, *The Letters of Peter the Venerable*, ed. Giles Constable, 2 vols (Cambridge, Mass., 1967)
Perceval de Cagny, *Chroniques de Perceval de Cagny, publiés pour la première fois*, ed. H. Moranville, SATF (Paris, 1902)
Philip of Novara: Filiopo da Novara, *Guerra di Federico II in Oriente (1223–1242)*, ed. Silvio Melani (Naples, 1994)
Pontus und Sidonia, ed. K. Schneider (Berlin, 1961)
Primat, 'Chronique', trans. Jean du Vignay, *RHGF* 23
Le Procès des Templiers, ed. Jules Michelet, 2 vols (Paris, 1841–51, reprinted Paris, 1987)
Les Prophecies de Merlin, ed. Lucy Allen Paton, 2 vols, Modern Language Association of America nos 1026, 1077 (London and New York, 1926–27)
Les Prophesies de Merlin (Cod. Bodmer 116), ed. Anne Berthelot, Biblioteca Bodmeriana textes 6 (Cologny-Geneva, 1992)
La Queste del Saint Graal, roman du XIIIe siècle, ed. A. Pauphilet, CFMA 33 (Paris, 1980). An English translation is available, *The Quest of the Holy Grail*, trans. Pauline M. Matarasso (Harmondsworth, 1969)
Ralph of Coggeshall, *Chronicon anglicanum*, ed. J. Stevenson, RS66 (London, 1875)
Ralph of Diss, *Opera historica*, ed. William Stubbs, 2 vols, RS 68 (London, 1876)

Raoul de Hodenc, *Le Roman des Eles*, in *Le Roman des Eles by Raoul de Hodenc and L'Ordene de Chevalerie*, ed. Keith Busby, Utrecht Publications in General and Comparative Literature no. 17 (Amsterdam, 1983)
Raoul de Cambrai, chanson de geste, ed. P. Meyer and A. Longnon, SATF (Paris, 1882)
Récits d'un ménestrel de Reims au treizième siècle, ed. Natalis de Wailly, SHF (Paris, 1876)
Recueil des Historiens des Croisades: Historiens Occidentaux, pub. L'Académie des Inscriptions et des Belles-Lettres, 5 vols (Paris, 1841–95)
Records of the Templars in England in the Twelfth Century: the Inquest of 1185 with illustrative charters and documents, ed. Beatrice A. Lees (London, 1935)
La Règle du Temple, ed. Henri de Curzon, SHF (Paris, 1886). An English translation is available: *The Rule of the Templars*, trans. J.M. Upton-Ward (Woodbridge, 1992)
'Regni Iherosolymitani brevis historia', in *Annali Genovesi di Caffaro e de'suoi continuatori dal MXCIX al MCCXCIII*, ed. L.T. Belgrano and C.I. di Sant'Angelo, new edn, 5 vols, Fonti per la Storia Italia nos 11–14bis (Rome, 1890–1929)
'Regni Iherosolymitani brevis historia', ed. G.H. Pertz, *MGHS*, 18
Reinfrid von Braunschweig, ed. K. Bartsch, BLVS 109 (Tübingen, 1871)
Reinolt von Montelban oder die Heimonskinder, ed. Fridrich Pfaff, BLVS 174 (Tübingen, 1885: reprinted Amsterdam, 1969)
Renaus de Montauban, oder die Haimonskinder, Altfranzösisches Gedicht, ed. H. Michelant, BLVS 67 (Stuttgart, 1862)
Renaut de Montauban, édition critique du manuscrit Douce, ed. J. Thomas, TLF 371 (Geneva, 1989)
<Renaut de Montauban>: edition critique du ms de Paris, B.N., fr. 764 (R), ed. Philippe Verelst (Ghent, 1988)
Ricaut Bonomel, 'Ir'e dolors s'es dins mon cor asseza', in Antoine de Bastard, 'La colère et la douleur d'un templier en Terre Sainte: *<Ir'e dolors s'es dins mon cor asseza>*', *Revue des Langues Romanes*, 81 (1974), 333–73
Ricoldo de Monte Cruce, 'Lettres de Ricoldo de Monte Cruce', ed. R. Röhricht, *Archives de l'Orient Latin*, 2 (1884), 258–96
The Rise of Gawain, Nephew of Arthur (De ortu Waluuanii nepotis Arturi), ed. and trans. Mildred Leake Day (New York and London, 1984)
Robert de Boron, *Le Roman de l'Estoire dou Graal*, ed. William A. Nitze, CFMA 57 (Paris, 1983)
Robert de Clari, *La Conquête de Constantinople*, ed. Philippe Lauer, CLMA 40 (Paris, 1924)
Roger of Howden, *Chronica*, ed. William Stubbs, 4 vols, RS 51 (London, 1868–71)
———, *Gesta regis Henrici Secundi: The chronicle of the reigns of Henry II and Richard I*, ed. William Stubbs, 2 vols, RS 49 (London, 1867)
Roger of Wendover, in *Roger de Wendover liber qui dicitur flores historiarum: The Flowers of History by Roger of Wendover*, ed. Henry G. Hewlett, 3 vols, RS 84 (London, 1886–89)
Li Romans de Bauduin de Sebourc, IIIe roy de Jhérusalem; poëme du XIVe siècle, publié pour la première fois d'après les manuscrits de la Bibliothèque Royale [ed. anon: in fact ed. Louis Napoléon Boca], 2 vols (Valenciennes, 1841)
Le Roman de Cassiodorus, ed. Joseph Palermo, 2 vols, SATF (Paris, 1963–64)
Le Roman du Comte d'Artois (XVe siècle), ed. Jean-Charles Seigneuret, TLF 142 (Geneva, 1966)
Li Romans de Claris et Laris, ed. J. Alton, BLVS 169 (Tübingen, 1884; reprinted Amsterdam, 1966)
Le Roman de Laurin, fils de Marques le sénéchal, ed. Lewis Thorpe (Cambridge, 1958)
Dal Roman de Palamedés al Cantari di Febus-el-Forte, ed. Alberto Limentani (Bologna, 1962)
Le Roman de Pontus et Sidoine, ed. M.-C. de Crécy, TLF 475 (Geneva, 1998)
Le Roman de Silence, see Heldris de Cornuälle
Le Roman de Tristan en prose, ed. Renée L. Curtis, 3 vols (Cambridge, 1985)
Le Roman de Tristan en prose, ed. Philippe Ménard *et al.*, 9 vols, TLF 353 etc. (Geneva, 1987–97)
The Romance of Morien, a metrical romance rendered into English prose from the Medieval Dutch, by Jessie Weston (London, 1901)
'Rothelin', in *RHC Occ*, 2. There is an English translation available: *Crusader Syria in the Thirteenth Century: the Rothelin Continuation of the History of William of Tyre with part of the Eracles or Acre Text*, trans. Janet Shirley (Aldershot, 1999)

Rutebuef, *Oeuvres complètes de Rutebuef*, ed. Edmond Faral and Julia Bastin, 2 vols (Paris, 1959–60)
Le Saint Voyage de Jherusalem du seigneur d'Anglure, ed. François Bounardot and Auguste Longnon, SATF (Paris, 1878)
Saladin, suite et fin du deuxième cycle de la Croisade, ed. Larry S. Crist, TLF (Geneva, 1972)
'Sir Perceval of Galles' in *Middle English Metrical Romances*, ed. Walter Hoyt French and Charles Brockway Hale, 2 vols in 1 (New York, 1964), pp. 531–603
Sone von Nausay, ed. M. Goldschmidt, BLVS 216 (Tübingen, 1899)
La Suite du roman de Merlin, ed. Gilles Roussineau, 2 vols, TLF 472 (Geneva, 1996)
Tabulae ordinis theutonici ex tabularii regii Berolinensis codice potissimum, ed. Ernest Strehlke (Berlin, 1869: reprinted Toronto and Jerusalem, 1975)
Textes latins et vieux français relatifs aux Cyranides, ed. Louis Delatte (Liège and Paris, 1942)
Thaddeo of Naples, *Historia de desolacione et conculcacione civitatis Acconensis et tocius terre sancte in AD MCCXCI*, ed. Paul Riant (Geneva, 1873)
Theséus de Cologne:
Theseus de Cologne: Fragment of a Lost Edition, and Unknown Version of the Romance. Printed Apparently by or for Jehan Trepperel, Paris, 1504, ed. F.W. Bourdillon (typescript in British Library and the National Library of Wales)
Hystoire Tresrecreative: traictant des faictz et gestes du Noble et Vaillant chevalier Theseus de Coulongne par sa prouesse Empereur de Rome. Et aussi de son filz Gadifer Empereur de Grece. Pareillement des trois enfans dudit Gadifer cest ascavoir Regnault, Regnier et Regnesson: lesquels firent plusieurs beaulx faictz darmes comme pourrez veoir ci apres (Paris, 1534)
Hystoire Tresrecreative: traictant des faictz et gestes du Noble et Vaillant chevalier Theseus de Coulongne par sa prouesse Empereur de Rome. Et aussi de son filz Gadifer Empereur de Grece. Pareillement des trois enfans dudit Gadifer cest ascavoir Regnault, Regnier et Regnesson: lesquels firent plusieurs beaulx faictz darmes comme pourrez veoir ci apres (Paris, 1550)
'Theséus de Cologne', in André Guillaume Contant d'Orville, *Mélanges tirés d'une grande Bibliothèque. De lecture des livres français, huitième partie: livres de Philosophie, Sciences et Arts du Seizième Siècle*, vol. 14 (Paris, 1781).
Thomas Aquinas, *Summa theologiae*, Blackfriars edn. (London, 1963)
Thomas Malory, 'The Tale of King Arthur' in *The Works of Sir Thomas Malory*, ed. Eugène Vinaver, 3 vols, 2nd edn (Oxford, 1967)
——, *Le Morte d'Arthur*, ed. Janet Cowen, 2 vols (Harmondsworth, 1969)
Thomas Walsingham, *Chronica monasterii S. Albani. Thomas Walsingham, quondam monachi S. Albani, Historia anglicana*, ed. Henry Thomas Riley, 2 vols, RS 28 (London, 1863–64)
'Tractatus de locis et statu sancte terre ierosolimitanae', ed. Benjamin Z. Kedar, in *The Crusades and Their Sources*, ed. J. France and W.G. Zajac, pp. 111–33
Ulrich von Etzenbach, *Wilhelm von Wenden*, ed. H.-F. Rosenfeld, Deutsche Texte des Mittelalters 49 (Berlin, 1957)
Ulrich Füetrer, *Das Buch der Abenteuer*, ed. Heinz Thoelen, with Bernd Bastert, 2 vols (Göppingen, 1997)
Der Untergang des Templerordens mit urkundlichen und kritischen Beiträgen, ed. Konrad Schottmüller, 2 vols (Berlin, 1887, reprinted Vaduz, Lichtenstein, 1991)
Urban IV, *Les Registres d'Urbain IV*, ed. Jean Guiraud *et al.*, 5 vols, BEFAR (Paris, 1899–1958)
Usāmah ibn Munqidh, *An Arab-Syrian Gentleman and Warrior in the Period of the Crusades: Memoirs of Usâmah ibn-Munqidh*, ed. Philip K. Hitti (Princeton, 1929, 1987)
Valentin et Orson (Jacques Maillet, Lyons, 1489)
Valentine and Orson, translated from the French by Henry Watson, ed. Arthur Dickson, EETS 204 (London, 1937)
La Version Post-Vulgate de la Queste del Saint Graal *et de la* Mort Artu: *troisième partie du Roman du Graal*, ed. Fanni Bogdanow, 3 vols to date, numbered 1, 2 and 4 part 1, SATF (Paris, 1991)
The Vulgate Version of the Arthurian Romances, edited from Manuscripts in the British Museum, ed. H. Oskar Sommer, 8 vols (Washington, 1908–16)

Wace, *Le Roman de Brut de Wace*, ed. Ivor Arnold, SATF, 2 vols (Paris, 1938–40)
'Du bon William Longespee', in A. Jubinal, ed., *Nouveau recueil de contes, dits, fabliaux, et autres pièces inédits des XIIIe, XIVe et XV siècles, pour faire suite aux collections Legrand d'Aussy, Barbazan et Méon, mis au jor pour la première fois*, 2 vols (Paris, 1839–42), 2, pp.339–353
'Du bon William Longespee', ed. Simon Lloyd, 'William Longespee II: The Making of an English Crusading Hero', *Nottingham Medieval Studies*, 34 (1991), 41–70; 35 (1992), 79–125
William, archbishop of Tyre, *Willelmi Tyrensis archiepiscopi chronicon; Guillaume de Tyre, Chronique*, ed. R.B.C. Huygens, CCCM LXIII–LXIIIa (Turnholt, 1986)
——, *Guillaume de Tyre et ses continuateurs*, ed. Paulin Paris, 2 vols (Paris, 1879–80)
——, trans. E.A. Babcock and A.C. Krey, *A History of the Deeds Done Beyond the Sea, by William of Tyre*, 2 vols (Columbia, 1944)
Wirnt von Grafenberg, *Wigalois: the Knight of Fortune's Wheel*, trans. J.W. Thomas (Lincoln and London, 1977)
Wolfram von Eschenbach, *Parzival*, ed. K. Lachmann and W. Spiewok, 2 vols (Stuttgart, 1981)
——, *Parzival*, in *Wolfram's von Eschenbach Parzival und Titurel*, ed. Karl Bartsch, Deutsche Classiker des Mittelalters, 9 (Leipzig, 1875)
——, *Willehalm, Titurel*, ed. Walter Johannes Schröder and Gisela Hollandt (Darmstadt, 1971)
——, *Parzival*, trans. A.T. Hatto (Harmondsworth, 1980)
——, *Willehalm*, trans. Marion E. Gibbs and Sidney M. Johnson (Harmondsworth, 1984)
'Ein zeitgenössisches Gedicht auf die Belagerung Accons', ed. Hans Prutz, *Forschungen zur deutschen Geschichte*, 21 (1889), 449–94

Secondary works

Adolf, Helen, 'An Historical Background for Chrétien's Perceval', *Publications of the Modern Language Association of America*, 58 (1943), 597–620
——, *Visio Pacis: Holy City and Grail: an attempt at an Inner History of the Grail Legend* (Philadelphia, 1960)
Appleby, John T., *England Without Richard, 1189–1199* (London, 1965)
Arnold, Udo, 'Eight Hundred Years of the Teutonic Order', in *The Military Orders: Fighting for the Faith*, ed. M. Barber, pp. 223–35
Barber, Malcolm, 'The Origins of the Order of the Temple', *Studia Monastica*, 12 (1970), 219–40; reprinted in his *Crusaders and Heretics*
——, 'Propaganda in the Middle Ages: the Charges Against the Templars', *Nottingham Medieval Studies*, 17 (1973), 42–57
——, *The Trial of the Templars* (Cambridge, 1978)
——, 'The Templars and the Turin Shroud', *Catholic Historical Review*, 68 (1982), 206–25; reprinted in his *Crusaders and Heretics*
——, 'The Social Context of the Templars', *Transactions of the Royal Historical Society*, 34 (1984), 27–46; reprinted in his *Crusaders and Heretics*
——, *The Two Cities: Medieval Europe 1050–1320* (London, 1992)
——, *The New Knighthood: a History of the Order of the Temple* (Cambridge, 1994)
——, *Crusaders and Heretics, 12th–14th Centuries* (Aldershot, 1995)
——, ed., *The Military Orders: Fighting for the Faith and Caring for the Sick* (Aldershot, 1994)
——, 'The Trial of the Templars Revisited', in *The Military Orders*, vol. 2, ed. H. Nicholson, pp. 329–42
Barber, Richard and Barker, Juliet, *Tournaments: Jousts, Chivalry and Pageants in the Middle Ages* (Woodbridge, 1989)
Barker, Juliet, *The Tournament in England, 1100–1400* (Woodbridge, 1986)
Barlow, Frank, *Thomas Becket* (London, 1986)
Baumgartner, Emmanuel, 'Les techniques narratives dans le roman en prose', in *The Legacy of Chrétien de Troyes*, ed. N.J. Lacy, D. Kelly and K. Busby, 2 vols (Amsterdam, 1987)
——, *Le 'Tristan en Prose', essai d'interpretation d'un roman médiéval* (Geneva, 1975)

Beer, Jeanette M.A., *Narrative Conventions of Truth in the Middle Ages* (Geneva, 1981)
——, 'Women, Authority and the Book in the Middle Ages', in *Women, the Book and the Worldly*, ed. L. Smith and J.H.M. Taylor, pp. 61–9.
Bender, Karl-Heinz, 'Retour à l'histoire: les dernières épopées du premier cycle de la croisade', *Les Épopées de la croisade. Premier colloque international (Trèves, 6–11 août, 1984)*, ed. Karl-Heinz Bender and Hermann Kleber, *Zeitscrift für französische Sprache und Literatur, Beiheft*, neue Folge Helf 11 (Stuttgart, 1987), pp. 98–104
Bennett, Philip E., 'Female Readers in Froissart: Implied, Fictive and Other', in *Women, the Book and the Worldly*, ed. L. Smith and J.H.M. Taylor, pp. 13–23
Berard, R.N., 'Grapes of the Cask: a Triptych of Medieval English Monastic Historiography', *Studia Monastica*, 24 (1982), 75–103
Berg, Evert van den, 'La littérature chevaleresque dans la Flandre du 14e siècle: épopée ou roman?' in *Aspects de l'épopée romane*, ed. H. van Dijk and W. Noomen, pp. 331–8
Biller, Peter and Hudson, Anne, eds, *Heresy and Literacy, 1000–1530* (Cambridge, 1994)
Biller, Peter, 'The Cathars of Languedoc and written materials', in his *Heresy and Literacy*, pp. 61–82
Birkhan, Helmut, 'Les croisades contre des païens de Lituanie et de Prusse. Idéologie et réalité', in *La Croisade: réalités et fictions*, ed. D. Buschinger, pp. 31–50
Blaess, M., 'L'abbaye de Bordesley et les livres de Guy de Beauchamp', *Romania*, 78 (1957), 511–18
Boase, T.S.R., ed., *The Cilician Kingdom of Armenia* (Edinburgh and London, 1978)
——, 'The History of the Kingdom', in his *The Cilician Kingdom of Armenia*, pp. 1–33
Bogdanow, Fanni, *The Romance of the Grail – a Study of the Structure and Genesis of a Thirteenth-Century Arthurian Prose Romance* (Manchester, 1966)
——, 'Robert de Boron's vision of Arthurian History', in *Arthurian Literature XIV*, ed. James P. Carley and Felicity Riddy (Cambridge, 1996), pp. 19–52
Boor, H. de, ed., *Geschichte der Deutschen Literatur 1: Der Deutsche Literatur von Karl dem Grossen bis zum beginn der Höfischen Dichtung, 770–1170* (Munich, 1949)
Borchardt, Karl, 'Two Forged Alms-Raising Letters used by the Hospitallers in Franconia', in *The Military Orders: Fighting for the Faith*, ed. M. Barber, pp. 52–6
Bossuat, Robert, 'La Chanson de Hugues Capet', *Romania*, 71 (1950), 450–81
——, 'Théseus de Cologne', *Le Moyen Age*, 65 (1959), 97–133, 293–320, 539–77
Bouchard, C.B., *Sword, Miter and Cloister: Nobility and the Church in Burgundy, 980–1198* (Ithaca and London, 1987)
Boulton, D'Arcy Jonathan Dacre, *The Knights of the Crown: The Monarchial Orders of Knighthood in Europe, 1325–1520* (Woodbridge, 1987)
Bromberg, B., 'The Financial and Administrative Importance of the Knights Hospitaller to the English Crown', *Economic History*, 4 no. 15 (Feb. 1940), 307–11
Bruce, James Douglas, *The Evolution of Arthurian Romance From the Beginnings Down to the Year 1300*, 2 vols (Baltimore, 1923; 2nd edn 1928; repr. 1959)
Brundage, James, 'The Lawyers of the Military Orders', in *The Military Orders: Fighting for the Faith*, ed. M. Barber, pp. 346–57
Bulst-Thiele, Marie Luise, 'Zur Geschichte der Ritterorden und des Konigreichs Jerusalem in 13. Jahrhundert bis zur Schlacht bei La Forbie am 17. Okt 1244', *Deutsches Archiv für Erforschung des Mittelalters*, 22 (1966), 197–226
——, *Sacrae domus militiae templi Hierosolymitani magistri: Untersuchungen zur Geschichte des Templerordens 1118/9–1314* (Göttingen, 1974)
——, 'Der Prozess gegen den Templerorden', in *Die geistlichen Ritterorden Europas*, ed. Josef Fleckenstein and Manfred Hellmann, Vorträge und Forschungen 26 (Sigmaringen, 1980), pp. 375–402
——, 'Templer in königlichen und päpstlichen Diensten', in *Festscrift Percy Ernst Schramm*, ed. Peter Classen and Peter Scheibert, 2 vols (Wiesbaden, 1964), 1, pp. 289–308
Bull, Marcus, 'The Confraternity of La Sauve-Majeure: a Foreshadowing of the Military Order?' in *The Military Orders: Fighting for the Faith*, ed. M. Barber, pp. 313–19
Bumke, Joachim, *Wolfram von Eschenbach: Forschung seit 1945: Bericht und Bibliographie* (Munich, 1970)

Burleigh, Michael, *Prussian Society and the German Order. An Aristocratic Corporation in Crisis, c. 1410–1466* (Cambridge, 1984)
Buschinger, Danielle, ed., *La Croisade: réalités et fictions* (Göppingen, 1989)
——, 'La signification de la croisade dans la littérature allemande du moyen âge tardif', in her *La Croisade*, pp. 51–60
——, 'Deux témoins de la réception des *Aliscans* en Allemagne au moyen âge tardif: l'*Arabel* d'Ulrich von dem Türlin et *Die Schlacht von Alischanz*', in *Aspects de l'épopée romane*, ed. H. van Dijk and W. Noomen, pp. 339–44
Butler, Christopher, *Number Symbolism* (London, 1970)
Bynum, Caroline Walker, *Fragmentation and Redemption: Essays on Gender and the Human Body in Medieval Religion* (New York, 1992)
Christiansen, Eric, *The Northern Crusades: the Baltic and the Catholic Frontier, 1100–1525* (Basingstoke, 1980: 2nd edn Harmondsworth, 1997)
Cigaar, Krijnie, 'Robert de Boron en Outremer? Le Culte de Joseph d'Arimathie dans le monde Byzantin et en Outremer', *Polyphonia Byzantina: Studies in Honour of Willem J. Aerts*, ed. Hero Hokwerda, Edmé R. Smits and Marinus M. Woesthuis (Groningen, 1993), pp. 145–59
——, 'Le Royaume des Lusignans: terre de littérature et de traditions échanges littéraires et culturels', *Actes du Colloque: Les Lusignans et L'Outre-Mer* (Poitiers, 1995), pp. 89–98
——, 'Flemish Counts and Emperors: Friends and foreigners in Byzantium', in *The Latin Empire: Some Contributions*, ed. V.D. Van Aalst and K.N. Cigaar (Hernen, 1990), pp. 33–62
Claasens, Geert H.M., 'Some notes on the Proto-Saladin', in *Aspects de l'épopée romane*, ed. H. van Dijk and W. Noomen, 131–40
Clanchy, Michael, *From Memory to Written Record: England, 1066–1307*, (London, 1979)
Cohn, Norman, *Europe's Inner Demons: the Demonization of Christians in Medieval Christendom* (London, 1975, 1993)
——, *The Pursuit of the Millenium: Revolutionary millenarians and mystical anarchists of the Middle Ages* (London, 1957; revised edn., 1993)
Cole, Penny J., *The Preaching of the Crusades to the Holy Land, 1095–1270* (Cambridge, Mass., 1991)
Cook, Robert F. and Crist, Larry S., *Le Deuxième cycle de la croisade* (Geneva, 1972)
Cook, Robert Francis, 'Crusade Propaganda in the Epic Cycles of the Crusade', in *Journeys Towards God*, ed. B.N. Sargent-Baur, pp. 157–75
Coss, Peter, *The Knight in Medieval England, 1000–1400* (Stroud, 1993)
——, *The Lady in Medieval England, 1000–1500* (Stroud, 1998),
Coureas, Nicholas and Riley-Smith, Jonathan, eds, *Cyprus and the Crusades* (Nicosia, 1995)
Cowdrey, H.E.J., 'Cluny and the First Cruasade', *Révue Benedictine*, 83 (1973), 285–311; reprinted in his *Popes, Monks and Crusaders* (London, 1984), XV
Crist, Larry S., 'On Structuring *Baudouin de Sebourc*', in *Romance Epic: Essays on a Medieval Literary Genre*, ed. Hans-Erich Keller (Kalamazoo, Michigan, 1987), pp. 49–55
Curtis, Renée, 'The Problems of the Authorship of the Prose *Tristan*', *Romania*, 79 (1958), 314–35
Curtius, Ernst Robert, *European Literature and the Latin Middle Ages*, trans. Willard R. Trask, Bollingen Series 36 (Princeton, 1953)
Davis, J.G., 'Pilgrimage and Crusade Literature', in *Journeys Towards God*, ed. B. N. Sargent-Baur, pp. 1–30
Davis, R.H.C., 'William of Tyre', in *Relations between East and West in the Middle Ages*, ed. Derek Baker (Edinburgh, 1987), pp. 64–76
Delaville le Roulx, Jean, *Les Hospitaliers à Rhodes (1310–1421)* (Paris, 1913, reprinted London, 1974)
Delisle, L., 'Mémoire sur les opérations financières des Templiers', *Mémoires de l'Institut National de France, Académie des Inscriptions et Belles–Lettres*, 33, 2 (1889)
Demurger, Alain, *Vie et mort de l'ordre du Temple*, 3rd edn (Paris, 1993)
——, *A Brief History of Religious Military Orders: Hospitallers, Templars, Teutonic ...* , trans. Beryl Degans (Paris, 1997): originally published in French as *Brève Histoire des ordres religieux-militaires* (Paris, 1997)
Dickson, Arthur, *Valentine and Orson: a Study in Late Medieval Romance* (New York, 1929)

Dijk, Hans van and Noomen, Willem, eds, *Aspects de l'épopée romane: mentalités, idéologiés, intertexualités* (Groningen, 1995)
Diverres, Armel, 'The Grail and the Third Crusade: Thoughts on *Le Conte del Graal* by Chrétien de Troyes', *Arthurian Literature X*, ed. Richard Barber (Cambridge, 1990), pp.13–109
Dobson, R.B., *The Peasants' Revolt of 1381* (Basingstoke, 1970, 1983)
Dronke, Peter, ed., *A History of Twelfth-Century Western Philosophy* (Cambridge, 1988)
Duby, George, 'The transformation of the aristocracy: France at the beginning of the thirteenth century', in his *The Chivalrous Society*, trans. Cynthia Postan (London, 1977), pp. 178–85
Duparc-Quioc, Suzanne, *Le Cycle de la croisade* (Paris, 1955)
——, *La Chanson d'Antioche: étude critique* (Paris, 1978)
Edbury, Peter W. and Rowe, John, *William of Tyre: Historian of the Latin East* (Cambridge, 1988)
Edbury, Peter W., *The Kingdom of Cyprus and the Crusades, 1191–1374* (Cambridge, 1991)
——, 'Propaganda and Faction in the Kingdom of Jerusalem: the Background to Hattin', in *Crusaders and Muslims in Twelfth-Century Syria*, ed. M. Shatzmiller (Leiden, 1993), pp. 172–89
——, 'The Templars in Cyprus', in *The Military Orders: Fighting for the Faith*, ed. M. Barber, pp. 189–95
——, *John of Ibelin and the Kingdom of Jerusalem* (Woodbridge, 1997)
——, 'The Lyon *Eracles* and the Old French Continuations of William of Tyre', in *Montjoie: Studies in Crusade History in Honour of Hans Eberhard Mayer*, ed. Benjamin Z. Kedar, Jonathan Riley-Smith and Rudolf Hiestand (Aldershot, 1997), pp. 139–53
Emplaincourt, Edmond A., 'Le Parfait du Paon', *Romania*, 102 (1981), 396–405
Eubel, C., *Hierarchia Catholica Medii Aevi*, 2nd edn (Münster, 1908)
Ferrante, J., 'The Influence of Women Patrons', in *Literary Aspects of Courtly Culture*, ed. D. Maddox and S. Sturm Maddox (Cambridge, 1994)
Fincham, H.W., *The Order of the Hospital of St John of Jerusalem and its Grand Priory of England* (London, 1933)
Finlayson, John, *Morte Arthure* (London, 1967)
Fischer, Mary, 'Criticism of Church and Crusade in Ottokar's Osterreichische Reimchronik,' *Forum for Modern Language Studies*, 22 (1986), 157–71
Fletcher, Robert Huntingdon, *Arthurian Material in the Chronicles, especially those of Great Britain and France*, Studies and Notes in Philology and Literature (Boston, 1906)
Flori, Jean, 'La notion de chevalerie dans les chansons de geste du XII siècle. Étude historique de vocabulaire', *Le Moyen Age*, 81 (1975), 211–44, 407–45
——, 'Pour une histoire de la chevalerie: l'adoubement dans les romans de Chrétien de Troyes', *Romania*, 100 (1979), 21–53
——, *Idéologie du Glaive: Préhistoire de la Chevalerie* (Geneva, 1983)
——, *L'Essor de la Chevalerie, XIe–XIIe siècles* (Geneva, 1986)
——, 'Du nouveau sur les origines de la première croisade', *Le Moyen Age*, 101 (1995), 103–11
Flutre, L.-F., *Table des noms propres avec toutes leurs variantes figurant dans des romans du moyen âge* (Poitiers, 1962)
——, 'Études sur le Roman de Perceforêt (huitième et dernier article)', *Romania*, 91 (1970), 189–226
Folda Jaroslav, *Crusader Manuscript Illumination at Saint-Jean d'Acre, 1275–1291* (Princeton, 1976)
Forey, Alan, *The Templars in the Corona de Aragón* (London, 1973)
——, 'The Emergence of the Military Order in the twelfth century', *Journal of Ecclesiastical History*, 36 (1985), 175–95; reprinted in his *Military Orders and Crusades*
——, 'Recruitment to the Military Orders (twelfth to mid-fourteenth centuries)', *Viator*, 17 (1986), 139–71; reprinted in his *Military Orders and Crusades*
——, 'Women and the Military Orders in the Twelfth and Thirteenth Centuries', *Studia Monastica*, 29 (1987), 63–92; reprinted in his *Military Orders and Crusades*
——, 'The Military Orders and the ransoming of captives from Islam (twelfth to early fourteenth centuries)', *Studia Monastica*, 33 (1991), 259–79; reprinted in his *Military Orders and Crusades*

——, *The Military Orders: From the Twelfth to the Early Fourteenth Centuries* (Basingstoke, 1992)
——, *Military Orders and Crusades* (Aldershot, 1994)
——, 'Literacy and Learning in the Military Orders during the Twelfth and Thirteenth Centuries', in *The Military Orders*, vol. 2, ed. H. Nicholson, pp. 185–206.
Fowden, Garth, *The Egyptian Hermes: A Historical Approach to the late Pagan Mind* (Cambridge, 1986: new edn Princeton, 1993)
Frappier, Jean, 'Le Graal et la chevalerie', *Romania*, 75 (1954), 165–210
——, 'Chrétien de Troyes', in *Arthurian Literature in the Middle Ages*, ed. R.S. Loomis, pp. 157–91
Frappier, Jean and Grimm, Reinhold R., eds, *Grundriss der romanischen Literaturen des Mittelalters*, vol. IV: *Le Roman jusqu'à la fin du XIII siècle* (Heidelberg, 1978)
Fryde, Natalie, 'King John and the Empire', in *King John: New Interpretations*, ed. S.D. Church (Woodbridge, 1999), pp. 335–46
Gallais, Pierre, 'Robert de Boron en Orient', in *Mélanges de Langue et de Littérature du Moyen Age et de la Renaissance offerts à Jean Frappier*, 2 vols (Geneva, 1970), 1, pp. 313–19
García, José Manuel Rodríguez, 'Alfonso X and the Teutonic Order: an Example of the Role of the International Military Orders in Mid-Thirteenth Century Castile', in *The Military Orders*, vol. 2, ed. H. Nicholson, pp. 319–27
Geary, P., *Living with the Dead in the Middle Ages* (Ithaca, 1994)
Gervers, Michael, ed., *The Second Crusade and the Cistercians* (New York, 1991),
——, 'Donations to the Hospitallers in England in the Wake of the Second Crusade', in his *The Second Crusade and the Cistercians*, pp. 155–61
Gilchrist, John, 'The Papacy and the War against the 'Saracens', *International History Review*, 10 (1998), 174–97
Gilchrist, Roberta, *Contemplation and Action: the Other Monasticism* (London, 1995)
Gillingham, John, *Richard the Lionheart* (London, 1978)
——, 'Roger of Howden on Crusade', in *Medieval Historical Writing in the Christian and Islamic Worlds*, ed. D.O. Morgan (London, 1982), pp. 60–75; reprinted in his *Richard Coeur de Lion*, pp. 141–53
——, *Richard Coeur de Lion: Kingship, Chivalry and War in the Twelfth Century* (London and Rio Grande, 1994)
——, *Richard I* (New Haven and London, 1999)
Gladstone, R., 'Early Charters of the Knights Hospitallers relating to Much Woolton, nr Liverpool', *Transactions of the Historic Society of Lancashire and Cheshire*, 56 (1903), 1–24
Gransden, Antonia, *Historical Writing in England, c. 550 to c. 1307* (London, 1974)
Green, D.H., *Medieval Listening and Reading: the Primary Reception of German Literature, 800–1300* (Cambridge, 1994)
Haferland, Harald, 'Die Geheimnisse des Grals. Wolframs 'Parzifal' als Lesemysterium?', *Zeitschrift für deutsche Philologie*, 13 (1994), 23–57
Hallam, Elizabeth M., *Capetian France, 987–1328* (London, 1980)
Hamel, Mary, '*The Siege of Jerusalem* as a crusading poem', in *Journeys Towards God*, ed. B.N. Sargent-Baur, pp. 177–94
Hamilton, Bernard, *The Albigensian Crusade*, Historical Association Pamphlet no. 85 (London, 1974)
——, 'Prester John and the Three Kings of Cologne', in *Prester John, the Mongols and the Ten Lost Tribes*, ed. Charles F. Beckingham and Bernard Hamilton (Aldershot, 1996), pp. 171–85, previously published in *Studies in Medieval History presented to R.H.C. Davis*, ed. H. Mayr-Harting and R. I. Moore (London, 1985), pp. 177–91
——, 'The Impact of Crusader Jerusalem on Western Christendom', *Catholic Historical Review*, 80 (1994), 695–713
Hampe, Karl, *Germany under the Salian and Hohenstaufen Emperors*, trans. Ralph Bennett (Oxford, 1973)
Harf-Lancner, Laurence, *Les Fées au Moyen Age. Morgane et Mélusine. La naissance des fées* (Geneva, 1984),

Hasenhoir, Geneviève, 'Religious reading amongst the laity in France in the fifteenth century', in *Heresy and Literacy, 1000–1530*, ed. P. Biller and A. Hudson, pp. 205–21
Haverkamp, Alfred, *Medieval Germany*, translated Helga Braun and Richard Mortimer (Oxford, 1988)
Helm, K. and Ziesemer, W., *Die Literatur des Deutschen Ritterordens* (Giessen, 1951)
Hiestand, Rudolf, 'Kingship and Crusade in twelfth-century Germany', in *England and Germany in the High Middle Ages*, ed. Alfred Haverkamp and Hanna Vollrath (Oxford, 1996), pp. 235–65
Hillenbrand, Carole, *The Crusades: Islamic Perspectives* (Edinburgh, 1999)
Hobsbaum, Eric, 'Introduction: Inventing Traditions', in *The Invention of Tradition*, ed. Eric Hobsbaum and Terence Ranger (Cambridge, 1983), pp. 1–14
Holmes, Urban T., *A New Interpretation of Chrétien's Conte del Graal*, Studies in the Romance Languages and Literature, pamphlet no. 8 (1948)
Holmes, Urban T. and Klenke, Sister M. Amelia, *Chrétien, Troyes and the Grail* (Chapel Hill, 1959)
Housley, Norman, 'Politics and Heresy in Italy: anti-heretical crusades, orders and confraternities, 1200–1500', *Journal of Ecclesiastical History*, 33 (1982), 193–208
——, *The Avignon Papacy and the Crusades, 1305–1378* (Oxford, 1986)
——, *The Later Crusades: From Lyons to Alcazar, 1274–1580* (Oxford, 1992)
——, 'Cyprus and the Crusades, 1291–1571', in *Cyprus and the Crusades*, ed. Nicholas Coureas and Jonathan Riley-Smith, pp. 187–206
Hucker, Bernd Ulrich, *Kaiser Otto IV*, MGH Schriften, 34 (Hanover, 1990)
Jackson, Peter, 'The Crusades of 1239–41 and their Aftermath', *Bulletin of the School of Oriental and African Studies*, 50 (1987), 32–60
Jackson, W.T.H., *The Literature of the Middle Ages* (New York and London, 1960)
Jacoby, David, 'La littérature française dans les états latins de la Méditerranée orientale à l'époque des croisades: diffusion et création', in *Essor et fortune de la chanson de geste dans l'Europe et l'Orient latin. Acts du IXe Congrès International de la Société Rencesvals pour l'Étude des Épopées Romanes* (Padua and Venice, 1982), pp. 617–646; reprinted in his *Studies on the Crusader States and on Venetian Expansion* (Northampton, 1989), II
——, 'Knightly Values and Class Consciousness in the Crusader States of the Eastern Mediterranean', *Mediterranean Historical Review*, 1 (1986), 158–86; reprinted in his *Studies on the Crusader States and on Venetian Expansion* (Northampton, 1989), I
Jan, Libor and Jesensky, Vít, 'Hospitaller and Templar commanderies in Bohemia and Moravia: their Structure and Architectural Forms', in *The Military Orders*, vol. 2, ed. H. Nicholson, pp. 235–49
Jefferson, Lisa, 'Tournaments, Heraldry, and the Knights of the Round Table: a fifteenth-century Armorial with two accompanying texts', in *Arthurian Literature XIV*, ed. James P. Carley and Felicity Riddy (Cambridge, 1996), 69–157
Jolivet, Jean, 'The Arabic Inheritance', in *A History of Twelfth-Century Western Philosophy*, ed. P. Dronke, pp. 113–48
Jones, Martin H., 'Richard the Lionheart in German Literature of the Middle Ages', in *Richard Coeur de Lion in History and Myth*, ed. Janet L. Nelson (London, 1992), pp. 70–116
Joranson, Einar, 'The Palestine Pilgrimage of Henry the Lion', in *Medieval and Historiographical Essays in Honor of James Westfall Thompson*, ed. James Lea Cate and Eugene N. Anderson (Port Washington, New York, 1966), pp. 146–225
Jordan, Karl, *Henry the Lion: a biography* (Oxford, 1986)
Jotischky, Andrew, *The Perfection of Solitude: Hermits and Monks in the Crusader States* (Philadelphia, 1995)
Jubb, Margaret A., 'Enemies in Holy War, but brothers in chivalry; the crusaders' view of their Saracen opponents', in *Aspects de l'épopée romane*, ed. H. van Dijk and W. Noomen, pp. 251–9
Kay, Sarah, 'Le Problème de l'ennemi dans les chansons de geste', in *Aspects de l'épopée romane*, ed. H. van Dijk and W. Noomen, pp. 261–8
Kedar, Benjamin Z., *Crusade and Mission: European Approaches Towards the Muslims* (Princeton, 1984)

——, 'A Twelfth-Century Description of the Jerusalem Hospital', in *The Military Orders*, vol. 2, ed. H. Nicholson, pp. 3–26
——, 'The *Tractatus de locis et statu sancte terre ierosolimitanae*', in *The Crusades and Their Sources: Essays Presented to Bernard Hamilton*, ed. John France and William G. Zajac (Aldershot, 1998), pp. 111–33
Keen, Maurice, 'Chivalry and Courtly Love', *History*, 47 (1964), 1–17, reprinted in his *Nobles, Knights and Men-at-Arms*, pp. 21–42
——, 'Chivalry, Heralds and History', in *The Writing of History in the Middle Ages: Essays Presented to R. W. Southern*, ed. R.H.C. Davis and J.M. Wallace-Hadrill (Oxford, 1981), pp. 393–41 and reprinted in his *Nobles, Knights and Men-at-Arms*, pp. 63–81
——, 'Chaucer's Knight, the English Aristocracy and the Crusade', in *English Court Culture in the Later Middle Ages*, ed. V.J. Scattergood and J.W. Sherborne (London, 1983), pp. 45–61
——, *Chivalry* (New Haven and London, 1984)
——, *Nobles, Knights and Men-at-Arms in the Middle Ages* (London, 1996)
Keller, Hans-Erich, 'The *Song of Roland*: a mid-twelfth century song of propaganda for the Capetian kingdom', *Oliphant*, 3 (1976), 242–58
Kelly, Thomas E., *Le Haut Livre du Graal: Perlesvaus. A Structural Study* (Geneva, 1974)
Kennedy, Beverly, *Knighthood in the Morte Darthur*, 2nd edn (Cambridge, 1992)
Kennedy, Elspeth, 'The Knight as Reader of Arthurian Romance', in *Culture and the King. The Social Implications of the Arthurian Legend; Essays in Honor of Valerie M. Lagorio*, ed. Martin B. Shichtman and James P. Carley (New York, 1994), pp. 70–90
Kieckhefer, Richard, *Magic in the Middle Ages* (Cambridge, 1989)
Knight, Stephen, 'From Jerusalem to Camelot: King Arthur and the Crusades', in *Medieval Codicology, Iconography, Literature and Translation: Studies for Keith Val Sinclair*, ed. Peter Roufe Monks and D.D.R. Owen (Leiden, 1994), pp. 223–32
Kolb, Herbert, *Munsalvaesche: Studien zur Kyot Problem* (Munich, 1963)
Kuhn, Walter, 'Ritterorden als Grenzhüter des Abendlandes gegen das östliche Heidentum', *Ostdeutsche Wissenschaft*, 6 (1959), 7–70
Labande, Edmond-René, *Étude sur Baudouin de Sebourc, chanson de geste. Légende poetique de Baudouin II du Bourq, roi de Jérusalem* (Paris, 1940)
Lachet, Claude, *Sone de Nansay et le roman d'aventures en vers au XIII siècle*, Nouvelle Bibliothèque du Moyen Age, 19 (Paris, 1992)
Langlois, E., *Table des noms propres de toute nature compris dans les chansons de geste* (Paris, 1904)
Lassus, Jean, *Landmarks of the World's Art: The Early Christian and Byzantine World* (London, 1966)
Lathuillère, Roger, *Guiron le Courtois. Étude de la tradition manuscrite et analyse critique* (Geneva, 1966)
Lawrence, C.H., *Medieval Monasticism: Forms of Religious Life in Western Europe in the Middle Ages*, 2nd edn (London, 1989)
Leclercq, J., 'Monks and Hermits in Medieval Love Stories', *Journal of Medieval History*, 18 (1992), 341–56
Leff, Gordon, *Medieval Thought from Saint Augustine to Ockham* (Harmondsworth, 1958)
Gentil, Pierre le, 'The work of Robert de Boron and the *Didot Perceval*', in *Arthurian Literature in the Middle Ages*, ed. R. Loomis, pp. 251–62
Legros, Huguette, 'Entre Chrétiens et Sarrasins, des amités paradoxales: liberté de l'imaginaire ou rêve d'un monde réconcilié', in *Aspects de l'épopée romane*, ed. H. van Dijk and W. Noomen, pp. 269–78
Lejeune, Rita, *L'Oeuvre de Jean Renart*, Bibliothèque de la Faculté de Philosophie et Lettres de l'Université de Liège, fascicule 61 (Liège, 1935)
——, 'The Troubadours', in *Arthurian Literature in the Middle Ages*, ed. R.S. Loomis, pp. 392–9
Lejeune, Rita and Stiennon, Jacques, *The Legend of Roland in the Middle Ages*, trans. Christine Trollope, 2 vols (London, 1971)
Leyser, Henrietta, *Hermits and the New Monasticism: a Study of Religious Communities in Western Europe, 1000–1150* (London, 1984)

———, *Medieval Women: A Social History of Women in England, 450–1500* (London, 1995
Lloyd, Simon, *English Society and the Crusade, 1216–1307* (Oxford, 1988)
———, 'William Longespee II: the Making of an English Crusading Hero', *Nottingham Medieval Studies*, 34 (1991), 41–70, 35 (1992), 79–125
Lock, Peter, *The Franks in the Aegean, 1204–1500* (London, 1995)
Locke, Frederick W., *The Quest for the Holy Grail: A Literary Study of a thirteenth-century Romance* (Stanford, California, 1960)
Lods, Jeanne, *Le Roman de Perceforest: origines – composition – caratères – valeur et influence*, Publications Romanes et Françaises 32 (Geneva, 1951)
Longnon, Jean, *Les Companions de Villehardouin: recherches sur les croisiés de la quatrième croisade* (Geneva, 1979)
Loomis, Roger Sherman, 'Edward I, Arthurian Enthusiast', *Speculum*, 28 (1953), 114–27
———, ed., *Arthurian Literature in the Middle Ages: A Collaborative History* (Oxford, 1959)
———, 'The Oral Diffusion of the Arthurian Legend', in his *Arthurian Literature in the Middle Ages*, pp. 52–63
———, 'Arthurian Influence on Sport and Spectacle', in his *Arthurian Literature in the Middle Ages*, pp. 553–63
Löseth, Eilert, *Le Roman en prose de Tristan, le roman de Palamède et la compilation de Rusticien de Pise: analyse critique d'après des manuscrits de Paris* (Paris, 1890; Geneva, 1974)
Lüpke, Helmut, *Untersuchungen zur Geschichte des Templerordens im Gebiet der nordostdeutschen Kolonisation: Inaugural-Dissertation* (Bernburg, 1933)
———, 'Das Land Tempelburg. Ein historisch-geographische Untersuchung', *Baltische Studien*, 35 (1933), 43–97
Luscombe, D.E., 'Peter Abelard', in *A History of Twelfth-Century Philosophy*, ed. Dronke, pp. 279–307
Luttrell, Anthony, 'The Aragonese Crown and the Hospitallers of Rhodes, 1314–1332', *English Historical Review*, 76 (1961), 1–19, reprinted in his *The Hospitallers in Cyprus, Rhodes, Greece and the West (1291–1440)* (London, 1978)
———, 'The Hospitallers' Historical Activities, 1291–1400', in *Annales de l'ordre souverain et militaire de Malte*, 24 (1966), 126–9, reprinted in his *The Hospitallers in Cyprus, Rhodes, Greece and the West, 1291–1440* (London, 1978), XVII
———, *The Hospitallers in Cyprus, Rhodes, Greece and the West, 1291–1440* (London, 1978)
———, *Latin Greece, the Hospitallers and the Crusades, 1291–1440* (Aldershot, 1982)
———, 'The Hospitallers in Cyprus, 1310–1378', *Kypriakai Spoudai*, 50 (1986), 155–84, reprinted in his *The Hospitallers of Rhodes and their Mediterranean World* (Aldershot, 1992), IX
———, *The Hospitallers of Rhodes and their Mediterranean World* (Aldershot, 1992)
———, *The Hospitaller State on Rhodes and its Western Provinces, 1306–1462* (Aldershot, 1999)
———, 'The Hospitallers in Cyprus after 1386', in *Cyprus and the Crusades*, ed. N. Coureas and J. Riley-Smith, pp. 125–41
———, 'The Military Orders, 1312–1798', in *The Oxford Illustrated History of the Crusades*, ed. Jonathan Riley-Smith (Oxford, 1995), pp. 326–64
———, 'The Earliest Templars', in *Autour de la Première Croisade*, ed. Michel Balard (Paris, 1996), pp. 193–202
———, 'The Earliest Hospitallers', in *Montjoie: Studies in Crusade History in Honour of Hans Eberhard Mayer*, ed. Benjamin Z. Kedar, Jonathan Riley-Smith and Rudolf Hiestand (Aldershot, 1997), pp. 37–54
Luttrell, Claude A., *The Creation of the First Arthurian Romance: a Quest* (London, 1974), pp. 27–32
———, 'The Prologue of Crestien's *Li Contes del Graal*', *Arthurian Literature III*, ed. Richard Barber (Cambridge, 1984), pp. 1–25
Mahoney, Dhiva B., 'The Truest and Holiest Tale: Malory's Transformation of the *Queste del Saint Graal*', in *Studies in Malory*, ed. James W. Spisak (Kalamazoo, Michigan, 1985), pp. 109–28
Mann, Jill, 'Malory and the Grail Legend', in *A Companion to Malory*, ed. E. Archibald and A.S.G. Edwards (Cambridge, 1996), pp. 203–20

Mason, Emma, 'Timeo barones et dona ferentes', in *Religious Motivation: Biographical and Sociological Problems for the Church Historian*, ed. Derek Baker, Studies in Church History, 15 (1978), pp. 61–75
——, 'The Hero's Invincible Weapon: an Aspect of Angevin Propaganda', *Ideas and Practice of Medieval Knighthood III, papers from the fourth Strawberry Hill Conference, 1988*, ed. Christopher Harper-Bill and Ruth Harvey (Woodbridge, 1990), pp. 121–37
Matarasso, Pauline, *The Redemption of Chivalry: a Study of the Queste del Saint Graal* (Geneva, 1979)
Matthews, William, *The Tragedy of Arthur: A study of the Alliterative 'Morte Arthure'* (Berkeley and Los Angeles, 1960)
Mayer, Hans Eberhard, 'Henry II of England and the Holy Land', *English Historical Review*, 97 (1982), 721–39
——, *The Crusades*, trans. John Gillingham, 2nd edn (Oxford, 1988)
McNiven, Peter, *Heresy and Politics in the Reign of Henry IV: the Burning of John Badby* (Woodbridge, 1987)
Melville, Marian, *La Vie des Templiers* (Paris, 1951)
Menache, Sophia, *The Vox Dei: Communication in the Middle Ages* (Oxford, 1990)
Ménard, Philippe, *Les Fabliaux: contes à rire du moyen âge* (Paris, 1983)
——, 'La réception des romans de chevalerie à la fin du Moyen Age et au XVIe siècle', *The Bibliographical Bulletin of the International Arthurian Society*, 49 (1997), 234–73
Micha, Alexandre, 'Sone de Nansay', in *Grundriss der romanischen Literaturen des Mittelalters*, vol. IV: *Le Roman jusqu'à la fin du XIII siècle*, ed Jean Frappier and Reinhold R. Grimm (Heidelberg, 1978), pp. 490–91
——, *Étude sur le <Merlin> de Robert de Boron: Roman du XIIIe siècle* (Geneva, 1980)
——, *Essais sur le cycle du Lancelot-Graal* (Geneva, 1987)
Michael, Ian, 'The Spanish Perceforest: a recent discovery', *Studies in Medieval Literature and Languages in Memory of Frederick Whitehead*, ed. W. Rothwell, W.R.J. Barron, David Blamires and Lewis Thorpe (Manchester, 1973), pp. 209–18
Mickel, Lesley, *Ben Jonson's Antimasques: a History of Growth and Decline* (Aldershot, 1999)
Milburn, Robert, *Early Christian Art and Architecture* (Aldershot, 1988)
Militzer, Klaus, 'From the Holy Land to Prussia: the Teutonic Knights between Emperors and Popes and their Policies until 1309', in *Mendicants, Military Orders and Regionalism*, ed. J. Sarnowsky, pp. 71–81
Minnis, A.J. and Scott, A.B., eds, *Medieval Literary Theory and Criticism, c. 1100–c. 1375: The Commentary Tradition* (Oxford, 1988)
Moisan, André, *Répertoire des nons propres de personnes et de lieux cités dans les chansons de geste françaises et les oeuvres étrangères dérivées*, 2 tomes in 5 vols (Geneva, 1986)
——, 'Les traditions rolandienne et turpinienne dans les croniques et conquestes de Charlemaine de David Aubert', in *Aspects de l'épopée romane*, ed. H. van Dijk and W. Noomen, pp. 399–408
Moore, R.I., *The Formation of a Persecuting Society* (Oxford, 1987)
Morgan, M. Ruth, *The Chronicle of Ernoul and the Continuations of William of Tyre* (Oxford, 1973)
——, 'The Rothelin Continuation of William of Tyre', in *Outremer: Studies in the History of the Crusading Kingdom of Jerusalem presented to Joshua Prawer*, ed. Benjamin Z. Kedar, Hans E. Mayer and R.C. Smail (Jerusalem, 1982), pp. 244–57
Morris, Rosemary, 'King Arthur and the Growth of French Nationalism', in *France and the British Isles in the Middle Ages and Renaissance: Essays by members of Girton College, Cambridge, in memory of Ruth Morgan*, ed. Gillian Jondorf and D.N. Dumville (Woodbridge, 1991), pp.115–30
Murray, Alexander, *Reason and Society in the Middle Ages* (Oxford, 1978)
Myers, G.M. '*Les Chétifs* – Étude sur le développement de la chanson,' *Romania*, 105 (1984), 65–75
Naumann, Claudia, *Der Kreuzzug Kaiser Heinrichs VI* (Frankfurt am Main, 1994)
Nicholson, Helen, 'Templar Attitudes towards Women', *Medieval History*, 1, 3 (1991), 74–80

——, *Templars, Hospitallers and Teutonic Knights: Images of the Military Orders, 1128–1291* (London, 1993)
——, 'Knights and Lovers: the Military Orders in the Romantic Literature of the Thirteenth Century', in *The Military Orders: Fighting for the Faith*, ed. M. Barber, pp. 340–45
——, 'Women on the Third Crusade', *Journal of Medieval History*, 23 (1997), 335–49
——, *Chronicle of the Third Crusade: a Translation of the Itinerarium Peregrinorum et Gesta Regis Ricardi* (Aldershot, 1997)
——, ed., *The Military Orders*, volume 2: *Welfare and Warfare* (Aldershot, 1998)
——, 'The Military Orders and the Kings of England in the Twelfth and Thirteenth Centuries', in *From Clermont to Jerusalem: the Crusades and Crusader Societies, 1095–1500*, ed. Alan V. Murray, International Medieval Research, 3 (Turnhout, 1998), pp. 203–28
——, 'The Knights Hospitaller on the frontiers of the British Isles', in *Mendicants, Military Orders and Regionalism in Medieval Europe*, ed. J. Sarnowsky, pp. 47–57
Nutt, Alfred, *Studies in the Legends of the Holy Grail, with especial reference to the hypothesis of its Celtic Origin* (London, 1888)
Olschki, Leonardo, *The Grail Castle and its Mysteries*, trans. J. A. Scott (Manchester, 1966)
Olson, Glending, *Literature as Recreation in the Later Middle Ages* (Ithaca and London, 1982)
Oman, Charles, *The Great Revolt of 1381*, new edition with introduction by E.B. Fryde (Oxford, 1969)
Paolini, Lorenzo, 'Italian Catharism and written culture', *Heresy and Literacy*, ed. P. Biller and A. Hudson, pp. 83–103
Parkes, M.B., 'The Literacy of the Laity', in *Literature and Western Civilisation: the Medieval World*, ed. David Daiches and Anthony Thorlby (London, 1993), pp. 555–75
Patschovsky, Alexander, 'The literacy of Waldensianism from Valdes to *c.* 1400', *Heresy and Literacy*, ed. P. Biller and A. Hudson, pp. 112–36
Pauphilet, Albert, 'La Queste du Saint Graal du MS Bibl Nat Fr. 343', *Romania*, 36 (1907), 591–609
——, *Études sur la Queste del Saint Graal attribuée a Gautier Map* (Paris, 1921)
Perman, R.C.D., *see* Henri d'Arci
Petit-Dutaillis, Charles, *Étude sur la vie et le règne de Louis VIII (1187–1226)* (Paris, 1894)
Phillips, Jonathan, *Defenders of the Holy Land: Relations Between the Latin East and the West, 1119–1187* (Oxford, 1996)
——, 'Archbishop Henry of Reims and the Militarization of the Hospitallers', in *The Military Orders*, vol. 2, ed. H. Nicholson, pp. 83–8
Piquet, J., *Des banquiers au moyen âge: Les Templiers: Étude sur leur opérations financières* (Paris, 1939)
Potthast, Augustus, *Regesta pontificum Romanorum inde ab a. post Christum natum MCXCVIII ad a. MCCCIV*, 2 vols (Graz, 1957)
Powell, James M., 'The role of women in the Fifth Crusade', in *The Horns of Hattin*, ed. Benjamin Z. Kedar (Jerusalem and London, 1992), pp. 294–301
Pratt, Karen, 'The Cistercians and the *Queste del Saint Graal*', *Reading Medieval Studies*, 21 (1995), 69–96
Prestwich, John, 'Richard Coeur de Lion: *Rex Bellicosus*', in *Richard Coeur de Lion in History and Myth*, ed. Janet L. Nelson (London, 1992), pp. 1–16
Prestwich, Michael, *Edward I* (London, 1988)
Pringle, Denys, 'King Richard and the Walls of Ascalon', *Palestine Exploration Quarterly*, 116 (1984), 133–47, here 136; reprinted in his *Fortification and Settlement in Crusader Palestine* (Aldershot, 2000)
Pryor, John H., *Geography, Technology and War: Studies in the Maritime History of the Mediterranean, 649–1571* (Cambridge, 1988)
Pugh, R.B., 'The Knights Hospitallers as Undertakers', *Speculum*, 53 (1978), 566–74
Queller, Donald E., *The Fourth Crusade: The Conquest of Constantinople, 1201–1204* (Leicester, 1978)
Queller, Donald E. and Madden, Thomas F., *The Fourth Crusade and the Conquest of Constantinople* (Philadelphia, 1997)
Reeves, Marjorie, 'Originality and Influence of Joachim of Fiore', *Traditio*, 36 (1980), 269–316

Reville, André, *Le Soulèvement des travailleurs d'Angleterre en 1381, études et documents publiés avec un introduction historique par Charles Petit-Dutaillis*, Mémoires et Documents Publiés par la Société de l'école des Chartes, 2 (Paris, 1898)
Richey, Margaret Fitzgerald, *Studies of Wolfram von Eschenbach* (London, 1957)
Richter, Horst, '*Militia Dei*: a central concept for the religious ideas of the early crusades and the German *Rolandslied*', in *Journeys Towards God*, ed. B.N. Sargent-Baur, pp. 107–26
Riley-Smith, Jonathan, *The Knights of St John in Jerusalem and Cyprus, c. 1050–1310* (London, 1967)
—— *The Feudal Nobility and the Kingdom of Jerusalem, 1174–1277* (London and Basingstoke, 1973), pp. 121–44
——, 'The Templars and the Teutonic Knights in Cilician Armenia', in *The Cilician Kingdom of Armenia*, ed. T. Boase, pp. 92–117
——, 'Crusading as an Act of Love', *History*, 65 (1980), 177–92
——, *The First Crusade and the Idea of Crusading* (London, 1986)
——, 'Family tradition and participation in the Second Crusade', in *The Second Crusade and the Cistercians*, ed. M. Gervers, pp. 101–8
——, *What were the Crusades?* 2nd edn (Basingstoke, 1992)
——, *The First Crusaders, 1095–1131* (Cambridge, 1997)
——, *Hospitallers: The History of the Order of St John* (London, 1999)
Roob, Alexander, *Alchemy and Mysticism: the Hermetic Museum* (Cologne, 1997)
Roques, Mario, 'Ronsavals: poème épique provençal', *Romania*, 58 (1932), 1–28, 161–89
Roussel, Claude, *Conter de geste au XIV siècle: Inspiration folklorique et écriture épique dans La Belle Hélène de Constantinople*, Publications romanes et françaises 222 (Geneva, 1998)
Sandys, A., 'The Financial and Administrative Importance of the London Temple in the Thirteenth Century', in *Essays in Medieval History presented to Thomas Frederick Tout*, ed. A.G. Little and F.M. Powicke (Manchester, 1925), pp. 147–62
Sargent-Baur, Barbara N., 'Alexander and the *Conte du Graal*', in *Arthurian Literature XIV*, ed. James P. Carley and Felicity Riddy (Cambridge, 1996), pp. 1–18
——, ed., *Journeys Towards God: Pilgrimage and Crusade* (Kalamazoo, Michigan, 1992)
Sarnowsky, Jürgen, ed., *Mendicants, Military Orders and Regionalism in Medieval Europe* (Aldershot, 1999),
——, 'Kings and Priors. The Hospitaller Priory of England in the Later Fifteenth Century, in his *Mendicants, Military Orders and Regionalism*, pp. 83–102
Schein, Silvia, 'The Templars: the Regular Army of the Holy Land and the Spearhead of the Army of its Reconquest', in *I Templari: Mito e Storia, Atti del Convegno Internazionale di Studi alli Magione Templari di Poggibonsi-Siena, 29–31 Maggio 1987*, ed. Giovanni Minnucci and Franca Sardi (Siena, 1989), pp. 15–25
——, *Fideles Crucis: The Papacy, the West, and the Recovery of the Holy Land, 1274–1314* (Oxford, 1991)
Schirok, Bernd, *Parzivalrezeption im Mittelalter* (Darmstadt, 1984)
Schmolke-Hasselmann, Beate, *Der arthurische Versroman von Chrestien bis Froissart: zur Geschichte einer Gattung* (Tübingen, 1980), pp. 190–208, 222–32, translated by Margaret and Roger Middleton as *The Evolution of Arthurian Romance: Verse Tradition from Chrétien to Froissart* (Cambridge, 1998)
——, 'The Round Table: Ideal, Fiction, Reality', in *Arthurian Literature*, 2, ed. Richard Barber (Cambridge, 1982), pp. 41–75
Schulze-Busaker, Elisabeth, 'La datation de *Ronsavals*', *Romania*, 110 (1989), 127–66, 396–425
Schüpferling, Michael, *Der Tempel-herren Orden in Deutschland. Dissertation zur Erlangung der Doktorwürde von der philos. Fakultät der Universität Freiburg in der Schweiz* (Bamberg, 1915)
Selwood, Dominic, *Knights of the Cloister: Templars and Hospitallers in Central-Southern Occitania 1100–1300* (Woodbridge, 1999)
Siberry, Elizabeth, *Criticism of Crusading, 1095–1274* (Oxford, 1985)
Smail, R.C., 'Latin Syria and the West, 1149–1187', *Transactions of the Royal Historical Society*, 5th series 19 (1969), 1–21

Smith, Lesley and Taylor, Jane H.M., eds, *Women, the Book and the Worldly: Selected Proceedings of the St Hilda's Conference, 1993, vol. 2* (Cambridge, 1995)
——, eds, *Women and the Book: Assessing the Visual Evidence* (London, 1996)
Snelleman, Willem, *Das Haus Anjou und der Orient in Wolframs 'Parzival'* (Nijkerk, 1941)
Sparnaay, Hendricus, 'The Dutch Romances', in *Arthurian Literature in the Middle Ages*, ed. R.S. Loomis, pp. 443–61
Spiewok, Wolfgang, 'L'importance de la croisade pour l'evolution de l'idéologie courtoise et le développement de la littérature médiévale allemande – du dogme à la tolérance', in *Aspects de l'épopée romane*, ed. H. van Dijk and W. Noomen, pp. 301–7
Starkey, David, 'King Henry and King Arthur', in *Arthurian Literature XVI*, ed. James P. Carley and Felicity Riddy (Cambridge, 1998), pp. 171–96
Stock, Brian, *The Implications of Literacy: Written Language and Models of Interpretation in the Eleventh and Twelfth Centuries* (Princeton, 1983)
Suard, François, 'Les héroes Chrétiens face au monde Sarracin', in *Aspects de l'épopée romane*, ed. H. van Dijk and W. Noomen, pp. 187–208
Sumption, Jonathan, *Pilgrimage: an Image of Medieval Religion* (London, 1975)
Tester, Jim, *A History of Western Astrology* (Woodbridge, 1987)
Thomson, W.R., 'The Image of the Mendicants in the Chronicles of Matthew Paris', *Archivum Franciscanum Historicum*, 70 (1977), 3–34
Tillmann, Helene, *Innocent III*, trans. Walter Sax (Amsterdam, 1980)
Tommasi, Francesco, 'Uomini e donne negli ordini militari di Terrasanta: Per il problema delle case doppie e miste negli ordini giovannita, templare e teutonico (secc. XII–XIV), in *Doppelkloster und andere Formen der symbiose mannlicher und weiblicher Religiosen in Mittelalter*, ed. Kaspar Elm and Michel Parisse, Berliner historische Studien, 18 (1992), pp. 177–202
Trotter, David, *Medieval French Literature and the Crusades (1100–1300)* (Geneva, 1987)
——, 'La mythologie arthurienne et la prédication de la croisade', in *Pour une mythologie du Moyen Age*, ed. Laurence Harf-Lancer and Dominique Boutet (Paris, 1988), pp. 155–77
Tunison, J.S., *The Graal Problem – From Walter Map to Richard Wagner* (Cincinnati, 1904)
Turner, Ralph V., *King John* (London, 1994)
Tyerman, Christopher, *England and the Crusades, 1095–1588* (Chicago, 1988)
——, *The Invention of the Crusades* (Basingstoke, 1998)
Tyson, Diana B., 'Patronage of French Vernacular History Writers in the Twelfth and Thirteenth Centuries', *Romania*, 100 (1979), 180–222
Vaughan, Richard, *Matthew Paris* (Cambridge, 1958)
Vessey, D.W.T.C., 'William of Tyre and the Art of Historiography', *Medieval Studies*, 35 (1973), 433–55
Vial, Guy, *Le Conte du Graal: sens et unité* (Geneva, 1987)
Vinaver, Eugène, *Études sur le Tristan en Prose* (Paris, 1925)
——, 'The Prose *Tristan*', in *Arthurian Literature in the Middle Ages*, ed. R.S. Loomis, pp. 339–47
Walker, John, 'Crusaders and Patrons: the Influence of the Crusades on the Patronage of the Military Order of St Lazarus in England', in *The Military Orders: Fighting for the Faith*, ed. M. Barber, pp. 327–32
Ward, Benedicta, *Miracles and the Medieval Mind* (London, 1982)
Warren, W.L., *King John* (London, 1961)
——, *Henry II* (London, 1973)
Wentzlaff-Eggebert, Friedrich-Wilhelm, *Kreuzzugsdichtung des Mittelalters: Studien zu ihrer geschichtlichen und dichterischen Wirklichkeit* (Berlin, 1960)
Weston, Jessie, *The Quest of the Holy Grail* (London, 1913, reprinted 1964)
——, 'Notes on the Grail Romances – *Sone de Nansai*, *Parzival* and *Perlesvaus*', *Romania*, 43 (1914), 403–26
——, *From Ritual to Romance: An Account of the Holy Grail From Ancient Ritual to Christian Symbol* (new edn, New York, 1957)
——, 'Notes on the Grail Romances: Caput Johannis=Corpus Christi', *Romania*, 49 (1923), 273–9

Wightman, W.E., *The Lacy Family in England and Normandy, 1066–1194* (Oxford, 1966)
Wildermann, Ansgar Konrad, *Die Beurteilung des Templerprozesses bis zum 17. Jahrhundert* (Freiburg, 1971)
Wilkin, Gregory J., 'The Dissolution of the Templar Ideal in "Sir Gawain and the Green Knight"', *English Studies*, 63 (1982), 109–21
Wojtecki, Dieter, *Studien zur Personengeschichte des Deutschen Ordens im 13 Jahrhundert*, Quellen und Studien zur Geschichte des östlichen Europa, 3 (Wiesbaden, 1971)
Woledge, Brian and Clive, H.P., *Répertoire des plus anciens textes en prose française depuis 842 jusqu'aux premières années du XIII siècle* (Geneva, 1964)

Unpublished Theses

Cook, Barry John, 'The Transmission of knowledge about the Holy Land through Europe, 1271–1314', PhD thesis, University of Manchester, 1985
Prescott, Andrew John, 'Judicial Records of the Rising of 1381', PhD thesis, Bedford College, University of London, 1984
Rosenthal, Elizabeth E., 'Théseus de Cologne, a general study and partial edition', PhD thesis, Birkbeck College, University of London, 1975

INDEX

Entries are listed under first name of medieval characters, and surname of modern writers. Titles of books are listed under the first word of the title excluding the article (so *Diu Crône* is found under 'c'). For readers' convenience, dates of death of historical characters are included where possible. For fictional characters, the work in which they appear follows the name in brackets.

Abbreviations:

H = Order of Hospital of St John;   T = Order of the Temple;   TK = Teutonic Order

Abilan of Damascus (First Crusade Cycle), 70, 78, 217
Acre, city of, 35, 40, 44, 45, 65, 66, 79, 92, 98, 116–17, 144, 151
  loss of (1291), 3, 4, 24, 26, 71, 82–5, 92, 228
  siege of (1189–91), 26, 51, 52, 64, 81, 118, 124, 130
Adam of Murimuth (d. 1347), 229
Adolf, Helen, 111, 112–17, 119, 122, 131, 143
Agnes of Burgundy, duchess of Bourbon and Auvergne (married 1425), 89
Aimery of Lusignan, king of Cyprus, king of Jerusalem (d. 1205), 111, 120–21, 124, 136, 138, 151
al-'Adil I, Ayyubid sultan of Egypt (d. 1218), 125, 132–3
al-Aqsa mosque ['Temple of Solomon'], 26, 38–42, 59, 61, 64, 94, 111, 167, 169, 219, 231
Albrecht IV, duke of Bavaria, 107
Albrecht (von Scharfenberg), 23, 52–5, 76, 106, 107, 109, 188
Alexander III (d. 1181), pope, 123
Alexander Giffard (d. 1250), 77
Alexander the Great, legend of, 19, 21, 148, 149, 158
Alexandria, 99, 226
Alfonse, count of Poitiers (d. 1270), 224
Alfonso VIII, king of Castile (d. 1214), 133
Alfonso XI, king of Castile (d. 1350), 91, 94, 224–5
Alfonso de Cartagena, bishop of Burgos (d. 1456), 206
Alice of France (fl. 1195), 132

Aliscans, 20, 201
alliterative *Morte Arthure*, 1, 23, 72, 98, 187, 189, 212, 220
Amaury, king of Jerusalem (d. 1174), 78, 94
Amaury, king of Jerusalem (First Crusade Cycle), 44, 67
Amaury de la Roche, brother of T, 223
Ambroise, 9, 52
Andrew of Chavigny, 64
Anfortas (*Parzival*), 131–2, 142
Anglo-Scottish war, 148
Anne, master of T (Ottokar's *Reimchronik*), 85
Antioch, 72, 96, 97
Antoine de la Sale (fl. 1460), 9, 89–90, 188, 205, 216, 226 *and see his individual works*
Aragon, kingdom of, 63
Armenia, *see* Cilician Armenia
Arnold of Lubeck (fl. 1209), 145
Arsūf, battle of (1191), 67, 85–6
Arthur, king, ix, 14, 19, 21, 22, 53, 65, 72, 98–100, 112, 118, 139, 148, 152, 153, 169, 173, 175, 191, 212–14
Arthurian literature and its impact on society, 14–15 and nn 46–51, 19, 21–3, 28, 118, 152, 178, 180, 191, 192, 198, 204–15, 220, 235
Artois, count of, 90, 91, *and see* Robert, count of Artois
Ascalon, 70, 111
audiences of literature, 2, 4, 9, 11, 18, 29, 30, 37, 104, 171, 180, 187, 219, 234–7
authors, 2, 4, 9–12, 18, 42, 104, 171, 180, 187, 203–5, 219, 234 *and see individual authors*

Bahā' al-Dīn (d. 1234), 132
Bait Gibrin, castle of H, 85
Baldwin IV, king of Jerusalem, 'the leper' (d. 1185), 109–14, 117, 126, 130, 131
Baldwin V, king of Jerusalem (d. 1186), 86, 131
Baldwin VI of Flanders and Hainaut, emperor of Constantinople (d. c. 1205), 43
Baldwin de Beauvais (*Les Chétifs*), 45
Baldwin of Edessa, king of Jerusalem (d. 1118), 44, 136, 203, 217
Baldwin of Ford, archbishop of Canterbury (d. 1190), 130
Balian of Ibelin (d. 1193), 46
Balkans, 27, *and see* 'Romania'
Baltic States, 28 *and see* Livonia, Lithuanians
Le Bastard de Bouillon, 218–19, 221
Baudouin de Sebourc (Crusade Cycle), 44, 67, *and see Le Roman de Baudouin de Sebourc*
Bavaria, 107, 139
Beatrice of Jerusalem (First Crusade Cycle), 44, 66
Beatrice of Swabia (d. 1212), 139
Beauvais, bishop of, 37, 43
Beirut, 48 n 35, 116–17, 124, 138, 183, 201, 204
Belacâne (*Parzival*), 122
La Belle Hélène de Constantinople, 20, 200, 202
Benedictine order, 152–3
Berengaria of Navarre (d. 1230), 132
Bernard, abbot of Clairvaux (d. 1153), 5–6, 36, 49, 73, 169, 193, 195
Blanche of Castile, queen of France (d. 1252), 133
Boccaccio, *see Decameron*
Bohemia, 71 *and see* Ottokar, Waclaw
Bohort de Gaunes/Bors de Gaunes (Arthurian legend), 153–4, 170, 171, 176, 182, 208, 211, 212
Boniface VIII, pope (d. 1303), 42
Boucicaut (d. 1421), 226
Botron, heiress of, 46
Bouvines, battle of (1214), 95, 126, 139, 144
Brabant, 55, 138, 142
  duchess of, 122
  and see Henry of, Maria of
Brehus sans Pitié (Arthurian legend), 11, 175, 206–7
Bride, queen of Jerusalem (*Orendal*), 74, 93
Brittany, 98
Bruce, John Douglas, 1 n 1, 116, 169, 177
Buch der Abenteuer, by Ulrich Füetrer, 23, 107, 189
Bueve de Hantone ('Bueve of Hampton'), 43, 48, 64, 67, 91, 93

Burgundy, 90, 91, 222
  and see Charles of Charolais, Philip the Good
Caesarius of Heisterbach, 52, 145, 194
Calabre, queen (First Crusade Cycle), 11, 217
Calatrava, order of, 27, 91
The Canterbury Tales, by Geoffrey Chaucer, 99
Capetian kings and legend, 14 n 47
Carmelite friars, 17
Castile, 91, 174, *and see* Alfonso
Catalonia, 133
Celestine II, pope (d. 1144), 50
Cent Nouvelles Nouvelles, 90–91
La Chanson d'Antioche, 14, 161–2
La Chanson de Jérusalem, 45, 157
  second continuations branch ('Second State' of First Crusade Cycle), 44–5, 66, 67, 200, 217
  London-Turin continuation ('Third State' of First Crusade Cycle), 11, 45, 70, 77–9, 93–4, 188, 200, 203, 217, 218
'La Chanson des rois Baudouin', 44, 66, 67
La Chanson de Roland, 74, 77, 224
Charles V, emperor (d. 1556), 27
Charles V, king of France (d. 1380), 58
Charles, count of Anjou (d. 1285), 223
Charles, count of Charolais (later Charles the Bold, duke of Burgundy, d. 1477), 42
Charles Martel (d. 714), 37
Charlemagne, emperor of the West (d. 814), 14 and n 47, 19, 20, 37, 39, 67, 125
La Chastelaine de Vergi, 47, 53, 57
Chaucer, *see The Canterbury Tales*
Les Chétifs, 45
La Chevalerie d'Ogier de Danemarche, 37–8, 39
Le Chevalier au Cygne et Godefroid de Bouillon, 64, 72, 100, 157, 158, 189–90
chivalry, 5–7, 14–16, 102–3, 108, 147–50, 152, 153, 159–60, 168–71, 173–4, 177, 180, 182, 204–19, 220, 224–6, 234–7
Chrétien de Troyes (d. after 1192?), 9, 21, 52, 104, 108, 112–20, 121–3, 126, 130, 131, 133, 135–6, 141, 143, 150, 152, 180–83, 211
Christ, 39, 41, 50, 51, 56, 70, 74, 87, 93, 104, 110, 118–19, 135, 154, 157–62, 166–7, 175, 177, 210, 212, 225
Christ, order of, 82
chronicles, viii–ix, 2, 8, 12, 67, 236
Chronique d'Ernoul et de Bernard le trésorier, ix, 46, 133, 200, 216
Cilician Armenia ('Hermine'), 64, 87, 124

Circe (*Perceforest*), 91, 150
Cistercian order, 2, 17, 25, 153, 169
Clement IV, pope (d. 1268), 223
Clement V, pope (d. 1314), 189, 228
Clementia of Zähringen, 129
Cleriadus et Meliadice, 23
Cluny, abbot of, 36, 42, 170
confraternities, secular, *see* fraternities
Conrad III, king of the Romans (d. 1152), 110, 121, 124
Conrad, landgrave of Thuringia, master of TK (d. 1240), 81
Conrad, marquis of Montferrat (d. 1192), 121, 130, 140, 141
Conrad of Querfurt, imperial chancellor, bishop of Hildesheim, 121, 124, 136
Constantinople, 59–60, 72, 74, 88, 97, 199, 203
Le Conte du Graal, or *Perceval*, by Chrétien de Troyes, 21, 23, 112–20, 126, 130, 131, 133, 141, 143, 150, 152, 181, 183, 211
  continuations of, 109, 120, 160, 182, 206
convention, literary, vii–ix, 2, 4, 9, 13–14, 17, 18, 20–21, 27–9, 46, 49–58, 71, 78, 87, 105, 187, 191, 234–7
conversion, 68–71, 117, 121–2, 147, 150, 153–4, 170–73, 177–8, 181, 208, 211, 213–14, 217–18, 235
Condwîrâmûrs (*Parzival*), 49, 122
Constantine the Great, emperor (d. 337), 158–9
Corbaran (Crusade Cycle), 45, 217
Corbenic (*Queste*, etc.), 153–4, 176, 208, 210–11
Crécy, battle of (1346), 219, 224, 232
Diu Crône, by Heinrich von dem Türlin, 104, 112, 150
crosses:
  gold, 157, 158, 168
  red, 29, 102, 153–63
  white, 88, 156
crusades, 4, 5, 24, 40, 50, 71, 79, 98, 110–11, 124–5, 144, 145, 200–204, 212, 213, 220, 225–6, 234–7
  first crusade (1095–99), 24, 25, 72, 110, 125, 152
  second crusade (1147–48), 64, 110, 124, 125
  third crusade (1189–92), 26, 51, 56, 64, 65, 67, 81, 85–6, 94, 110, 114, 117–21, 124, 126, 127, 132, 143–4, 146, 179, 217, 218
  German crusade (1197–98), 81, 108, 111, 121, 124, 129, 136, 138, 143, 145
  fourth crusade (1201–4), 43, 110–11, 120, 125, 151, 178–9, 203
  fifth crusade (1218–21), 64, 67, 81, 203
  Frederick II's crusade (1228–29), 81, 124, 125, 147
  Louis IX's first crusade (1248–54), 77, 78
  Louis IX's second crusade (1270), 223
Crusade Cycle
  first Crusade Cycle, 11, 13, 20, 21, 44–5, 66, 70, 77–9, 93–4, 156, 161–2, 188, 200, 203, 217, 218, 220
  'second Crusade Cycle', 41, 64 and n 79, 66–7, 72, 86, 94, 100, 157, 158, 189, 200–201, 203, 218–19, 220
Cyprus, 27, 57–8, 87, 116, 121, 124–5, 146, 151, 152, 166, 177, 180, 181, 201, 226

Dagobert, cycle of, 20, 58
Damascus, 57, 61, 67, 70
Damietta, 81
Decameron, by Giovanni Boccaccio, 42, 91
De laude novae militiae, by Bernard, abbot of Clairvaux, 5–6, 36, 49
La Déliverance Ogier le Danois, 92, 236
A Demanda do Santo Graal, 150, 172, 214
'Didot' *Perceval*, 23, 105, 150
Le Dis du chevalier à la mance, 47–8, 57, 91
Diverres, Armel, 117–20, 121, 122, 143
Doon of Mayence (*Bueve*), 48
Dodequin (Crusade Cycle), 11, 217, 218–19
Dome of the Rock [Omar mosque, 'Lord's Temple', *Templum Domini*], 42, 111
Du bon William Longespee, 77, 188, 220

Edward I, king of England (d. 1307), 223
Edward III, king of England (d. 1377), 148, 232
Egypt, 78, 94
Ela, countess of Salisbury (d. 1261), 77
Eleanor of Castile, queen of England (d. 1290), 9
Eleanor of England, queen of Castile (d. 1215), 133, 142
Eleanor of Provence, queen of England (d. 1291), 12
Elizabeth, countess of Champagne (fl. 1125), 46
Elizabeth of Hungary, landgräfin of Thuringia (d. 1231), 81
Elucidation, 181–2
empire, western, 55, 123–6, 130–31, 136, 142, 145, 165
Les Enfances Renier, 157
England, monarchs of, and Arthurian tradition, pp. 14–15 n 47, 118, 148
Ernoul, ix, 9, 46, 67, 133, 200, 216
Escanor, by Girart d'Amiens, 9
Esclarmonde, 78–9, 187, 200, 219

L'Escoufle, by Jean Renart, 43, 76, 93, 200, 203, 220
L'Estoire del Saint Graal (in prose), 22, 148, 150, 152, 157, 158, 192, 198
Estoire dou Graal, by Robert de Boron, *see* Roman de l'Estoire dou Graal
Estoires d'Outremer et de la Naissance Saladin, 42, 46, 64, 218
Eugenius III, pope (d. 1153), 155, 170
Eustace III of Boulogne (d. after 1125), 136, 138
Eustace Deschamps (d. c. 1406), 229
Everard des Barres, master of the T (d. c. 1176), 64, 170

Feirefîz (*Parzival*), 110, 122–3, 132–3, 211 n 81
Felix Fabri (fl. 1484), 128
Ferran (Fernando) prince of Portugal (d. 1470), 63
Ferrand of Portugal, count of Flanders, husband of Joanna (d. 1233), 95
La Fille du comte de Ponthieu, 41–2, 64, 100, 187, 190
Fischer, Mary, 82
Flanders, *see* Ferrand; Joanna; Philip of Alsace
Florent et Octavien, 40, 94
Florie (Crusade Cycle), 11, 217
Florinde of Edessa (*Théséus*), 59, 60, 72, 96, 97
Folda, Jaroslav, 179
Four Sons of Aymon, *see* Renaut de Montauban
Franc Palais (*Perceforest*), 148, 150
France, 39, 60, 87, 94, 95, 97, 192, 219, 223–4, 231–2
Francesc Ferrer, 63
Frappier, Jean, 169
fraternities and orders of secular knights, 25–6, 103, 148, 173–4, 225
Frederick I Barbarossa, emperor (d. 1189), 14 n 47, 81, 110, 121, 123, 124, 126, 129
Frederick II of Hohenstaufen, emperor (d. 1250), 81, 124–6, 130, 131, 139, 144, 147
Frederick, duke of Swabia (d. 1191), 124
friars, 2, 17, 195, 228, 229, 230
Froissart, *see* Jean Froissart
Fulk, count of Anjou, king of Jerusalem (d. 1143), 85, 126

Gahmuret (*Parzival*), 121, 122, 126, 140, 142
Galaad [Galahad] (*Queste*, etc.), 7, 102, 116, 151, 153–4, 157, 159, 160, 163, 169–77, 179–80, 182, 208–11, 214, 218

Gallafur (*Perceforest*), 158, 159
Gallais, Pierre, 151, 177–8
Garin the Hospitaller [Guérin de Glapion], bishop of Senlis (d. 1227), 69, 95, 223
Garnier de Nablûs, master of the H (d. 1192), 67, 86, 92
Gastria, castle of the T, 151
Gaufrey, 92–3
Gauvain (King Arthur's nephew: French version), 112, 115, 118–20, 171, 172, 205, 206, 208, 213
Gawân (*Parzival*), 111, 120, 122, 124, 139–42
Gawain (King Arthur's nephew: English version), 167–9, 212
Gaza, battle at (1239), 78
Genoa, 27, 199, 226
Genoese, 62, 88, 116, 199
Geoffrey, count of Anjou (d. 1151), 126
Geoffrey, brother of T, almoner, 224
Geoffrey 'Bigtooth' of Lusignan, son of Mélusine (*Mélusine*), 87
Geoffrey Chaucer, *see* Canterbury Tales
Geoffrey of Lusignan (fl. 1192), 111
Geoffrey of Lusignan (fl. 1262), 224
Geoffrey of Monmouth, *Historia regum Britanniae*, 212–14
Geoffrey of Paris, 229
Geoffrey de Villehardouin (d. c. 1212–18), 9
Geoffroi de Charny (d. 1356), 225
Gerart de Ridefort, master of the T (d. 1189), 46, 51–2
Gerbert de Montreuil, 160
Gilles de Chin, *see* L'Histoire de Gilles de Chyn
Gillette of Narbonne (*Decameron*), 91
Gillingham, John, 128
Giovanni Boccaccio, *see* Decameron
Giuletta of Hohenstaufen, 121, 140
Godfrey of Bouillon, ruler of Jerusalem (d. 1100), 110, 136, 157, 217
Gontier de Soignies, 46, 53
Grail romances, 21, 22, 28, 52–3, 55, 76, 102–83, 192, 196–8, 208–11
Granada, 91, 99, 226
Greece, 27; *and see* 'Romania'
Green, D.H., 19, 191
Grunwald, battle of (1410) [Tannenberg], 27
Guérin de Glapion, *see* Garin the Hospitaller
Gui de Buci, brother of T, 224
Guillaume de Dole [*Le Roman de la Rose*], by Jean Renart, 41, 43, 46, 48, 203, 220
Guillaume de Nangis, Latin continuation of his chronicle, 97
Guillaume d'Orange (historically, Duke William of Toulouse, d. 812), 20, 77, 198, 201, 224, 235

Guiot of Provins, 109, 206
Guinevere, queen (Arthurian legend), 170, 205
Guiron le Courtois (*Meliadus-Gyron*), 11, 22, 205, 210
Guy Cornelly, knight, 45–6
Guy de Beauchamp, earl of Warwick (d. 1315), 44, 77
Guy of Lusignan, king of Jerusalem (d. 1194), 58, 86, 111, 131
Guy of Lusignan, son of Mélusine (*Mélusine*), 66, 87
Gyron le Courtoys, 10, 28, 206–7, 210

Haferland, Harald, 134
Harpin de Bourges, brother of T (Crusade Cycle), 45, 70–71, 73, 77–8, 94, 188, 217, 222
Hartwig II, archbishop of Bremen, 136
Hattin, battle of (1187), 51, 70, 215
Haut Livre du Graal, see *Perlesvaus*
Heinrich von dem Türlin, see *Diu Crône*
Heldris de Cornualle, 10 and n 30
Helie de Boron, 10, 177–9
Helinand de Froidmont, 192, 198
Henry II, king of Cyprus and Jerusalem (d. 1324), 152
Henry II, king of England (d. 1189), 36, 94, 121, 126, 130, 202, 210
Henry [III], the Young King (d. 1170), 116
Henry VI, emperor (d. 1197), 121, 124, 126, 129, 144
Henry, count of Champagne, ruler of Jerusalem (d. 1197), 118–21, 126–8, 136
Henry, count Palatine of the Rhine (d. 1227), 129, 136, 145, 146
Henry, duke of Brabant and Lotharingia (d. 1235), 136, 138, 139, 146
Henry Bolinbroke, earl of Derby, king Henry IV of England (d. 1413), 99
Henry the Black, duke of Bavaria (d. 1126), 139
Henry the Lion, duke of Saxony (d. 1195), 19, 129, 130
Hermann I, landgrave of Thuringia (d. 1217), 81, 105, 108, 111, 143–6, 204
hermits, 54, 133–5, 149, 154, 171, 182, 206
Herzeloyde (*Parzival*), 122, 129, 142
L'Histoire de Gilles de Chyn by Gautier de Tournai, 76, 200, 219
L'Histoire des princes de Déols de seigneurs de Chasteauroux, by Jean la Gougue, 64
Hobsbawm, Eric, 14
Holmes, Urban, 117
Holy Land, 5, 24, 26, 36–7, 41, 47, 50, 65, 76, 79, 81–5, 93, 97–9, 103–4, 110–14, 116–18, 124, 129, 138, 145–7, 151, 178–80, 182, 202, 204, 211–12, 223, 227–9, *and see* Acre, Holy Sepulchre, Jerusalem, Latin East
Holy Sepulchre, 37–40, 47, 56, 100, 110–11, 148–9, 173, 181, 213
Holy war, 24, 25, 76–101, 153, 155–63, 172, 178, 180, 181, 190, 211–15, 218, 220, 225–6, 235–6
Honorius III, pope (d. 1227), 36
Hospital of St John of Jerusalem [Hospitallers], 1, 26, 27, 38, 56–9, 61, 71, 76, 77, 81, 83–9, 92–8, 156, 188–90, 199–202, 204, 221–4, 227–35
    charitable and hospital work, 57, 66
    criticism of, 72–4, 78, 84
    discipline of, 62
    individual brothers of, *see* Garnier, Garin [Guérin], Joseph of Chauncy, Matthew, Philip d'Eglis, Robert Hales; fictional brothers, *see* Simó de Far
    lovers and, 47–9, 57–64
    lodging travellers/pilgrims, 65, 66
    Malta, 27
    martyrs, 57
    messengers, 61, 95–7
    militarisation, 26, 76, 97, 200
    origins, 26, 38, 67, 204, 220
    place of penance, 38, 39, 42–3
    place of retirement, 44, 45, 47–8
    protecting fugitives, 65
    ransoming prisoners, 66–7
    Rhodes, 27, 57, 61–3, 66, 69, 87–9, 94, 199, 201, 202, 221, 222, 231
    sisters of, 44, 45
    and see Military Orders
Hubert de Burgh, justiciar of England (d. 1243), 224
Hugh, bishop of Jabala in the principality of Antioch, 123
Hugh, count of Champagne (fl. 1125), 46
Hugh of Lusignan, I king of Cyprus (d. 1218), 151
Hugh of Tiberias (fl. 1204), 217–18
Hugues Capet, 20
Humbert of Beaujeu, 36, 170
Humfrey II of Toron (d. 1179), 217
Hundred Years War, 148
Huon de Bourdeaux (*Esclarmonde*), 78–9

Iberian peninsula, 82, *and see* Aragon, Castile, Catalonia, Granada, Spain, Valencia
Ida, queen of Jerusalem (First Crusade Cycle), 44, 45, 66
'Imād al-Dīn (d. 1201), 132

Innocent II, pope (d. 1143), 49
Innocent III, pope (d. 1216), 56 n 59, 125, 135 n 76, 139
invented tradition, 14–16
Ireland, 54–5
Isabel I of Jerusalem (d. 1205), 114, 118, 121, 130, 131, 136, 138, 140
Isabel II of Jerusalem (d. 1228), 125, 130
Iseut, queen of Cornwall (*Tristan*), 7, 205, 206, 209
Ithêr of Gaheviez (*Parzival*), 140–41
Itinerarium peregrinorum I, 51, 56, 217

Jacquemart Giélée, 227
Jacques d'Avesnes (d. 1191), 67, 81, 86, 92
Jaffa, battle of (1192), 85
  city of, 111, 124
Jake de Neys, *see* Jacques d'Avesnes
Jakelin de Mailly, marshal of the T (d. 1187), 51
James of Vitry, bishop of Acre, cardinal-bishop of Tusculanum (d. 1240), 25, 52, 121
Jaufré Rudel (fl. 1147), 54
Jean d'Arras, *see Mélusine*
Jean de Berri, 58
Jean de Condé (d. c. 1345), 47–8, 86
Jean de Kays, brother of T, 224
Jean Dupin, 229
Jean Froissart (d. c. 1400/1401), 21, 98, 218, 226, 230, 231–2
Jean le Bel (d. 1370), 98
Jean Renart, 43, 46, 48, 203, 220, *and see* individual works
Jeanne of Boulogne, queen of France (d. 1360), 91 and n 41
Jehan d'Avesnes, 23, 42, 100, 190
Jehan de Saintré, by Antoine de la Sale, 23, 89–90, 188, 189, 191, 205, 216, 219, 226
Jem, Ottoman pretender (d. 1495), 69
Jerusalem, city/kingdom of, 24, 26, 35–41, 44, 46, 50, 56–7, 59–61, 64, 67, 68, 74, 76, 86, 92, 94, 100, 103, 109–32, 136, 138–47, 151–4, 157, 161, 165, 170, 172, 181–3, 187, 200, 203, 212, 235, *and see* Holy Land, Holy Sepulchre, Latin East
  patriarch of, 26, 59, 130
Joachim, abbot of Fiore (d. 1202), 121
Joanna, countess of Flanders (d. 1244), 120
Joanna, queen of Sicily, countess of Toulouse (d. 1199), 132–3, 142
Joanot Martorell (d. 1468), 61, 63, 87–8, 199, 231, *and see Tirant lo Blanc*
John, king of England (d. 1216), 126, 133 and n 73

John, master of the T (First Crusade Cycle), 78, 94
John XXII, pope (d. 1334), 82
John Coke (fl. 1549), 176
John, duke of Normandy, II king of France (d. 1364), 97–8, 148
John Hardyng (d. 1465?), 128, 176
John of Brienne, king of Jerusalem (d. 1237), p. 131 n 67, 151
John of Hildesheim, 230
John of Ibelin, old lord of Beirut (d. 1236), 44, 152, 201
John of Ibelin, count of Jaffa (d. 1266), 10
Joseph, see *Roman de l'Estoire dou Graal*
Joseph of Arimathea, 152, 153, 163, 176, 181
Joseph of Chauncy, treasurer of H, 223
Josiane (*Bueve*), 91
Jubail, 138
Judas Maccabaeus (d. 161/160 BC), 50–51
Jüngerer Titurel, by Albrecht, 23, 52–4, 106, 188
Justinian, emperor (d. 565), 159

Keen, Maurice, 16
Kelly, Thomas, 162–3
Knight, Stephen, 111, 117
knighthood, ideals of, *see* chivalry
knightly class, 3 n 6, 5–7, 9–10, 14–16, 30–31, 222–6, 234–7
Knights of the Band, secular order of chivalry, 174, 224–5
Kolb, Herbert, 111
Konrad the priest, 19
Die Kreuzfahrt des Landgrafen Ludwigs des Frommen von Thüringen, 80–81, 94, 107, 188
Kyôt of Katelangen (*Parzival*), 133
Kyôt of Provence (*Parzival*), 108–9, 120

Lachet, Claude, 55
Lactantius (d. c. 320), 134, 158–9
Lancelot (Arthurian legend), 54, 63, 99–100, 152, 153, 171, 205, 206, 210, 212, 218
Lancelot (non-cyclic), 153, 213–14, 225
Lancelot (Vulgate), 18, 22, 23, 214, 225
'Lan quant voi esclarcir', 46 and n 31
Lanzelet, 23
Latin East, 151–2, 178–80
Layamon, 213
Leon, king of Cilician Armenia (d. 1219), 124
Leopold V, duke of Austria (d. 1194), 81, 140
leprosy, 112, 117, 196
literature as history, viii, 8–18, 29–30, 191–2, 203, 219–20
Lithuanians, 26–7, 89–90, 99

Philip IV, king of France (d. 1314), 4, 27, 109, 166, 219, 220–21
Philip VI, king of France (d. 1350), 231
Philip d'Eglis, brother of H, 223
Philip of Alsace, count of Flanders (d. 1191), 21, 112, 114–18, 135, 141
Philip of Burgundy (d. 1346), 91
Philip of Novara (d. 1266), 10, 201
Philip of Swabia, king of the Romans (d. 1208), 111, 125–6, 136, 139, 142, 143
Philip the Good, duke of Burgundy (d. 1467), 42, 90, 91, 148 n 99, 204
pilgrimage, 24, 35–7, 41, 98, 129
pilgrims, 26, 28, 59, 61, 64–6, 97, 146, 170
Poitiers, battle of (1356), 218, 219
Poland, 27, 90
Pontus et Sidoine, 23, 200, 205
popes, viii, 27, 49–51, 56, 63, 73, 220, *and see individual popes*
Post Vulgate, *see Roman du Graal*
Prester John, 122–4, 142
Les Prophecies de Merlin, 8, 23, 158, 175, 211, 212, 213
Prussia, crusade in, 5, 26, 27, 69, 84, 85, 89–90, 98, 226, 230, 234

La Queste del Saint Graal, 17, 18, 22, 54, 105, 109, 116, 150, 152–4, 157, 159–60, 163, 169–72, 177–8, 180–82, 197–8, 204, 205, 211, 220, 235

Raoul de Cambrai, 35–7
Raoul de Hodenc, *Roman des Eles*, 6–7, 205, 224
reality in fictional literature, vii–ix, 190–203, 219–21, 234–5
Regni Iherosolymitani brevis historia, 46
Regnier the charcoalburner (*Theséus*), 20, 61, 67, 72–4, 96–7
Reinolt von Montelban, 39–40
Reisen, 27
Renaut de Montauban, 20, 37–40, 66, 75
Renaut of Montauban (St Reinold), 37–41, 66
Renechon (*Theséus*), 59, 60, 68
Repanse de Schoye (*Parzival*), 122, 131–3, 142
Rhodes, *see* Hospital of St John: Rhodes
Richard I, king of England, 'the Lionheart' (d. 1199), 58, 64–5, 85–6, 94, 98, 116, 118–19, 121–2, 126–30, 132, 136, 140–42, 146, 212
Richard Coeur de Lion, Middle-English verse romance, 65, 67, 85–6, 92, 94, 220
Richard of Ascalon, brother of T (*Bon William Longespee*), 77
Richard of Montivilliers (*L'Escoufle*), 76

Richey, Margaret Fitzgerald, 109, 111
Ricoldo of Monte Cruce (d. 1320), 228
The Right Plesaunt and Goodly Historie of the Foure Sonnes of Aymon, by William Caxton, 40
Robert, count of Artois (d. 1250), 78, 83
Robert de Boron, 22, 150–52, 173, 177, 178, 181, 204
[pseudo] Robert de Boron, 10, 22, 177–9
Robert de Clari (d. after 1216), 9
Robert de Sablé, master of T (d. 1193), 146
Robert Hales, prior of H in England (d. 1381), 224
Roger of Howden (d. *c*. 1201), 36, 138
Roland (d. 778), ix, 14 nn 46–7, 19, 20, 67
Rolandslied, by Konrad the priest, 19
Roman de Baudouin de Sebourc, 41, 86, 189
Roman de la Rose, see Guillaume de Dole
Roman de l'Estoire dou Graal, by Robert de Boron [*Joseph*], 22, 150–52, 181, 204
Roman de Laurin, 23, 53–4, 204
Roman de Perceforest, 23, 89, 91, 147–50, 158, 181, 219, 224
Roman du Graal, by ?Robert de Boron, 22, 105, 150, 152, 171–4, 177–82, 208–11, 224
Romanç de l'armada del Soldà contra Rodes, by Francesc Ferrer, 63, 199
Li Romans de Claris et Laris, 54–6, 188, 204, 220
'Romania', 178–9
Rome, 60, 73–4
Roncesvalles, battle of (778), 67
Ronsavals, 67
Rosenthal, Elizabeth, 58, 97
Round Table, 103, 148, 151, 153, 173–4, 180
Russians, 26, 99
Rusticien de Pise [Rustichello of Pisa], 8, 9
Rutebeuf (fl. 1277), 227–8

St Augustine of Hippo (d. 430), 134
St Euphemia of Chalcedon (d. 303), 166
St Demetrius (3rd century AD?) 162
St George (d. 303?), 79, 82, 156, 162
St James of Compostella, order of, *see* Santiago
St James of Santiago, order of, *see* Santiago
St John of Jerusalem, Hospital of, *see* Hospital
St John the Baptist, 88, 164–5
St Lazarus, Order of, 81
St Maurice (d. 287?), 162
St Mercurius (3rd century AD?), 162
St Michael, 77
St Ursula (4th–5th century AD), 166
Le Saint Voyage de Jherusalem du seigneur d'Anglure, 88–9

saints' relics, adoration of in Middle Ages, 164–7, 207
Saladin, 64, 66–7, 179, 189, 200, 218
Saladin, sultan of Cairo and Damascus (d. 1193), 41–2, 65, 67, 80, 86, 94, 111, 119, 125, 132, 147, 203, 215, 216, 217–18
Santiago, order of, 27, 91, 94
Saphet, castle of T, 68
Sarraz (*Queste*, etc.), 105, 154, 157, 170, 175–7, 182, 208
satire, 2, 18, 237
Segurades le Brun (*Prophecies*), 175
Seven Sages of Rome, cycle of, 19, 23, 53, 204
Schîânatulander (*Parzival*), 49, 52–3
Schoysîâne (*Parzival*), 133, 142
Sicily, 65, 87, 126, 130, 223
Sigûne (*Parzival*), 49, 52–3, 146
Silence, by Heldris de Cornualle, 10, 21
Simó de Far [Simon de Far], brother of H (*Tirant lo Blanc*), 61–3, 187
Sir Gawain and the Green Knight, 167–9
Sir Perceval de Galles, 150
Snelleman, Willem, 111, 121–3, 126
Solomon, king of Israel, 153, 167–9
Sone de Nausay [*Nansay*], 1, 21, 48, 53–5, 57, 79, 93, 188, 204, 220, 224
Spain, 5, 26, 85, 99, 230, 234, *and see* Iberian Peninsula
Spring of Cresson, battle at (1187), 51
Stephen of Bourbon, Dominican friar (d. 1261), 65
Suite du Merlin, 22–3
Suleiman the Magnificent (d. 1566), 27
Swan Knight, 122–3, 137–8, 142, 156–7
Swordbrothers of Livonia, 68
Sybil of Anjou (d. 1165), 112
Sybil, queen of Jerusalem (d. 1190), 111–14, 131, 140

Tancred (d. 1112; Crusade Cycle), 11, 217, 218–19, 221
Tannenberg, battle of [Grunwald] (1410), 27
Temple of Solomon, *see* al-Aqsa mosque
Templars [Order of the Temple, Knights of the Temple], 1–8, 26–7, 28, 58, 69, 76–87, 92–100, 102–11, 120–23, 138, 142, 145–51, 154–6, 159–70, 173, 174, 181–3, 187–90, 198–202, 219, 221, 223–4, 227–33, 234–6
banner of, 74–5, 155, 220
burying dead, 54, 55–6, 67
and conversion, 68–9
criticism of, 72–5, 78, 82–4, 86, 92–3, 109, 138
dissolution of (1312), 27, 59, 71, 86, 189–90, 201, 202, 219, 220–21, 227–32
epitome of Military Orders, 71
helping travellers/pilgrims, 53–4, 64–5, 146
individual brothers, *see* Amaury de la Roche, Everard des Barres, Geoffrey, Gerart de Ridefort, Gui de Buci, Jakelin de Mailly, Jean de Kays, Nicholas, Robert de Sablé; fictional brothers, *see* Anne, Harpin de Bourges, John, Margon, Richard, Wymound, Walter von Spetten
knightly ideal, as , 5–7
'knights of the Temple', 147–50
lovers and, 28, 45–57, 59–61, 63, 65, 224
martyrs, 49–52, 70–71, 77, 109, 146, 162–3, 168, 174, 182
messengers, 39, 60–61, 72, 95–7
money-lending, 94
origins, 26, 38, 45, 67
place of penance, 35–43, 189, 199
place of retirement, 43–9, 199
priests, 60
privileges of, ix, 49–50
protecting fugitives, 64–5
ransoming prisoners, 66–7, 200
rule of, 5, 49
spirituality of, 67, 70–72, *and see* martyrs
trial of (1307–12), 1, 3–4, 27, 71, 73, 79–80, 82–3, 85, 92, 107, 236
veneration of saints, 166–8
and see Military Orders
Templum Domini [Lord's Temple], *see* Dome of the Rock
Teutonic Order, 1, 26–8, 69, 71, 79–81, 83–5, 87, 89–90, 145–6, 188–9, 221, 227–8, 230
banner of, 89
bishops of, 69
criticism of, 28, 83, 85, 236
individual brothers of, *see* Conrad, landgrave of Thuringia
origins, 26, 145
militarisation, 26, 81, 146
and see Military Orders
Thaddeo of Naples (fl. 1291), 228
Theobald IV, count of Champagne and king of Navarre (d. 1253), 78
Theséus de Cologne, 20, 21, 39, 58–61, 63, 66, 68–9, 72–5, 88, 95–8, 100, 188–90, 220, 231
Thuringia, 80–81, 143–5, *and see* Conrad, Hermann, Ludwig
Thomas Becket, archbishop of Canterbury (d. 1170), 36
Thomas Malory, 23, 99–100, 171, 212
Thomas Walsingham (d. 1422?), 229

INDEX 273

Thorn, second treaty of (1466), 27, 90
Thorpe, Lewis, 17
Tîbnîn [Toron], 124, 139
Tirant lo Blanc, by Joanot Martorell and Martí Joan Galba, 61–4, 87–8, 92, 188, 189, 191, 220, 222, 231
Titurel by Wolfram von Eschenbach, 106
Trevrizent the hermit (*Parzival*), 133–5, 140
Trier, 74, 135
  archbishops of, 135 and n 76
Tripoli, city of, 138
  countess of, 54
Tristan, 10, 18, 22, 150, 174–5, 177–80, 197–8, 206, 208–12, 214
Tristan (Arthurian legend), 7, 21–2, 28, 152, 172, 205, 206, 208–10, 212, 214
Trotter, David, 2
Troyes, council of (1129), 49
Tunison, J.S., 116
Tyre, archbishop of, 94; *and see* William, archbishop of Tyre

Ulrich Füetrer, 21, 23, 53, 76, 80, 107, 109, 188, 189
Ulrich von Etzenbach, 71
Urban IV, pope (d. 1264), 223
Urien of Lusignan (*Mélusine*), 57
Usamāh ibn Munqidh, 216

Valencia, 63
Valentin et Orson, 37
Venice, 27
Vial, Guy, 119
Vienne, council of (1311–12), 189, *and see* Templars: dissolution of
Die Vier Heymons Kindern, by Paul von der Aelst, 41
Vinaver, Eugène, 115
Virgin Mary, 77, 158, 168, 212, 225
Vulgate cycle of Arthurian romance, 18, 21–2, 28, 190, 212–14, 218

Wace, 213

Waclaw [Wenzel] II, king of Bohemia (d. 1305), 71
Walter Map (d. *c*. 1209/10), 19, 116, 210
Walter de Montbéliard (d. *c*. 1212), 151
Walter von Spelton, count, master of T (*Kreuzfahrt*), 81–2
Walther von der Vogelweide (d. *c*. 1230), 145 n 93
Wayland the smith [Galaan] (Crusade Cycle, etc.), 200
Weston, Jessie, 109, 164–5
Wildermann, Ansgar Konrad, 1–2
Wilhelm von Wenden, by Ulrich von Etzenbach, 71
Willehalm, by Wolfram von Eschenbach, 81, 108, 144, 204
William, archbishop of Tyre (d. *c*. 1184), 12, 116, 199–200
William Caxton (d. 1491), 40
William des Barres (fl. 1216), 64, 95, 179
William Longespee II (d. 1250), 77
William Marshal (d. 1219), 44, 224
William of Beaujeu, master of T (d. 1291), 228
William of Montferrat (d. 1177), 140
William of Newburgh (d. 1198), 51
Wolfdietrich, 79–80
Wolfram von Eschenbach, 1, 4, 9, 49, 52, 56–7, 63, 76, 80–81, 104, 105–12, 120–47, 149–50, 165, 180, 183, 188, 189, 196, 204, 211, 215, 220, 224, 234, 235, *and see individual works*
women, in audience, 3 and n 6
  as authors, 9–11, 196
  in literature, 11, 73, 119, 158, 170, 206, 218–19, *and see individual characters*
  as patrons of literature, 8–11 and n 30, 21, 58, 89, 118, 120, 194
  as patrons of Military Orders, 3 and n 6
Wymound of Ascalon, brother of T (*Bon William Longespee*), 77

Ydain (*Sone*), 48
Yvain, by Chrétien de Troyes, 52